Narratives on Defining Moments for Women Leaders in Higher Education

Heidi L. Schnackenberg
SUNY Plattsburgh, USA

Published in the United States of America by
IGI Global
701 E. Chocolate Avenue
Hershey PA, USA 17033
Tel: 717-533-8845
Fax: 717-533-8661
E-mail: cust@igi-global.com
Web site: https://www.igi-global.com

Copyright © 2025 by IGI Global. All rights reserved. No part of this publication may be reproduced, stored or distributed in any form or by any means, electronic or mechanical, including photocopying, without written permission from the publisher.
Product or company names used in this set are for identification purposes only. Inclusion of the names of the products or companies does not indicate a claim of ownership by IGI Global of the trademark or registered trademark.

Library of Congress Cataloging-in-Publication Data

CIP Pending
ISBN: 979-8-3693-3144-6
EISBN: 979-8-3693-3145-3

Vice President of Editorial: Melissa Wagner
Managing Editor of Acquisitions: Mikaela Felty
Managing Editor of Book Development: Jocelynn Hessler
Production Manager: Mike Brehm
Cover Design: Phillip Shickler

British Cataloguing in Publication Data
A Cataloguing in Publication record for this book is available from the British Library.

All work contributed to this book is new, previously-unpublished material.
The views expressed in this book are those of the authors, but not necessarily of the publisher.

Table of Contents

Preface xiii

Chapter 1
Provoked The Power of Conflict and Change for Women in Higher Education Leadership 1
    Lolita L. Kincade, SUNY Plattsburgh, USA

Chapter 2
motherscholar and MotherLeader The Day That Changed Everything 25
    Heidi L. Schnackenberg, SUNY Plattsburgh, USA

Chapter 3
Self-Care and Emotional Well-Being of a Women Educators An Interpretative Phenomenological Analysis 47
    Elsy N. J., Christ University, India

Chapter 4
Overcoming Imposter Syndrome Exploring the Challenges Women Leaders Face in Confronting Self-Doubt and Internalized Biases 65
    Mohit Yadav, O.P. Jindal Global University, India
    Preet Kanwal, Lovely Professional University, India
    Thi Minh Ngoc Luu, International School, Vietnam National University, Hanoi, Vietnam

Chapter 5
Two Centuries of Defining Moments for Black Women Higher Education Leaders in the United States 91
    Natasha N. Johnson, Georgia State University, USA

Chapter 6
One Bad Mother How One New Mother in Academia Realized She Was 'Mothered' Out 113
    Ashley Gambino, SUNY Plattsburgh, USA

Chapter 7
Narratives of Women Higher Education Teachers in Karnataka: A Study on Self-Esteem, Small Group Socialization, and Workplace Communication Behaviour... 127
> Vishnu Achutha Menon, Institute for Educational and Developmental Studies, Noida, India

Chapter 8
Dichotomies, Power Structures, and Change-Focused Intentionality: A Personal Narrative in Support of Ongoing Student Status and Reflection While Simultaneously Serving in Leadership Roles in Higher Education........ 155
> Jennifer Schneider, Community College of Philadelphia, USA

Chapter 9
Mentoring the Next Generation of Women Leaders Investigating the Role of Women Leaders in Supporting the Development of Future Generations.......... 195
> Mohit Yadav, O.P. Jindal Global University, India
> Parth Sharma, University of Petroleum and Energy Studies, India
> Phuong Mai Nguyen, International School, Vietnam National University, Hanoi, Vietnam

Chapter 10
Empowered to Lead Navigating Psychological Safety and Resilience as a Black Woman Leader.. 221
> Kendra Lewis-Strickland, Independent Researcher, USA

Chapter 11
Where There's a Will, There's a Way 241
> Julie Lynn Richards, SUNY Plattsburgh, USA

Chapter 12
Balancing Lives: A Thematic Analysis of Self-Care and Emotional Balance Among Female Professors 255
> Shravani Minesh Kapse, Banasthali Vidyapith, India
> Sandhya Gupta, Banasthali Vidyapith, India
> Anu Raj Singh, Banasthali Vidyapith, India
> Priyesh Kumar Singh, Banasthali Vidyapith, India

Chapter 13
Becoming How Leadership and Mentoring Influence the Perception of Self ... 275
  Clair A. Stocks, Chapman University, USA

Compilation of References 291

About the Contributors 335

Index 341

Detailed Table of Contents

Preface xiii

Chapter 1
Provoked The Power of Conflict and Change for Women in Higher Education Leadership 1
    Lolita L. Kincade, SUNY Plattsburgh, USA

With growing research on the adverse effects of gendered racism impacting Black women in higher education, this chapter explores the author's lived experiences navigating such challenges, drawing connections to relevant empirical findings. This chapter further provides a thorough examination of mental health, and an in-depth exploration of measures to support mental wellness, well-being, and retention of Black women in the academy, including conditions of psychological safety. The Social-Ecological Model (SEM) of Support for Women of Color is used to guide the development of effective interventions through social environments at individual and interpersonal levels.

Chapter 2
motherscholar and MotherLeader The Day That Changed Everything 25
    Heidi L. Schnackenberg, SUNY Plattsburgh, USA

"I love you more than you know." Those were the last words I read from my son, my only child, for an hour and a half, as I watched law enforcement equipped with bullet proof vests and armed with high-powered weapons enter my son's high school across the street from my office. I didn't know at the time that it was just a swatting prank call, and I couldn't get in touch with my son to find out if he was ok. If I had ever felt the typical academic mother work-family guilt, resulting from the struggle between work and family commitments (Borelli et al., 2017), I surely never have since. That day changed everything.

Chapter 3
Self-Care and Emotional Well-Being of a Women Educators An
Interpretative Phenomenological Analysis 47
    Elsy N. J., Christ University, India

Women educators play a vital role in universities, yet their demanding careers can significantly impact their emotional well-being. This paper explores the challenges they face, including societal expectations, workload pressures, and the potential consequences of neglecting self-care. This research delves deeper into the lived experiences of self-care through an interpretative phenomenological analysis. By analyzing the narrative of a female educator, gain insights into the complex interplay between self-care practices, emotional wellbeing, and the demands of academia. The study reveals the constant struggle to balance professional obligations with personal well-being, highlighting the need for supportive structures to prioritize women educators' mental health. Universities also play a crucial role by implementing policies that address workload management, fostering an inclusive culture, and demonstrating leadership commitment to well-being. The findings call for increased institutional support and a cultural shift towards prioritizing well-being for women in academia.

Chapter 4
Overcoming Imposter Syndrome Exploring the Challenges Women Leaders
Face in Confronting Self-Doubt and Internalized Biases 65
    Mohit Yadav, O.P. Jindal Global University, India
    Preet Kanwal, Lovely Professional University, India
    Thi Minh Ngoc Luu, International School, Vietnam National University,
      Hanoi, Vietnam

Imposter Syndrome significantly impacts women leaders, manifesting as persistent self-doubt and internalized biases despite their professional achievements. This chapter explores the complexities of Imposter Syndrome by examining personal, professional, and systemic challenges faced by women in leadership roles. It delves into personal development strategies, such as cognitive restructuring and self-compassion, as well as organizational support mechanisms, including mentorship programs and inclusive cultures. The chapter emphasizes the need for systemic changes and further research into intersectionality and emerging interventions. Future research directions include longitudinal studies, the role of digital platforms, and empirical validation of coping strategies. By addressing these dimensions, the chapter aims to provide a comprehensive understanding of Imposter Syndrome and offer practical insights for supporting women leaders in overcoming self-doubt and enhancing their professional growth.

Chapter 5

Two Centuries of Defining Moments for Black Women Higher Education
Leaders in the United States 91
> *Natasha N. Johnson, Georgia State University, USA*

Black women have made significant strides in their representation in higher education leadership in the United States over the past two centuries. They have faced barriers, yet they have also made substantial contributions to the field. Historically, Black women remain at the forefront of the struggle for equal access to education, with many earning degrees, becoming educators, and founding higher education institutions. However, their leadership roles have often been marginalized and overlooked. Despite this, Black women have persevered and made advancements in higher education administration, but they continue to face obstacles in their career paths and leadership progression. The experiences of Black women higher education leaders, including the challenges they encounter and the strategies they employ to overcome them, can provide valuable insights for improving the retention and advancement of Black women leaders. Achieving gender equality in leadership positions in higher education is a matter of fairness, and it is essential to advancing the evolving higher education landscape.

Chapter 6

One Bad Mother How One New Mother in Academia Realized She Was
'Mothered' Out... 113
> *Ashley Gambino, SUNY Plattsburgh, USA*

This chapter explores the lived experience of a transitional time period for the author: becoming a new mother during an unprecedented period in history, the COVID19 pandemic. While much has been discussed about working mothers during the pandemic, the author discusses how the pandemic and motherhood were only two of the factors contributing toward a feeling of burn-out toward academic care work. Ultimately, a changing student demographic and new leadership duties coupled with the sexist role assignments and expectations of academia combined with the transition to motherhood and a pandemic were simply too much to cope with. The author recognizes that while she is certainly not the first woman to have been overburdened by the misogyny of academic care work, there is a cohort of academic leaders who became mothers and leaders during a time unlike any other in history.

Chapter 7
Narratives of Women Higher Education Teachers in Karnataka: A Study on Self-Esteem, Small Group Socialization, and Workplace Communication Behaviour 127
Vishnu Achutha Menon, Institute for Educational and Developmental Studies, Noida, India

This chapter investigates the relationships between self-esteem, small group socialization, and workplace communication behaviour among women teachers in higher education institutions in Karnataka, India. Using standardized instruments, data was collected from 509 participants through offline and online surveys. Results reveal strong positive correlations between self-esteem and both small group socialization and workplace communication behaviour. Linear regression analyses confirm the predictive capabilities of self-esteem on these variables. The findings contribute to understanding professional dynamics among women educators and offer insights for supporting their career development.

Chapter 8
Dichotomies, Power Structures, and Change-Focused Intentionality: A Personal Narrative in Support of Ongoing Student Status and Reflection While Simultaneously Serving in Leadership Roles in Higher Education 155
Jennifer Schneider, Community College of Philadelphia, USA

This chapter shares a blend of evidence-based theory and reflexive, narrative first-person experiences in support of simultaneously adopting a formal position of student while serving as a leader and teacher in systems of higher education. The article does not argue for any one particular approach to intentionally adopting and maintaining an identity and status as student while also leading in teaching and administrative roles. Instead, the breadth of possible ways to simultaneously adopt a student identity while teaching and leading is highlighted and an ongoing state of reflexive and iterative student status is encouraged. The focus is on spaces in which the intersection of dual identities can further support and strengthen individual experiences as student, leader, and teacher within educational institutions.

Chapter 9
Mentoring the Next Generation of Women Leaders Investigating the Role of
Women Leaders in Supporting the Development of Future Generations 195
    Mohit Yadav, O.P. Jindal Global University, India
    Parth Sharma, University of Petroleum and Energy Studies, India
    Phuong Mai Nguyen, International School, Vietnam National
        University, Hanoi, Vietnam

This chapter explores the pivotal role of mentorship in developing the next generation of women leaders. It examines how mentorship programs can empower women to overcome barriers, build confidence, and advance in their careers. Key themes include the integration of technological advancements, the emphasis on diversity and inclusivity, and the evolution of mentorship models. The chapter also addresses the future of mentorship, focusing on global networks, the impact of remote work, and emerging challenges. By analyzing best practices and providing actionable insights, this chapter offers a roadmap for organizations to create effective mentorship programs that support women's leadership development. The ultimate goal is to foster a more equitable and innovative leadership landscape, where diverse voices and experiences contribute to organizational success and societal progress.

Chapter 10
Empowered to Lead Navigating Psychological Safety and Resilience as a
Black Woman Leader 221
    Kendra Lewis-Strickland, Independent Researcher, USA

This chapter, written by a Black woman mid-career leader with more than a decade of experience in higher education, explores the intersection of resilience, psychological safety, and the challenges faced by Black women professionals. Through two defining moments in her career, the author highlights the crucial role of psychological safety in shaping her personal and professional journey. This chapter positions psychological safety and resilience as vital for Black women in higher education. It combines personal narratives, research, and practical strategies, stressing the need for leaders to create empowering environments and for institutions to be intentionally designed with Black women in mind. The author's two pivotal experiences—early career challenges and navigating personal difficulties —illustrate the impact of psychological safety on her confidence and professional growth. These accounts provide insights into resilient coping mechanisms and institutional culture change.

Chapter 11
Where There's a Will, There's a Way 241
   Julie Lynn Richards, SUNY Plattsburgh, USA

This chapter traces my transformative journey to a leadership position in higher education. Unlike a singular defining moment, my path unfolded through events and a significant leap of faith, guiding me back to academia and culminating in a leadership role. Embracing change and adventure laid the groundwork, while an unwavering commitment to continuous learning became foundational. "Where There's a Will, There's a Way" explores the instrumental role of networking and mentorship in shaping my leadership trajectory, highlighting flexibility and adaptability through overcoming struggles. Defying age stereotypes and persevering formed another crucial aspect. Emphasizing personal fulfillment alongside professional achievement became pivotal, underscoring the multifaceted nature of my worldview. The continuous pursuit of harmonizing personal passions acted as a driving force, propelling me into leadership in higher education. This narrative provides insights into the interconnected dynamics of personal growth, resilience, and passion pursuit in academic leadership development.

Chapter 12
Balancing Lives: A Thematic Analysis of Self-Care and Emotional Balance
Among Female Professors 255
   Shravani Minesh Kapse, Banasthali Vidyapith, India
   Sandhya Gupta, Banasthali Vidyapith, India
   Anu Raj Singh, Banasthali Vidyapith, India
   Priyesh Kumar Singh, Banasthali Vidyapith, India

Female professors frequently experience extreme pressure and stressors when managing multiple duties, both personal and professional. They also think that they are more constrained because of their domestic duties. In fulfilling the demands of their personal and professional roles, female professors often struggle to maintain their self-care and emotional balance. This chapter has attempted to look into the self-care and emotional balance among female professors of two distinct groups, viz., 10 married female professors and 10 unmarried female professors, to explore whether there are any similarities and/or differences in their themes, and with the help of this thematic analysis, findings will be discussed.

Chapter 13
Becoming How Leadership and Mentoring Influence the Perception of Self ... 275
Clair A. Stocks, Chapman University, USA

This chapter will use a single personal narrative and case study approach to analyze the challenges often faced by women in higher education and the impact of leadership in influencing the perception of self. A pivotal experience with a transformational leader and engaged mentor was the impetus for deep reflection that shepherded an evolution of individuals, teams, and an entire institution. This defining experience in the author's career will serve as a guide through literature that emphasizes the influence of leadership on individual perceptions and performance, cohesive team formation, and institutional success. The far-reaching effect of transformational leadership will be considered, as those who experience it adopt the practices of effective leadership and bring them to new teams and institutions. This chapter will include a specific focus on the lasting impact positive experiences with leadership and mentoring can have on confidence, achievement, and new leader development among women in higher education.

Compilation of References 291

About the Contributors 335

Index 341

Preface

It is often said that we are the sum of our experiences. If that is true, then it is both the little and the big events that create our persona. As humans, we often find that big events can change us - how we perceive ourselves, how we act and react in certain situations, and how we navigate our world. These circumstances can be pivotal in our lives and development. In many ways, they are defining moments in our lives. Moments, events, and circumstances that are so impactful that they change the very essence of who we are and how we see ourselves. Life shifted on its axis and we are redefined at our core.

While these defining moments clearly impact us personally, they can also impact us professionally. Particularly those who identify as women, the personal and the professional are intertwined, often inextricably, whether we want them to be or not. We are a whole, and more than the sum of our parts. This phenomena is never more real than for women in higher education, and women in leadership in higher education. The defining moments in our lives can affect us in equal measure, both personally and professionally. These moments can cause us to dig in and push forward stronger and harder. They can nudge us to pivot and choose a related path, or *swerve,* as Michelle Obama (2018) says, and follow a new path. Or we can walk off the path altogether until we figure out in which new direction we want to go. A hiatus is ok. So is a full-stop. Defining moments can do that to us, and these experiences are important.

Narratives on Defining Moments for Women Leaders in Higher Education captures those pivotal, defining moments, events, or times in the lives of women in higher education and women leaders in higher education. The stories included here represent the fascinating experiences and moments that define powerful women and women leaders in higher education. They reveal how these academics became who they are as people and as leaders. This book is different from other publicatiions because it focuses on women leaders in education and the ways in which specific moments, circumstances, or seasons in their lives have defined and/or brought about changes to their sense of self, work-life balance, and priorities. While a host of other books and articles have focused on the the work lives of women, and women in higher education, this volume is centered on the process and evolution of their Identities through their lived experiences.

Through this volume, readers expand their understanding about specific challenges, issues, strategies, and solutions that are associated with women leaders in higher education, and the particular implications of the moments that define women, as leaders and as people. *Narratives on Defining Moments for Women Leaders in Higher Education* includes a variety of emerging evidence-based professional practice and narrative personal accounts as written by administrators, faculty, and staff - individuals who are keenly aware of the challenges faced by women leaders in the academy. It is hoped that this work is of value to instructors, administrators, professional staff, graduate students, and truly anyone navigating the personal and professional changes that are wrought by impactful life experiences.

Heidi L. Schnackenberg
SUNY Plattsburgh, USA

REFERENCE

Obama, M. (2018). *Becoming*. Crown.

Chapter 1
Provoked
The Power of Conflict and Change for Women in Higher Education Leadership

Lolita L. Kincade
https://orcid.org/0009-0007-5070-4806
SUNY Plattsburgh, USA

ABSTRACT

With growing research on the adverse effects of gendered racism impacting Black women in higher education, this chapter explores the author's lived experiences navigating such challenges, drawing connections to relevant empirical findings. This chapter further provides a thorough examination of mental health, and an in-depth exploration of measures to support mental wellness, well-being, and retention of Black women in the academy, including conditions of psychological safety. The Social-Ecological Model (SEM) of Support for Women of Color is used to guide the development of effective interventions through social environments at individual and interpersonal levels.

THE POWER OF CONFLICT AND CHANGE FOR WOMEN IN HIGHER EDUCATION LEADERSHIP

Help us to be ever faithful gardeners of the spirit, who know that without darkness nothing comes to birth, and without light nothing flowers. – May Sarton

I don't have a green thumb. Over the years, I have likely invested hundreds of dollars in forgiving low-maintenance, trouble-free, easy-care, low-light, drought-tolerant, tough-to-kill plants. Despite my best efforts, I always beat the odds. I've

DOI: 10.4018/979-8-3693-3144-6.ch001

resorted to sprucing up my family home with silk and artificial plants. When my daughter was around four years old, she began participating in gardening activities at school. One day I spotted her watering one of our best plastic potted plants. Poor baby, "How does your garden grow?" I said jokingly while sharing with family and friends about her efforts to maintain our vibrant and thriving faux houseplants.

While I don't personally have a green thumb, I do have a deep appreciation and respect for gardening and agriculture. I subscribe to the notion that the process of "growing" is profoundly spiritual and gives us insight into the nature of God as the creator. Further, I view the basic principles of tilling and cultivating soil as a metaphor for life, that can also be applied to the experiences of women in higher education leadership, particularly women of color.

When land is cultivated, weeds are destroyed, and the soil is being prepared for an impressive yield. While cultivation indeed promotes development, plants, or crops still undergo pressure and change, and they must adapt to survive and thrive. In some ways, they are provoked to growth. This understanding has led me to recognize and appreciate the power of conflict and change in my role as a higher education leader.

In this essay, I reflect on some of these experiences, drawing connections to relevant empirical findings, synthesizing this information, and making meaning as it relates to my personal and professional development. I explore mental health challenges among Black women in higher education and share a Social-Ecological Model (SEM) of Support for women in higher education leadership navigating similar experiences. It is my intention to nurture the confidence I need to continue this work. I also hope to encourage others to grow from adversity, while engaging in radical self-care. I believe that this practice is fundamental to leading a life and professional career that is happy, healthy, and whole.

RECOUNTING

For nearly two weeks, I cried myself to sleep with deep regret. "What have I gotten my family into?" I whispered in a painful and quiet prayer. I groaned in silence, my pillow drenched in tears. "I can't just quit!" I said in a failed attempt to counter thoughts and feelings of hopelessness and defeat. I reflected on the fact that I have always used my faith in Jesus Christ as a guide, leading me to be extremely conscientious; making careful and deliberate attempts to create a life that is purpose-driven, safe, and secure. Only, what resulted from the recent shift in my life was a challenging time of uncertainty that felt anything but purposeful, pleasant, or psychologically safe.

Just one year earlier I began my journey in higher education leadership. My spouse extended his support, agreeing to uproot our family and leave a diverse community we had come to love, to move to a remote part of the country where American Black families like ours were few and far between. In retrospect, while I anticipated some challenges, I generally underestimated the magnitude of the burden we would carry; the emotional, psychological, and physical toll. I was also not fully prepared for the dynamics of the community at large, or the resistance and racism (whether conscious or unconscious) I would encounter in my new professional role.

As community members, my family experienced implicit bias in healthcare and racial discrimination in housing. Intentional efforts to undermine access to homeownership resulted in us living in a hotel with our two small children for the first couple of months we were in town. Eventually, we were forced to use a mortgage lender in a different state, because of systemic denial of services in the local area. Our new lender processed our application and loan almost immediately, unable to identify any challenges or reasons as to why the processing of our initial home loan was being delayed. Even in the context of this very convoluted experience, our ability to achieve homeownership success is increasingly rare for Black Americans.

Historically, racial restrictions in housing have limited homeownership and wealth building among Black Americans across generations. When homeownership was an option, we were prohibited from purchasing homes in well-appointed communities. Many systems and practices, however, were designed and implemented to block homeownership altogether. Federal Housing Authority (FHA) guidelines, for example, prohibited loans to Black borrowers. As a result of the Fair Housing Act of 1968, it became unlawful to discriminate based on race or ethnicity in the sale or rental of housing, but even today only 45% of Black Americans own homes, compared to 75% of White Americans (Harvard Public Health, 2023). According to a report sponsored by the National Association of Real Estate Brokers (2023) Black loan applicants in the United States are more than twice as likely to be denied a home mortgage as White applicants. These data point to the persistence of discrimination and systemic racism impacting home-buying experiences for thousands of Black families like mine.

As it relates to healthcare, race-related attitudes among providers largely impacted medical interactions and the outcomes that followed. Identifiable concerns included implicit racial bias in medical encounters, poor and unresponsive provider communication, non-active listening, and a lack of patient-centered care. Experiences of being overlooked or discredited during medical visits are common among Black patients and can be attributed to discrimination (Micthell & Perry, 2020). These issues were even more prominent for my spouse, as a Black male. Mitchell and Perry

(2020) further explain that both systemic racism and perceived discrimination are determinants of health, and they are also determinants of health communication experiences for Black males. A failure to recognize diversity among Black men and physicians' lack of sociocultural awareness about the challenges they regularly face is most salient (Kramer et al, 2021).

In addition to these concerns, we were targeted by racial profiling, including unwarranted traffic stops, and racist calls to the police for apparently asserting our rights in "White spaces." This was extremely concerning to my family since the system of police deployment in America is fundamentally dangerous to Black lives (Feldkamp & Neusteter, 2021). Comprehensive data on police violence across the United States reveals that police have killed 1,351 people between March 2023-2024, and Black Americans are being killed by police at 2.9 times the rate of their White counterparts (Mapping Police Violence, 2024). Feldkamp & Neusteter (2021) suggest that police officers have become the weaponized embodiment of social and racial bias, dispatched at the request of semi-anonymous callers who either knowingly, or unknowingly release devastating outcomes, including potential police violence against Black citizens that can be fatal.

We navigated racial hierarchies and stigma in commercial spaces while eating at restaurants, shopping, and/or procuring goods. We struggled to find beauty products and services, as there was little to no representation or options for Black hair or skin care in the community. Further, we discovered that places where we would typically find in-group solidarity were severely lacking. Most church congregations and places of worship that we encountered were predominantly and almost solely White. The same was true for many community organizations and institutions. Our children were among the only Black kids in school, and there was no diverse representation among teachers. No children were participating in sports, dance, or other extracurricular activities that looked like them. We were the only Black family in our neighborhood, and apparently the first. Sociologist Anderson (2022) explains that when Black people are outnumbered by White people in community or social spaces, we feel a peculiar vulnerability. I believe it is this deep sense of vulnerability that made moving to this area by far one of the most significant and challenging changes of my life.

Virtually every place we went, we experienced some degree of scrutiny that the average White community member does not need to endure. We desired to go about our daily lives uneventfully, but on too many occasions we did not. Anderson (2022) suggests that White people typically avoid Black space, but Black people are required to navigate the White space as a condition of our existence. This is described as "the Black tax," and we were feeling every bit of it. Meanwhile, life was happening. Several relatives back home suffered serious medical conditions, and we grieved the loss of a close loved one. I also learned of an abnormal growth on my liver and was awaiting news as to whether the lesion was cancerous or benign. In my field of Human Development and Family Science, this piling up of varying amounts and types of demands is referred to as "stressor overload."

At work, it felt as though I was also on the front line of an uphill battle. As an outsider, I readily recognized that entrenched thinking, systems, and culture were negatively impacting productivity in the workplace. Subgroups were already formed and divided, and our faculty team was polarized. As a new leader, I tried to lean into innovation and transformation, but it was clear from my perspective that people were only interested in maintaining the status quo and doing things the way they have always been done. My interpersonal and professional interactions were largely impacted by issues including, but not limited to ageism, gendered racism, and implicit bias.

Perceived youthfulness of professional Black workers can shape our subjective experience in the workplace, as we are confronted with prejudicial attitudes and interactions based on perceptions about our age (Smith-Tran, 2023). Drawing from semi-structured interviews with professional Black women, a study by Smith-Tran (2023) contributes to our understanding of how gendered racism and ageism intersect when Black women's chronological ages differ from how we are perceived. For example, in some instances, I may have been told that I looked like a student, or that I *didn't* look like a professor. If I were correctly characterized as a professional, I was assumed to be at entry-level rank, on a non-tenure track, or informed that I appeared "too young" to lead. For Black women in academia, perceived youthfulness creates problems that commonly undermine our authority in profound and exhausting ways. In my case, the implicit assumptions were that I was not only less competent or capable of leadership because of my chronological or *perceived* chronological age, but that I was also somehow worthy of less respect and consideration. In higher education settings where wisdom, experience, and expertise are rewarded, this infantilization of Black women in professional leadership positions is disempowering, hindering our ability to be fully regarded in the workplace.

Unable to separate the individual effects of each aspect of my identity (Sanchez-Hucles & Davis, 2010), I often struggled to identify whether my age, race, or gender were responsible for the reactions of my colleagues. Sanchez-Hucles and Davis (2010) explain that the joint possibility of both gender and racial discrimination makes it difficult for Black women to make accurate attributions concerning potential discrimination. Thus, determining an appropriate response is even more challenging. Their study fully captures the complex experiences of women of color who serve as leaders. The researchers use ideas concerning identity and the intersection of multiple identities to understand how these factors shape the experiences of women of color in the workplace. Their study concludes that it is more difficult for women to be seen as effective leaders compared to men, and hurdles are higher for women of color than for White women and men. As leaders, Black women feel greater pressure to make fewer mistakes and to conform to conventional prototypes, ignoring important aspects of our identities, beliefs, cultural competencies, and values (McCluney & Rabelo, 2019; Sanchez-Hucles & Davis, 2010). Reports of greater isolation, difficulty being perceived as credible, and having limited power are common. Black women are also more likely to face misperceptions of their identities and roles, experience greater stereotyping, and generally endure more stress (Sanchez-Hucles & Davis, 2010; Turner, 2002). Dimensions of race, gender, and related challenges impacting the leadership experiences of racially diverse women are now being addressed with greater attention.

A growing body of literature highlights experiences of subtle, everyday forms of racism and racial slights against Black women, as well as gendered racial microaggressions (Lewis et al., 2016; Sue et al., 2007). We are frequently stereotyped as overly dominant or aggressive, ignored, silenced, and marginalized in the workplace (Lewis et al., 2016). I experienced no shortage of micro-aggressive, hostile, patronizing, and subtle bullying behaviors among colleagues, or in other cases what I interpreted as a lack of regard and collegiality. My leadership, decision-making, and expertise were constantly called into question and challenged on every side. I was regularly dismissed or outright ignored when making requests, recommendations, or sharing plans regarding the future direction of the unit. I did not feel seen, heard, or respected. These circumstances seem to mirror many empirical studies that have examined Black women's experiences, including subtle and intersecting forms of discrimination in higher education (Hill et al., 2016; Johnson & Joseph-Salisbury, 2018; Love et al., 2020; Moody & Lewis, 2019).

The growing tension of racial stress became so intolerable for my White counterparts, that it triggered a range of defensive moves, including outward displays of emotions such as anger, fear, guilt, stonewalling, and silence (DiAngelo, 2015). Attempts to confront these concerns sparked conversation but resulted in only temporary adjustments and little accountability. These interactions led to accusations and further criticism about my leadership capabilities, personal and professional disposition, and communication style. For example, assumptions perpetuated by media about Black women's communication styles include that we are loud and use nonverbal expressiveness such as shaking or waving hands and fingers (Lewis et al., 2016). Being told that one's speaking tone is aggressive or challenging is another example. Tone policing, as well as pathologizing cultural values and communication styles in this way are common racial microaggressions, (Kincade, 2023) that propagate bias and discrimination. People generally react more negatively to Black women who express indignation (while advocating for ourselves) because we activate the stereotype of an "angry Black woman" and internal attributions (Motro, Evans, Ellis, & Benson, 2022). In workplace settings, these widely held assumptions can lead to poor performance evaluations and/or poor assessments of leadership capability (Motro et al., 2022). Due to this stigma, I felt demonized and entreated as though I were bad-tempered, hostile, and threatening to others.

On one occasion a colleague suggested that I get to know another member of our professional community, who they believed had a unique way of directly addressing conflict (e.g., racial stress) in ways that made others feel more comfortable. The individual they described as extremely polite, kind, and *humble*, happens to be a member of a racial/ethnic group stereotypically characterized as being less assertive and more positive in nature. While perhaps not intended, this statement echoes the narrative of the Black *problem minority* versus the exemplary *model minority*. The assertion is that members of the model minority group should be viewed as a standard or ideal example to imitate. The other notable concern with this interaction is the expectation that people should be made to "feel good" when being challenged to confront privilege, racism, unconscious bias, or how they see themselves and others in the world. It reinforces White expectations of racial comfort and White racial equilibrium (DiAngelo, 2015). DiAngelo (2015) explains how this need for an insulated environment of racial protection and comfortability is used to protect the racial interests and perspectives of White Americans, ultimately impeding learning, growth, racial healing, and transformation.

Aside from the impact and emotional labor of harmful stereotypes and assertions, I was routinely the only person of color in various spaces across campus, which lends itself to issues of both hypervisibility and invisibility (Buchanan & Settles, 2019). I experienced being misidentified by name and repeatedly called the name of "the other" Black woman on campus. Others were just so insatiably curious about my culture and identity, that it led to offensive questions, comments, or unsolicited attempts to touch my hair. While seemingly harmless, unwelcomed hair touching is a deeply rooted cultural and political issue for many Black women, and just one more assertion of power and privilege (Collier, 2021). In a world of commonplace, subtle prejudice and pointed insults, this can feel like an absolute final straw.

Despite intense distress and simmering negative emotions, I continued the practice of showing up, fully present, engaged in my work, and performing to the best of my ability. After all, what other choice did I have, except to persevere and survive? This is the archetype of the *strong*, Black woman. However, even in my attempts to overlook the negative experiences and focus on the work, I was characterized as aloof, impersonal, "disinterested," or "*too* professional." Suddenly, I perfectly understood the idiomatic expression I heard my father say as a child on many occasions to vent his frustration regarding his experiences as a Black man in America: "I can't win for losing."

RELATING

As much as I hated to admit it, I was deeply hurt and discouraged by the issues I faced both personally and professionally. I would feel deflated, offended, and provoked on almost a daily basis. Racial battle fatigue was at an all-time high. That is the physical, mental, and emotional stress of coping with the constant stream of microaggressions and overt racism for people of color (Arnold et al, 2016). I also feared the pervasiveness of "the angry Black woman" stereotype. As such, I suppressed my emotions and parts of myself, so as not to display traits or characteristics that could be misused to damage or destroy my professional reputation, undermine my role, impede the work I was hoping to accomplish, or have other deleterious consequences. Researchers Quaye and colleagues (2020) characterize this as "suppressed rage," which can also be associated with racial battle fatigue.

I was losing sleep and motivation, and my overall well-being and mental health were negatively impacted. A vast body of empirical evidence has revealed the harmful effects of gendered racism on the physical and psychological well-being of Black women (Jerald et al., 2017; Spates et al., 2020). The effects can be even more damaging when certain culturally specific measures are not in place, such as a collective community identity and social connectedness (Spates et al., 2020), which was the case in my experience.

This "interdependent phenomena" of oppressions (Collins, 1990) is seemingly commonplace for women like me. The pressure to subdue my truth, anger, and pain substantiates how I experience the compounding effects of racism and sexism in my role in higher education, in the community, and my daily life. So, what is the remedy? How can I begin to reclaim my power? Perhaps I begin by amplifying my Black voice; breaking free of suppression; reconciling my strength and acknowledging my humanity. The cultural trope of the *Black Superwoman* with supernatural strength and resiliency is not who I aspire to be. The consequences and negative psychological outcomes are far too great (Liao, Wei, & Yin, 2020). The real "badge of honor" is not in being strong, but in being whole. *This* is the power of conflict and change. Secondly, I empower others by spotlighting this larger issue of worsening mental health among Black women in higher education, resulting from the kind of emotional injury and trauma illustrated in this chapter. A thorough examination of mental health, as well as an in-depth exploration of measures to support the mental health and retention of Black women in higher education, is of great importance.

REASONING

Stepping onto a brand-new path is difficult, but not more difficult than remaining in a situation, which is not nurturing to the whole woman. – Maya Angelou

The world of academia was thrown into shock upon learning of the tragic death of Dr. Antoniette "Bonnie" Candia-Bailey in January 2024. The former Lincoln University Vice President of Student Affairs died by suicide. BIPOC (Black, Indigenous, People of Color) women higher education leaders, however, were not surprised by the circumstances surrounding her death. It was reported that Dr. Bonnie endured severe bullying and harassment by the president of the university and that she also experienced challenges with her mental health. Many women of color not only empathize with Dr. Bonnie, but we identify with her because witnessing her pain compounds our own. We relate to the individual trauma that often results from challenges associated with our intersecting and historically oppressed identities. I was certainly able to draw personal connections to her layered experiences, and the detrimental effects. In recent years, there have been several other media reports of the sudden deaths of Black women in academia. While the causes of death were not always revealed, commonalities among women were their notable positions in higher education leadership. It feels as though for years Black women have been sounding the alarm, requesting emergency help. But, only in the wake of someone's death is there an uprising.

Dr. Bonnie's unfortunate and consequential death has sparked a national conversation, and a call to improve the treatment of Black women in higher education. However, it has also shown a greater light on barriers to mental health among this population and the importance of psychological safety in the workplace as racially diverse women ascend to senior-level positions in higher education. Spotlighting the role of mental health in the workplace, the United States Surgeon General provides a well-researched and evidence-based guide that outlines the importance of employer responsibility in supporting employee health (U. S. Office of the Surgeon General, 2022). Cultivating academic cultures and environments that promote well-being, safety, and a sense of belonging can help improve employees' mental health outcomes while supporting organizational productivity and success.

MENTAL HEALTH

According to the United States Office of the Surgeon General (2022), workplace mental health is a critical priority for public health, as it largely impacts individual workers, their children, families, productivity, and organizational performance. Hostile and dangerous working conditions, including harassment, microaggressions, and discrimination are examples of daily stressors that impact the health of workers and organizational performance. Workers can face different challenges based on personal characteristics such as age, race, and gender. For example, it was reported that women and people of color are more likely to experience threats to their physical and psychological safety in the workplace. These individuals are also part of larger communities, where their mental health can be negatively impacted by socioeconomic, political, and cultural factors. As it relates to this chapter, structural racism is an example of this, which reinforces the racial hierarchy established through slavery and colonialism in the Americas dating back to the early 17th century. Structural racism has perpetuated trauma and discrimination for African Americans, (Scott-Jones & Karma, 2020), and mental health disparities based on minority racial status are well-identified, including inequities in access, symptom severity, diagnosis, and treatment (Scott-Jones & Karma, 2020).

The impact of the conditions described is also noteworthy since chronic stress that results from harassment, microaggressions, and discrimination in the workplace has been linked to sleep disruptions, muscle tension, and impaired metabolic functioning. Stress further increases vulnerability to infection, diabetes, high blood pressure, high cholesterol, heart disease, obesity, cancer, and other chronic health conditions. Such conditions are also associated with increases in depression, anxiety, suicidal ideation, and substance abuse which impacts workers, their children, and families (American Psychological Association, 2018).

Given the challenges outlined, the United States Office of the Surgeon General (2022) developed a Framework for Workplace Mental Health and Well-being, which is intended to spark critical dialogue and organizational change in the workplace. This framework identifies five essentials for workplace mental health and well-being, including (1) protection from harm (2) connection and community (3) work-life harmony (4) mattering at work, and (5) growth opportunities. The Framework can be viewed as a starting point for organizations in amending and implementing policies, processes, and practices to best support the mental health and well-being of workers. Organizations are encouraged to build systems for accountability, engage in data disaggregation to better understand the needs among disproportionately impacted groups, utilize validated tools for measuring worker well-being, and ensure processes for continuous quality improvement. These systems are identified as being critical to sustaining workplace structures and practices that advance rather than harm the health and well-being of all workers over time.

PSYCHOLOGICAL SAFETY

A 2022 report and call to action from Black Women Thriving (2022) highlights that 66% of Black women report not feeling emotionally safe at work. Dr. Candia-Bailey's case is a prime example of this. Reports indicate that "Dr. Bonnie" contacted senior–level leadership and the University's board president to express concerns about bullying, harassment, and racial discrimination. It is believed that she suffered severe depression and anxiety resulting from workplace interactions. Though leadership was reportedly unresponsive "Dr. Bonnie" also made requests for mental health-related job accommodations covered under Family and Medical Leave (FMLA) and the Americans with Disabilities Act (ADA), indicative of a perceived lack of support and psychological safety. This is important to note, as the first essential of the Framework for Workplace Mental Health and Well-being emphasizes two basic human needs: Safety and security (US Office of the Surgeon General, 2022). Workplace safety suggests that:

All workers are in a safe and healthful work environment, protected from physical harm, injury, illness, and death. This is done through continued efforts to minimize occupational hazards and physical workplace violence, as well as psychological harm such as bias, discrimination, emotional hostility, bullying, and harassment. Security builds on safety to include financial and job security, given the negative effects that layoffs and job loss can have on workers and their families (US Office of the Surgeon General, 2022, p. 12).

Additional components of protection from harm emphasize psychological safety, mental health support, and operationalized policies and programs rooted in Diversity, Equity, Inclusion, and Accessibility (DEIA). Research by Edmonson and Bresman (2022) suggests that Black women require differentiated solutions to feel psychologically safe at both the interpersonal and organizational levels at work, and this tailored approach is important to boosting the well-being and work outcomes of Black women in the workplace.

With psychological health and safety as a priority, the author encourages the use of a Social-Ecological Model of Support (SEM) that aims to inform the development of systems and structures that mitigate harmful effects and foster well-being among Black women. This model identifies interventions at interactive and reinforcing levels (e.g., individual, interpersonal, organizational, community, society, and public policy) to support Black women in reaching their full personal and professional potential in the higher education sector (Kincade, 2023). The recommendations proposed in this model are also adeptly aligned with the five essentials for workplace mental health and well-being proposed by the United States Office of the Surgeon General.

RESTRUCTURING

A Social-Ecological Framework

Kincade's (2023) Social-Ecological Model (SEM) of Support for Women of Color is an extension of bioecological models that emphasize the influence of social environments on human development (Bookchin, 1980; Bronfenbrenner, 1977; Bronfenbrenner, 2001; Ruffin, 2010). This model centers on the experiences of racially diverse women at intersections of race and gender.

A defining feature of this and any ecological model is that it considers the physical environment and its relationship to people at individual, interpersonal, organizational, community, and societal levels. Based on this understanding we can conclude that the environmental context of colleges and universities is embedded in larger social structures that that can negatively impact the mental health of Black women, as demonstrated by my narrative and what we have learned throughout this chapter regarding the unique challenges of Black women in higher education overall. Developing successful interventions through social environments, then, can help to buffer some of these concerns. The SEM model for Women of Color is organized into five nested, hierarchical levels:

1. The individual level consists of specific characteristics that combat race-based stress, including self-care practices and healthy work-life balance.
2. The interpersonal level promotes increased understanding of institutional culture and climate, as well as relationships and social networks among people of shared identities to foster a supportive and collegial workplace.
3. The organizational level considers practices that can be adopted by higher education institutions, including upholding protections for professionals victimized by discrimination and workplace bullying, providing professional development opportunities, and engaging in equity practices.
4. Community structures offer relationships with professionals across universities and opportunities to engage with organizations and networks geared specifically toward women of color.
5. Equal opportunity for women of color to advance in public sectors is important, as it relates to society and public policy (Kincade, 2023). See *Table 1*.

The current chapter emphasizes the individual and interpersonal levels, which identify specific recommendations that foster positive mental health. Explicit examples from my lived experiences are included to demonstrate how these factors can promote resiliency. Transformative interventions at interactive and reinforcing levels can support the long-term health and well-being of Black women, as we navigate our complex roles as higher education faculty and campus leaders. While this is essential to the practice of radical self-care among members of this group, it in turn supports the advancement of higher education systems. University institutions and structures directly benefit from the valuable contributions made by Black women, who are commonly driving positive organizational change.

Individual Level

Self-care including mindfulness and/or meditation practices are encouraged at the individual level of the SEM model. Since racial microaggressions and other daily challenges can negatively impact the self-esteem and self-efficacy of Black women, these practices are important to countering challenging experiences. Further, they serve to empower women to address issues of race-based stress, hostilities, and related physical and psychological effects (Kincade, 2023).

Faith and spirituality are not explicit examples of self-care included in the SEM model. However, for Black women especially, there is empirical evidence that supports the notion that self-care encompasses spiritual health, which commonly serves as a coping mechanism for stress (La Freada, 2021). Collective and spiritual coping reflects an African-centered worldview that includes participation in a spiritual community, and a connection with God as creator (Greer, 2011; Liao et al., 2020). Employing higher levels of spirituality relevant to self-care might include prayer and pondering scriptures (Shahid, 2014). Liao and colleagues explain that these practices predict quality of life among African American women, indicating that there is a correlation to positive mental health. According to the research, these coping responses were directly associated with decreased depression, as well as decreased symptoms of anxiety and loneliness. I emphasize spiritual health here, since spiritual coping measures like those described reduced stress, improved my intrinsic motivation, and enhanced my quality of life as I navigated many of the challenges outlined in this chapter. Dedicated spiritual practice increased my feelings of resilience and strength. It led me to rediscover the essence of purpose in my career, improving my overall job satisfaction and contributing positively to my mental health and well-being.

Creating a delicate balance between home and work is another important practice of self-care according to the SEM model (Kincade, 2023). Being confronted with incompatible role obligations and the stress associated with having the ability to fulfill only a limited number of those obligations is a major source of stress. Therefore, managing the amount of time devoted to work can be helpful. I made several minor adjustments to create a healthier work-life balance. This included clearly defining my work hours and communicating them to students, staff, and faculty colleagues. I practiced maintaining these hours, and leveraging technology to my advantage, setting notifications and away messages to filter non-urgent, work-related communication. I was intentional with my "no," assisting me to prioritize and evaluate commitments, and in some cases avoid over-commitment. These and similar actions helped to decrease stress and avoid burnout.

Role compartmentalization can enable Black women to mentally separate and organize their lives in ways that prevent interference and becoming overwhelmed. Effective time management can also assist in striking a healthier balance. Finally, therapeutic, or other relevant mental health services can be beneficial in addressing internalized oppression. Only, there is a need for the use of culturally competent, trauma-informed practitioners. These professionals should be trained to recognize Race-Based Traumatic Stress, and the unique psychological and emotional distress and maladaptive outcomes that result from racism and discrimination (Kincade, 2023).

While individual self-care emphasized in the SEM model is essential, an important argument made by Wyatt and Ampadu (2022) is that current discourse on mental health and well-being relative to the lived experiences of members of the Black community often ignores

systemic and community-level factors that encourage, sustain, or inhibit self-care practices. They utilize the theory of intersectionality and the psychology of liberation framework to underscore the importance of self and community care as a tool for social justice, preservation, and resistance against oppressive systems that threaten the mental health and wellness of the Black community. These scholars encourage information, training, and resources about self-care, which have important implications for higher education programs and institutions:

From a systems perspective, self-care support requires systems, institutions, and communities to implement programs and/or initiatives that support individuals' self-care needs. Self-care support also requires that systems, institutions, and communities respond to the unique wellness needs of individuals. For example, a system that is supportive of self-care recognizes the impact of oppression and intersectional identities on the lived experiences of communities of color and how this can influence self-care practices. Self-care support can also take the form of community building that prioritizes increasing self-care capacities and sustainability within Black communities (Wyatt & Ampadu, 2022, p. 216).

Interpersonal Level

At the interpersonal level measures of preparedness for working in Predominantly White Institutions (PWIs) should include increasing one's understanding of the institutional climate and culture, and its potential to significantly influence diversity experiences among Black women in higher education. According to the SEM model, a college or university's climate is operationalized as its expression of identity and purpose. That is the impressions, beliefs, and expectations held by students, staff, faculty, and administrators as it relates to the work and learning environment, and factors that represent expressions of the institution's identity and purpose (Piggot & Cariaga, 2019; Schneier, Ehrhart & Macey, 2013). Further, the institutional climate includes the explicit mission and policies that drive institutional goals.

Actions to achieve strong member identification with the mission and goals of the institution are significant to ensuring a strong sense of belonging. Also, Black women can navigate their various roles in higher education more successfully when they have an increased understanding of the institutional support that may or may not be available to them. This can aid in combating the invisibility, isolation, and racial stigma that is commonly experienced among women of color in higher education. Scholars and leaders will be able to identify if the institutional climate will support their identity, beliefs, cultural competencies, and values, or if there will be pressure to ignore aspects of their cultural or ethnic identity to achieve success. This is essential since women of color often draw from racial and cultural assets to achieve and maintain their success as faculty and higher education leaders (Kincade, 2023).

Formal and informal networks and social support systems can also be helpful at the interpersonal level. I sought formal support and communicated openly with my direct supervisor, particularly as it related to managing race-based stress and personnel issues. I needed to facilitate difficult conversations about race, that required both will and skill. With adequate preparation and support, I would eventually be able to engage my colleagues in ways that led to deeper understanding, empathy, and transformation. Formal support from a member of senior-level leadership supported my well-being, and what was in the best interest of my academic unit. Moreover, my university sponsored equity advocate workshops, where campus and community participants learned about valuable race-conscious, equitable practices. As a result, I was able to find support and community among equity-minded allies, professionals, and leaders. This helped to strengthen my informal support network as well, leading to trusting and reliable connections beyond the workplace. Collectively, these networks helped to reinvigorate me, increasing my sense of belonging and reducing my isolation. A greater sense of belongingness led me to feel as though I could be my authentic self at work, without fear of repercussions. This in turn positively impacted my overall mental health, work performance, and productivity.

While allies have an important role in offering solidarity-based support, networks of persons with shared gender, racial, ethnic, immigrant, and class-based identities are critical to building a network of support, friendships, and professional collaborations. Members of these networks can be intentional in creating safe spaces to share their experiences, vulnerabilities, and needs. This will aid in developing a supportive and collegial community among Black women. Those who have already successfully navigated unique challenges and climbed the ranks of academia can serve as models, mentors, and leaders for others. They can help to build a bridge for new and rising professionals. When networking and mentorship efforts identified at the interpersonal level are committed and sustained over time, they can contribute positively to mental health (Kincade, 2023).

RECAPITULATION

"Gardening adds years to your life and life to your years." – Unknown.

Black women *must* be a target of systemic changes and interventions. It is imperative to confront concerns of chronic stress, workplace bullying, and everyday racism, as these factors are leading to maladaptive and even fatal outcomes. Further, without comprehensive solutions, the landscape of higher education will continue to change, as a growing number of Black women resign from their positions and institutions as a bold act of self-preservation (Johnson et al., 2024). Given that Black women are already grossly underrepresented in the academy, this effect is highly concerning. Moreover, this will negatively impact strategic planning goals and initiatives across colleges and universities, as Black women play a critical role in shaping academic and institutional success.

The recommendations from the SEM model of support are not intended to be exhaustive. Instead, they are fundamental practices that can help to increase psychological safety and improve overall mental health and wellness among racially diverse women in higher education. While many Black women experience debilitating transformational experiences in academia and yet emerge anew with enhanced leadership potential (Bennis & Thomas, 2002; Chance, 2021), the high risk of this intense pressure is causing severe harm, including poorer mental health, shorter life expectancy, and other physical health symptoms that impair our ability to thrive (Chinn, Martin & Redmond, 2021; Liao et al., 2022). This may be particularly true when we internalize or conform to prescribed societal expectations of self-sacrificing, or unyielding strength. Therefore, as highlighted in the SEM model, individual and interpersonal systems of advocacy and support are critical to mental health promotion.

Black women who currently work or who are entering academia and/or higher education leadership can utilize the SEM framework as a tool to assess the supports that are available to them at each level of the model. If any necessary support is lacking, the model can also serve as a guide for education, prevention, or intervention needed to improve social and structural environments across institutions. Professionals might consider a few key actions or questions for reflection:

1. How does the institution encourage self-care in the workplace to strengthen a culture of well-being?
2. What employee mental health supports or services are in place? Is there an emphasis on multicultural approaches and competencies?
3. Consider reviewing previous and current culture climate survey results. What validated tools are used to measure professional well-being? How has the institution used the data to improve its response to critical issues, and/or to develop prevention or intervention programs? What actions have been taken to ensure processes for continuous quality improvement? What organizational studies are available? What values are reflected in the institution's strategic priorities? What can you learn from the institution's web and social media pages?
4. Are there program institutes or research centers affiliated with the university that promote diversity, equity, and inclusion efforts?
5. Are there opportunities available to engage with women of shared racial/ethnic/immigrant and/or class-based identities?
6. Is there demonstrated support or leadership in the workplace by Black women or other women of color?
7. Does the institution support or provide opportunities for peer mentorship and/or sponsorship?

These fundamental inquiries are particularly geared toward developing the individual and interpersonal levels of support that have been emphasized in this chapter, where there is a focus on understanding university climate and culture, building social support networks, and garnering peer support. Professionals can consider engaging in critical inquiry at additional levels of the SEM model, including the organizational, community, and societal levels. See *Table 1*. It will also be important for higher education academicians and leaders to consider the five essentials for workplace mental health and well-being. That is, available support systems that ensure (1) protection from harm (2) connection and community (3) work-life harmony (4) mattering at work, and (5) growth opportunities (U. S. Office of the Surgeon General, 2022) as previously described. These factors can help to promote resiliency and mitigate issues of race-based stress.

Mounting evidence of the adverse effects of race and gender bias in higher education demonstrates how essential it is for Black women to continue to acknowledge our truth and share our personal stories. This allows us and others to better understand the significance and impact of these life experiences. Further, the emphasis on resiliency in this narrative is to serve as an example that a healthy and thriving career in higher education leadership is feasible, with adequate support. As we learned at the beginning of this chapter, gardening can teach us a powerful life lesson about growth and development. Just as gardens require careful tending, nurturing, and the right environment to grow and flourish, Black women faculty and leaders also need proper maintenance, protection, and just the right amount of care.

REFERENCES

American Psychological Association. (2018). Stress affects on the body. Retrieved from: https://www.apa.org/topics/stress/body

Anderson, E. (2022). *Black in white space: The enduring impact of color in everyday life*. University of Chicago Press.

Arnold, N. W., Crawford, E. R., & Khalifa, M. (2016). Psychological heuristics and Faculty of Color: Racial battle fatigue and tenure/promotion. *The Journal of Higher Education*, 87(6), 890–919. DOI: 10.1080/00221546.2016.11780891

Bennis, W. G., & Thomas, R. J. (2002). *Geeks and Geezers: How Era, Values, and Defining Moments Shape Leaders*. Harvard Business School Publishing.

Black, W. T. R. (2022). Retrieved from https://everylevelleads.com/wp-content/uploads/2022/06/Black-Women-Thriving-Report_2022.pdf

Bookchin, M. (1980). *Toward an ecological society*. Black Rose.

Bresman, H., & Edmondson, A. C. (2022). Research: To excel, diverse teams need psychological safety. *Harvard Business Review*. https://hbr.org/2022/03/research-to-excel-diverse-teams-need-psychological-safety

Bronfenbrenner, U. (1977). Toward an experimental ecology of human development. *The American Psychologist*, 32(7), 513–531. DOI: 10.1037/0003-066X.32.7.513

Bronfenbrenner, U. (2001). The bioecological theory of human development. In Smelser, N. J., & Baltes, P. B. (Eds.), *International encyclopedia of the social and behavioral sciences* (Vol. 10, pp. 6963–6970). Elsevier. DOI: 10.1016/B0-08-043076-7/00359-4

Buchanan, N. T., & Settles, I. H. (2019). Managing (in) visibility and hypervisibility in the workplace. *Journal of Vocational Behavior*, 113, 1–5. DOI: 10.1016/j.jvb.2018.11.001

Chance, N. L. (2021). A phenomenological inquiry into the influence of crucible experiences on the leadership development of Black women in higher education senior leadership. *Educational Management Administration & Leadership*, 49(4), 601–623. DOI: 10.1177/17411432211019417

Chinn, J. J., Martin, I. K., & Redmond, N. (2021). Health equity among Black women in the United States. *Journal of Women's Health*, 30(2), 212–219. DOI: 10.1089/jwh.2020.8868 PMID: 33237831

Collier, Z. (2021). "Don't Touch My Hair": An Examination of the Exercise of Privilege and Power Through Interracial Hair-Centered Communication Interactions. *Proceedings of the New York State Communication Association*, 2017(1), 11.

Collins, P. H. (1990). Black feminist thought in the matrix of domination. *Black feminist thought: Knowledge, consciousness, and the politics of empowerment, 138*(1990), 221-238.

DiAngelo, R. (2015). White fragility: Why it's so hard to talk to White people about racism. *The Good Men Project,* 9.

Feldkamp, K., & Neusteter, S. B. (2021). *The little-known, racist history of the 911 emergency call system* (Doctoral dissertation, These Times).

Goodreads. (2024). Popular quotes. Retrieved from https://www.goodreads.com/quotes

Greer, T. M. (2011). Coping strategies as moderators of the relationship between race-and gender-based discrimination and psychological symptoms for African American women. *The Journal of Black Psychology*, 37(1), 42–54. DOI: 10.1177/0095798410380202

Harvard Public Health. (2023). For Black Americans, homeownership can mean better health. Retrieved from: https://harvardpublichealth.org/equity/fighting-for-more-black-homeownership-and-less-systemic-racism/

Hill, C., Miller, K., Benson, K., & Handley, G. (2016). *Barriers and bias: The status of women in leadership*. American Association of University Women. https://www.aauw.org/resources/research/barrier-bias/

Jerald, M. C., Cole, E. R., Ward, L. M., & Avery, L. R. (2017). Controlling images: How awareness of group stereotypes affects Black women's well-being. *Journal of Counseling Psychology,* 64(5), 487–499. DOI: 10.1037/cou0000233 PMID: 29048195

Johnson, A., & Joseph-Salisbury, R. (2018). 'Are You Supposed to Be in Here?' Racial microaggressions and knowledge production in higher education. In *Dismantling race in higher education* (pp. 143–160). Palgrave Macmillan. DOI: 10.1007/978-3-319-60261-5_8

Johnson, J. B., Castillo, N., Nagthall, N., & Negussie, H. (2024). Safeguarding black women educators' mental health. Retrieved from https://www.insidehighered.com/opinion/career-advice/conditionally-accepted/2024/03/01/how-and-why-advocate-and-support-black

Kincade, L. L. (2023). At the Crossroads: A Social-Ecological Model of Support for Women of Color in Higher Education Leadership. In *Stabilizing and Empowering Women in Higher Education: Realigning, Recentering, and Rebuilding* (pp. 87-105). IGI Global. DOI:DOI: 10.4018/978-1-6684-8597-2.ch006

Kramer, J., Yinusa-Nyahkoon, L., Olafsson, S., Penti, B., Woodhams, E., Bickmore, T., & Jack, B. W. (2021). Black men's experiences with health care: Individuals' accounts of challenges, suggestions for change, and the potential utility of virtual agent technology to assist black men with health management. *Qualitative Health Research*, 31(10), 1772–1785. DOI: 10.1177/10497323211013323 PMID: 34092141

La Freada, F. R. (2021). *Equipping African American Christian Women to Succeed in Predominantly White Institutions of Higher Education Within the United States of America* (Doctoral dissertation, Regent University).

Lewis, J. A., Mendenhall, R., Harwood, S. A., & Browne Huntt, M. (2016). "Ain't I a woman?" Perceived gendered racial microaggressions experienced by Black women. *The Counseling Psychologist*, 44(5), 758–780. DOI: 10.1177/0011000016641193

Liao, K. Y. H., Wei, M., & Yin, M. (2020). The misunderstood schema of the strong Black woman: Exploring its mental health consequences and coping responses among African American women. *Psychology of Women Quarterly*, 44(1), 84–104. DOI: 10.1177/0361684319883198

Love, B. H., Templeton, E., Ault, S., & Johnson, O. (2021). Bruised, not broken: Scholarly personal narratives of Black women in the academy. *International Journal of Qualitative Studies in Education : QSE*, •••, 1–23.

Mapping Police Violence. (2024). Retrieved from https://mappingpoliceviolence.org

McCluney, C. L., & Rabelo, V. C. (2019). Conditions of visibility: An intersectional examination of Black women's belongingness and distinctiveness at work. *Journal of Vocational Behavior*, 113, 143–152. DOI: 10.1016/j.jvb.2018.09.008

Mitchell, J. A., & Perry, R. (2020). Disparities in patient-centered communication for Black and Latino men in the US: Cross-sectional results from the 2010 health and retirement study. *PLoS One*, 15(9), e0238356. DOI: 10.1371/journal.pone.0238356 PMID: 32991624

Moody, A. T., & Lewis, J. A. (2019). Gendered racial microaggressions and traumatic stress symptoms among Black women. *Psychology of Women Quarterly*, 43(2), 201–214. DOI: 10.1177/0361684319828288

Motro, D., Evans, J. B., Ellis, A. P., & Benson, L.III. (2022). Race and reactions to women's expressions of anger at work: Examining the effects of the "angry Black woman" stereotype. *The Journal of Applied Psychology*, 107(1), 142–152. DOI: 10.1037/apl0000884 PMID: 33793257

National Association of Real Estate Brokers. (2023). 2023 state of housing in black America. Retrieved from https://www.nareb.com/site-files/uploads/2023/11/SHIBA-Report-2023.pdf

Quaye, S. J., Karikari, S. N., Carter, K. D., Okello, W. K., & Allen, C. (2020). Why can't I just chill?": The visceral nature of racial battle fatigue. *Journal of College Student Development*, 61(5), 609–623. DOI: 10.1353/csd.2020.0058

Ruffin, K. N. (2010). *Black on earth: African American ecoliterary traditions*. University of Georgia Press. DOI: 10.1353/book11452

Ryan, M., & Ryan, M. (2015). A model for reflection in the pedagogic field of higher education. In Ryan, M. E. (Ed.), *Teaching reflective learning in higher education* (pp. 15–27). Springer., DOI: 10.1007/978-3-319-09271-3_2

Sanchez-Hucles, J. V., & Davis, D. D. (2010). Women and women of color in leadership: Complexity, identity, and intersectionality. *The American Psychologist*, 65(3), 171–181. DOI: 10.1037/a0017459 PMID: 20350016

Scott-Jones, G., & Kamara, M. R. (2020). The traumatic impact of structural racism on African Americans. *Delaware Journal of Public Health*, 6(5), 80–82. DOI: 10.32481/djph.2020.11.019 PMID: 34467171

Shahid, K. T. (2014). *Finding Eden: How Black women use spirituality to navigate academia* (Doctoral dissertation, Miami University).

Smith-Tran, A. (2023). "There's the Black Woman Thing, and There's the Age Thing": Professional Black Women on the Downsides of "Black Don't Crack" and Strategies for Confronting Ageism at Work. *Sociological Perspectives*, 66(3), 419–433. DOI: 10.1177/07311214221139441

Spates, K., Evans, N. T., James, T. A., & Martinez, K. (2020). Gendered racism in the lives of Black women: A qualitative exploration. *The Journal of Black Psychology*, 46(8), 583–606. DOI: 10.1177/0095798420962257

Turner, C. S. V. (2002). Women of color in academe: Living with multiple marginality. *The Journal of Higher Education*, 73(1), 74–93. DOI: 10.1080/00221546.2002.11777131

U. S. Office of the Surgeon General. (2022). *The US Surgeon General's framework for workplace mental health & well-being*. Department of Health and Human Services.

Wyatt, J. P., & Ampadu, G. G. (2022). Reclaiming self-care: Self-care as a social justice tool for Black wellness. *Community Mental Health Journal*, 58(2), 213–221. DOI: 10.1007/s10597-021-00884-9 PMID: 34478022

APPENDIX

Table 1. A Social Ecological Model (SEM) of Support for Women of Color in Higher Education

Level [1] Individual	Level [2] Interpersonal	Level [3] Organizational	Level [4] Community	Level [5] Society & Public Policy
1a. **Practice self-care** ■ Mindfulness ■ Meditation ■ Managing the amount of time devoted to work *1b.* **Address internalized oppression** ■ Relevant mental health services, including therapy with a focus on Race-Based Traumatic Stress	*2a.* **Increase knowledge & understanding of the culture and climate of predominantly White institutions** *2b.* **Build social support networks** ■ Shared gender, racial/ethnic/immigrant and class-based identities ■ Friendships with other faculty/research colleagues of color ■ Safe and private venting spaces to discuss similarities in experiences *2c.* **Demonstrated support in the workplace by women of color** *2d.* **Peer Mentoring** ■ Other women of color in higher education leadership/administration	*3a.* **Greater representation of women of color** *3b.* **Address wage inequity issues** *3c.* **Uphold protections for those facing discrimination, bullying & verbal abuse** *3d.* **Professional development training addressing:** ■ Cultural humility ■ Unconscious bias ■ Collegiality ■ Intersectional experiences	*4a.* **Peer mentoring and support groups across universities** ■ Virtually or on social media ■ Face-to-face gatherings by region *4b.* **Empowerment seminars aimed at racially diverse women** *4c.* **Formal and professional organizations geared toward women of color employed in higher education**	*5a.* **Proactive plan of action to ensure equal opportunity in employment & university programs and activities** *5b.* **Support for women of color in politics** *5c.* **Acknowledge and address racial capitalism** ■ White allies to relinquish power and reallocate resources to minority populations.

Chapter 2
motherscholar and MotherLeader
The Day That Changed Everything

Heidi L. Schnackenberg
SUNY Plattsburgh, USA

ABSTRACT

"I love you more than you know." Those were the last words I read from my son, my only child, for an hour and a half, as I watched law enforcement equipped with bullet proof vests and armed with high-powered weapons enter my son's high school across the street from my office. I didn't know at the time that it was just a swatting prank call, and I couldn't get in touch with my son to find out if he was ok. If I had ever felt the typical academic mother work-family guilt, resulting from the struggle between work and family commitments (Borelli et al., 2017), I surely never have since. That day changed everything.

INTRODUCTION

It was April of 2023 and as far as I knew that morning, it was a typical spring day. I got up and splashed water on my face to wake up because I never sleep enough during the week. I then woke up my 15 year old son for high school. As he rolled over and pulled up the blankets in an effort to ignore me and squeak out a few more minutes of sleep, it occurred to me, as it does every morning, how he is the delight of my heart. I love to give him a kiss to wake him up, in an effort to disguise the fact that I get to inhale his still-clean scent from his shower the night before. After I finally pester him enough, my son gets up and I go downstairs to heat up his breakfast. Not that he can't do it himself, but because I like to do it. He's my only child

DOI: 10.4018/979-8-3693-3144-6.ch002

- I'm a stereotypical female academic in that way, either childless or having a single child (Mason, Wolfinger, & Goulden, 2013) - and I consider every moment with him precious. It's a bonus that I actually like my own kid and enjoy being with him.

After he eats and finishes getting ready, he hops in the car with his Dad to go to yet another day of his sophomore year of high school. I wave out the window, and he waves back, as we always do, and then I go upstairs to get myself ready for work. While I'm getting showered and changed, I leave my email open just to see who needs what when I get to work, and I leave my Google Chat open just in case any of my friends, or my son, messages me. Will, my son, typically messages me throughout the day, mostly because he claims he's bored and not paying attention in class. I do instigate it though by sending the first "I love you have a great day" message in the chat each morning. Which I did that morning too, as always. He messaged back that he'll "try" to have a good day and that he loved me too. After that, we sent little emojis to each other. Then, at about 10:30 am, he sent me what reads like a very endearing message, but felt heavier, and cryptic, to me. Will wrote "I love you more than you know." Of course I wrote him back that I loved him too, but that was the last I heard from him for an hour and a half. The longest 90 minutes of my life.

Although I didn't know what was happening at the time, I tried to keep calm despite my growing alarm that Will wasn't responding to my "is everything alright, honey?" and "I need you to write back to me please, sweetie" messages. I quickly got into my car and drove the seven minutes to campus, and walked into my office. I found out at work that there was a threat called into the school and it was on lockdown. While this has happened before, this one was much more credible and the authorities were alerted. My building and office is directly across the street from my son's high school, so as I walked to the side of the building facing the high school, I watched as both uniformed and plain-clothed police officers arrived, in squad cars and personal vehicles. Border patrol and customs officers in the area also came to the school. Most frightening were the authorities who parked their cars outside of the school and proceeded to put on bulletproof vests, flak jackets, and pull out guns, most notably AK-47s. (Look these up if you've never seen one. It will add an unsettling visual detail for you.) As I watched the authorities run into my son's school, I was relieved, horrified, frightened, numb, and feeling absolutely alone even though my colleagues were all around me, and another colleague also had a son at the high school. I still couldn't get a hold of my son. I had no idea what was happening in that building that was so close to me that I could literally run to it in 60 seconds. And my only child was in there with god knows what happening. I didn't know if he was ok and I had no ability to help or protect him, even though I was so close. I was the most frightened I had ever been.

This part of the story is told from my son's perspective, since all I could do during those 90 minutes was work to tamp down the tears and fears and continue to message him. Will told me that there was a message over the loudspeaker that the school was on lockdown. There are so many lockdown drills in schools these days that I think kids are fairly desensitized to them. But this one was different since they had a hold in place, students had to stay in their classrooms, and they knew that authorities were called. Students of course also knew that theirs could be the next school-shooting so they were also petrified. Will was in his Global History class, luckily with a teacher who was also his varsity soccer coach so he knew and trusted him and that gave him some small sliver of peace. (My understanding is that his teacher handled things very well.) Will also had a class full of his close friends and buddies in Global with him so it helped that they were already a community by that time of the year. My son said that as they waited, no one told them any information so the students didn't know what was happening. All they knew was that they had to stay where they were, very still, and that the police were in the building. Note that their principal was off-site that day, down the street, at a district meeting, and couldn't re-enter the building to be with his students. The students really like this principal, as do I, so another source of calm and comfort was inadvertently denied them. Or perhaps it was intentional by the swatter(s)? We may never know.

Soon, but for what seemed like an eternity, Will said he heard classroom doors being kicked in and could hear people storming down the halls. When they finally got to his door, it was kicked in and the teacher and kids were forced to stand with their arms in the air while four policemen with AK-47s trained on them surveyed the room. Will said at that moment all the tension burst and he began to cry. An officer told him that "it was going to be alright, son" and he said that gave him some relief. But not knowing if it was the good guys or the bad guys kicking that door in with guns pointed at him scared him beyond reason. As it should have. No teenager - no human - should ever have to experience that.

Will said after he started to cry, everyone in the room began to cry, his tears seeming to give permission to everyone else to feel and release their fears. I couldn't have been prouder when he told me he had openly cried out of fear and panic. My son is 6'1" and a varsity athlete in two sports. He also sits first trombone in his band and jazz band, takes advanced and college-level classes, is a member of the National Honor Society, and has attended no less than three proms and several homecoming dances. He could have easily played the tough, popular kid and hidden his tears and brushed it off and joked about what happened. But he didn't. He showed how he felt and he let it out by crying. And showed all the other kids in his class it was ok to do the same thing. That single, organically brave, act probably helped both my son and a lot of other kids to start processing what happened there and then. I know a lot of his classmates went to therapy for a long time after that incident. I offered therapy to my son as well, but he declined. Luckily, he did talk with me at length, many times, about what happened so I knew he was thinking and feeling it and trying to make sense of the senseless. He was scared to go back to school for a long time, but now, a year later, he feels more confident.

Of course, all of what happened in the school was relayed to me from Will's point of view. I had no idea what was happening for quite a while. Finally, around 12pm, I received a Google Chat message and phone call from him. To be honest, I don't remember the chat message specifically, but it was something to the effect of "I'm ok." The phone call was "can you come pick me up" and then a little bit of adolescent griping that I was walking over rather than driving my car across the street to get him. The teenager was back:-) When I went to sign him out of school however, he saw why I walked instead of drove. Cars were lined down the block and across the street, with parents inside their vehicles waiting to get their kids. My feet were faster than their engines and I was surely going to use them since I had the good fortune of both geography and physical well-being.

Once I got Will and brought him back to my office, my partner met us on campus and we all just hugged and talked for a while. Finally, being the 15-year old that he was, my son informed us that he was hungry and his food of choice was right on campus in one of our dining halls. So we went to get him his chicken strips and fries and just sat in the seating area on campus where the college hubbub continued, and the overhead TVs blared withmovies and the cartoons of the moment.

While that situation turned out to be nothing more than swatting, which was happening with unfortunate frequency in schools in northern New York that spring, it was still one of the most terrifying moments of my life, and I've had a few. It did, however, solidify my life's priorities, if they had actually been in question up to that time. I love my job and am proud of the work that I do and the credentials that I've earned, but I've always known my son came first. What accompanied that choice was a healthy dose of mother-guilt for not being able to be both the perfect parent and the perfect worker. At that moment, on that day, I knew that I would never again feel guilty for choosing my son over my work. And I never have.

BACKGROUND

I've always found the phrase "working mother" to be redundant. To me, *all* mothers are working mothers. Some women also are employed, either by themselves or someone else. Some mothers also travel away from their homes to their employment, while other mothers perform their employment within their homes. While the latter sounds very convenient, during the COVID-19 pandemic, most working mothers, along with the rest of the world, found out how utterly maddening it is to try to both parent and work in the same physical space during the same hours. While children and adolescents are now back in school, much about the employment lives of mothers has not changed from pre-pandemic life (Schnackenberg, 2023).

Female-identifying parents who are employed by colleges or universities are often dubbed "motherscholars." Motherscholars (Matias, 2011; Matias, 2022; Matias & Nishi, 2018) are thought to possess a symbiotically beneficial relationship between their employment in the academy and their role as maternal caregivers. It is said that the qualities of a successful academic both inform and uplift motherhood, and that the skills and talents required of mothering positively impact the life of an instructor and a scholar. The life of a motherscholar is a whole, not made of two different roles and parts, but a complete entity where all the various aspects of one's life positively influence the other. Motherscholars are a wonderful asset and integral to the life of of the academy. They/we deserve to be seen (CohenMiller, 2019). It is a great privilege to be a motherscholar.

Much has been written about the lives of academic mothers. The late Maryann Mason co-authored several high-profile, comprehensive, works on the effects of motherhood on the professional lives of academic women. She and her co-authors (Mason & Goulden, 2002; Mason & Goulden, 2004; Mason, Wolfinger, & Goulden, 2013) found that women in higher education were less likely to have children and families, less likely to be married, and more likely to wait to have families or be childless than men of the same academic rank. In fact, where having children is an asset to academic men's careers, it is a hindrance to women's (Budig, 2014). The more highly skilled the professional woman, the more motherhood negatively affects salary and earnings (England, Bearak, Budig, & Hodges, 2016).

In addition to economic challenges, a host of other barriers to mothering in the academy have been identified. A primary hindrance to the harmonious work-life balance of motherscholars is the long held ideology that women take primary responsibility for the domestic affairs of the home, and males are the breadwinners and source of economic stability. Despite women entering the workforce in droves, this gender ideology has attached itself to working women and remains to the present day. Academic mothers are expected to be both the managers of their own careers, as well as the functioning of all things on the homefront (Hunt, 2015). In her seminal work on the subject, Arlie Hochschild (2012) called this phenomena "the second shift" and it plagues working women across the globe, in a vast variety of careers. Each of these identities - domestic manager and career women - are full-time jobs. Add caregiving and/or parenting on top of these roles and there simply aren't enough hours in the day to accomplish all of them. Each role requires long hours and full attention, and the academy expects and privileges those who can dedicate long, focused hours, to their work (Isgro & Casteñeda, 2015). Flaherty (20154) also notes that academics spend a considerable amount of time in meetings and performing other service work, which also goes professionally uncredited. Given that much of the service work, both credited and uncredited, falls to academic women (Guarino & Borden, 2017), this again leaves the housekeeping - in this case academic housekeeping - as the job of females in the academy. So not only are academic women caregivers at home, they appear to be caregivers in higher education as well, doing the domestic work in the institution. Perhaps this adds yet another dimension to the carework of motherscholars.

These many claims on the time of academic mothers are not only stressful, and impossible, but they also consume valuable hours that could and need to be spent on scholarly investigation. Academic research takes time to do well. Dedicated hours are needed in which to think and ponder, and wander around questions that spark curiosity. It takes significant (often quiet) time to formulate original hypotheses and create appropriate methodologies with which to investigate them. Data collection and analysis are not something done with attention split into many directions. Equally time-intensive is understanding what the data is saying and forming conclusions. Then, of course, there is the time needed to write about these original works of scholarship. Adding to the challenges of dedicated research time, is the dated perception for the need of a constant "campus presence" from faculty. Often, it is better for motherscholars to write and do scholarly work in a more secluded location, away from both family and other work obligations, but they dare not work remotely for fear of the perception that they are just staying home to do care work. In a time where the vast majority of professional communication occurs virtually, and coursework is also done online, it is a deep shame that aspersions are cast on academic mothers for needing solitary, quiet spaces, to complete their scholarship. Academic men largely do not suffer such suspicions about their work time being used for family matters. Correspondingly, Derrick, Chen, van leeuwen, Lariviiere, and Sugimoto (2018) found that the level of parental engagement is negatively associated with scholarly productivity. Ward and Wolf-Wendel (2012) ground their widely publicized work, *Academic Motherhood: How Faculty Manage Work and Family*, in the idea that academic women are the primary child and elder caregivers. Together, these two works establish that caregiving academic women, i.e. motherscholars, suffer lower levels of scholarly productivity than their male counterparts. If this finding was ever in question, the COVID-19 pandemic exacerbated this phenomenon exponentially (Bender, Brown, Hensley Kasitz, & Vega, 2022; Cui, Ding, & Zhu, 2022; Krukowski, Jagsi, & Cardel; 2021).

Cohenmiller, Demers, Schnackenberg and Izekenova (2022) found that a lack of systematized maternity and parental leave is another notable hindrance to the careers of academic mothers. Similarly, a practice that presents itself as a support, but more often than not, hurts academic mothers professionally are stop-the-clock policies. These types of options, where individuals are allowed to pause or prolong the time to tenure, are perfect examples of how policies in higher education are still rife with implicit bias. Winslow and Davis (2016) discuss how clock-stopping policies have not been shown to be a hindrance to tenure, but can affect the overall salaries (including annual percentage increases) of those who take advantage of them. Sallee, Ward, & Wolf-Wendel (2016) report that academic mothers were hesitant to take advantage of stop-the-clock policies due to the perception that they were less dedicated to their careers than their male colleagues. Williams and Lee (2015) offer anecdotal evidence on how female academics are consistently driven out of higher education once they become pregnant. In fact, Antecol, Bedard, and Stearns (2018) found that not only do gender-neutral clock stopping policies reduce motherscholar tenure rates, they increase academic male tenure rates. Perhaps these policies are not so subtly biased afterall.

Other, more overt, examples of gender/mother-bias in higher education reveal themselves in the smaller, day-to-day job expectations of academics. Simple, but often overlooked practices, such as scheduling work meetings in the evening when daycares and after-school programs are closed limits the participation of academic mothers. Similarly, the lack of childcare on college campuses restricts the flexibility of motherscholars to fully engage in campus life. While unfortunate, these occurrences are not uncommon or surprising since the idea that faculty have flexible schedules undergirds some of the lack of consideration around evening scheduling and lack of childcare. Academic women who are also caregivers do not have flexible schedules. In fact, it is just the opposite. Motherscholars, indeed most working mothers, often talk about how when one meeting or appointment needs to be changed, the balance of an entire day or week can fall crumbling at their feet. Male academics rarely discuss this phenomenon since it is not their lived experience, Work policies that interfere with family responsibilities remain prevalent in higher education since the academy continues to be a highly gendered institution.

MAIN FOCUS OF THE CHAPTER

Issues, Controversies, Problems

The concept of MotherLeader emerged from the motherscholar domain (Schnackenberg, 2018; Schnackenberg, 2020; Schnackenberg, 2021; Schnackenberg, 2022; Schnackenberg, 2023). It's clear that the professional and personal lives of motherscholars are overwhelming, yet some academic mothers still choose to pursue leadership roles in the academy. Just as motherhood can inform academic and professional life, motherhood can also inform and enhance leadership. The relationship is mutually beneficial since the qualities that make a good leader are also the qualities needed to be a competent caregiver. Perspective gained while both leading and caring is bi-directional and adds depth to decision-making in every context. While motherhood and caregiving is often invisible in higher education (Laapayese, 2017), the skills, knowledge, empathy, and strength gained from these experiences don't simply disappear once a woman walks into the ivory tower. The skills needed to mother are also beneficial when running an academic department, division, or institution. Caregivers need to be organized and have deep wells of energy (as well as devise ways to protect their own energy and well-being). They also need to be able to carefully listen, read between the lines, and be attentive to non-verbal cues. Mothers are resourceful, critical-thinkers, and exceptional problem-solvers. They know when to let others attempt to solve problems and learn from the process and from failure. MotherLeaders and motherscholars develop thick skins and work hard not to let nonsense, both personal and institutional, negatively affect them. Importantly, caregivers know when and how to say "no" and to be consistent in their decisions and refusals. All of these skills, truly all of them, are endlessly useful in leadership in academic settings. The active listening, decision-making, kindness, firmness, consistency, etc. are all deeply important leadership skills that mothers possess or develop as they nurture those in their care. These abilities translate directly from the home into the office, often with relatively little modification. The context, setting, and venue just change. Not the basic leadership abilities.

While the coexistence of leading and mothering is intensely beneficial, the same challenges are faced by MotherLeaders and motherscholars. Perhaps the thing that motherscholars and MotherLeaders suffer from most is "work-family guilt" (Korabik, 2015). This guilt stems from many causes, but at the root is having to make difficult decisions regarding priorities. Work versus children and family is generally the typical dichotomous choice that puts academic mothers in an impossible position. For MotherLeaders, it's often the choice between doing something to care for the institution, or to care for their loved ones. A deeply troubling decision for highly educated, ambitious, dedicated, caring, academic mothers. This feeling is not new, and it is well-documented. Sallee, Ward and Wolf-Wendel found in two qualitative studies that motherscholars often feel guilty about their parenting and professor-ing, where men feel pride at doing and being both (2016). This experience crosses international boundaries since Santos (2015) found Portuguese academic mothers experience feelings of guilt for being neither the perfect worker nor the perfect parent. In their quantitative, correlational, study, Borelli, et al. (2017) found that mothers of young children had significantly higher levels of work-family guilt and work-interfering-with-family-guilt than did fathers. Collins (2021) found that the guilt that working mothers feel crosses international boundaries, but that supportive workplace policies can mitigate that guilt. Brooks (2014) reported similar findings with international collegiate student mothers - the feeling of maternal work-family guilt can be alleviated through institutional, state, and/or national policies, as well as reframed social norms with regard to the role of a "good mother." CohenMiller, Demers, Schnackenberg, and Izekenova (2022) support this finding in their work, where motherscholars describe supportive and helpful workplace policies that occur either organically or at lower levels in the academy (i.e. departmental levels), but are rarely institutionalized throughout colleges and universities to provide help to all. Holm, Prosek, and Godwin Weisberger (2015) go so far as to call these organic support systems and/or workplace policies "protective factors." They explain that their participants named specific individuals and/or resources as the reasons they felt safe enough to have children while studying in graduate programs in higher education. Their participants felt safe enough to become doctoral student mothers, or DocMamas (CohenMiller, 2018). This finding begs the question - why in the world do motherscholars or DocMamas need to feel safe and protected from a workplace and institution like *higher education* in order to be comfortable enough to have children while also being or becoming highly educated?

It is clear that academic women are fearful of becoming mothers while also working in colleges and universities. If and when they do decide to become motherscholars, and eventually MotherLeaders, they then suffer from a host of workplace challenges not present for their male counterparts, including a lesser rate of scholarly productivity, a higher rate of uncompensated service work, and an evident lack of representation in the upper echelons of leadership, just to name a few. A most glaring disparity between motherscholars/MotherLeaders and male parent academics is the amount of work-family guilt that women caregivers feel. While often being overworked both at home and in academia, motherscholars and MotherLeaders also suffer from the feeling of doing none of it well, when no single person could or should have to do half of what's expected of these fierce women. It appears that a forward-thinking institution like higher education, that should be on the forefront of creating a better society for all of its members, is failing miserably. We should expect and insist on better treatment and policies from academic establishments that have the power to shape and change culture.

Solutions and Recommendations

As a parent, and a professor, I often hear academic mothers struggle over the constant competing demands of caregiving and employment. This life and career comes with the ever-present guilt of not giving 100% to both the greedy ivory tower, and our deserving loved ones. Where the expectation of this type of perfection came from is likely a powerful mix of media influence, popular narrative, and the socialization of stereotypical men's and women's roles in society. Regardless of its origins, the fact remains that motherscholars and MotherLeaders do not have unlimited amounts of time, energy or attention to give to any set of demands on their lives. Nor should they be expected to give their all to everyone and everything. As with anything in life, it's important to prioritize. Not just for time management or sanity reasons, though those are important too. It's important to prioritize so we know what means the most to us and that we feel good putting our attention in those places, rather than where we feel we are expected to focus our energy. Clarity of priorities helps to rid us of work-family guilt because, once we're certain of where we choose to put our time and energy, there simply is no reason to feel guilty about who we are and what we do. Institutions of higher education can support motherscholars and MotherLeaders as they aspire to manageable work and family lives. By respecting the boundaries academic mothers set on their time and responsibilities, and instituting structures to help alleviate some of the unnecessary burdens faced by motherscholars and MotherLeaders, higher education can begin to show that it values the academic women who are an integral fabric of the colleges and universities at which they work.

CONCLUSION

Circling back to that terrible day for my family and I one year ago, it's clearly important that schools and communities do all that we can do rally around our children and adolescents to keep them safe. Unfortunately, in the current times, this means putting in place protective measures and protocols, often involving law enforcement, in P-12 schools. While effective in both combating and preventing violence in and attacks on schools, these measures can frequently be alarming for both students and their caregivers. It is therefore equally important to have mental health support and counseling services available on both a consistent and as needed basis for individuals in the school community. While it is a shame that schools in the United States have become targets for those wishing to inflict irreversible harm to our most vulnerable citizens (children and adolescents), it is to our credit that caregivers feel passionate enough about the right to and need for an education that we continue to send our youth to schools. It is our continued collective duty to ensure that these spaces for learning and growing remain safe and nurturing environments, where perpetrators dare not tread.

For me, my commitment to my only child was always, and still remains, my primary focus. His needs are prioritized above my work demands every time. And I make no apology nor offer unneeded explanation for that choice. I was almost 40 years old when he was born, and he is the only child I had and ever will have. I have had many decades to establish my career and give the full of my energy and talents to the academy. I have no qualms in reclaiming and refocusing those priorities to the individual whom I love most in the world. Sadly, I have watched both of my parents pass away and when they each were at the end of their lives, neither ever regretted the meetings they missed or work responsibilities or professional opportunities that slipped through their fingers. They did regret the events or opportunities they missed that involved my sister and I. And they especially regretted all the life moments of their young grandchildren that they would miss in the future. My parent's clarity at the end of their lives confirmed what I had suspected all along - it's the lives of those I love that are the most important. Work and career come far, far, second to that. I am therefore comfortable, and in fact proud, of the work choices that I make, or don't make, that enable (or force) me to prioritize my son. Faced with the possibility of losing him on that spring day in 2023 solidified my priorities for me one thousand times over. I am here for the good that I can put into the world through the people I care about most. If I make some career contributions along the way also, then that's good too. But that's not what will make me smile at the end of the day and not what fills my heart each day until then. My priorities, and my conscience, are clear. That day changed everything.

REFERENCES

Antecol, H., Bedard, K., & Stearns, J. (2018). Equal but inequitable: Who benefits from gender-neutral tenure clock stopping policies? *The American Economic Review*, 108(9), 2420–2441. DOI: 10.1257/aer.20160613

Bender, S., Brown, K. S., Hensley Kasitz, D. L., & Vega, O. (2022). Academic women and their children: Parenting during COVID-19 and the impact on scholarly productivity. *Family Relations*, 71(1), 46–67. DOI: 10.1111/fare.12632

Borelli, J. L., Nelson, S. K., River, L. M., Birken, S. A., & Moss-Racusin, C. (2017). Gender differences in work-family guilt in parents of young children. *Sex Roles*, 76(5-6), 356–368. DOI: 10.1007/s11199-016-0579-0

Brooks, R. (2014). Social and spatial disparities in emotional responses to education: Feelings of guilt among student parents. *British Educational Research Journal*, 41(3), 505–519. DOI: 10.1002/berj.3154

Budig, M. (2014). *The fatherhood bonus and the motherhood penalty: Parenthood and the gender gap in pay*. The Way. https://www.thirdway.org/report/the-fatherhood-bonus-and-the-motherhood-penalty-parenthood-and-the-gender-gap-in-pay?tpcc=nlbroadsheet

CohenMiller. A.S. (October 25, 2019). *Gender equality & social justice: Raising awareness & empowering community*. Nazarbayev University Media and Information Literacy Forum 2019, Astana, Kazakhstan. DOI:DOI: 10.13140/RG.2.2.15965.15842

CohenMiller, A. S., Demers, D., Schnackenberg, H., & Izekenova, Z.CohenMiller. (2022). "You are seen; you matter": Applying the theory of gendered organizations to equity and inclusion for motherscholars in higher education. *Journal of Women and Gender in Higher Education*, 15(1), 87–109. DOI: 10.1080/26379112.2022.2025816

Collins, C. (2021). Is maternal guilt a cross-national experience? *Qualitative Sociology*, 44(1), 1–29. DOI: 10.1007/s11133-020-09451-2

Cui, R., Ding, H., & Zhu, F. (2022). Gender inequality in research productivity during the COVID-19 pandemic. *Manufacturing & Service Operations Management*, 24(2), 707–726. DOI: 10.1287/msom.2021.0991

Derrick, G.E., Chen, P., Leeuwen, T.N., Larivière, V., & Sugimoto, C.R. (2018). The academic motherload: Models of parenting engagement and the effect on academic productivity and performance. *ArXiv, abs/2108.05376*.

England, P., Bearak, J., Budig, M. J., & Hodges, M. J. (2016). Do highly paid, highly skilled women experience the largest motherhood penalty? *American Sociological Review*, 81(6), 146–167. DOI: 10.1177/0003122416673598

Flaherty, C. (April 9, 2014). So much to do so little time. *Inside Higher Ed*. https://www.insidehighered.com/news/2014/04/09/research-shows-professors-work-long-hours-and-spend-much-day-meetings

Guarino, C. M., & Borden, V. M. H. (2017). Faculty service loads and gender: Are women taking care of the academic family? *Research in Higher Education*, 58(6), 672–694. DOI: 10.1007/s11162-017-9454-2

Hochschild, A. (2012). The second shift: Working families and the revolution at home. Penguin Group., 978-0-14-312033-9.

Holm, J. M., Prosek, E. A., & Godwin Weisberger, A. C. (2015). A phenomenological investigation of counseling doctoral students becoming mothers. *Counselor Education and Supervision*, 54(1), 2–16. DOI: 10.1002/j.1556-6978.2015.00066.x

Hunt, A. N. (2015). The role of theory in understanding the lived experiences of mothering in the academy. In Young, A. M. (Ed.), *Teacher, scholar, mother: Re-envisioning motherhood in the academy* (pp. 3–12). Lexington Books.

Isgro, K., & Casteñeda, M. (2015). Mothers in U.S. academia: Insights from lived experiences. *Women's Studies International Forum*, 53, 174–181. DOI: 10.1016/j.wsif.2014.12.002

Korabik, K. (2015). The intersection of gender and work–family guilt. In Mills, M. (Ed.), *Gender and the work-family experience*. Springer., DOI: 10.1007/978-3-319-08891-4_8

Krukowski, R. A., Jagsi, R., & Cardel, M. I. (2021). Academic productivity differences by gender and child age in science, technology, engineering, mathematics, and medicine faculty during the COVID-19 pandemic. *Journal of Women's Health*, 30(3), 341–347. DOI: 10.1089/jwh.2020.8710 PMID: 33216682

Lapayese, Y. (2017). Mother-scholars: Thinking and being in higher education. Cole, K. & Hassel, H. (Eds.) *Surviving sexism in academia: Strategies for feminist leadership*. Routledge.

Mason, M. A., & Goulden, M. (2002). Do babies matter? The effect of family formation on the lifelong careers of academic men and women. *Academe*, 88(6), 21–27. DOI: 10.2307/40252436

Mason, M. A., & Goulden, M. (2004). Do babies matter (Part 2)? Closing the baby gap. *Academe*, 90(6), 1–10. DOI: 10.2307/40252699

Mason, M. A., Wolfinger, N. H., & Goulden, M. (2013). *Do babies matter? Gender and family in the ivory tower*. Rutgers University Press.

Matias, C. E. (2022). Birthing the motherscholar and motherscholarship. *Peabody Journal of Education*, 97(2), 246–250. DOI: 10.1080/0161956X.2022.2055897

Matias, C. E. (2011, April 7 - April 11). *Paying it forward: Motherscholars navigating the academic terrain*. AERA Division G Highlighted Panel. American Educational Research Association 2011, Annual Meeting, New Orleans, LA, United States.

Matias, C. E., & Nishi, N. W. (2018). ParentCrit epilog. *International Journal of Qualitative Studies in Education : QSE*, 31(1), 82–85. DOI: 10.1080/09518398.2017.1379625

Sallee, M., Ward, K., & Wolf-Wendel, L. (2016). Can anyone have it all? Gendered views on parenting and academic careers. *Innovative Higher Education*, 41(3), 187–202. DOI: 10.1007/s10755-015-9345-4

Santos, G. G. (2015). Narratives about work and family life among Portuguese academics. *Gender, Work and Organization*, 22(1), 1–15. DOI: 10.1111/gwao.12061

Schnackenberg, H. L. (2018) motherscholar:MotherLeader. In Schnackenberg, H.L. & Simard, D.A. (Eds.), *Challenges and Opportunities for Women in Higher Education Leadership,* Hershey, PA: IGI Global.

Schnackenberg, H. L. (2020). motherscholar: MotherLeader and the Ethical Double-Bind. In Squires, M.E. & Yu, Y., & Schnackenberg, H.L. (Eds), *Ethics in Higher Education*, New York, NY: Nova Science Publishers.

Schnackenberg, H. L. (2021). motherscholar: MotherLeader and the Pandemic. In Schnackenberg, H.L. & Simard, D.A. (Eds), *Women and Leadership in Higher Education During Global Crises*. Hershey, PA: IGI Global.

Schnackenberg, H. L. (2022). motherscholar: MotherLeader Reflections from a Little Past the Middle. In Schnackenberg, H.L. (Ed.) *Women in Higher Education and the Journey to Mid-Career*. Hershey, PA: IGI Global.

Schnackenberg, H. L. (2023). motherscholar and MotherLeader: The more things change, the more they stay the same. In H.L. Schnackenberg & D.A. Simard (Eds), *Stabilizing and empowering women in higher education: Realigning, recentering, and rebuilding* (pp. 284-295). IGI Global. DOI: DOI: 10.4018/978-1-6684-8597-2

Ward, K., & Wolf-Wendel, L. (2012). *Academic motherhood: How faculty manage work and family*. Rutgers University Press.

Williams, J. C., & Jessica, L. (September 28, 2015). It's illegal, Yet it happens all the time: How Pregnant women and mothers get hounded out of higher education. *Chronicle of Higher Education*. https://www.chronicle.com/article/Its-Illegal-Yet-It-Happens/233445

Winslow, S., & Davis, S. N. (2016). Gender inequality across the academic life course. *Sociology Compass*, 10(5), 404–416. DOI: 10.1111/soc4.12372

ADDITIONAL READING

American Council on Education. (2017). *American college president study 2017*. http://www.aceacps.org

Anderson, N. (September 11, 2012). American university professor breast-fed baby in class, sparking debate. *The Washington Post*. https://www.washingtonpost.com/local/education/american-university-professor-breast-feeds-sick-baby-in-class-sparking-debate/2012/09/11/54a06856-fc12-11e1-8adc-499661afe377_story.html?utm_term=.29c67ed75a81

Baker, M. (2010). Choices or constraints? Family responsibilities, gender and academic careers. *Journal of Comparative Family Studies*, 41(1), 1–18. DOI: 10.3138/jcfs.41.1.1

Baker, M. (2012). Gendered families, academic work, and the motherhood penalty. *Women's Studies Journal*, 26(1), 11–24.

Baker, M. (2016). Women graduates and the workplace: Continuing challenges for academic women. *Studies in Higher Education*, 41(5), 887–900. DOI: 10.1080/03075079.2016.1147718

Bassett, R. H. (2005). *Parenting and professing: Balancing family work with an academic career*. Vanderbilt University Press. DOI: 10.2307/j.ctv17vf5r6

Belkin, L. (October 26, 2003). The opt-out revolution. *The New York Times Magazine*.https://www.nytimes.com/2003/10/26/magazine/the-opt-out-revolution.html

Birken, S., & Borelli, J. L. (January 14, 2015). Coming out as academic mothers: What happens when two highly driven women in academe decide to have children? *The Chronicle of Higher Education*. https://www.chronicle.com/article/Coming-Out-as-Academic-Mothers/151157

Bonawitz, M. & Andel, N. (2009). The Glass Ceiling Is Made Of Concrete: The barriers to promotion and tenure of women in american academia. *Forum on Public Policy: A Journal of the Oxford Round Table, 5*(2), 1-16.

Casteneda, M., & Isgro, K. (2013). *Mothers in academia*. Columbia University Press.

Chavez-Garcia, M. (September 28, 2009). Superprofessor meets supermom. *The Chronicle of Higher Education*. https://www.chronicle.com/article/Superprofessor-Meets-Supermom/48613

Cohen, H. (2002). *The baby bias*. The New York Times. https://www.nytimes.com/2002/08/04/education/the-baby-bias.html

Colbeck, C. L., & Drago, R. (2005). Accept, avoid, resist: How faculty members respond to bias against caregiving . . . and how departments can help. *Change*, 37(6), 10–17. DOI: 10.3200/CHNG.37.6.10-17

Dominici, F., Fried, L. P., & Zeger, S. L. (July-August, 2009). So few women leaders. *American Association of University Professors*. https://www.aaup.org/article/so-few-women-leaders#.We-bdrVrwy4

Drago, R., & Williams, J. (2000). A half-time tenure track proposal. *Change*, 32(6), 46–51. DOI: 10.1080/00091380009601767

Eagly, A. H., & Karau, S. J. (2002). Role congruity theory of prejudice toward female leaders. *Psychological Review*, 109(3), 573–598. DOI: 10.1037/0033-295X.109.3.573 PMID: 12088246

Eddy, P. L. (2010). *Community college leadership: A multidimensional model for leading change*. Stylus Publications.

Etzkowitz, H., Kelmelgor, C., & Uzzi, B. (2000). *Athena unbound: The advancement of women in science and technology*. Cambridge University Press. DOI: 10.1017/CBO9780511541414

Evans, E., Grant, C., & Pescowitz, M. (2008). *Mama PhD: Women write about motherhood and academic life*. Rutgers University Press.

Fothergill, A., & Felty, K. (2003). I've worked very hard and slept very little: Mothers on the tenure track in academia. *Journal of the Association for Research on Mothering*, 5(2), 7–19.

Gee, M. V., & Norton, S. M. (2009). Improving the Status of Women in the Academy. *The NEA Higher Education Journal*, (Fall), 163–170.

Gomez, M. L. (2017). "I Have Always Felt Like a Trespasser": Life Histories from Latina Staff Members in Higher Education. In Cole, K., & Hassel, H. (Eds.), *Surviving sexism in academia: Strategies for feminist leadership*. Routledge.

Harris, R. S. (September 16, 2015). Childcare shouldn't be an issue. *Inside Higher Ed*. https://www.insidehighered.com/views/2015/09/16/essay-says-child-care-shouldnt-still-be-issue-scholarly-meetings

Hodge, D. M. (2017). Motherhood and leadership in academia: Getting beyond personal survival mode. In Cole, K., & Hassel, H. (Eds.), *Surviving sexism in academia: Strategies for feminist leadership*. Routledge. DOI: 10.4324/9781315523217-21

Ibarra, H., Carter, N. M., & Silva, C. (2010). Why Men Still Get More Promotions Than Women. *Harvard Business Review*, •••, 1–6. PMID: 20821967

Jacobs, J. A. (2004). The faculty time divide. *Sociological Forum*, 19(1), 3–27. DOI: 10.1023/B:SOFO.0000019646.82538.cc

Jaschik, S. (June 14, 2012). A stop the clock penalty. *Inside Higher Ed*. https://www.insidehighered.com/news/2012/06/14/study-finds-those-who-stop-tenure-clock-earn-less-those-who-dont

Jaschik, S. (October 27, 2017). But will her husband move? Study suggests women with male partners face bias in searches for junior faculty members. *Inside Higher Ed*. https://www.insidehighered.com/news/2017/10/27/hiring-junior-faculty-positions-study-finds-bias-against-female-candidates-who-have?utm_content=buffere28e6&utm_medium=social&utm_source=twitter&utm_campaign=IHEbuffer

Jones, B. D. (2012). *Women who opt out: The debate over working mothers and work-family balance*. New York University Press.

Kajitani, M. P. (2006). Finding a parent friendly place. *The Chronicle of Higher Education*. https://www.chronicle.com/article/Finding-A-Parent-Friendly/46855

Kajitani, M. P. (2006). Bring the kids. *The Chronicle of Higher Education*. from https://www.chronicle.com/article/Bring-the-Kids/46445

Kittelstrom, A. (February, 2010). The academic-motherhood handicap. *The Chronicle of Higher Education*. https://www.chronicle.com/article/The-Academic-Motherhood/64073

Klein, T. (July 22, 2010). Why women leaders are MIA from academic life. *Washington Post*. http://views.washingtonpost.com/leadership/guestinsights/2010/07/why-women-leaders-are-mia-from-academic-life.html

Kozma, M. M., & Schroer, J. W. (2017). For the love of the feminist killjoy: Solving philosophy's white male problem. In Cole, K., & Hassel, H. (Eds.), *Surviving sexism in academia: Strategies for feminist leadership*. Routledge. DOI: 10.4324/9781315523217-8

Lapayese, Y. (2017). Mother-scholars: Thinking and being in higher education. Cole, K. & Hassel, H. (Eds.) *Surviving sexism in academia: Strategies for feminist leadership*. Routledge.

Laypayese, Y. (2012). *Mother-scholar: (Re)Imagining K-12 education*. Springer Publishing. DOI: 10.1007/978-94-6091-891-9

Leonard, D. J. (July 26, 2013). Blame the institution, not just the fathers. *Chronicle of Higher Education*. https://www.chronicle.com/article/Blame-the-Institution-Not/140405

Lubrano, S. (October 31, 2012). Tenure and gender. *The Harvard Crimson*. https://www.thecrimson.com/column/exodoxa/article/2012/10/31/gender-tenure-women-professors

Marine, S. B., & Aleman, A. M. (2018). Women faculty, professional identity, and gender disposition. *Review of Higher Education*, 41(2), 217–252. DOI: 10.1353/rhe.2018.0002

Mason, M. A. (June 17, 2013). In the Ivory Tower, men only. *Slate*. https://www.slate.com/articles/double_x/doublex/2013/06/female_academics_pay_a_heavy_baby_penalty.html

Mason, M. A., & Ekman, E. M. (2007). *Mothers on the fast track*. Oxford University Press.

McGranahan, C. (March 22, 2017). *Yes, you can: Being an academic and a mother – redux. AllegraLab*. https://allegralaboratory.net/yes-you-can-being-an-academic-and-a-mother

Monosson, E. (2010). *Motherhood, the elephant in the laboratory: Women scientists speak out*. ILR Press.

Nakhaie, M. R. (2002). Gender differences in publication among university professors in Canada. *Canadian Review of Sociology*, 39(2), 151–179. DOI: 10.1111/j.1755-618X.2002.tb00615.x

National Center for Education Statistics, IPEDS Data Center (2016). Full-time instructional staff, by faculty and tenure status, academic rank, race/ethnicity, and gender (degree-granting institutions): Fall 2015.

National Education Association. (2009). Special salary issue 2009: Women and minority faculty members. https://www.nea.org/home/33837.htm/

Newman, J. (April 11, 2014). There is a gender pay gap in academe but it may not be the gap that matters. *Chronicle of Higher Education*. https://www.chronicle.com/blogs/data/2014/04/11/there-is-a-gender-pay-gap-in-academe-but-it-may-not-be-the-gap-that-matters

Nora, K., Rochelle, G., Lopez, A.-M., & Williams, N. A. (2017). Surviving sexism to inspire change: Stories and reflections from mothers on the tenure track. In Cole, K., & Hassel, H. (Eds.), *Surviving Surviving sexism in academia: Strategies for feminist leadership*. Routledge. DOI: 10.4324/9781315523217-13

O'Laughlin, E. M., & Bischoff, L. G. (2005). Balancing parenthood and academia: Work/family stress as influenced by gender and tenure status. *Journal of Family Issues*, 26(1), 79–106. DOI: 10.1177/0192513X04265942

O'Reilly, A. (Ed.). (2003). Mother in the academy [special issue]. *Journal of the Association for Research on Mothering*, 5(2).

Pfannenstiel, B. (February 21, 2018). Baby in the house: Iowa legislature welcomes its newest (and smallest) member. *The Des Moines Register*. https://www.desmoinesregister.com/story/news/politics/2018/02/21/baby-house-iowa-legislature-welcomes-its-newest-and-smallest-member/356010002/

Rhoads, S. E., & Rhoads, C. H. (2012). Gender roles and infant/toddler care: Male and female professors on the tenure track. *Journal of Social, Evolutionary, & Cultural Psychology*, 6(1), 13–31. DOI: 10.1037/h0099227

Rios, C. (2015). *You call it professionalism; i call it oppression in a three-piece suit, everyday feminism*. https://everydayfeminism.com/2015/02/professionalism-and-oppression

Rivera, L. A. (2017, October 25). When two bodies are (not) a problem: Gender and relationship status discrimination in academic hiring. *American Sociological Review*, 82(6), 1111–1138. DOI: 10.1177/0003122417739294

Rodino-Colocino, M., Niesen, M., Noble, S. U., & Quail, C. (2017). Smashing the "Maternal Wall.". In Cole, K., & Hassel, H. (Eds.), *Surviving sexism in academia: Strategies for feminist leadership*. Routledge.

Rosen, R. (1999, July 30). Secrets of the second sex in scholarly life. *The Chronicle of Higher Education*, 45(46), A48.

Sallee, M., Ward, K., & Wolf-Wendel, L. (2016). Can anyone have it all? Gendered views on parenting and academic careers. *Innovative Higher Education*, 41(3), 187–202. DOI: 10.1007/s10755-015-9345-4

Samble, J. N. (2008). Female faculty: Challenges and choices in the United States and beyond. *New Directions for Higher Education*, 143(143), 55–62. DOI: 10.1002/he.313

Schiebinger, L. L., Henderson, A. D., & Gilmartin, S. K. (2008). *Dual-career academic couples: What universities need to know*. Michelle R. Clayman Institute for Gender Research, Stanford University.

Schnackenberg, H. L., & Simard, D. A. (2016). *Challenges facing female department chairs in higher education: Emerging research and opportunities*. IGI Global.

Sepler, F. (2017). The bullying we don't talk about: Women bullying women in the academy. In Cole, K., & Hassel, H. (Eds.), *Surviving sexism in academia: Strategies for feminist leadership*. Routledge. DOI: 10.4324/9781315523217-31

Skurzewski-Servant, M., & Bugenhagen, M. J. (2017). Career navigation of female leaders in higher education. In Cole, K., & Hassel, H. (Eds.), *Surviving sexism in academia: Strategies for feminist leadership*. Routledge. DOI: 10.4324/9781315523217-23

Slaughter, A.-M. (2013). Why women still can't have it all. *The Atlantic*. https://www.theatlantic.com/magazine/archive/2012/07/why-women-still-cant-have-it-all/309020/

Spalter-Roth, R., & Erskine, W. (2005). Beyond the fear factor: Work/family policies in academia— resources or rewards? *Change*, 37(6), 18–25.

Stone-Mediatore, S. (2016). Storytelling/narrative. In Disch, L., & Hawkesworth, M. (Eds.), *The Oxford handbook of feminist theory*. Oxford University Press.

The Council of Graduate Schools. (September, 2017). Graduate enrollment and degrees: 2006-2016. https://cgsnet.org/ckfinder/userfiles/files/CGS_GED16_Report_Final.pdf

Turban, S., Freeman, L., & Waber, B. (October 23, 2017). A study used sensors to show that men and women are treated differently at work. *Harvard Business Review*. https://hbr.org/2017/10/a-study-used-sensors-to-show-that-men-and-women-are-treated-differently-at-work

Vancour, M. L., & Sherman, W. M. (2010). Academic life balance for mothers: Pipeline or pipe cream? In O'Reilly, A. (Ed.), *21st century motherhood: Experience, identity, policy, agency*. Columbia University Press.

Walden, G. (January 31, 2002). Hiding the baby. *Chronicle of Higher Education*. https://www.chronicle.com/article/Hiding-the-Baby/46228

Wamsley, L. (April 9, 2018). Tammy Duckworth becomes first U.S. senator to give birth while in office. *National Public Radio*. https://www.npr.org/sections/thetwo-way/2018/04/09/600896586/tammy-duckworth-becomes-first-u-s-senator-to-give-birth-while-in-office

Ward, K., & Eddy, P. L. (December, 2013). Women and academic leadership: learning out. *The Chronicle of Higher Education*. https://www.chronicle.com/article/WomenAcademic-Leadership-/143503

White, M. (April 27, 2016). Academia and motherhood: We can have both. *Washington Post*. https://www.washingtonpost.com/news/grade-point/wp/2016/04/27/academia-and-motherhood-we-can-have-both/?utm_term=.2e95b36b4c60

Williams, J. (2000). *Unbending gender: Why work and family conflict and what to do about it*. Oxford University Press.

Williams, J. (June 17, 2002). How academe treats mothers. *Chronicle of Higher Education*. https://www.chronicle.com/article/How-Academe-Treats-Mothers/46133

Williams, J. (2004). Hitting the maternal wall-before they reach a "Glass Ceiling" in their careers, women faculty may hit a "Maternal Wall. *Academe*, 90(6), 16–20. DOI: 10.2307/40252700

Williams, J. (2005). The Glass Ceiling and the Maternal Wall in academia. *New Directions for Higher Education*, 130(130), 91–110. DOI: 10.1002/he.181

Wilson, R. (2001a, November 9). A push to help new parents prepare for tenure reviews. *The Chronicle of Higher Education*, 48(11), A10–A12.

Wilson, R. (2001b, November 9). For women with tenure and families, moving up the ranks is challenging. *The Chronicle of Higher Education*, 48(11).

Wilson, R. (2002, December 13). Papers and pampers. *The Chronicle of Higher Education*, ●●●, A8–A11.

Wolf-Wendel, L., & Ward, K. (2006). Academic life and motherhood: Variations by institutional type. *Higher Education*, 52(3), 487–521. DOI: 10.1007/s10734-005-0364-4

Wolfinger, N. J., Goulden, M., & Mason, M. A. (2010). Alone in the Ivory Tower. *Journal of Family Issues*, 31(12), 1652–1670. DOI: 10.1177/0192513X10374939

Wolfinger, N. J., Mason, M. A., & Goulden, M. (2009). Stay in the game: Gender, family formation and alternative trajectories in the academic life course. *Social Forces*, 87(30), 1591–1621. DOI: 10.1353/sof.0.0182

Yoest, C., & Rhoads, S. (2004). *Parental leave in academia*. Report to the Alfred P. Sloan Foundation and the Bankard Fund at the University of Virginia. https://www.faculty.virginia.edu/familyandtenure/institutional%20report.pdf

Young, A. M. (2015). *Teacher, scholar, mother: Re-envisioning motherhood in the academy*. Lexington Books.

Young, D. S., & Wright, E. M. (2001). Mothers making tenure. *Journal of Social Work Education*, 27(3), 555–568. DOI: 10.1080/10437797.2001.10779074

Chapter 3
Self-Care and Emotional Well-Being of a Women Educators
An Interpretative Phenomenological Analysis

Elsy N. J.
https://orcid.org/0000-0003-2807-8734
Christ University, India

ABSTRACT

Women educators play a vital role in universities, yet their demanding careers can significantly impact their emotional well-being. This paper explores the challenges they face, including societal expectations, workload pressures, and the potential consequences of neglecting self-care. This research delves deeper into the lived experiences of self-care through an interpretative phenomenological analysis. By analyzing the narrative of a female educator, gain insights into the complex interplay between self-care practices, emotional wellbeing, and the demands of academia. The study reveals the constant struggle to balance professional obligations with personal well-being, highlighting the need for supportive structures to prioritize women educators' mental health. Universities also play a crucial role by implementing policies that address workload management, fostering an inclusive culture, and demonstrating leadership commitment to well-being. The findings call for increased institutional support and a cultural shift towards prioritizing well-being for women in academia.

DOI: 10.4018/979-8-3693-3144-6.ch003

INTRODUCTION

Universities, with their heavy workloads and high expectations, provide distinct challenges for female academics. The demanding nature of academic life, along with the unique challenges that women confront in professional contexts, has pushed the subject of self-care and emotional well-being among female educators to the forefront of conversation. This chapter delves into the experiences of female university educator, examining the challenges they face in maintaining a healthy work-life balance, as well as the potential consequences of ignoring self-care for their mental health and the impact on their emotional well-being in this demanding environment. It aims to learn how women view and deal with the difficulties that come with balancing research, teaching, service, and administrative responsibilities while having little personal time. The study also looks into how women educators define and incorporate self-care practices into their lives, as well as the possible benefits and obstacles of prioritizing self-care in the face of academic constraints. By identifying perceived facilitators and barriers to self-care, the study hopes to shed insight on the variables that permit or hinder women educators from prioritizing their well-being in the demanding university setting.

The Job Demands-Resources (JD-R) model provides a valuable framework for understanding the relationship between work environment and employee well-being, particularly pertinent to women educators. This model posits that job strain arises from an imbalance between demanding work conditions and available job resources. Women educators often grapple with heavy workloads, classroom management challenges, and work-life balance issues, which can contribute to burnout. Conversely, adequate administrative support, professional development, and supportive colleagues can mitigate these stressors. Building on the JD-R model, Stress and Coping Theory illuminates how women educators perceive and manage stress. Individuals appraise situations as stressful when demands exceed perceived resources. Women educators frequently encounter multiple stressors, and their coping mechanisms significantly influence their emotional well-being and job satisfaction. Role theory offers a lens to examine the multifaceted nature of a woman educator's role. Juggling teaching responsibilities, administrative tasks, and often caregiving roles can impact self-care. Spillover theory further emphasizes the interconnectedness of work and personal life. Work-related stress, satisfaction, or challenges can influence personal well-being, and vice versa. Understanding these dynamics is crucial for comprehending the complexities of women educators' experiences.

Women educators face a complex web of factors that may negatively impact their mental well-being. Gender prejudices in academics frequently result in unequal workloads, limited possibilities for progress, and an ongoing demand to prove themselves. Societal expectations of women as caregivers add to the strain, leading to feelings of guilt and inadequacy when prioritizing self-care. Furthermore, the challenging nature of academic work, which includes long hours, administrative responsibilities, and an emotional stake in student success, can easily result in burnout, stress, anxiety, and depression.

Self-care is a crucial tool for female educators to maintain their well-being and succeed in their employment. It includes a variety of activities that improve physical, mental, and emotional wellness. Women educators frequently lack self-care, which can lead to high levels of stress and negatively impact their health, well-being, job satisfaction, and performance. According to research, self-care and stress management are vital for educators' overall well-being and productivity. Furthermore, poor support, severe workloads, and insufficient time for duties all contribute to educators ignoring self-care practices, which eventually affects their retention in the field (Miller, 2018). The pressure on educators to prioritize self-care above tackling structural concerns can be interpreted as gaslighting, worsened by a neoliberal education system that values individualistic approaches to teaching and learning (Dunn, 2023). Addressing the absence of self-care among female educators is critical to enhancing their quality of life, job happiness, and overall efficacy in the educational sector.

Self-care is essential for women educators because it helps them maintain their mental well-being and avoid burnout (Nguyen, 2023). Women academic leaders confront unique challenges and stressors, particularly during emergencies such as the COVID-19 pandemic, making self-care critical to their well-being and efficacy in leading students and faculty (Puliatte, 2021). Neglecting self-care can result in high levels of stress, burnout (Metz & Jarvie, 2022), job unhappiness, and poor performance among educators. Implementing self-care practices at both the personal and university levels can help prevent burnout, boost work satisfaction, and provide a healthier learning environment for students (Rose et al., 2022). As a result, emphasizing self-care benefits both individual educators and the educational community as a whole.

Self-care practices for female educators include a variety of approaches to maintaining well-being and preventing burnout. These strategies include self-directed learning, feedback, and critical reflection (Fox, 2022), striving for continuous improvement to nurture oneself and others (Cardinal & Thomas, 2016), and participating in supervision to receive professional support and improve stress resilience (Liepina & Martinsone, 2022). Creating a community of practice based on mutual support, reciprocity, and lifelong learning can help increase work satisfaction among educators (Metz & Jarvie, 2022). Furthermore, employing self-care techniques at both the personal and institutional levels, while taking ecological implications into account, is vital for reducing burnout and maintaining overall wellness in the teaching profession (Rose et al., 2022).

The emotional well-being of female educators is an important factor that has been addressed in numerous research. According to a study, women academics experienced emotional stress during lockdown because to the blending of work and family obligations, resulting in irritation, fatigue, and worry (Ronnie et al., 2022). Furthermore, the emotional well-being of teachers is critical to the health of school organizations, and organizational cultures must be changed to better support teachers' emotional well-being (Stark et al., 2022). A study of school teachers in Bangalore found an important relationship between psychological well-being and mindfulness, underlining the importance of mindfulness and emotional intelligence for teachers' well-being. Female further education teachers' well-being influences their career choices and professional growth, which has an impact on college staff retention (Rasheed-Karim, 2023).

Universities have an important role in supporting the mental health of women educators, recognizing the issues they encounter, and actively encouraging self-care activities. As a result, universities should prioritize providing resources, support systems, and training to assist female educators in efficiently managing their mental health (Eltayeb, 2022). It is critical to foster an open communication culture and encourage academics to prioritize their own well-being without fear of being judged. By emphasizing self-care and emotional well-being among female educators, institutions can foster a more inclusive and supportive environment that allows these individuals to succeed personally and professionally.

In this context this chapter tries to explore and understand how do female university educators experience and manage their self-care and emotional well-being in the context of their demanding academic roles?

METHOD

Participant

This study used a purposive sample strategy to select a participant, Ann, a 45-year-old married professor with two children who works at a prestigious university in Bangalore, India. Ann has been worked at the university for 15 years and was diagnosed with anxiety two years ago. Through in-depth, semi-structured interviews, the study dives into Ann's experiences with her workload, service expectations, self-care practices, and how these aspects affect her emotional well-being.

Data Collection

The empirical data for this study consists of three transcribed, semi-structured interviews with the participant, Ann. Each interview focused on certain components of self-care practices and their effects on emotional well-being. The first interview focused on Ann's personal history, which led to her academic experiences and challenges. The second interview focused on Ann's self-care techniques and how they help her cope more effectively. Finally, the final interview focused on the relationship between self-care activities and their ability to improve emotional well-being. While the interview schedules were partially planned, they retained some flexibility to allow for in-depth study of developing themes and narratives (Kvale, 1996).

Analysis

This study uses Interpretive Phenomenological Analysis (IPA) as a qualitative research methodology to investigate the lived experiences of female university professors. The study investigates how Ann handle problems in the university environment and engage in self-care practices by meticulously analysing her narratives. To ensure reliability, the study involved several rigorous steps. Complete interview transcripts were meticulously analyzed through multiple readings to develop a deep understanding of the participant's experiences. Initial codes were identified and grouped into emergent themes, followed by an examination of their interconnections. Superordinate themes and sub-themes were then defined. Member checking was conducted to validate the findings with the participant. Themes are carefully retrieved from the transcripts, with an emphasis on recurring patterns and key components of the narratives. Throughout the study, the researcher revisited the transcripts to ensure that the selected themes appropriately reflect the participants' experiences, resulting in coherent and data-supported final interpretations. To avoid researcher bias, the entire research process, including data collection, analysis, and interpretation, was checked by an independent expert in qualitative research.

Results

This analysis examines Ann's university experiences through the lens of four major themes: the perpetual balancing act of work-life integration, fragmentation of self, self-care as resistance, and enhanced emotional wellbeing. These topics, along with their sub-themes highlight the ongoing battle to prioritize self-care in the face of academic obligations. Ann's story typifies the difficulties that many female academics face: juggling research, teaching, committee work, and administrative responsibilities leaves little time for personal activities. The pressure to publish, acquire funding, and be accessible to students generates a constant state of "on," resulting in internal tension between career goals and cultural expectations of parenthood and wifehood. This constant juggling act ultimately results in feelings of exhaustion, frustration, and a sense of falling behind, highlighting the detrimental impact of neglecting self-care in the academic environment.

THE PERPETUAL BALANCING ACT OF WORK-LIFE INTEGRATION

Ann described feeling like a constant juggler, prioritizing work demands over self-care. This metaphor highlights the immense pressure Ann experiences in managing numerous responsibilities. The lack of sufficient time emerges as a significant challenge, often leading to the prioritization of work demands over self-care.

Work-life Balance. This sub-theme explores the challenges of juggling personal life with the demands of a demanding academic career. It could delve into issues like maintaining relationships, managing childcare responsibilities, and finding time for personal hobbies and interests.

"There's never enough time in the day. It feels like I'm constantly running behind. To meet all the deadlines and demands, I often end up not getting enough sleep, skipping healthy meals, or missing out on exercise. It's a constant struggle to fit everything in."

She emphasizes the emotional burden associated with the pressure to constantly publish and secure grants within academia. These unrealistic expectations can contribute to feelings of inadequacy and burnout, further exacerbating the challenges of maintaining a healthy work-life balance.

"There's this constant pressure to keep churning out research papers and get grants. It's like you have to publish all the time, or else you fall behind. It's really easy to start feeling like you're not good enough, and just completely drained from trying to keep up."

The Disconnect Between Ideal and Reality. In the interview Ann outlined her challenges managing personal and professional life. She aspired to maintain a healthy lifestyle, but the reality often fell short. Ann expresses a clear desire to maintain a healthy lifestyle, including regular exercise and healthy eating. However, the reality of her academic workload often creates a significant disconnect between this ideal and her lived experience.

> *"I know I should work out and eat healthy, but by the end of the day, I'm just totally beat. It's easier to grab something quick than cook a healthy meal. Ideally, I'd love to do yoga every morning, but grading papers often takes up that time. Taking care of myself feels like a constant struggle - like I have to squeeze it in after everything else is done, and even then I feel a bit guilty about it."*

This disconnect between the ideal and reality of self-care is a common challenge faced by many academics, particularly women. The immense workload and pressure to publish can make it difficult to carve out time for personal well-being, leading to feelings of guilt and a sense of constantly falling short of self-care goals. Ann's statement paints a vivid picture of the constant pressure and lack of breathing space she experiences within her academic environment. The workload feels never-ending, with an endless stream of papers to grade, committee meetings to attend, and students requiring support. This constant demand on her time and energy creates a sense of being perpetually overwhelmed and leaves little room for self-care or personal well-being.

> *"There's always another paper to grade, another committee meeting, another student needing help. It feels like there's no time to breathe, let alone take care of myself."*

Identity and self-worth. This sub-theme examines how women educators perceive themselves both inside and outside of their professional roles. It could explore the influence of societal expectations, the pressures of balancing motherhood and career, and the challenges of maintaining a sense of self amidst the demands of academia.

> *"It's a constant battle to carve out time for myself, to remember who Ann is outside of academia. The societal expectation is to be this superwoman, juggling everything flawlessly. But the guilt creeps in when I miss a school play or have to cancel a family dinner because of a work deadline."*

The Emotional Toll. Professor Ann spoke of the emotional toll the constant pressure took on her well-being.

> *"The constant feeling of not being enough, of not meeting expectations, it takes a real emotional toll. I sometimes feel anxious and burnt out. A student confided in me about a personal crisis yesterday. While offering support, I felt a wave of exhaustion. It's emotionally draining to constantly pour into others while neglecting my own needs."*

This emotional labor can contribute to feelings of isolation and burnout. The lack of readily available support systems within the university environment further exacerbates these challenges. This struggle highlights the institutional culture's role in shaping self-care practices. University structures often prioritize productivity over well-being, creating an implicit pressure to prioritize work.

FRAGMENTATION OF SELF

Fragmentation of the self refers to a state where a person's sense of self feels divided or broken into separate parts. Ann was struggling to reconcile different aspects of her personality, leading to feelings of inconsistency and confusion about who she is.

Role-Playing and Identity Performance. Ann spoke about adopting different personas in different contexts. The use of the metaphor "wearing different masks" highlights a performative approach to identity, where the she feels the need to project specific versions of herself depending on the situation.

"It's like I'm wearing different masks all the time. At work, I'm Professor, the expert, the one with all the answers. But then I come home, and I'm just... lost."

This suggests that she may struggle to maintain a sense of authenticity and coherence across different social spheres. The constant need to perform specific roles can contribute to feelings of disconnection from one's true self.

Internal Conflict and Dissonance. Ann spoke about internal conflict arising from the contrasting demands and expectations associated with her professional and personal roles. The stark difference between the "strong, capable woman" she projects at work and the "exhausted, overwhelmed mess" she feels inside highlights a sense of dissonance within her self-perception.

"I don't know who I am anymore. Am I the strong, capable woman I project at the university, or the exhausted, overwhelmed mess I feel inside?"

This internal conflict can lead to confusion, anxiety, and difficulty reconciling the different aspects of her identity. The pressure to maintain these contrasting facades can contribute to the fragmentation of her sense of self. Despite the internal conflict, her questioning ("Am I...?") suggests a desire to reconcile these different parts of herself. This yearning for integration highlights the potential for healing and the possibility of achieving a more unified sense of self. By delving deeper into this internal conflict, arriving a clearer understanding of the psychological distress associated with her fragmented sense of self. It reveals the struggle to reconcile contrasting self-images, the impact on mental health, and the potential for further fragmentation or a journey towards integration.

Dissociation and Emotional Detachment. This sub-theme explores the potential for dissociation, where Ann feels disconnected from her thoughts, emotions, or sense of self. Phrases like "going through the motions" and "not really present in my own life" suggest a disengagement from her immediate experience.

"It's like there are these different parts of me, and they don't always connect. Sometimes, I feel like I'm just going through the motions, like I'm not really present in my own life. It's scary, because I don't know how to bring these pieces back together. It's like I've been shattered, and I don't know how to pick up the pieces."

Dissociation can be a coping mechanism for dealing with overwhelming emotions or experiences. In this case, it may be a way for the her to manage the internal conflict and emotional distress associated with her fragmented sense of self. This also provide a deeper understanding of her internal struggle and the psychological processes underlying her experience. It highlights the performative nature of her identity, the internal conflict arising from contrasting roles, and the potential for dissociation as a coping mechanism.

SELF-CARE AS RESISTANCE

Self-care as resistance is a powerful concept that challenges the traditional notion of self-care as simply pampering or indulgence. It reframes self-care as a radical act. She expressed a sense of guilt associated with prioritizing self-care a year before.

"Sometimes I felt like if I take time for myself, I'm letting colleagues and students down. There was an unspoken pressure to be constantly available."

When Ann found herself struggling to manage her emotions, she embarked on a journey of self-care that proved to be a powerful tool for coping. Initially, she might have felt overwhelmed by the intensity of her emotions, perhaps experiencing overwhelming anxiety, sadness, or anger. However, instead of ignoring or suppressing these feelings, Ann actively sought ways to nurture her well-being. Ann gradually developed a healthier relationship with her emotions. Instead of feeling overwhelmed and controlled by them, she learned to manage them with greater awareness and self-compassion. This newfound ability to regulate her emotions allowed her to navigate challenging situations with greater clarity and resilience, ultimately leading to a greater sense of well-being and a stronger sense of control over her life.

Ann began to view self-care not just as a personal act but also as an act of resistance against an unsupportive work culture. This reframing of self-care emphasizes the notion that prioritizing her well-being is not a luxury but a necessity in the face of demanding and potentially unsupportive work environments. By taking care of herself, she empowers herself to be a more effective educator and role model for her students, demonstrating the importance of self-care within the broader context of professional responsibility.

"I used to think self-care was just a luxury, something I could fit in when I had time. But now I realize it's absolutely essential. Taking care of myself, whether it's getting enough sleep, exercising, or just taking a few minutes to breathe, allows me to be a better educator and role model for my students. When I'm well-rested and feeling good, I can show up with more energy and focus, and that translates into a more positive learning environment for everyone."

Support network. The verbatim highlights the profound impact of Ann's support network of fellow female educators. Sharing her experiences and coping strategies with colleagues who understand the unique pressures of her profession provided invaluable support and validation. This sense of belonging and shared understanding likely helped her feel less alone and isolated in her struggles.

"Sharing experiences and strategies with colleagues who understand the pressure is invaluable. It helps me feel less alone."

Micro-self-care. Despite the challenges she faced, Ann discovered the importance of finding solace in small, everyday acts of self-care. Activities like taking a walk in the park or connecting with friends over coffee, seemingly insignificant in the grand scheme of things, held significant value for her emotional well-being. This highlights the concept of "micro-self-care," recognizing that even small, intentional acts of self-nurturing can have a cumulative positive impact on mental health.

"It might seem small, but taking a walk in the park or just grabbing coffee with friends makes a big difference in how I feel. These little things help me manage stress and stay positive, even when things get hectic at work. It's like taking a mini-vacation from the pressure, and it really helps me recharge."

By prioritizing these small moments of joy and connection, Ann likely created pockets of respite within her demanding professional life. These moments of self-care served as a source of emotional refuge, allowing her to recharge and maintain her resilience in the face of ongoing challenges.

The Longing for Support. Ann's statement reveals a yearning for greater institutional support for well-being initiatives within academia. She acknowledges the significant pressure placed on academics, particularly the expectation to embody a "superwoman" persona. However, she emphasizes the human limitations inherent in this expectation and expresses a desire for universities to play a more active role in promoting work-life balance and providing comprehensive mental health support

"There's a lot of pressure to be this superwoman figure, but we're human. Universities could do more to promote work-life balance and mental health support."

ENHANCED EMOTIONAL WELLBEING

Stress management. Ann's quote reveals a significant positive impact of incorporating simple stress management techniques into her daily life. She emphasizes the effectiveness of deep breathing and meditation in reducing her anxiety and promoting a sense of calmness, even amidst the pressures of her work environment. The use of the phrase "magic trick" highlights the transformative power of these practices in managing her emotional state. This suggests that Ann has found a practical and accessible way to cope with stress, leading to a noticeable improvement in her overall well-being.

"Taking a few minutes to breathe deeply and meditate has made a huge difference for me. It helps me stay calm and manage my anxiety, even when things get crazy at work. It's like a magic trick for me"

It highlights the transformative power of simple practices like deep breathing and meditation, emphasizing their effectiveness in reducing anxiety and promoting emotional stability. This interpretation also acknowledges the sense of empowerment Ann experiences by finding practical tools to manage her stress, suggesting a newfound sense of control over her emotional well-being.

Happiness and life satisfaction. Ann acknowledges the ongoing nature of personal growth while emphasizing the positive changes she has experienced in her overall happiness and life satisfaction. The verbatim quote capture Ann's personal journey towards greater happiness and life satisfaction, highlighting the positive impact of prioritizing her well-being and managing her stress effectively.

"I'm still a work in progress, but I definitely feel happier and more satisfied with my life overall. It's a journey, but I'm learning to prioritize my well-being and create a life that feels good for me."

Ann's narrative reflects a sense of self-awareness and a commitment to ongoing personal growth. While acknowledging that she is still on a journey, she emphasizes a significant improvement in her overall happiness and life satisfaction. This shift is attributed to her conscious effort to prioritize her well-being, suggesting that taking care of her emotional needs has led to a more fulfilling and meaningful life. The use of the phrase "create a life that feels good for me" highlights Ann's active role in shaping her own happiness and taking ownership of her well-being.

It highlights Ann's recognition of her progress, her commitment to continued growth, and the positive impact of prioritizing her well-being on her overall happiness and life satisfaction. This interpretation also emphasizes Ann's sense of agency and empowerment in creating a life that aligns with her values and brings her fulfillment.

Self-compassion. This sub-theme emphasizes the importance of treating oneself with kindness and understanding, particularly in the face of setbacks or challenges. Cultivating self-compassion allowed Ann to acknowledge her struggles without judgment and treat herself with kindness, especially during challenging times.

"You know, practicing self-compassion helps me acknowledge my struggles without beating myself up. It's like being my own best friend, especially when things get tough.... Mindfulness meditation is a great tool for this, allowing me to observe my emotions without judgment and just be present with what is."

Ann's verbatim reveals a conscious effort to move away from self-criticism and towards a more accepting and understanding relationship with herself. She emphasizes the importance of acknowledging her struggles without judgment, suggesting a past tendency towards harsh self-evaluation. This shift in perspective is likened to being her "own best friend," highlighting the desire for internal support and kindness, particularly during challenging times. Additionally, the mention of mindfulness meditation signifies a chosen practice that facilitates greater awareness and acceptance of her emotions, allowing her to observe them without judgment and fostering a more compassionate inner dialogue.

Meaning and purpose. This focuses on the sense of meaning and purpose derived from one's work and personal life, contributing to a sense of overall well-being.

"Taking care of myself has allowed me to rediscover my passion for teaching. I feel more engaged with my students and the impact I can have on their lives, which gives me a sense of purpose that I was missing before."

Narratives of Ann emphasizes how prioritizing her well-being has translated into a positive impact on her students, further reinforcing the sense of purpose she derives from her work. These verbatim quotes capture Ann's journey towards finding meaning and purpose in her life, highlighting the positive impact of prioritizing her well-being and managing her stress effectively.

"Now that I'm managing my stress better, I feel more fulfilled in my role as a professor. It's not just a job anymore; it's something I truly value and find meaning in. Taking care of myself has made me a better educator. I have more energy and focus to dedicate to my students, which ultimately allows me to make a bigger contribution to their lives".

DISCUSSION

The findings of this case study illuminate the challenges faced by women educators in universities and the crucial role of self-care in maintaining their emotional well-being. The pressure of workload and service expectations resonate with broader research on faculty burnout. The participant's self-care practices offer valuable insights for other women faculty. Establishing boundaries, engaging in mind-body practices, and nurturing social support networks were crucial for Ann's well-being. Universities can play a vital role by promoting these practices and fostering a culture that prioritizes faculty well-being.

Ann's narrative paints a vivid picture of the constant struggle she faces in balancing the demands of her academic career with the need for personal well-being. This theme, aptly named "The Perpetual Balancing Act of Work-Life Integration," highlights the numerous challenges she encounters in juggling various responsibilities. The sub-theme of "Work-life balance" delves deeper into the specific difficulties associated with maintaining a healthy equilibrium between professional and personal life. Ann mentions the challenges of nurturing personal relationships, managing childcare responsibilities (if applicable), and finding time for hobbies and interests that bring her joy and fulfillment. The constant pressure to excel in academia often leads Ann to feel like a "constant juggler," prioritizing work demands over self-care. The relentless pursuit of publishing, securing grants, and maintaining accessibility to students creates a state of perpetual "on-ness," leaving little room for personal well-being. This internal tension between career goals and societal expectations can be immensely draining, ultimately resulting in feelings of exhaustion, frustration, and a sense of falling behind.

Ann experience serves as a stark reminder of the detrimental impact neglecting self-care can have within the academic environment. The constant pressure to prioritize work over personal needs can lead to burnout, negatively affecting both physical and mental health. It is crucial to acknowledge the importance of striking a healthy balance between professional obligations and personal well-being, ensuring that both aspects of life receive the necessary attention and care.

Ann's narrative reveals a deep internal conflict arising from the contrasting demands and expectations associated with her professional and personal roles. This conflict manifests in the sub-theme of "Role-Playing and Identity Performance," where she describes feeling the need to adopt different personas in different contexts. This constant "wearing of masks" creates a performative approach to identity, where she projects a specific version of herself depending on the situation.

This performative approach can lead to a sense of disconnection from one's true self. The sub-theme of "Internal Conflict and Dissonance" highlights the stark contrast between the "strong, capable woman" Dr. Elsy portrays at work and the "exhausted, overwhelmed mess" she feels inside. This dissonance creates a sense of fragmentation within her sense of self, as she struggles to reconcile these contrasting self-images.

Furthermore, the sub-theme of "Dissociation and Emotional Detachment" suggests that Ann may utilize dissociation as a coping mechanism to deal with the overwhelming emotions and experiences associated with her fragmented self. Dissociation is a psychological process where individuals disconnect from their thoughts, emotions, or sense of self, potentially as a way to manage intense or overwhelming experiences. In Ann's case, it might be a way to cope with the internal conflict and emotional distress arising from the fragmentation of her identity.

By examining these sub-themes, we gain a deeper understanding of the internal struggle Ann faces as she navigates the contrasting demands of her professional and personal life. The constant need to perform different roles, the dissonance between her projected and internal self-image, and the potential use of dissociation as a coping mechanism all contribute to a sense of fragmentation within her sense of self. This analysis highlights the complex psychological impact of balancing multiple roles and the potential consequences for one's mental health and well-being.

Ann's story exemplifies the transformative power of self-care within a demanding academic environment. Initially, she felt guilt associated with prioritizing her well-being. This guilt likely stemmed from the immense pressure to publish, secure grants, and be constantly available to students. The academic culture often implicitly expects work to be prioritized above all else, leading to feelings of self-neglect and internal conflict for those who prioritize self-care.

However, Ann's journey demonstrates a shift in perspective. As she embarked on a path of prioritizing her well-being, she discovered a powerful tool for managing her emotions. Practices like deep breathing and meditation provided her with a sense of control and emotional regulation, fostering a healthier relationship with herself. Additionally, she recognized the value of seemingly insignificant acts of self-care, such as taking walks or connecting with friends. These small, everyday moments functioned as emotional refuges, building resilience in the face of ongoing work pressures.

Furthermore, Ann's case highlights the need for a more supportive academic culture. Her desire for greater institutional support for well-being initiatives reveals a crucial gap in the current system. The pressure to constantly perform and maintain an image of unwavering productivity often leaves academics feeling like they must embody an unsustainable "superwoman" persona. Ann's longing for change emphasizes the responsibility universities hold in promoting work-life balance and providing comprehensive mental health support for their faculty. By prioritizing self-care, Ann not only benefits her own well-being but also challenges the traditional academic narrative that prioritizes productivity over personal health. This act of resistance sets a precedent for a more sustainable and supportive academic environment for future generations.

The theme of Enhanced Emotional Wellbeing in Ann's case highlights the transformative impact of self-care practices and stress management techniques on her overall well-being. Her narrative emphasizes the positive changes she experienced in managing anxiety, finding greater happiness, and achieving a sense of self-acceptance.

One key element of this theme is the power of simple practices like deep breathing and meditation. Ann's quote reveals how these techniques helped her manage her anxiety and maintain composure even amidst the pressures of her academic environment. By incorporating these practices into her daily routine, she discovered a practical and accessible way to regulate her emotions, leading to a noticeable improvement in her overall emotional stability. This newfound ability to manage stress likely empowered her to navigate challenging situations with greater clarity and resilience.

Furthermore, the sub-themes of Happiness and Life Satisfaction and Self-compassion showcase Ann's journey towards a more fulfilling and meaningful life. While acknowledging the ongoing nature of personal growth, she emphasizes a significant improvement in her overall happiness and life satisfaction. This shift is directly attributed to her conscious decision to prioritize her well-being. By taking care of her emotional needs, Ann created space for a more positive and fulfilling life experience.

The emphasis on self-compassion highlights a crucial shift in Ann's internal perspective. She moved away from self-criticism and towards a more accepting and understanding relationship with herself. This change is evident in her description of treating herself "like her own best friend," especially during challenging times. By practicing self-compassion, Ann fostered a kinder and more supportive inner dialogue, further contributing to her overall emotional well-being.

Overall, Ann's narrative demonstrates the profound impact of self-care on emotional well-being. Through the integration of stress management practices and a shift towards self-compassion, she discovered a path towards greater happiness, life satisfaction, and a more fulfilling sense of self. This journey highlights the importance of prioritizing self-care not just as a means of survival in a demanding environment, but as a key element in creating a life that aligns with one's values and brings genuine joy.

Through a single case study, it reveals the delicate balance these women navigate and the institutional factors influencing their experiences. By promoting self-care through supportive structures and cultural shifts, universities can empower women faculty members to thrive in their academic endeavors.

CONCLUSION

This study offers a glimpse into the lived experiences of self-care and emotional well-being among a female university educator. The findings highlight the need for universities to create a more supportive environment for women. This includes promoting flexible work arrangements, fostering a culture of collaboration and support, and encouraging self-care practices. By identifying specific challenges faced by women educators and the strategies they employ to cope, institutions can develop targeted interventions. For instance, increased access to mental health resources, flexible work arrangements, and supportive leadership could be implemented. Moreover, by fostering a culture that prioritizes well-being, universities can create a more inclusive and supportive environment for all faculty members. Ultimately, the goal is to use these insights to inform policies and practices that enhance the overall quality of life for women educators. Further research with a larger sample size could provide valuable insights into the diverse experiences of women in academia. By prioritizing well-being, universities can not only support their female faculty but also create a more positive and sustainable work environment for all.

REFERENCES

Cardinal, B. J., & Thomas, J. D. (2016). Self-care strategies for maximizing human potential. *Journal of Physical Education, Recreation & Dance*, 87(9), 5–7. DOI: 10.1080/07303084.2016.1227198

Dunn, A. H. (2023). Teacher Self-Care Mandates as Institutional Gaslighting in a Neoliberal System. *Educational Researcher*, 52(8), 491–499. DOI: 10.3102/0013189X231174804

Eltayeb, S. (2022). Recognizing the University's Role in Mental Health Promotion. 132, *(57)*6, , 143.

Essed, P., & Carberry, K. (2020). In the name of our humanity: Challenging academic racism and its effects on the emotional wellbeing of women of colour professors. In *The international handbook of black community mental health* (pp. 61–81). Emerald Publishing Limited. DOI: 10.1108/978-1-83909-964-920201005

Fox, M. (2022). 7 A community of practice-educators as self-care. *Reflections on Valuing Wellbeing in Higher Education: Reforming our Acts of Self-care*.

Kvale, S. (1996). *Interviews: An Introduction to Qualitative Research Interviewing*. Sage.

Liepina, E., & Martinsone, K. (2022, May). Teachers' self-Care Strategies And Supervision As A Self-Care Activity For Teachers. In *Society. Integration. Education.Proceedings of the International Scientific Conference* (Vol. 1, pp. 426-441).

Metz, C. L., & Jarvie, S. H. (2022). Ecological Approach to Higher Educator Wellness and Self-Care. In *Self-Care and Stress Management for Academic Well-Being* (pp. 214–229). IGI Global. DOI: 10.4018/978-1-6684-2334-9.ch013

Miller, R. A., Jones, V. A., Reddick, R. J., Lowe, T., Franks Flunder, B., Hogan, K., & Rosal, A. I. (2018). Educating through microaggressions: Self-care for diversity educators. *Journal of Student Affairs Research and Practice*, 55(1), 14–26. DOI: 10.1080/19496591.2017.1358634

Nataraj, B. M., & Reddy, K. J. (2022). Psychological Well-Being of School Teachers: Predictive Role of Mindfulness and Emotional Intelligence. *MIER Journal of Educational Studies Trends and Practices*, 242-262.

Nguyen, M. (2023). Managing Our Mental Health Needs in Turbulent Times Through Self-Care: Importance of Practicing Self-Care in Education. In *Cases on Current Issues, Challenges, and Opportunities in School Counseling* (pp. 250-262). IGI Global.

Puliatte, A. (2021). Women Academic Leaders and Self-Care During a Crisis. In *Women and Leadership in Higher Education During Global Crises* (pp. 175–189). IGI Global. DOI: 10.4018/978-1-7998-6491-2.ch011

Rasheed-Karim, W. (2023). Further Education Teachers' Wellbeing: A Discussion of Equal Opportunities and Career Progression. *Brock Journal of Education*, 11(8), 22–48. DOI: 10.37745/bje.2013/vol11n82248

Ronnie, L., Bam, A., & Walters, C. (2022, May). Emotional wellbeing: The impact of the COVID-19 pandemic on women academics in South Africa. [). Frontiers.]. *Frontiers in Education*, 7, 770447. DOI: 10.3389/feduc.2022.770447

Rose, N. N., Ishak, A. S., Ismail, F., Basir, S. N. M., & Ismail, N. Q. A. (2022). Self-Care and Stress Management for Educators in Public Universities. In *Self-Care and Stress Management for Academic Well-Being* (pp. 157–174). IGI Global. DOI: 10.4018/978-1-6684-2334-9.ch010

Stark, K., Daulat, N., & King, S. (2022). A vision for teachers' emotional well-being. *Phi Delta Kappan*, 103(5), 24–30. DOI: 10.1177/00317217221079975

Chapter 4
Overcoming Imposter Syndrome
Exploring the Challenges Women Leaders Face in Confronting Self-Doubt and Internalized Biases

Mohit Yadav
https://orcid.org/0000-0002-9341-2527
O.P. Jindal Global University, India

Preet Kanwal
https://orcid.org/0009-0006-5114-8381
Lovely Professional University, India

Thi Minh Ngoc Luu
https://orcid.org/0000-0002-5972-7752
International School, Vietnam National University, Hanoi, Vietnam

ABSTRACT

Imposter Syndrome significantly impacts women leaders, manifesting as persistent self-doubt and internalized biases despite their professional achievements. This chapter explores the complexities of Imposter Syndrome by examining personal, professional, and systemic challenges faced by women in leadership roles. It delves into personal development strategies, such as cognitive restructuring and self-compassion, as well as organizational support mechanisms, including mentorship programs and inclusive cultures. The chapter emphasizes the need for systemic changes and further research into intersectionality and emerging interventions. Future research directions include longitudinal studies, the role of digital platforms, and empirical validation of coping strategies. By addressing these dimensions, the

DOI: 10.4018/979-8-3693-3144-6.ch004

chapter aims to provide a comprehensive understanding of Imposter Syndrome and offer practical insights for supporting women leaders in overcoming self-doubt and enhancing their professional growth.

INTRODUCTION

Impostor Syndrome is the all-pervasive feeling of self-doubt and the belief that whatever achievements one has are by luck rather than competence. This becomes a huge psychological challenge for many individuals in their leadership, particularly for women. Women executives achieve a lot, but in their leadership, they experience internal dialogues that degrade their confidence and success, though they are given external validity. It explores this heterogeneous nature of Imposter Syndrome, focusing on the unique experiences of women leaders in facing self-doubt and internalized biases in their life journeys. It will use narrations as a research methodology to demonstrate the symptoms of personal and professional struggles related to Impostor Syndrome with the authentic voices of several women leaders. This approach in the narrative makes the reader understand the way in which such challenges are brought out and the possible ways or support systems from which coping mechanisms can be provided to overcome such internal barriers. In the end, the chapter will show that it is very essential to address Imposter Syndrome in order to have more effective and resilient leadership among women, which should overall lead to an even better and more inclusive professional life (Costa, 2024; Tao & Gloria, 2018).

THEORETICAL FRAMEWORK

The traceable theoretical framework contextually supports the existence of Imposter Syndrome with its different leading theories and related concepts, which give insight into the underlying psychological and social roles such dynamics play. This section will outline the theories relevant to women's experiences in leadership roles.

1. Imposter Syndrome Theories

- **Imposter Phenomenon Theory:** The Imposter Phenomenon originally came from psychologists Pauline Clance and Suzanne Imes during the 1970s. Impostor feelings may lead one to feel like a fraud due to knowing that there is enough evidence in competence or success. Most of the time, one feels that their achievements are mitigated by factors—luck, or even something else—other than his/her abilities. This theory underlines the internal choice

they have to make in going along with their self-perception or their outer validation but is more prevalent in women leadership members under societal expectations and pressure.
- **Social Role Theory:** This theory claims that the norms and role expectations within society may consciously determine the conception of a person's self-identity and actions. Women in leadership positions live with the unfortunate situation of societal role expectations to be female, and yet meet all the demands of being an effective leader. This, in most cases, reinforces their feelings of being inadequate with not self-assurance on most issues because women leaders sometimes feel it is a must to deliver all that they lead in a men-dominant working environment (Pillay & Vermeulen, 2023).

2. Self-Doubt and Self-Efficacy

- **Self-efficacy theory,** originally put forward by Albert Bandura, concerns the beliefs of an individual in the ability to carry out tasks and achieve goals. Women leaders subscribing to Imposter Syndrome may thus have low self-efficacy, have low or diminished confidence in their capabilities. The lack of self-belief, therefore, hinders the willingness to perform and take up new chances (Bravata et al., 2019).
- **Cognitive Dissonance Theory:** According to the theory of Leo Festinger, it occurs when one's beliefs and actions are inconsistent with each other. Women leaders, who feel competent but get wracked with self-doubts, would also experience cognitive dissonance. That might very well be what contributes to imposterism. Resolution of these feelings generally leads to a change in self-perception, or at times, to seeking external validation (Nuelle et al., 2023).

3. Internalized Biases and Stereotypes

- **Stereotype Threat Theory:** This is a theory put forward by Claude Steele and Joshua Aronson, focusing on how people perform poorly if they believe that they are relevant to negative stereotypes. The stereotype threat might hit women leaders hardest when one takes into consideration social stereotypes about gender and leadership likely to create the beliefs 'I am inadequate' and 'I doubt myself'.
- **Internalized Misogyny**: This is where societal biases against women are so internalized, and in the process, self-sabotage and low self-worth may result. Women leaders internalize such biases and therefore lack the courage to effectively lead. This internalized misogyny can manifest as imposter feelings,

where women wonder whether they really are entitled to be leaders (Breeze et al., 2022; Hutchins, 2015).

4. Intersectionality

- **Intersectional Theory:** This theory, which is proposed by Kimberlé Crenshaw, examines the interconnection of diverse social identities such as race, gender, and class in the life of an individual. For women leaders, intersectionality can explain how more than one identity will change their experiences with Imposter Syndrome. An organization littered with prejudice or a toxic organizational culture will only serve to amplify these sorts of experiences for women who are marginalized (Gorsi, 2023).

5. Organizational and Cultural Context

- **Organizational Culture Theory:** This theory stipulates organizational norms and practices linked to behavioral and attitudinal consequences toward work. Women leaders function within a variety of organizational cultures and within those that do not specifically favor, support, or encourage the recognition and support of female leadership; the levels of imposter feelings are heightened. Clearly then, an understanding of the organizational environment is critical for a successful intervention in addressing and alleviating Imposter Syndrome (Canli, 2023).

By merging these theoretical perspectives, the framework developed will be well placed to afford a comprehensive understanding of psychological and social factors contributing to Imposter Syndrome in women leaders. This would also provide the basis necessary to explore the ways in which such interrelationships play out in actual real-world experience, the ways in which it influences leadership effectiveness, and shapes career progression (Ruple, 2020).

METHODOLOGY

The general aim of the narrations in this chapter is the illustration of the experiences of women leaders confronting Imposter Syndrome. Narrations are the stories told that present the rich qualitative method that personal and professional experiences are understood through personal experience; that is, offering a more intensive look into the world of particular persons. In the following parts, information is provided that concerns the rationale of applying narrations, the ways of data collection, and the ethical considerations approached through this research.

1. Rationale for Using Narrations

- Depth of Understanding: Narratives are a way for researchers to understand the tortuosity of the experience of Imposter Syndrome as women leaders understand it. Focusing on personal stories, therefore, the methodology will dig its way through the internal and external factors of influences that inform self-doubt and internalized bias.
- Authenticity of Experience: Through narratives, an avenue is opened for women leaders to be able to talk about their authentic voices, which are reflections of their lived experiences in life, struggles, and coping strategies. Valuing lived experience, this approach adds to a holistic and empathetic understanding of Imposter Syndrome.
- Contextual Relevance: Narrations offer a way to place Imposter Syndrome with the organizational and cultural environments where it occurs. An understanding of the context in which women leaders function could be gained, and the research can draw upon the identification of how organizational cultures and social expectations impact their experiences.

2. Description of Narrative Collection Methods

- Interviews: Semi-structured interviews with women leaders across industry have been used. The interviews are generally cathartic; that is, the intention is to bring out narratives, in-depth and elaborate, about their experiences with Imposter Syndrome, feelings of self-doubt, and biases which have been internalized, and how they work through them. This semi-structured approach will leave a certain amount of flexibility, so the participants may share their experiences in their own terms, while still managing the key themes to be found in the researcher's study (Chapman, 2015).
- Personal Stories and Case Studies: Beyond interviews, submission calls for personal stories and case studies can be carried out to share a diversity of perspectives. Submissions can be in the form of written stories, personal reflections, or full case studies showing a full picture of individual experiences.
- Focused Group Discussions: Focused group discussions with women leaders provide a scope for the possibility of collective discussion per se, where the experience may thus be shared. This will induce common denominators and differences as far as experiences are concerned with the concept of Imposter

Syndrome. The focused group also helps participants to interact, which may reveal how the feeling is shaped further by social and organizational contexts.

3. Data Analysis

- Thematic Analysis: The thematic analysis of the collected narratives will be conducted to identify and analyze recurring themes and patterns. It will include coding of data, with similar codes being categorized into themes, and these themes interpreted to explain reasons and experiences undergirding imposter syndrome.
- Narrative Analysis: Narrative analysis for this research is an enquiry into the way narratives are narrated or the narrated matter of the narratives. In this respect, how the stories of women leaders are narrated and presented are examined. This discussion focus with reference to the language, metaphors and storytelling technique and what they imply about experience an emotional nature of Impostor Syndrome.

4. Ethical Considerations

- Informed Consent: The participants will be clearly informed on the research in place, what participation involves, and how their narratives will be used. Full consent will be acquired from each of the participants in terms of their involvement.
- Confidentiality and Anonymity: All personal identifying information will be held confidential and anonymous to protect the privacy of participants. Pseudonyms will also assigned in the reporting of their narratives so that their real identities will remain anonymous.
- Sensitive Topics: Discussion around Imposter Syndrome can be of a sensitive nature, involving possibly upsetting topics. Researchers take great care to approach the interviews and data collection sensitively and respectfully. Participants are able to elect to leave the study at any time without any consequence to them.

5. Data Validation

- Member Checking: Provides respondents with an opportunity to confirm or validate their provided stories are as reflected in the research. This, therefore, assures the experiences in context are well represented and interpreted.
- Triangulation: Data is cross-validated with various sources like interviews, personal vignettes, and focus group discussion. This approach solidifies the

credibility and reliability of the findings as it is a mirror image of what occurs, giving an even greater view of Imposter Syndrome.

Through such application, the chapter provides more in-depth and empathetic insights into the phenomenon of Imposter Syndrome—value added through a perspective of women leaders' personal experience and interwoven with its generalist arguments for leadership authenticity and wider org[anizational] culture.

Narrations of 7 participants in different professional fields are-

1. Laura, Senior Marketing Executive

Laura was awarded and considered an innovator in her field of marketing for a global tech company. Despite all these successes, Laura always succumbs to self-defeating self-doubt. She recounts how she managed a high-stakes ad campaign that actually outperformed but she became so anxious that she wasn't thrilled by her success because, rather than lucking out, her success could be due to her incompetence. Laura's self-limiting belief emanates from the notion that her success could be due to her gender and not her competence. For instance, she copes with her internal feeling by engaging in self-reflection and asking a trusted colleague for feedback to affirm her contributions. Laura's story brings back the struggle between how we perceive ourselves and how others validate our work.

> "I was super excited when our project beat estimates, but instead of being proud, the only thing I could think about was how it must have been a fluke. The anxiety that I am not actually deserving of my accomplishments is always there. I wonder, is it all really about me? Or am I just a fake?"

---

2. Aisha, Engineering Manager

As though she did not belong there, Aisha was out of place with other professionals and leaders in her industry. She recalls the need to prove herself in each project meeting or conversation. The basis of Aisha's experience resonates in which she upheld and internalized the stereotype of her belonging in a technical area. A woman in a technical area, how can this be? Things are worse when her imposter feelings were further accentuated during one of many encounters by a junior male colleague attacking a technical decision she had made. To deal with such feelings, Aisha sought mentorship from female leaders in the field, who taught her strategies to deal with the doubts she holds, and she also joined women's leadership networks. Her story is clearly a tale of the kind of influence organizational cultures and gender biases have in leading women to self-doubt (Pillay & Vermeulen, 2023; McCullough, 2020).

"I feel like I have to work twice as hard to prove myself every time I walk into a meeting. When a junior colleague made a quizzical gesture about my technical choices, it felt like a blow to my already-fragile confidence. I have to remind myself that I've earned my place here, but the struggle is real."

---

3. Emily, Nonprofit Director

Emily works as a director at a nonprofit organization that deals with its fair share of territory taxations. Combined with the inappropriateness of having high expectations and limited resources, she brought up a self-doubting moment right after the first big grant proposal she had led was rejected. Even as her team offered supportive feedback, Emily has felt like she wants to admit to the fullness of her feelings of inadequacy, fearing her leadership was not effective. Emily's story epitomizes the way a performance environment, coupled with lack of acknowledgment, builds the viciousness of Imposter Syndrome. She depends on self-compassion strategies and practices thankfulness to neutralize her feelings of being an imposter.

"I felt that my failures were personal after the grant proposal rejection. Although my team reassured me that the rejection was not a reflection of my abilities, it could not shake off the feeling that perhaps I was not doing enough. It's an endless cycle; I constantly have to keep telling myself my successes to shut these thoughts out."

---

4. Priya, Tech Startup Founder

Her tech startup is wildly successful, amazing in so many ways, yet she often feels overwhelmed with the responsibility of running the company. She recounts during a high-stakes pitch some investor when the fears of being just competent enough used to weigh heavy on her. What the story of Priya shows is how being a woman of color and a startup founder means the intersection contributes to imposter feelings. She gains comfort from her support system and practices mindfulness quite frequently to handle her stress. Priya's experience is characteristic of the amplified challenges presented by intersectionality in the entrepreneurial environment.

"It was the most harrowing experience I have ever had in my professional life. All I could think was that maybe I don't belong here, despite everything that I have achieved. Being a woman of color in the startup space can accentuate that feeling, but being rooted in my support network and mindfulness helps keep me centered."

---

5. Sophia, University Professor

Sophia is a tenured university professor, and her career is highlighted with achievements. However, she is often fraught with self-doubt, referring to the fact that on a recent academic conference she attended, though people appreciated her hard work, she felt that people around her were more capable. What the story of Sophia indicates is: the realization of one's achievements which are not real but rather based on others' help or liking for her. She joins various professional development workshops, apart from shadowing with other senior colleagues, to overcome her imposter venom feeling. Her narrative helps reveal how the setting of a higher academic and professional tiered environment would influence someone in terms of their self-esteem (Leong & Smallwood, 2021; Hideg & Shen, 2019).

"At the seminar, I felt like a fraud in front of my colleagues. I was already a many-time awardee. I published serious papers, but still remain trapped in the notion that other factors count for my success, not my abilities. I told myself that my work can speak for itself, especially when I don't believe in it."

---

6. Mia, Corporate HR Director

Mia, an HR director in a big company, at times second guesses her decisions in a lead role, particularly in difficult personnel-related matters. She remembers a point when she needed to resolve an intense conflict in her team. She felt lost in how to control the situation. The intrapersonal scripting of Mia's biases results from the expectations and pressure that the society around her company has set toward women holding lead roles. She kept her feelings of being an imposter under control by taking care of learning and peer support. Mia's experience has shown the impact of organizational pressures and the importance of continuing professional development.

"Managing a major team conflict left me questioning my abilities. Despite my experience and training—msw, I often wonder—can I really cut it as a leader? I focus on learning and seek support from colleagues to remind myself that my decisions on leadership are valid and reflect what it means to lead."

---

7. Jenna, Creative Director in Fashion

Jenna, working as a creative director in the fashion industry, has been awarded as an innovator for her designs, but she feels mostly that she doesn't deserve the award. She can recollect those moments when she was worried about her success at ruling the major fashion show for which she was responsible, and how it would open up her work for inspection or not be good enough. Jenna's story underscores the impact of vocational-type pressures and daily comparison with peers as contributing factors to her feelings of being an impostor. What Jenna found as a coping response was affirmation—affirming herself and utilizing a support system in a network of fellow creatives. It's quite a representative story for the kind of problems that happen a lot in these industries.

"Even after our fashion show got good reviews, I felt like a fraud. I was trying to measure up to others and worrying that eventually, everyone would find me out. The fashion industry is really tough, and the pressure to always outdo yourself does not help you find the confidence in success. My creative network helps me stay confident."

Overall, these narratives will give an inside view of how Imposter Syndrome affects women leaders working in a wide and diverse variety of fields and organizational environments, yet listing their personal and professional struggles, coping strategies, and the broader implications for leadership and organizational culture.

IMPOSTER SYNDROME IN WOMEN LEADERS: A NARRATIVE ANALYSIS

Thematic Analysis of the Narratives about the Imposter Syndrome in Women Leaders: This section gives voice to the meaning of the rich narrative data the women leaders provided about self-doubt and the antics of internalized bias. The analysis of the interview data is aimed at laying bare the commonalities, patterns, and nuances of the experiences of Impostor Syndrome among women leaders sampled. This section is, in addition, broken down into a few rudimentary subsections in order to bring a clear perspective on the narratives.

1. Presentation of Key Narratives

- Selection of Narratives: The narratives under this section are those that match up and relate to the research questions and thus well placed in carrying the curiosity, indicating the wide distribution of experience with the Imposter Syndrome. The narratives are sourced from the interviews, personal submissions, and focus group discussions.
- Narrative Summaries: Summaries of each narrative are made to follow the general story of an individual experiencing Imposter Syndrome. Summaries highlight features of nature of self-doubt, stages, triggers, or the impact of certain incidents on the professional and personal lives of individuals.

2. Common Themes and Patterns

- Self-doubt Experiences, a Major Theme: The sense of self-doubt that pervades experiences of women in leadership is a very strong theme. Illustrations often include how such feelings never dissipate, even after outward forms of validation. Other common patterns include doubts regarding their very competence, fear about being exposed as a fraud, and a need to always prove one's worth (Chapman, 2015; Kolontari et al., 2023).
- Internalized Biases: Another important theme is bias internalization and self-perception of women leaders. Narratives show how deeply the societal norms and stereotypes embed their impressions in societies. They explain how they have internalized those biases, which negatively affect their level of confidence, and therefore their effectiveness as leaders.
- Organizational Culture Impact: Many narratives describe how organizational culture impacted their experience of Imposter Syndrome. The women leaders speak to their organizations not offering support or recognition, being inclusive, where inner self-doubt and imposter syndrome are worse.
- Coping Strategies and Resilience: On the other hand, the narratives also tell about the number of coping strategies and sources of resilience despite the adversities that are shown. Personal strategies of dealing with self-doubt by the women leaders are shown on mentorship, self-reflection, and self-compassion and so on. The item also examines the patterns of resilience including the reshaping of negative thoughts and reliance on support systems (Baumann et al., 2020;, Maqsood et al., 2018).

3. Individual vs. Collective Experiences

- Personal Accounts: Elaborate personal experiences of how individual women suffer from the syndrome, with unique differences. These stories illustrate differences based on personal background, career trajectory, and individual coping mechanisms.
- Collective Insights: The analysis also identified collective experiences shared by multiple women leaders. The research uncovered themes and patterns that reflected broader trends in the experiences of women leaders with Imposter Syndrome by analyzing shared verse overlying experiences.

4. Variations Accordingly to the Industry, Position, and Background

- Provenance of Negative Experience: How the people narrated the stories revealed that the imposter syndrome was different within the experience accrued from the different industries. For example, a female leader in a particularly male-biased industry faces very different challenges and pressures than other female leaders in more gender-balanced industries (Taylor & Breeze, 2020;, Murray et al., 2022).
- Position-Level Differences: The following elaborates on how Impostor Syndrome experiences may differ by organizational levels. Women at the highest level of leadership may feel qualitatively different self-doubts than women in midlevel or entry-level positions.
- Background and Intersectionality – This research would consider how such intersecting identities like Race, Ethnicity, and background regarding social-economic status influence experiences of Imposter Syndrome. Narratives from women of all diversities background-wise present a very fine line of understanding about how these combine and coalesce with gender and leadership challenges.

5. Implications for Leadership and Organizational Culture

- Impact on Leadership Effectiveness: This paper discusses how Imposter Syndrome impacts the performance, decision-making, and leadership style of women leaders. Insights from these narratives help one understand how self-doubt and internalized biases by such women leaders shape the ability to deliver desired results.
- Organizational Interventions: Learning from the stories, this study also points toward the organizational interventions that treatment of women leaders hav-

ing Imposter Syndrome in order to fight it. Creating an inclusive culture, designing mentorship programs, and providing environments that acknowledge and appreciate varied contributions are some of them.

An attempt to draw an in-depth understanding of the complexity and challenge that women leaders face with self-doubt and internalized biases, by reading through the lined narratives of women leaders experiencing Imposter Syndrome. Insights gained from these narratives contribute to broader discussions around how to address Imposter Syndrome and support women leaders in their professional journeys.

CHALLENGES FACED BY WOMEN LEADERS

The section "Challenges Faced by Women Leaders" explains the multilevel challenges women face in leadership and—more precisely—the influences and effects of Imposter Syndrome, which may include personal, professional, and structural challenges that lead to and compound feelings related to low confidence and internalized bias.

1. Personal Challenges

- Self-Doubt and Confidence Issues: Women leaders often face a great deal of inner self-doubt. Whether a person is qualified and has achieved whatever else, it plagues her from within and can be quite self-undermining. The causes of this syndrome can be one of many, including failure in the past, huge expectations that she has to live up to, and the pressure to continually sustain demanding standards that she herself has raised. Women have self-doubt that they aren't able to deliver, and the whole bubbling issue is the fear that probably they are not all that worth the status, which seems to be basically carried forward to other domains.
- Internalized Biases: Such internalized biases as success being a function of luck and not skill adversely affect the self-esteem being enhanced or addressed by women leaders. Women leaders may internalize stereotypes of the gender role that society propagates, which forms the backdrop against which they will view their achievements. The kind of biases as described above can translate into imposter feelings—women not being where they ought to be, or not being as competent as their colleagues (Murray et al., 2022;, Friedman et al., 2021).

2. Professional Challenges

- Perfectionism and Overachievement: A lot of the female leaders are perfectionists in nature, setting the bars to an extremely high level; as such, they feel great pressure to perform at or over such standards. The attempt to reach perfection will cause another source for burnout and enhance further inefficacy.
    Obstacles that could bar women leaders from moving up the career ladder include less opportunity for progression, lack of mentorship, and exclusion from informal networks. These barriers could really hurt their career and, in return, spur the feelings that they may really be an imposter, as they may feel that their career is stagnating because they are actually not good enough.
- Workplace Discrimination and Bias: At the workplace, gender-based discrimination and bias can very simply undercut the authority and the contributions that a woman is making. Women leaders are likely to experience some of the very subtle or overt discrimination typical of this, including not being considered for promotion, devaluation of concepts, and reinforcing imposter feelings. These add stress and self-doubt.
- Balancing Leadership and Personal Life: Balancing the demands of leadership with personal responsibilities proves an uphill task, especially for women. In most cases, expectations of the family and household upkeep weigh on a woman's mind, pushing her toward meeting set goals that could be unattainable, bringing on more stress and leaving one with a sense of failure when the personal and professional expectations are not met.

3. Systemic Challenges

- Organizational Culture and Climate: The organizational culture has a huge impact on the way women leaders feel within the organization. Men-dominated cultures or a lack of support for diversity and inclusion create conditions that enhance imposter feelings among women leaders. A hostile or non-welcome stance can be ascribed to a lack of recognition, support, or mentorship, where it becomes harder for women to prevail.
- Stereotypes and Expectations: Societal and organizational stereotypes regarding gender roles and leadership can contribute to the challenges that women leaders face. Stereotypes that question the leadership capacity of women or are normative in terms of restrictive norms can affect perceptions about them and in turn their self-perceptions. Women may therefore find themselves pressed to adjust to conventional normed standards of leadership and be criticized for any deviation from this practice.

- Lack of Role Models in Top Positions: This underrepresentation of women in powerful positions creates a feeling of isolation and self-doubt in them. If the top posts do not consist of women leaders, then this situation may solidify the belief in many that such posts are not for women or they do not belong to such environments.

4. Intersectional Challenges

- Impact of Intersectionality: Women leaders from marginalized backgrounds related to race, class, or economic status face a compounded challenge because their gender intersects with other identities. Did the intersectionality make the challenges related to Imposter Syndrome even worse, considering that women leaders from such backgrounds experience additional discrimination and prejudices?.
- Cultural and Contextual Factors: Cultural and contextual factors can play a part in how women leaders experience and manage IS. Some cultures have very stereotypical gender roles that not only limit further opportunities for women but also may be a significant factor in causing feelings of self-doubt and ineffectiveness.

5. Coping with and Overcoming Challenges

- Personal Methods: The personal strategies that the women leaders design to overcome Imposter Syndrome include feedback seeking, self-reflection, and self-compassion. Resilience and self-affirmation practices are very important in dealing with self-deficiency and sustaining confidence.
- Organizational Support: Organizations can alleviate Imposter Syndrome by nurturing inclusive cultures, mentorship programs, and the recognition of diverse contributions. Creating a supportive environment that provides recognition, opportunities, and resources for development is one way of overcoming some of the challenges women leaders face.

With these challenges in mind, the chapter attempts to give a detailed understanding of the factors instigating Imposter Syndrome among women leaders and tries to point out the call for policies and personal strategies, both at the systemic and individual levels, that help provide support means that empower women in positions of leadership.

STRATEGIES FOR OVERCOMING IMPOSTER SYNDROME

"Strategies to Overcome Imposter Syndrome" This section enumerates ten practical and useful ways women leaders can practice to manage and reduce self-defeating sentiments like self-doubt and inadequacy. These methods encompass personal development, organizational support, and systemic changes to make the environment more conducive for being inclusive and supportive. I.

Personal Development Strategies

- Self-Reflection and Awareness: One of the significant factors to be considered in the process of recognition and fighting off these feelings of being an imposter is being aware of oneself. Women leaders can be able to self-reflect on a daily or regular basis to understand what is causing the self-doubt and fighting off irrational beliefs that marginalize their ability. Journaling, meditation, and other forms of mindfulness can offer deep insight into one's thought process and emotional standing, paving the way for a clear understanding of personal achievements and competence.
- Cognitive restructuring: This is the process of identifying and reframing the negative thought patterns blamed for creating the Imposter Syndrome. Female leaders journal about the ways they are challenging their automatic thoughts of inadequacies and replacing them with more balanced and realistic views. Some techniques to reframe negative beliefs and create a more affirmative self-image are used in cognitive-behavioural therapy.
- Setting Realistic Goals: Establishing and working toward realistic goals will help address feelings of inadequacy. Women leaders should set achievable and measurable objectives, focus on celebrating progress, and acknowledge their accomplishments. Breaking big goals into smaller tasks that one can manage will help in realizing achievement more tangibly and therefore reduce the pressure to achieve perfection.
- Developing Self-Compassion: It is about being kind to oneself and understanding in times of failure. In view of this, ways through which women leaders can be self-compassionate include recognizing that they did their best, forgive themselves for messing things up, and that imperfection is human and part of growth. Some tools that can help with this are self-compassion exercises and affirmations.
    - Sought-Out Feedback and Mentorship: It is helpful to task your colleagues, mentors, and supervisors with providing feedback on your performance to better understand from an outsider's perspective and to validate performance successes. Constructive feedback can provide additional reinforce-

ment of strengths and areas for improvement, and authentic mentorship offers guidance, support, and motivation from experienced professionals who are able share their own experiences with Imposter Syndrome.

Organizational Support Strategies

- Creating an Inclusive Culture: This is where an organization has in place an inclusive culture that embraces diversity and allows the growth of all the members of staff. The creation of an equitable opportunity, recognition, and advancement of culture importantly involves cleaning house of any gender biases and stereotypes that a culture can do to relieve tension, part of which drives Imposter Syndrome.
- Offer Mentorship and Sponsorship Programs: Women leaders get able to receive the desired support and guidance through setting up formal mentorship and sponsorship programs. There are two types of development approaches: mentoring, aimed at personal and professional development, and sponsoring, aimed at prompting a person's career growth. Such programs will help women pursue their careers gain confidence and visibility in the organizations.
- Recognition and Celebrating Achievements: The organization should practice recognizing and celebrating the achievements of its employees. Day-to-day congratulating of individual and group achievements by winning awards, public recognition, and performance appraisal goes a long way in enhancing the importance of the people's contribution and enhancing confidence.
- Professional Development Opportunities: Professional development opportunities that come in terms of trainings, workshops, and conferences that are accessible, help in the development of skills, information, and confidence among women leaders. Continuous learning and growth build confidence in women leaders, instilling a sense of competence in the work that they do.

Systemic Changes

- Fix the Bias and Discrimination Based on Gender: Basic changes in the system to fix this undercurrent of gender-based bias and discrimination within organizations. Only by imbibing policies and practices in promoting gender equity, like equal pay, transparent processes for promotion, and anti-discrimination training, will an environment friendlier to women leaders be created.
- Demonstrated Work-Life Flexibility: Assisting employees in gaining some work-life balance using flexible work options, parental leave, and family sup-

port schemes can help shore up the pressure and demands that sometimes create the stew of feelings supporting Imposter Syndrome. Assisting in providing more workable solutions to balance both options can enable women leaders to remain well and confident.
- Building Growth Mindset: While encouraging a growth mindset among organizations, it should make them believe that skills and abilities are developed through efforts and learning. At the same time, organizations that value continuous improvement should be resilient through their culture so that women leaders look at problems and failures not as inadequacies but as opportunities for growth.
- Improve Representation and Role Models: Better levels of representation of the female gender at higher positions and increased visibility of role models can help reduce impostorism. Growing numbers of women leaders who see other women like them succeed have improved their sense of belonging and faith that they too are rightfully there and capable of the same success.

Personal Stories and Peer Support

- Sharing Experiences: Women leaders can benefit by sharing their experiences with other women who have faced similar challenges. Spaces for open dialogue can be created through peer support groups or networking events where exchange personal stories and coping strategies. This communal support can provide validation, reduce isolation, and offer practical advice for managing Imposter Syndrome.
- Building Support Networks: Establish a strong support network among friends, coworkers, and with professional organizations for emotional and practical support as well. Networking with other such women could provide them with a feeling of being less isolated and more self-assured in their positions of power.

Through the application of these strategies, women leaders can start to counteract some of the problems associated with Imposter Syndrome and develop a more positive and confident perspective regarding their professional skills. These strategies do not only support well-being but are central to establishing more inclusive organizational environments.

FUTURE DIRECTIONS AND RESEARCH

This section flags a number of research areas that require further exploration to enable the understanding and addressing of imposter syndrome among women leaders. As such, research on this phenomenon should continue to allow it to be better understood and interventions developed accordingly. The generalizability of these findings must take place with caution due to the small sample size.

1. Exploring Intersectionality

Impact of Multiple Identities: For example, future research should examine how women leaders may experience Impostor Syndrome differently according to their race, ethnicity, sexual orientation, or socioeconomic status. Research on how such respective multiple identities influence self-doubt and internal biases can offer a much bigger view of the challenges being confronted by diverse groups of women leaders.

Compared Studies: Comparative studies of a different cultural and national context can unveil how cultural norms and societal expectations mould the phenomenon of the Imposter Syndrome. Such research may help explain differences in the performance of impostor syndrome and uncover culturally specific mechanisms of coping or sources of support.

2. Longitudinal Studies

- Follow Imposter Syndrome Over Time: Longitudinal studies will help us understand how the imposter phenomenon changes as one goes along their career track. Following the same women leaders over time will reveal how self-doubt appears to develop in response to changes in career step, moves to other organizations, and personal maturation.
- Intervention Effects: Impact of interventions in reducing the Imposter Syndrome. Longitudinal studies will also be able to access whether long-term sustainability of an intervention designed to reduce feelings of the Imposter experience. It will be possible to determine the women's change in confidence in different strategies and career paths over time for which strategies have long-term positive effects.

3. Organizational Culture and Climate

• Effectiveness of Organizational Interventions: Research will point to what organizational mentorship programs, interventions around issues of diversity, and recognition practices effectively lead to a decrease in Impostor experiences. It would be beneficial to evaluate how these interventions may not be effective or may be effective in the experiences and perceptions of women to develop best practices.

• Leadership Styles Related Implications: To understand better the implications of varied leadership styles and organizational climates on Imposter Syndrome to better understand how leadership practices impact the confidence and career satisfaction of women, the role which inclusive and supportive leadership styles play across the globe in remedying the feelings of inadequacy.

4. Technology and Imposter Syndrome

• The Role of Digital Platforms: Understanding if and how digital platforms work, including online communities, social media, and virtual mentoring, offers great potential for implementing new perspectives. Research could address how these platforms either support the feelings of inadequacy or exacerbate the same and can be harnessed for productive interventions.

• AI and Personalized Support: Another emergent area relates to the use of Artificial Intelligence for the delivery of personalized support in battling against Imposter Syndrome. There can be the development of an AI support system that administers tailored resources and strategies and delivers personal feedback and guidance adapted to individual experiences and features.

5. Intersection with Career Development

• Influence on Career Advancement: There is a need for future research that would be able to show how Imposter Syndrome goes a long way in impacting the career development and growth opportunities for women leaders. Clarification on the existence of self-doubt in impacting career movement should be done to enlighten ways that overcome women into getting rid of the barriers of career movement.

• Role of Professional Development: Imposter Syndrome can be further complicated by watching how professional development programs may modulate this impact. Efforts can focus on which forms of training and development activities are most successful at enhancing confidence and abilities in minimization of feelings of self-doubt.

6. Empirical Validation of Coping Strategies

• Effectiveness of Coping Mechanisms: More empirical research would have to be done to finally assert the coping mechanisms for this syndrome. This will involve looking at the effectiveness of such individual strategies as cognitive restructuring and self-compassion, and organizational strategies such as mentorship and recognition programs.

• Development of New Interventions: The innovative interventions for handling Imposter Syndrome and ways forward should be discussed in the study. It should concern development of new therapeutic approaches, training programs, or organizational policies that target the problems unique to women leaders.

7. Broader Implications for Leadership and Policy

• Impact on Leadership Effectiveness: How Imposter Syndrome impacts leadership effectiveness can be mainstreamed into leadership development practice that is either organizational or generic. If self-doubt can be shown to affect decisions, team working, and overall impact on effectiveness, we could contribute toward that understanding.

• Policy Recommendation: The research that is currently being done and research that will be carried out in the future will hopefully be able to develop working policy recommendations for organizations and institutions, including guidelines and best practices in the creation of support services that cater to women leaders who are currently experiencing Imposter Syndrome.

8. Case Studies and Applications in Real-Life Contexts

• Detailed Case Studies: A detailed case study of organizations and leaders who addressed imposter syndrome can bring fort practical insights and examples. They offer valuable lessons and strategies that may be adopted and implemented in a disparate context.

- Real-World Application: The research conducted will be translated into real-world application and actual tools that work towards increasing the actual impact on women in leadership. This includes resources, workshops, and programs developed to apply best practices to the specific needs of women leaders.

Pursuing these future directions would enlighten the researchers and practitioners towards gaining more authentic insights into Imposter Syndrome, thereby establishing supportive strategies towards women leaders. In its behalf, continued research such as this is crucial in establishing settings where women can thrive and perform to the fullest and lead with confidence.

CONCLUSION

In conclusion, Imposter Syndrome is a great challenge to women leaders. It is characterized by self-doubt, internalized biases, and deep feelings of insufficiency that women feel despite personal achievements and qualification. This phenomenon impacts personal mental health and goes on to influence professional development and organizational behavior. Research on the personal, professional, and systemic challenge of women as leaders suggests strongly that Imposter Syndrome cannot be addressed in isolation at the personal level. Developmental activities personally around critical self-reflection, cognitive reframing, and self-compassion-based work are necessarily individual to control the internalization of self-doubt. Organizational support—with regard to establishment of an inclusive culture, mentorship, and recognition of successes—then becomes greatly important as a step to mitigate these issues. Beyond this work, however, a more fundamental resolution to the problems at hand will require systemic changes and a comprehensive approach toward wider research on intersectionality and the effectiveness of the different needed interventions. Future research has to look toward longitudinal studies, the effect of emerging technologies, and the development of novel and evidence-based strategies in the support of women leaders. It calls for an understanding and management of the intrinsic complexities underlying Imposter Syndrome in creating an enabling environment where women leaders can realize their worth, get past self-doubt, and thrive.

REFERENCES

Baumann, N., Faulk, C., Vanderlan, J., & Bhayani, R. (2020). Small-group discussion sessions on imposter syndrome. *MedEdPORTAL: the Journal of Teaching and Learning Resources*, 11004. Advance online publication. DOI: 10.15766/mep_2374-8265.11004 PMID: 33204832

Bravata, D., Watts, S., Keefer, A., Madhusudhan, D., Taylor, K., Clark, D., Nelson, R. S., Cokley, K. O., & Hagg, H. (2019). Prevalence, predictors, and treatment of impostor syndrome: A systematic review. *Journal of General Internal Medicine*, 35(4), 1252–1275. DOI: 10.1007/s11606-019-05364-1 PMID: 31848865

Breeze, M., Taylor, Y., & Addison, M. (2022). Imposter agony aunts: ambivalent feminist advice., 611-630. DOI: 10.1007/978-3-030-86570-2_37

Canli, U., & Aquino, E. (2023). Barriers and challenges experienced by latina nurse leaders. *Hispanic Health Care International; the Official Journal of the National Association of Hispanic Nurses*, 22(2), 92–98. DOI: 10.1177/15404153231199175 PMID: 37728110

Chapman, A. (2015). Using the assessment process to overcome imposter syndrome in mature students. *Journal of Further and Higher Education*, 41(2), 112–119. DOI: 10.1080/0309877X.2015.1062851

Chapman, A. (2015). Using the assessment process to overcome imposter syndrome in mature students. *Journal of Further and Higher Education*, 41(2), 112–119. DOI: 10.1080/0309877X.2015.1062851

Costa, K. (2024). Study protocol of "exploring the interplay between family responsibilities, personal vulnerabilities, and motivational theories in the publishing endeavours of women scholars: a qualitative evidence synthesis". DOI: 10.20944/preprints202402.0680.v1

Friedman, S., O'Brien, D., & McDonald, I. (2021). Deflecting privilege: Class identity and the intergenerational self. *Sociology*, 55(4), 716–733. DOI: 10.1177/0038038520982225

Gorsi, H., Ali, S. A., & Tariq, S. (2023). A conceptual model of impostor phenomenon and job performance: Role of vicarious learning, impression management, and self-reflection. *Journal of Professional & Applied Psychology*, 4(3), 460–477. DOI: 10.52053/jpap.v4i3.183

Hideg, I., & Shen, W. (2019). Why still so few? a theoretical model of the role of benevolent sexism and career support in the continued underrepresentation of women in leadership positions. *Journal of Leadership & Organizational Studies*, 26(3), 287–303. DOI: 10.1177/1548051819849006

Hutchins, H. (2015). Outing the imposter: A study exploring imposter phenomenon among higher education faculty. *New Horizons in Adult Education and Human Resource Development*, 27(2), 3–12. DOI: 10.1002/nha3.20098

Kolontari, F., Lawton, M., & Rhodes, S. (2023). Using developmental mentoring and coaching approaches in academic and professional development to address feelings of 'imposter syndrome'. *Journal of Perspectives in Applied Academic Practice*, 11(1), 34–41. DOI: 10.56433/jpaap.v11i1.537

Leong, T., & Smallwood, N. (2021). Leading by example: The women of respiratory health in australia. *Respirology (Carlton, Vic.)*, 26(10), 997–998. DOI: 10.1111/resp.14135 PMID: 34459516

Maqsood, H., Shakeel, H., Hussain, H., Khan, A., Ali, B., Ishaq, A., & Shah, S. (2018). The descriptive study of imposter syndrome in medical students. *International Journal of Research in Medical Sciences*, 6(10), 3431. DOI: 10.18203/2320-6012.ijrms20184031

McCullough, L. (2020). Barriers and assistance for female leaders in academic stem in the us. *Education Sciences*, 10(10), 264. DOI: 10.3390/educsci10100264

Murray, Ó., Chiu, Y., Wong, B., & Horsburgh, J. (2022). Deindividualising imposter syndrome: Imposter work among marginalised stemm undergraduates in the uk. *Sociology*, 57(4), 749–766. DOI: 10.1177/00380385221117380

Nuelle, J., Agnew, S., & Fishman, F. (2023). Challenges for women in hand surgery: Our perspective. *Journal of Hand and Microsurgery*, 15(4), 258–260. DOI: 10.1055/s-0042-1744209 PMID: 37701318

Pillay, D., & Vermeulen, C. (2023). Seeking support through solidarity: Female leader's experiences of workplace solidarity in male-dominated professions. *Frontiers in Psychology*, 14, 1119911. Advance online publication. DOI: 10.3389/fpsyg.2023.1119911 PMID: 37457071

Ruple, A. (2020). Overcoming imposter syndrome., 2020 Recent Graduate Proceeding. https://doi.org/DOI: 10.21423/aabppro20207954

Tao, K., & Gloria, A. (2018). Should i stay or should i go? the role of impostorism in stem persistence. *Psychology of Women Quarterly*, 43(2), 151–164. DOI: 10.1177/0361684318802333

Taylor, Y., & Breeze, M. (2020). All imposters in the university? striking (out) claims on academic twitter. *Women's Studies International Forum*, 81, 102367. DOI: 10.1016/j.wsif.2020.102367

Chapter 5
Two Centuries of Defining Moments for Black Women Higher Education Leaders in the United States

Natasha N. Johnson
https://orcid.org/0000-0001-8145-2153
Georgia State University, USA

ABSTRACT

Black women have made significant strides in their representation in higher education leadership in the United States over the past two centuries. They have faced barriers, yet they have also made substantial contributions to the field. Historically, Black women remain at the forefront of the struggle for equal access to education, with many earning degrees, becoming educators, and founding higher education institutions. However, their leadership roles have often been marginalized and overlooked. Despite this, Black women have persevered and made advancements in higher education administration, but they continue to face obstacles in their career paths and leadership progression. The experiences of Black women higher education leaders, including the challenges they encounter and the strategies they employ to overcome them, can provide valuable insights for improving the retention and advancement of Black women leaders. Achieving gender equality in leadership positions in higher education is a matter of fairness, and it is essential to advancing the evolving higher education landscape.

DOI: 10.4018/979-8-3693-3144-6.ch005

INTRODUCTION

"I want history to remember me... not as the first Black woman to have made a bid for the presidency of the United States, but as a Black woman who lived in the 20th century and who dared to be herself. I want to be remembered as a catalyst for change in America."[2]– Shirley Anita St. Hill Chisholm, the first African American woman in US Congress (1968).

The journey of Black women in higher education leadership in the United States spans over two centuries, marked by considerable milestones and persistent challenges. Their dynamic roles and contributions were often marginalized in public Black colleges, where state educational administration was one of the few areas in which Black men could exert political influence, thus overshadowing the leadership roles of Black women. Theoretical lenses and historical advancements reveal that Black women in higher education leadership have faced critical barriers, including systemic racism and gender bias, which have hindered their career progression. In specific disciplines like engineering education, Black women leaders encounter unique challenges such as performance reviews, ethical decision-making, and the necessity of code-switching, highlighting the intersectionality of their experiences. Despite the increasing number of female students and novice faculty, the attainment of leadership positions by women, particularly Black women, remains limited due to hegemonic leadership practices that favor White men's and women's experiences, thus excluding them from mainstream leadership rhetoric and practice. This historical and ongoing struggle underscores the urgent need for more inclusive leadership theories and forums that support the advancement of Black women in higher education, ensuring their perspectives and contributions are recognized and valued.

Black women have made substantial strides in their career progression and representation in higher education leadership in the United States over the past two centuries (Johnson, 2023; Porter et al., 2022). They have faced challenges and barriers, yet they have also made significant contributions to the field. Despite the increasing number of female students and faculty in academia, there are still too few female leaders to promote and inspire diversity (Soares, 2023). Historically, Black women have been at the forefront of the struggle for equal access to education, with many earning degrees and becoming educators and founders of higher education institutions (Evans, 2016). However, their leadership roles have often been marginalized and overlooked (Walser-Smith, 2019). Despite this, Black women have persevered and made advancements in higher education administration. Their progress, though not without obstacles, is a testament to their resilience and the potential for further advancement. The experiences of Black women leaders in higher education, including the challenges they encounter and the strategies they use to overcome them, can provide valuable insights for improving the retention and advancement of Black women leaders (Gamble & Turner, 2015). Achieving gender equality in leadership positions in higher education is not only a matter of fairness but is also essential to advancing the current and evolving higher education landscape (Chamblin et al., 2022; Salinas, 2016; Wright & Salinas, 2016).

Defining moments for Black women higher education leaders in the United States have been shaped by historical achievements, challenges, and opportunities for reform. Black women have strived for higher education since before the Civil War, facing violence and daunting challenges but persisting in their pursuit of degrees (Williams, 2023). Despite these challenges, Black women have made advancements in higher education, with some becoming college administrators, presidents, and founders of institutions (Brubacher, 2017; Evans, 2016). Acquiring higher education was seen as a pathway to citizenship and freedom for Black Americans. Black women played a pivotal role in demanding access to education (Allen et al., 2023). However, the path for Black women in academic leadership is nuanced and multiplicative as they navigate gendered and racialized pathways to leadership (Johnson, 2024; Johnson & Johnson, 2024). Black women leaders in higher education face barriers and inequitable outcomes associated with the intersectionality of their race and gender (Showunmi, 2023). Understanding these barriers and identifying support is crucial for improving the retention of Black women leaders in higher education administration (Tevis et al., 2020).

Black women have faced numerous challenges in accessing and advancing in higher education leadership in the United States. Over the past two centuries, they have navigated cultural adversity and fought for equal opportunities, making notable strides despite systemic barriers. One particularly defining moment was the founding of Spelman College in 1881, a historically Black college for women that provided educational opportunities for Black women during a period of widespread exclusion from mainstream institutions (Mebane, 2019). Another milestone was the establishment of the Association for the Study of African American Life and History in 1915, advocating for the inclusion of Black historical experiences in higher education curricula (Dagbovie, 2003). Recent studies continue to explore the lived experiences of Black female faculty in leadership positions, highlighting the unique challenges they face, including racial and gender biases (Horhn & Lassiter, 2022). Despite this, Black women have ascended to prominent leadership positions as visible role models and advocates for diversity and inclusion in academia (Williams, 2023).

The literature on Black higher education leaders has focused primarily on Black men. Still, recent scholarship has highlighted the role of Black women – the good, the bad, and the ugly – in this field (Hailu & Cox, 2022). Challenges faced by Black women leaders include ethical decision-making, limited autonomy in selecting their administrative team, and code-switching (West, 2020). Despite being the most represented minoritized group among higher education administrators, Black women still lag behind White women and men in leadership positions (Grottis, 2022; Nickerson, 2020). Barriers to career progression for Black women administrators include systemic inequities and lack of support, but identifying these barriers can inform strategies to improve retention (Butcher, 2022; Richardson, 2023). The COVID-19 pandemic allowed African American women leaders in higher education to launch their businesses, driven by the familial history of entrepreneurship, workplace inequities, and a desire for authentic leadership (Baumgartner, 2022; Cottrill et al., 2014; Kapasi et al., 2016).

A BACKGROUND

"Slavery is the combination of all crime. It is War. Those who rob their fellow men of home, of liberty, of education, of life, are really at war against them as though they cleft them down upon the bloody field."[3]*– Lucy Stanton, the first African American woman in the US to complete a four-year collegiate course of study (1850).*

Black women have strived to secure higher education in the United States for over two centuries. These efforts began before the Civil War and continue to the present time. In the process, African American women have earned certificates, bachelor's degrees, and various graduate degrees and have become college administrators, presidents, and founders of higher education institutions. Multiple supporters, including Prudence Crandall, who dedicated their efforts to enlightening African American females during the nineteenth century, often encountered violence and hostility (Williams, 2023; Williams & Ziobro, 2023). Nevertheless, Black women persisted and began moving up the higher education ladder in the early nineteenth century despite facing these and other daunting challenges (Evans, 2016). Most women, revealingly, obtained their degrees in Northern states, including Ohio, and primarily at specific institutions such as Oberlin, Antioch, and Wilberforce.

During the period preceding the Civil War (1861-1865), Oberlin emerged as the preeminent institution in Antebellum America for conferring higher education degrees or certificates to Black women (Baumgartner, 2022; Terry, 2023). Notably, numerous Black women successfully attained literary degrees (L.D.s) from this esteemed institution. Notably, Lucy Ann Stanton is widely recognized as the inaugural Black woman to fulfill the requirements of a four-year curriculum and be awarded an L.D. from Oberlin, which occurred circa 1850. Concurrently, Sarah Jane Early pursued her studies at Oberlin, similarly to Ms. Stanton, ultimately obtaining a degree in classical studies in 1856. Moreover, Early achieved another historic milestone by assuming the first Black woman college instructor role in the annals of United States history, commencing her tenure at Wilberforce University in 1858. It is crucial to acknowledge that Stanton and Early rank among the pioneering Black women who were granted degrees from Oberlin, all of whom accomplished this feat before 1860.

Although Stanton is widely regarded as the inaugural Black woman in the United States to receive a certificate of completion from an institute of higher education, it was, in fact, Mary Jane Patterson who achieved the distinction of being the first Black woman to acquire a Bachelor of Arts (B.A.) degree in 1862, an accomplishment she accomplished at Oberlin. On the other hand, Lucy Ann earned what was then referred to as a literary degree, as opposed to a bachelor's degree, and thus, she is not recognized as the foremost Black woman to obtain a four-year degree. To this day, our knowledge is limited to the fact that she attained "a degree" in classical studies, and based on the accessible records, it was not designated as a B.A. Two years later, in 1864, Rebecca Lee completed her degree at the New England Female Medical College. Dr. Lee is the first documented Black woman in the United States of America to achieve a medical degree (Evans, 2007; Williams, 2023).

Prior to 1865, a minimum of twelve Black women successfully obtained their academic degrees from colleges in the southern region of the United States. By 1865, three noteworthy Black women educators, namely Patterson, Frances Josephine Norris, and Fanny Marion Jackson, achieved B.A. degrees from Oberlin College. From there, Patterson and Coppin began their teaching careers at the Institute for Colored Youth in Philadelphia, Pennsylvania, one of the country's earliest secondary educational institutions for African Americans, and eventually became known as Cheyney University. Following her graduation from Oberlin, Patterson dedicated five years to teaching at the Institute for Colored Youth. Subsequently, she taught at the Preparatory High School for Colored Youth, also known as M Street School, in Washington, DC, where she later assumed the position of school principal. During her tenure as principal, she worked tirelessly to elevate the status of the school, transforming it into one of the most esteemed high schools catering to African American students in the nation.

Coppin herself was born into slavery, eventually becoming a self-made woman. She worked to secure an education at the Rhode Island State Normal School, first, followed by Oberlin. She became a principal at the Institute of Colored Youth and substantively expanded the curriculum, making it one of the nation's more notable schools for African Americans. Her expansion included the development of a Women's Industrial Exchange and Industrial Department. Coppin State University in Baltimore, Maryland, is named for Fannie Jackson Coppin (Williams, 2023). The nineteenth century proved a crucial period of growth and progress for Black women in education, and Coppin serves as an example. Now spanning two hundred years of African American women in higher education, these women played indispensable roles in the establishment of Black educational institutions, with Oberlin and Wilberforce serving as notable platforms, as a noteworthy number of Black women who obtained degrees from these institutions went on to become educators, advocates for civil rights, and founders of schools (Thelin & Gasman, 2003; Williams, 2023).

A PRECARIOUS JOURNEY

> *"We needed to be assertive as women in those days - assertive and aggressive - and the degree to which we had to be that way depended on where you were. I had to be."*[4]*– Katherine Johnson, American mathematician whose calculations of orbital mechanics as a NASA employee were critical to the success of the first and subsequent US-crewed spaceflights (1961).*

Over the past two centuries, Black women in the United States have navigated a precarious journey toward securing higher education and leadership roles within this sphere. Initially, their quest was fundamentally a fight for access to a system from which they were systematically excluded. Mary Ann Shadd Carey's enrollment at Howard University in 1884 marked a significant milestone as she became the first Black woman to do so, symbolizing the breaking of gender and racial barriers in higher education. Before and after this period, African American women faced – and continue to face – considerable obstructions in accessing higher education due to systemic racial and gender biases. This struggle does not end with access. Black women in academia have continuously faced challenges related to race and gender, often finding themselves in precarious, part-time, and sometimes full-time positions with considerable instability. Despite these and other setbacks, there has been much progress in recruitment, retention, and career ascension for African American women at Predominantly White Institutions, albeit within a framework that often necessitates navigating systemic barriers and biases. Leadership roles for Black women in higher education have also evolved, with a growing recognition of their unique perspectives and contributions. Current studies employing theoretical frameworks like Critical Race Feminist Theory and Black Feminist Thought, among others, have helped illuminate how Black women leaders in postsecondary education define themselves and their leadership styles, contributing to a broader understanding of leadership, primarily inclusive of race and gender.

By demanding access to education, Black women were at the forefront of the fight for Black equality throughout the twentieth century. African Americans considered the quest for a quality education a prominent civil rights issue (McCluskey, 2014). In the early decades of the twentieth century, Black women began to acquire graduate degrees in more substantial numbers. In the 1900s, women such as Marion Thompson Wright, Constance Baker Motley, and Autherine Lucy demanded equal access to all educational facilities nationwide. For many Black Americans, acquiring a higher education was a pathway to citizenship and freedom. Most scholarly literature on Black Americans in higher education has focused primarily on Black men. However, more recently, scholars have explicitly focused on the role of Black women in higher education. The field is defined by intellectual biographies, social histories of pivotal institutions, including Oberlin and Spelman, edited volumes of interviews, personal narratives, autobiographies, and other qualitative works of women who participated in signature moments in the history of Black women in higher education. Reoccurring themes in this lived history include race consciousness, gender equity, and class awareness (Brock et al., 2019).

Equally important are the contributions and leadership evolution of Black women. A growing number of extant studies are examining and centering the accounts of African American women in higher education leadership, focusing on how they define job satisfaction and overcome professional challenges. Georgiana Simpson made history in 1921 as the first Black woman to receive a Ph.D. in the United States; from there, similar successes by other Black women scholars soon followed this achievement. Historically, Black women's participation in collegiate education in the U.S. continues to evolve significantly, dating from the earliest settlers in the USs to contemporary times (i.e., 21st century). Recent advancements include the furtherance of phenomenological studies designed to describe and uplift the lived experiences of Black women in education, faculty, and leadership positions, highlighting their rising influence in academia and academic leadership. Studies of this nature center on the experiences of Black women and offer insights into their advancement and continued impact in the educational sphere.

African American women's progression in higher education leadership in the United States has been undoubtedly meaningful and defining. Included among these milestones are the historical and contemporary struggles of Black female scholars who continue to overcome multiple forms of resistance in higher education, namely, Sadie Tanner Mossell Alexander, Eva Beatrice Dykes, and Georgiana Simpson—the first Black women in the United States to earn doctorate degrees (Howard-Baptiste & Harris, 2014). In the ongoing work to better understand the persistent challenges that Black female academics face, it is vital to acknowledge the pioneering efforts of those Black women who paved paths despite the many obstacles. The journey is a precarious one, to say the least. Black women in and beyond the realm of higher education can forge paths forward in solidarity (Horhn & Lassiter, 2022), appreciating those who came before, among the first Black women to earn bachelor's, master's, and doctoral degrees in the United States (Howard-Baptiste, 2014; Howard-Baptiste & Harris, 2014).

PRESENT-DAY

"I hope to inspire people to try to follow this path, because I love this country, because I love the law, because I think it is important that we all invest in our future. And the young people are the future. I am also ever buoyed by the leadership of generations past who helped to light the way."[5]*– Ketanji Brown, Lawyer, Jurist, and Justice of the United States Supreme Court (2022).*

Few texts speak directly to the history of Black women in higher education. Nevertheless, notable overviews generally tend to be social histories focused on a select few Black women, with some intellectual accounts focusing on Black women novelists, academics, thinkers, and leaders appearing more recurringly since the late 1900s. Moreover, the first book-length scholarly analysis of women in higher education focuses overwhelmingly on white women (Eisenmann, 2023; Solomon, 1985). Nevertheless, this work provides an essential framework for thinking more broadly about women in higher education. After Solomon's text was published, several overviews of educated Black women working in various capacities (e.g., novelists, writers, social workers, and public intellectuals) began appearing in growing fashion. Works that followed Solomon's book, though not always explicitly about Black women in higher education, continue to provide necessary context regarding the lived experiences of Black women who have had access to higher education spaces, many of whom became educators themselves and used their knowledge as writers, activists, and institution builders, to support and uplift other women (Brown, 2006; Butcher, 2022).

Other 20th and 21st-century works include Paula Giddings' text, one of the first scholarly surveys of Delta Sigma Theta, the oldest and largest Black women's organization in the United States. Giddings' work (1988) highlighted Black women's search for sisterhood and the challenges embedded in the Black sorority movement. It was soon followed by Carby's work (1987) on Black women novelists, many of whom were, themselves, holders of higher education degrees. In addition, Brown's 2006 text is a valuable overview of Black women professionals and their collective activism, focusing on their support of the war effort and social work. Scholars who study African American women in US history and higher education have not thoroughly covered this timeframe. This and other related works are among the first to examine African American women's intellectual, scholarly activity in the 19th century via a discussion of Black female novelists (Carby, 1987). In the 20th century, notable figures highlighted in this arena include pioneers such as Pauline Elizabeth Hopkins and Frances Ellen Watkins Harper. While much scholarship on race, politics, and African American history has focused on men such as W. E. B. Du Bois, Cooper's text (2017) critically examines race and gender in Black women's intellectual lives. Some individuals featured in Cooper's study were the first Black women to attain higher education degrees, including graduate degrees. These works cover a vast amount of information on the experience of Black women in higher education, including a discussion of the group's concern for Black civil rights and women's empowerment writ large.

Other relevant historical texts include Solomon's work, one of the more critical histories of women in higher education. This text provides vital historical information and context on women's opportunities and challenges in higher education. It remains an essential resource on the topic of women in the history of higher education (Solomon, 1985). Historian Deborah Gray White's work traverses one hundred years of Black women in US society, focusing on the Black women's club movement, including a discussion of Black women in higher education. Many women who formed literary clubs, self-help associations, and civil rights organizations (the NAACP included) were among the first Black women to obtain higher education degrees (White, 1999). Noble's work (1993) surveys Black women in higher education during the 20th century, serving as a helpful reference on this subject matter. This work uncovers much relevant information regarding African American women's higher education experiences and points current scholars to future directions in what remains an emergent field. Myers' text (2002) is a sociological study underscoring the interwoven systems of race and gender in academia in the US. Rooted in narrative inquiry and ranging across various disciplines, Black women employed at predominantly white colleges and universities provide recollections (i.e., primary sources of information) for historians examining Black women in higher education and their perspectives regarding academia in the twenty-first century. Perkins (2015) is a leading scholar on Black women and higher education. Authoring several works in this discipline, she uses an intersectional approach to understanding the quest for higher education by some leading Black women education activists embracing their collective work as a strategy toward Black women's empowerment. These timelines reflect a trajectory of perseverance, achievement, and increasing influence of Black women in higher education leadership as they continue shaping a more diverse academic landscape.

MANAGERIAL SIGNIFICANCE

"The greatness of Americans is that we are mosaic - we are diverse."[6] — *Sheila Jackson Lee, American lawyer and politician, U.S. representative for Texas' 18th congressional district (1995-2024).*

The paths of Black women in higher education leadership in the United States have evolved significantly over the past two centuries. Dating back to before the Civil War (1861–1865), Black women have persistently fought to acquire higher education in the U.S., demonstrating remarkable resilience in overcoming substantial barriers related to race and gender (Showunmi, 2023). Despite the educational advancements Black women have made, they are underrepresented at the highest levels of academic leadership (Grant, 2015). Nonetheless, Black women have made notable inroads as academic leaders. These roles shape student experiences and institutional policies and are critical to creating pipelines for emergent and future educational leaders (Grottis, 2022). In increasing fashion, emergent studies continue to reveal the unique challenges African American women face working to advance in predominantly white institutions. Particularly in recruitment, retention, and career advancement, recent research has focused on the intersection of race and gender in academia, highlighting the experiences of Black women and advocating for more inclusive environments (Barak, 2005).

Black women in higher education leadership roles in the United States hold pointed managerial importance due to their unique perspectives and the critical barriers they have overcome. Historically, Black women have been at the forefront of the struggle for educational equality, with pioneers setting foundational precedents in the 19th century by securing degrees and leading academic institutions (Showunmi, 2023). Their achievements are a source of pride and inspiration for all. Despite their historical contributions, Black women continue to face underrepresentation in senior leadership roles within higher education, a disparity that necessitates targeted identity-based leadership initiatives and structured mentoring programs to support their advancement (Pinto et al., 2024). However, the growing number of female students and novice faculty underscores the need for more women leaders to inspire and reflect the shifting demographics in higher education (Johnson, 2023; Johnson & Johnson, 2024). Research indicates that Black women are the most represented minoritized group among U.S. higher education administrators. Yet, they still lag behind their White counterparts in leadership positions, highlighting the need for policies that cultivate and retain their talent and leadership acumen (West, 2020). By understanding the trajectory of Black women leaders and identifying the support they use to remain in the administration, higher education institutions can develop strategies to improve their retention and success (Nickerson, 2020). Overall, the managerial significance of Black women in higher education lies in their ability to bring diverse perspectives, challenge entrenched leadership norms, and serve as role models for future generations, fostering a more inclusive and equitable academic environment.

A GLIMPSE INTO THE FUTURE

"The future never just happened. It was created."[7]— Mae Jemison, doctor, engineer, and America's first Black female astronaut, regarding serving on the crew of the shuttle Endeavour (1992).

Over the last two centuries, Black women have strived to secure higher education in the United States, facing a host of violence and challenges along the way (Winkle-Wagner, 2015). However, their dynamic roles in public colleges were often marginalized and obscured (Adekunle et al., 2023). The achievements and barriers Black women administrators face in higher education allow us to better understand their trajectories, identify career barriers, and consider how to support their retention (Butcher, 2022; DeWitt, 2016). The race-gender dyad is significant to the experiences of Black women and Black women leaders in higher education, particularly those operating in historically White institutions (Collins & Bilge, 2020). The presence of Black women in senior-level higher education leadership, especially at Predominantly White Institutions (PWIs), is minimal, and, unfortunately, their experiences in these positions are not well-known (Walser-Smith, 2019).

Black women in the United States have made great strides in higher education leadership over the past two centuries. The 20th century was a turning point, seeing a gradual increase in African American women's participation in higher education as students, educators, and educational leaders. In recent decades, leadership roles have opened up for Black women in academia. There has been a notable rise among Black women leaders in academic institutions, including roles as faculty members, deans, and senior student affairs officers (Barak, 2005; West, 2020). Other extant studies have used frameworks like Black Feminist Thought (BFT) to understand how Black women leaders in higher education define themselves and their roles (Allen et al., 2023; Collins, 2020). Despite this progress, Black women in academia still face challenges related to gender and racial biases. Research has examined these experiences and the resilience of Black women in these roles (Carducci et al., 2024; Evans, 2016).

Black women have historically played a pivotal role in higher education, yet their leadership roles have often been marginalized and overlooked. Despite the increasing number of female students and novice faculty, Black women remain underrepresented in leadership positions, facing systemic barriers rooted in both gender and racial discrimination. Studies reveal that Black women often ascend to leadership through academic pathways, and the challenges they face, including racial and gender harassment, microaggressions, and systemic oppression, are not only individual but also institutional. These barriers are compounded, again, by leadership practices that exclude those who do not fit the dominant cultural norms. Strategies to overcome these challenges include truth-telling about the impact of neoliberal institutions, creating support networks, and fostering environments that recognize and celebrate Black excellence. Achieving gender equality in leadership is not only a matter of fairness but also essential for the evolving landscape of higher education, necessitating reforms that support the advancement and retention of Black women leaders. By understanding and addressing these challenges, higher education institutions can create more inclusive and equitable environments that benefit from Black women's diverse perspectives and leadership.

Throughout the 21st century and beyond, we have seen substantial progress and notable milestones for African American women in higher education leadership in the United States (Idowu, 2023; Johnson, 2021, 2023, 2023; Johnson & Fournillier, 2022, 2023). Despite enduring systemic barriers, African American women continue to face the challenges of accessing higher education head-on. As a result of these struggles – and continued perseverance – Black women continue to work towards closing the gaps to their fundamental rights as equal members of and participants in academia. For example, social justice and other extant leadership ideologies serve as necessary frames, exploring African American women's experiences in educational leadership and highlighting their contributions and challenges in job satisfaction and career advancement. These and other historical milestones, such as landmark achievements such as Lila Fenwick becoming the first Black woman to graduate from Harvard Law School in 1956, continue demonstrating Black women's ability to break racial and gender barriers in and beyond the academic sphere.

CONCLUSION

"It isn't easy for Black women in the academy to love institutions that do not love us back. Yet, we persist because we are committed to holding institutions accountable for realizing their full potential, which includes creating space for and bringing out the richness in research and practice that comes from diverse perspectives and forms of knowledge. I've seen glimpses of this potential through various possibility models inside and outside the academy. I draw critical hope from them."[8]*– Dr. Joy Gaston Gales, president of the Association for the Study of Higher Education (ASHE) and Senior Advisor for Advancing Diversity, Equity, and Inclusion (2022).*

This chapter marks two centuries of defining moments for Black women in higher education. These significant historical benchmarks speak primarily to Black women's trajectories, experiences, and higher education (Soares, 2023; Thelin & Gasman, 2003). These signatory occurrences in African American life offer a timeline through the 19th century, the World War I and World War II eras, the Civil Rights and Post-Civil Rights eras, to the present day. A topical-chronological approach predominantly defines these analyses, allowing shareholders to understand the topic's historiography on a whole scale. Black women's history is still a relatively new, emergent field. Much of the work on Black women in higher education can be found in biographies, era-specific survey histories, and edited volumes, with a few pertinent monographs. The history of Black women advancing in higher education has only recently become a subfield in and beyond historical, era-specific studies. Only recently have a few survey and monograph studies begun appearing about Black women and higher education that have helped to move the historiography of this vital subject forward beyond oral histories, biographies, case studies, and edited volumes, to name a few (Williams, 2023).

The state of Black women in higher education remains complex and multifaceted. Despite growing relevant research and scholarship, this group continues to be marginalized in academic discourse and curriculum, with works too often relegated to less prestigious journals, which questions the value placed on critical research centered on their experiences (Patton et al., 2024; West & Porter, 2023). Black women in higher education navigate a landscape fraught with intersectional challenges, including historically rooted racial and gender discrimination. The persistence of these issues is evident in the discursive representations of Black women in academe, who are often depicted as resilient in the face of adversity, reliant on interdependent relationships, and defined by their intersectional identities of race and gender (Johnson, 2021, 2023, 2023). Furthermore, the experiences of Black women in academia are riddled with sophisticated racism and sexism, which not only undermine their career progression but also contribute to racial trauma and a decline in their well-being.

Nevertheless, Black women continue to disrupt monolithic perceptions and assert their full humanity, living integrated and complete lives while striving for success in predominantly White institutions, historically Black institutions, and other educational contexts (West & Porter, 2023). The need for more varied, nuanced, and intersectional literature is critical, as is the call for higher education institutions to critically engage with and support Black women's success and well-being both on and off campus. As Black feminist epistemologies and methodological approaches gain traction, future research must continue to innovate and rigorously address Black women's unique needs and experiences in higher education (Patton et al., 2024). The ongoing efforts to highlight and address these issues underscore the importance of creating inclusive and supportive environments for Black women in academia (Howard-Hamilton, 2023; West & Porter, 2023).

Understanding the multifaceted experiences and challenges Black women educators and leaders encounter can contribute to positive change and decrease workplace disparities in academia (Adekunle et al., 2023; Johnson, 2025). The underrepresentation of African American women in executive and administrative positions in colleges and universities highlights the need for effective and diverse leadership in contemporary higher education. To move this needle forward, and as a member of this same group myself, I highlight the criticality of understanding the challenges Black women leaders face en route to identifying strategies to improve their retention and advancement. By understanding and addressing these challenges, higher education institutions can create more inclusive and equitable environments that benefit from Black women's diverse perspectives and leadership. This is further evidenced by the creation of forums and spaces that value the perspectives and experiences of Black women leaders; in these and other ways, higher education institutions can do their part in the work towards achieving gender equity in leadership (Johnson, 2024; Schnackenberg, 2025).

REFERENCES

Adekunle, J. O., Campbell, K., Chapman, S. J., Chávez, M., Dooley, K. L., Liu, P., & Williams, H. V. (2023). *Inequality and Governance in an Uncertain World: Perspectives on Democratic and Autocratic Governments*. Rowman & Littlefield.

Allen, M., Smith, A., & Dika, S. (2023). Black Feminism and Black Women's Interactions With Faculty in Higher Education. In *Oxford Research Encyclopedia of Education*. DOI: 10.1093/acrefore/9780190264093.013.1723

Barak, M. (2005). *Managing Diversity: Toward a globally inclusive workplace*. SAGE.

Baumgartner, K. (2022). In pursuit of knowledge: Black women and educational activism in antebellum [). NYU Press.]. *America*, 5, •••.

Brock, R., Pratt-Clarke, M., & Maes, J. B. (Eds.). (2019). *Journeys of social justice: Women of color presidents in the academy*. Peter Lang Incorporated, International Academic Publishers.

Brown, N. (2006). *Private politics and public voices: Black women's activism from World War I to the New Deal*. Indiana University Press.

Brubacher, J. (2017). *Higher education in transition: History of American colleges and universities*. Routledge. DOI: 10.4324/9780203790076

Butcher, J. T. (Ed.). (2022). *Black Female Leaders in Academia: Eliminating the Glass Ceiling With Efficacy, Exuberance, and Excellence*. IGI Global., DOI: 10.4018/978-1-7998-9774-3

Carby, H. V. (1987). *Reconstructing womanhood: The emergence of the Afro-American woman novelist*. Oxford University Press.

Carducci, R., Harper, J., & Kezar, A. (2024). *Higher Education Leadership: Challenging Tradition and Forging Possibilities*. JHU Press. DOI: 10.56021/9781421448787

Chamblin, M., Newland, L. Z., Kelly, J., & Silva Thompson, L. M. (2022). Sistas in Action: Hearing the Call, Leading the Way. In Butcher, J. (Ed.), *Black Female Leaders in Academia: Eliminating the Glass Ceiling With Efficacy, Exuberance, and Excellence* (pp. 97–120). IGI Global., DOI: 10.4018/978-1-7998-9774-3.ch006

Clanton, T. L., Shelton, R. N., & Franz, N. E. (2023). Thriving Despite the Odds: A Review of Literature on the Experiences of Black Women at Predominately White Institutions. *Handbook of Research on Exploring Gender Equity, Diversity, and Inclusion Through an Intersectional Lens*, 423–437.

Collins, P. H. (2020). Defining black feminist thought. In *Feminist Theory Reader* (pp. 278–290). Routledge.

Collins, P. H., & Bilge, S. (2020). *Intersectionality*. John Wiley & Sons.

Cooper, B. C. (2017). *Beyond respectability: The intellectual thought of race women*. University of Illinois Press. DOI: 10.5406/illinois/9780252040993.001.0001

Cottrill, K., Denise Lopez, P., & Hoffman, C., C. (. (2014). How authentic leadership and inclusion benefit organizations. *Equality, Diversity and Inclusion*, 33(3), 275–292. DOI: 10.1108/EDI-05-2012-0041

Dagbovie, P. G. (2003). Black women, Carter G. Woodson, and the association for the study of Negro life and history, 1915-1950. *Journal of African American History*, 88(1), 21–41. DOI: 10.2307/3559046

Daniel, G. R., & Williams, H. V. (Eds.). (2014). *Race and the Obama phenomenon: The vision of a more perfect multiracial union*. Univ. Press of Mississippi. DOI: 10.14325/mississippi/9781628460216.001.0001

DeWitt, P. M. (2016). *Collaborative leadership: Six influences that matter most*. Corwin Press.

Eisenmann, L. (2023). Historical Considerations of Women and Gender in Higher Education. In Perna, L. W. (Ed.), *Higher Education: Handbook of Theory and Research. Higher Education: Handbook of Theory and Research* (Vol. 38). Springer., DOI: 10.1007/978-3-031-06696-2_6

Evans, S. Y. (2016). *Black women in the ivory tower, 1850–1954: An intellectual history*. University Press of Florida.

Gamble, E. D., & Turner, N. J. (2015). Career ascension of African American women in executive positions in postsecondary institutions. *Journal of Organizational Culture. Communications and Conflict*, 19(1), 82.

Giddings, P. (1988). In search of sisterhood: Delta Sigma Theta and the challenge of the Black sorority movement.

Grant, C. M. (2015). Smashing the glass ceiling: Accountability of institutional policies and practices to leadership diversity in higher education. In *Culturally Responsive Leadership in Higher Education* (pp. 167–179). Routledge. DOI: 10.4324/9781315720777-12

Gray-Nicolas, N. M., Modeste, M. E., Miles Nash, A., & Tabron, L. A. (2022). (Other) sistering: Black Women Education Leadership Faculty Aligning Identity, Scholarship, and Practice Through Peer Support and Accountability. *Journal of Education Human Resources*, 40(1), 90–113. DOI: 10.3138/jehr-2021-0017

Grottis, L. R. (2022). Black Women in Higher Education Leadership: A Critical Review of the Achievements and Barriers to Career Advancement. *Black Female Leaders in Academia: Eliminating the Glass Ceiling With Efficacy, Exuberance, and Excellence*, 58–72.

Hailu, M. F., & Cox, M. F. (2022). Black women in academic leadership: reflections of one department chair's journey in engineering. In *Black Feminist Epistemology, Research, and Praxis* (pp. 177–188). Routledge.

Hill, R. F. (2019). The danger of an untold story: Excerpts from my life as a Black academic. *Journal of Education for Library and Information Science*, 60(3), 208–214. DOI: 10.3138/jelis.2019-0008

Horhn, E. B., & Lassiter, S. (2022). A Tale of Two Black Women Seeking Solidarity within Academia. *The Ivory Tower: Perspectives of Women of Color in Higher Education*, 81.

Howard-Baptiste, S., & Harris, J. C. (2014). Teaching then and now: Black female scholars and the mission to move beyond borders. *Negro Educational Review*, 65(1–4), 5–22.

Howard-Baptiste, S. D. (2014). Arctic space, lonely place: "Mammy moments" in higher education. *The Urban Review*, 46(4), 764–782. DOI: 10.1007/s11256-014-0298-1

Howard-Hamilton, M. F. (2023). Black Women in higher education reclaiming our time. *New Directions for Student Services*, 2023(182), 5–8. DOI: 10.1002/ss.20462

Idowu, B. D. (2023). A personal reflection upon navigating into a senior academic role. *Frontiers in Sociology*, 8, 979691. DOI: 10.3389/fsoc.2023.979691 PMID: 37415874

Johnson, L. (2023). Black Women and Theoretical Frameworks. *The Scholarship Without Borders Journal*, 1(2), 1. DOI: 10.57229/2834-2267.1018

Johnson, N. N. (2021). Balancing race, gender, and responsibility: Conversations with four Black women in educational leadership in the United States of America. *Educational Management Administration & Leadership*, 49(4), 624–643. DOI: 10.1177/1741143221991839

Johnson, N. N. (2023). Intersectionality in Leadership: Spotlighting the Experiences of Black Women DEI Leaders in Historically White Academic Institutions. In *The Experiences of Black Women Diversity Practitioners in Historically White Institutions* (pp. 213–238). IGI Global.

Johnson, N. N. (2024). Rooted in justice: One Black woman's unique, intersectional educational leadership journey. *School Leadership & Management*, 44(2), 140–158. DOI: 10.1080/13632434.2023.2290512

Johnson, N. N. (2025). Two Centuries of Defining Moments for Black Women Higher Education Leaders in the United States. In Schnackenberg, H. L. (Ed.), *Narratives on Defining Moments for Women Leaders in Higher Education*. IGI Global.

Johnson, N. N., & Fournillier, J. B. (2022). Increasing diversity in leadership: Perspectives of four Black women educational leaders in the context of the United States. *Journal of Educational Administration and History*, 54(2), 174–192. DOI: 10.1080/00220620.2021.1985976

Johnson, N. N., & Fournillier, J. B. (2023). Intersectionality and leadership in context: Examining the intricate paths of four Black women in educational leadership in the United States. *International Journal of Leadership in Education*, 26(2), 296–317. DOI: 10.1080/13603124.2020.1818132

Johnson, N. N., & Johnson, T. L. (2024). The Race-Gender-Equity-Leadership Matrix: Intersectionality and Its Application in Higher Education Literature. *Journal of Black Studies*. Advance online publication. DOI: 10.1177/00219347241259454

Kapasi, I., Sang, K. J., & Sitko, R. (2016). Gender, authentic leadership and identity: Analysis of women leaders' autobiographies. *Gender in Management*, 31(5/6), 339–358. DOI: 10.1108/GM-06-2015-0058

Lawson, E. N. (1984). *The three Sarahs: Documents of antebellum black college women*. Mellen-Press.

Logan, S. W. (1999). *We are coming: The persuasive discourse of nineteenth-century Black women*. SIU Press.

McCluskey, A. T. (2014). *A forgotten sisterhood: Pioneering Black women educators and activists in the Jim Crow South*. Rowman & Littlefield. DOI: 10.5771/9781442211407

Mebane, B. (2019). *The Sisterhood Is Alive and Well at Spelman College: A Feminist Standpoint Case Study*. Ball State University.

Myers, L. (2002). *A broken silence: Voices of African American women in the academy*. Bloomsbury Publishing USA. DOI: 10.5040/9798400621802

Nickerson, J. C. (2020). Black women in higher education leadership: examining their lived experiences utilizing cross-race and cross-gender mentorship.

Noble, J. (1993). The higher education of African American women in the twentieth century. *Women in higher education: a feminist perspective*, 329-336.

Parfait-Davis, M. (2022). A Framework for Contextualizing Black Women's Negative Experiences in the Academy. *The Ivory Tower: Perspectives of Women of Color in Higher Education*, 55.

Patton, L. D., Davison, C. H., Mackie, T., McCollum, S., & Nelson, B. (2024). *Black Women in Academia*. Oxford Bibliographies., DOI: 10.1093/obo/9780199756810-0320

Perkins, L. M. (2015). "Bound to them by a common sorrow": African American women, higher education, and collective advancement. *Journal of African American History*, 100(4), 721–747. DOI: 10.5323/jafriamerhist.100.4.0721

Pinto, R., Douglas, T. R. M., Lane-Bonds, D., & McMillian, R. (2024). Yes She Can: Examining the Career Pathways of Black Women in Higher Education Senior Leadership Position. *Advances in Developing Human Resources*, 26(2-3), 15234223241254574. DOI: 10.1177/15234223241254574

Porter, C. J., Sulé, V. T., & Croom, N. N. (Eds.). (2022). *Black Feminist Epistemology, Research, and Praxis: Narratives in and Through the Academy*. Taylor & Francis. DOI: 10.4324/9781003184867

Richardson, S. D. (2023). Higher Education Leaders as Entre-Employees: A Narrative Study. *American Journal of Qualitative Research*, 7(3), 1–18. DOI: 10.29333/ajqr/13222

Schnackenberg, H. L. (Ed.). (2025). *Narratives on Defining Moments for Women Leaders in Higher Education*. IGI Global., DOI: 10.4018/979-8-3693-3144-6

Showunmi, V. (2023). Visible, invisible: Black women in higher education. *Frontiers in Sociology*, 8, 974617. DOI: 10.3389/fsoc.2023.974617 PMID: 37152206

Smith, J. C., & Phelps, S. (Eds.). (1992). *Notable Black American women* (Vol. 2). VNR AG.

Soares, L. (2023). "Tuskegee Is Her Monument": Gender and Leadership in Early Public Black Colleges. *History of Education Quarterly*, 63(3), 1–21. DOI: 10.1017/heq.2023.3

Solomon, B. M. (1985). *In the company of educated women: A history of women and higher education in America*. Yale University Press.

Terry, D. (2023). On the Threshold of Education: Race and Antebellum Schooling in the Text and Context of the Colored American. *CEA Critic*, 85(1), 58–83. DOI: 10.1353/cea.2023.0004

Tevis, T., Hernandez, M., & Bryant, R. (2020). Reclaiming our time: An autoethnographic exploration of Black women higher education administrators. *The Journal of Negro Education*, 89(3), 282–297.

Thelin, J. R., & Gasman, M. (2003). Historical overview of American higher education. *Student services: A handbook for the profession, 4*, 3-22.

Walkington, L. (2017). How far have we really come? Black women faculty and graduate students' experiences in higher education. *Humboldt Journal of Social Relations*, 39(39), 51–65. DOI: 10.55671/0160-4341.1022

Walser-Smith, J. (2019). *Transforming the Academy: Black Women Leaders at Predominantly White Institutions in the South* (Doctoral dissertation, Appalachian State University).

West, N. M. (2020). A contemporary portrait of Black women student affairs administrators in the United States. *Journal of Women and Gender in Higher Education*, 13(1), 72–92. DOI: 10.1080/26379112.2020.1728699

West, N. M., & Porter, C. J. (2023). The state of Black women in higher education: A critical perspective 20 years later. *New Directions for Student Services*, 2023(182), 9–13. DOI: 10.1002/ss.20463

White, D. G. (1999). *Too heavy a load: Black women in defense of themselves 1894-1994*. WW Norton & Company.

Wilder, J., Jones, T. B., & Osborne-Lampkin, L. T. (2013). A profile of Black women in the 21st-century academy: Still learning from the "Outsider-Within.". *Journal of Research Initiatives*, 1(1), 5.

Williams, H. V. (2023). *Black Women in Higher Education*. Oxford Bibliographies., DOI: 10.1093/obo/9780190280024-0115

Williams, H. V., & Ziobro, M. (Eds.). (2023). *A Seat at the Table: Black Women Public Intellectuals in US History and Culture*. Univ. Press of Mississippi. DOI: 10.14325/mississippi/9781496847515.001.0001

Winkle-Wagner, R. (2015). Having their lives narrowed down? The state of Black women's college success. *Review of Educational Research*, 85(2), 171–204. DOI: 10.3102/0034654314551065

Wright, D. A., & Salinas, C. (2016). African American women leaders in higher education. In *Racially and ethnically diverse women leading education* [). Emerald Group Publishing Limited.]. *Worldview*, 25, 91–105.

ENDNOTES

[1] To maintain continuity and consistency, the constructs "Black" and "African American" are used interchangeably throughout this chapter.

[2] https://www.brainyquote.com/authors/shirley-chisholm-quotes

[3] https://www.historyisaweapon.com/defcon1/stantonaplea.html#:~:text=Slavery%20is%20the%20combination%20of,down%20upon%20the%20bloody%20field

[4] https://www.brainyquote.com/authors/katherine-johnson-quotes

[5] https://people.com/politics/ketanji-brown-jackson-most-inspiring-quotes/#:~:text=%22I%20hope%20to%20inspire%20people,young%20people%20are%20the%20future.%22&text=%22I%20am%20also%20ever%20buoyed,helped%20to%20light%20the%20way

[6] https://quotefancy.com/quote/1290916/Sheila-Jackson-Lee-The-greatness-of-Americans-is-that-we-are-mosaic-we-are-diverse

[7] https://www.illumy.com/10-inspiring-quotes-by-black-women-in-stem-you-may-not-know/

[8] https://www.diverseeducation.com/opinion/article/15295726/does-anyone-see-us-disposability-of-black-women-faculty-in-the-academy

Chapter 6
One Bad Mother
How One New Mother in Academia Realized She Was 'Mothered' Out

Ashley Gambino
SUNY Plattsburgh, USA

ABSTRACT

This chapter explores the lived experience of a transitional time period for the author: becoming a new mother during an unprecedented period in history, the COVID19 pandemic. While much has been discussed about working mothers during the pandemic, the author discusses how the pandemic and motherhood were only two of the factors contributing toward a feeling of burn-out toward academic care work. Ultimately, a changing student demographic and new leadership duties coupled with the sexist role assignments and expectations of academia combined with the transition to motherhood and a pandemic were simply too much to cope with. The author recognizes that while she is certainly not the first woman to have been overburdened by the misogyny of academic care work, there is a cohort of academic leaders who became mothers and leaders during a time unlike any other in history.

INTRODUCTION

My path to academic leadership is unique, but ultimately, I ended up facing an issue that appears to be all too common among women academic leaders with children. I am 'mothered' out. At the time that I came to the realization that I was in this situation, it felt as though it had manifested itself overnight. It seemed that I went to sleep as a thriving mother, chair, experienced faculty member, and mentor and the next day I faced an email from a recent alumna looking for support and thought: I. JUST. CAN'T. DEAL.

I began my career in academia as a hybrid of sorts. I was on a professional line leading to permanency, a tenure-esque type of job security. My position was originally intended to be a largely clinical position, serving as an audiologist in our on-campus speech and hearing center, but quickly morphed into something different as it became clear that teaching and mentoring students, particularly undergraduates, were strengths of mine. And I loved every minute of it. I was young and fresh out of graduate school with an exuberant enthusiasm for my chosen profession: audiology. I was also fortunate enough to be employed at the university where I earned my undergraduate degree and was passionate about the education and opportunities that the institution had afforded me. These two passions came together to fuel an unflinching dedication to the education and support of my students.

In a rare moment of uncharacteristic cockiness, I will say this clearly and proudly: I was damn good at my job. I was killing it. Prospective students, current undergraduate students, current graduate students, alumni, it didn't matter. I was there for them. Touring, meeting, counseling, teaching, hugging, pushing, mentoring constantly. Teaching class in the evenings to allow for my students to have more clinical experiences with me during the day? Absolutely. Hosting virtual visits in the evenings for current students to connect with alums working in my field? You bet. Driving two and a half hours each way to have lunch and a mini reunion with alumni on a Saturday? Of course. Wandering around the building to the study spots the afternoon before my exams to check in with students preparing for said exams? For sure. Helping navigate students through various small and large scale personal crises? Undoubtedly. I did it all. And, despite being a raging introvert, I was thriving in a career that demanded a seemingly unending stream of human contact. The work had purpose. My legacy was clear as day: each student I helped to reach professional success would go on to serve patients seeking communication support for a better quality of life. My efforts at making individual impacts today would go on to create future smiles and tears of joy in patients that I would never meet or know. Who wouldn't bounce into their office loving life with that legacy playing itself out?

So what happened? How did I go from gleefully doing anything it takes to convince students to attend my university and to pursue my profession to ignoring an email from an alum asking a simple question about job opportunities because it put me over the edge? Perhaps the real question is, what didn't happen? For starters, time was catching up to me. I was no longer a millennial teaching millennials. And just as we settled in to see how the first few episodes of 'Gen Z Goes to College' would play out, the COVID-19 Pandemic hit. As we all pivoted so often and so swiftly that we wore holes in the soles of our shoes, we simultaneously came face to face with the mental health crisis facing this new generation of college students.

Amid all that, I became a first time mother and a first time chairperson. In fact, one of my first tasks upon returning from maternity leave was drafting 2020-2021 year end reports. My first time doing so. For the first 'full' pandemic year. In between overnight feedings, of course. None of which the previous all-male lineage of chairs for my department could even begin to imagine.

KEEPING MY DISTANCE

When I began my career in academia, I was 26 years old and very focused on fighting off imposter syndrome associated with my age. Imposter syndrome is a phenomenon, often seen in high achieving women, marked by the feeling that individuals are not worthy of their own success or capable of the positions they hold (Clance & Imes, 1978). To quell the overwhelming sensation that I was not prepared for academia, I leaned hard into presenting as professional a front as possible. Like other young academics my imposter syndrome was fueled in part by regularly being mistaken for a student (Wilkinson, 2020). I focused on doing everything I could to distance myself from the student body and present a professorial persona. This mostly consisted of me hiding any semblance of a personal life from my students and establishing (perhaps unrealistically) high expectations for their professionalism and academic work.

Despite these efforts at distance, I somehow managed to endear myself to students. As a seasoned colleague said to me "They know you don't take any sh*t, but they also know you care." As an elder millennial teaching younger millennials, the first decade of my career involved me easily ingratiating myself with my students. While I hated being mistaken for a student, my proximity to them in age was an asset. I understood them. I knew what they needed and wanted. I was them just a few short years ago, after all. I knew that the world saw them as entitled and lazy students who expected a trophy for showing up (Tulgan, 2016). But in reality, I knew that they were terrified of failure and afraid to look 'stupid.' Despite my efforts to keep my distance, my students and I quickly developed a mutual respect. I worked hard for them and they, in turn, worked hard for me. As Miller and Mills (2019) discussed, students saw my youth as an asset to my approachability and relatability while identifying my 'hustle' and dedication to them as reasons to care and put forth the effort to meet my clear, yet high, standards. As I crept closer to my 30th birthday and began to feel a bit more comfortable in my 'academic skin,' a student and I faced similar personal challenges. In the time-span of a year and a half, my parents passed away, first my father and then my mother. Shortly after my mother's passing, a student whom I had been mentoring and had a strong connection with lost her own mother to a similar disease process. Here we were, two bright and motivated women at opposite ends of our 20s, both facing the loss of our mothers - to whom we were exceptionally close. And somehow, we had to keep going. I had to keep teaching. She had to keep learning. Suddenly, I was an 'audiology mom.' This was the moment where those very intentional walls came tumbling down. This student needed to know that I understood how she felt. And she could only know that if I shared some of the personal details that I had fought so hard to contain. We worked closely together on a project and long hours spent in a lab forged a bond that forever changed both of our lives. Over a decade later, we are still extremely close. Our relationship has shifted, like many adult mother-daughter duos do, to a friendship with a dash of mothering when appropriate.

ENTER DEPARTMENT MOM

The mentor slash mother relationship that I developed with the student mentioned above was a catalyst for my promotion to 'department mom.' But no one called me that. I was too young for that. I was almost their peer and had let my armor down a bit, so of course they began to flood my office for non-academic support. And so, like so many before me, I became inundated with the 'women's work of academia.' I was the carer and the nurturer (in a tough love fashion as that is still what suited my personality). When a student needed to talk through a tough situation, they rounded the corner into my office with a quiet "Do you have a minute?" But it was never just a minute. It was many minutes and those added up. On top of those minutes, I began to be asked to take time to meet with prospective students, to arrange department social events, to buy the secretary's birthday card, and so on and so on. I was told "You are so good at this. The students really connect with you. Here is another event to attend or plan." I was too naive to realize that the male leadership was taking advantage of my appeal to our students. I had not yet read the literature indicating that women are expected by both students and male colleagues to be 'academic moms' instead of academic scholars (Bernard, 1964; Docka-Filipek & Stone, 2020).

I was so focused on overcoming my own imposter syndrome that I did not recognize the sexism in my colleagues and (internalized) sexism in my mostly women students. When my male chair often asked, "When are you going to work on some research?" I looked blankly at him and tried to imagine where I would find the time in my schedule to do this research that wasn't part of my job description. It did not occur to me that I could find the time to do this research he prioritized if he did more of the caring work of our department that I had taken on, which also wasn't in my job description. No, my mind simply turned to 'I just don't have what it takes to do that and I like what I am doing better.' While it may be true that I liked what I was doing better than research, it certainly wasn't true that I didn't have 'what it takes.' Unless what it takes is dedicated time to focus and develop scholarship and freedom from other burdens of academia. Oh, wait. I didn't have that because I was too busy being an academic mom. I found myself focused on "chores that tend to impede academic career making as they are time consuming and undervalued, but nevertheless crucial for the continuity of the academic institution (Heijstra, et al., 2017 p. 765)." I focused on the value that I was adding to the institution instead of the value that the institution could add to my career. Someone had to do it, I rationalized, and I am good at it and I like it, so why not me? Despite calling myself a feminist, at the start of my career I could not see how these men were letting me down instead of elevating me. As Vallaro (2008) wrote "when we find ourselves in caring situations, our choices are limited, and on many campuses, there's no tangible reward for these maternal practices." I had not yet realized this. Instead of recognizing that being pushed into departmental academic mom work was limiting my opportunities to advance my career or grow my skill set, I saw that I was praised by leadership for my efforts. That must mean I was a success, right? I did not see the patriarchal brush off that care work was getting from my male leadership in favor of activities that would get them more clout and more cash, not to mention a work life unburdened by the psychological and emotional needs of students.

EVERYTHING CHANGES. OR DOES IT?

As the years slipped by, I found a tribe of academic women who did elevate me. This led to a shift in my role to an academic tenured line and departmental chair. With this shift came new responsibilities. Suddenly research was in my job description. As were administrative and leadership duties. But it was still expected that I would do the academic housework that had been handed off to me by previous (male) chairs long ago. There was no 'me' behind me to pass the care work off to in favor of the work that would bring the clout and cash. I also felt as though I was also expected to express more 'feminine' attributes in my interactions with students as a chair. Students seemed frustrated with my matter-of-fact approach to their concerns. If students were not coddled and accommodated it was clear that I was not meeting their expectations of a departmental mom. However, after years of being the departmental mom, I knew that previous chairs did not even have such conversations with the students because as the students reported to me: 'he is busy' or 'he is intimidating' or some other combination of gendered tropes. My approach had not changed from years prior when I was considered 'firm but fair' or 'stern but supportive.' The only change was my title and the location of my office. Given that I was a woman in a role more often associated with men, the focus had apparently shifted to my agentic qualities, but no longer in a favorable light. After all, as a woman, I was supposed to be soft and gentle, not thorough and honest. Despite the fact that compared to my immediate predecessor, I was, in my humble opinion, the embodiment of a warm hug, student exit surveys no longer saw my virtues to the same degree as they did just a semester or two prior.

My first semester as a departmental chair was Fall 2020, when higher education was still attempting to determine 'how to do college' in a pandemic. Like much of the gendered work of higher ed, it has been noted that the pandemic appeared to follow the expected pattern with men seeing a higher rate of publishing productivity while women seemed to feel that their home life and work life became one with expectations to be even more accessible and available than prior to the pandemic (Chinetti, 2023; Docka-Filipek & Stone, 2020; Lopes & de Camargo Santos, 2023). It is also not surprising that women were providing the bulk of the emotional support and care for students (Docka-Filipek et al., 2023; Lopes & de Camargo Santos, 2023). This came in coordination with women parents facing the bulk of the childrearing and homeschooling as schools closed (Fan & Moen, 2024). All of the care work that women typically engage in was amplified. While an academic woman who was a parent could, in most situations, previously devote attention to her students during class hours and her children during home hours, the pandemic shifted the requirements to constant care and accessibility. Beyond the care work side of academia, we had to learn logistics of remote instruction. It was my experience that women appeared to put more stock in the questions of how to do these things well. In my department it was the women who explored remote learning opportunities and experiences to best serve our students and patients. We asked ourselves how we teach and engage our students. Whom we didn't even see in person. I was also learning how to be a leader among my faculty. Whom I didn't even see in person.

At the time, the introvert in me felt as though I was living my best life. I had quiet days at home working independently with Zoom meetings and classes mixed in. I was efficient and effective. But who were all these people on the other side of the screen? The pandemic created a great divide for me in regard to my academic momism. In the before-times my classroom was a place where the business of learning occurred in a fun and enthusiastic way while ensuring a high level of professionalism and academic standards. I knew my students well and could produce their names and personality quirks at will. In the throes of the pandemic, I had a series of Brady Bunch squares that stared at me blankly (or worse, fell asleep!) while I did everything I could muster to replicate the classroom atmosphere that seemed to work so well for me. I also didn't know who they were for another reason. They were now solidly Generation Z. Generation Z entered the higher education realm several years prior to the pandemic. The first few years of educating this group did not feel vastly different from educating millennials, as they were generational cuspers. But for me, the pandemic was a clear demarcation of the end of the millennial student and the appearance of the true Generation Z student. While I, like the younger millennials I had taught for a decade, was given a trophy regardless of how well my youth soccer team performed, I could not relate to the aggressive overparenting experienced by Generation Z. This parenting style had "interfered with their social, emotional, and intellectual development, making it difficult for them to become autonomous adults, able to navigate the challenges of life' (Gabrielova & Buchko, 2021, p. 493). Suddenly the mental health needs of the students in my courses skyrocketed while their desire and ability to be independent from their parents plummeted. Parents were texting them in class, making their course schedules for them, and at times strongly disagreeing with the expertise that the faculty offered. I began to regularly hear "Well, my mom thinks…" for everything from what to put in a graduate school letter of intent to what major to pick. Jean Twenge prepared us for this in 2017 when she described this generation in the very subtitle of her book "iGen: Why today's super-connected kids are growing up less rebellious, more tolerant, less happy - and completely unprepared for adulthood: and what it means for the rest of us." She also painted a picture of the average incoming first year college student having the maturity of a 14 year old. One can certainly imagine that the average 14 year old needs a bit more mothering (academic or otherwise) than an 18 or 19 year old. If this task falls overwhelmingly to the women over the men in academia, as discussed above, then certainly the burden was increasing with the generational changeover.

I'M NOT A REGULAR MOM, I'M AN ACADEMIC MOM.

If this isn't already feeling a little 'everything, everywhere all at once,' I was also pregnant in the Fall of 2020 and went on maternity leave in Spring 2021. As the world began its transition to a post pandemic 'new normal,' I began my transition to motherhood. As indicated by Hwang et al. (2020), "transition to motherhood is a continuous process of adapting to and responding to constantly changing physical, psychological, social, and relational dimensions (p.11, 2022)." Along with faculty everywhere, I was navigating the constantly changing realities of higher education. However, I was also navigating the constantly changing realities of my body, my mind, my identity, and my relationships. In the years prior to my motherhood journey, when I contemplated diving into parenting a child in my household versus the young adults in my classroom, I was hesitant. Like many millenial and Generation X women, I had personal and professional goals that I wanted to accomplish first. I had never been someone to make a decision without considering all of the options available and their various consequences and certainly would follow a similar path when considering motherhood. As Zabak et al (2023), put it "this intricate negotiation exemplifies the delicate interplay between embracing one's individuality and fulfilling the role of a parent, ultimately shaping the timeline of delayed childbearing" (para. 19). Given my aggressive contemplation of the pros and cons surrounding transitioning to motherhood, I felt that I was as ready as possible to begin the journey. While I, in no way, expected the experience to be effortless, I was not prepared for the onslaught of ch-ch-ch-ch changes, as David Bowie would say. I decided to begin my steps forward towards motherhood well before the pandemic, before Generation Z landed in my classrooms, and well before I knew I was to be chairperson. It just took some time to see to fruition. I thought I had my 'work-life' figured out and that I would continue to succeed in that realm while adding in a few 'mom-life' lessons. I had no way to see all the employment and societal changes coming my way.

And then, because why not tackle one more thing, along came an unexpected postpartum mental health deterioration. Prior to becoming a mother, I was terrified of certain aspects of the experience of being a parent (giving birth and surviving on less than ideal sleep conditions were my main concerns). But, as someone who had suffered significant personal stressors in my 20s with no significant mental health implications, I did not see the changes to my mental health coming. This is not to say I was ignorant to the possibility. I would skim that section of whatever book or article I was reading with the expectation that it was information that was irrelevant to me. I was solid as a rock! If anything, I was too consistent and reliable. Two of the key implications for maternal well-being when struggling with postpartum mood disorders are emotional distress and mood fluctuations and impact on self-esteem (Modak et al., 2023). It is difficult to feel like you have anything figured out or under control when you find yourself sitting on the floor literally crying over spilt (breast) milk. It is not unreasonable for a high achieving academic woman to begin to question her ability to continue to lead a department when she suddenly felt like a hysterical mess at unexpected moments. Hwang et al (2022) identified the transition to motherhood as a period of changes beyond merely the often mentioned physical and psychological. They suggested that defining attributes of the transition also include changes to relationships and social perceptions with women redefining their self-identity during this transition. My self-identity was, for better or worse, largely interwoven with my academic and professional successes. I was able to compartmentalize emotional devastation related to personal loss early in my career because my career depended on it. And I depended on my career for a sense of purpose and identity. While the expected statement from a mother would be 'but now I had a greater purpose at home,' I didn't say this, because I didn't feel this way. I had been conditioned through circumstances and sexism to be the academic mom and I still wanted to be this. For my students. For me. Who was I without all of the academic mom hustle mentioned in the introduction of this chapter?

Because of my desire to cling to my professional identity while undergoing a tumultuous transition to motherhood, I did not turn my back on my academic mom title as quickly as I should have. Instead, I spent a few painful semesters trying to be everything to everyone. As most women attempting this feat discover, I found out that this was impossible (Philipsen et al., 2017). I was lucky enough to have my child enrolled in the campus childcare center down the hall from my office. This allowed me to schedule my days around feedings and had the added bonus that my son could spend time at my office. I worked in a speech and hearing clinic with an extremely family friendly vibe from the students up to the Dean. I was eager to be able to integrate my work family with my home family. It seemed that my child was quickly embraced by my colleagues and students. I thought that as a working mother I was demonstrating a way to 'have it all' to my students. Perhaps it was naive, but I thought that I was finally demonstrating to my students that women have lives outside of work and sometimes those lives include children. And wouldn't it be easier if they were allowed to be a part of our work lives instead of hidden away? I was giving myself gold stars for demonstrating a positive view of working motherhood and family friendly workplaces. But instead, some students saw this as evidence that I was not dedicated to my job. In an exit survey for our graduate program a student expressed frustration over another faculty member's (perceived) misstep by missing an email. The student gave this other faculty member grace by suggesting that she was overworked (something I don't dispute, to be fair) and commented "And where was the chair? In her office with her baby." I wasn't sure what the student expected of me to fix this situation given that it was not within my job description to answer my colleague's emails and the student had certainly not alerted me to concerns in my role as chair. In a moment of women supporting women through humor, the faculty member who allegedly missed an email said, "To be honest, your baby was in my office more than yours!" While my colleague and I attempted to laugh it off, I had to admit that reading this student comment hurt (clearly it still stings a bit). Though subconsciously I knew I wasn't doing everything to my previous levels of performance, it was apparent that simply having a visible child was a strike against me. Two commonly recognized misogynistic occurrences ran headfirst into each other in this one comment: women faculty are more likely to receive negative feedback on surveys and working mothers are more likely to be perceived as preoccupied or less dedicated. (Heffernan, 2022; Grummell et al., 2009). It didn't matter to the student that I was often breastfeeding and checking work emails at the same time or that my after work hours communication with an alum is what scored an internship for her. To the student my flexible work schedule was invisible and perceived simply as incompetence and shirking of duties.

MOTHERED OUT

At that time, I could not come to terms with the fact that "Maybe what I'm doing isn't what I'm capable of doing under the best of conditions (the best of conditions including being ten years younger, averaging at least seven hours of sleep a night, and having no responsibility to anyone but myself), but it's the best I can do right now (Gilbert, 2008)." I was running myself into the ground physically, emotionally, and psychologically in order to continue to be both an academic mom and a mom to my son. In addition to those titles, I was also trying to fulfill my duties as an instructor, a clinician, a departmental chair, and a spouse. Forget about sister, aunt, or friend, the folks on the other side of those dyads were woefully ignored. Eventually, I began to see the sexism for what it was. I was 'doing good and feeling bad,' like many women in academia feeling overwhelmed with departmental care work and the realization that it did not benefit career advancement (Acker & Feuerverger, 1996). Despite my slow awakening to my true circumstances, I felt as though I couldn't get off the mommy merry-go round without taking someone down with me. The guilt for disappointing all whom I mothered felt insurmountable. As Dunn (2020) wrote "the time and effort I dedicated to eliminating my professor guilt during the onset of the pandemic fueled my mom guilt. My work–life balance no longer existed as the pandemic eradicated the idea and possibility of balance. Work became life, and life became work" (p. 495). I faced a version of Sophie's Choice between my academic children and my own child that is not unusual for academic women, but was intensified by the circumstances of the pandemic, the generational shift in my students, and new leadership roles. I had also come to the realization that I had been forced into this situation by the sexism of many of my colleagues and society and the academy in general.

A recent continuing education webinar began with the following quote: "In traditional Native American teaching it is told that each time you heal someone, you give away a piece of yourself until, at some point, you will require healing (Stebnicki, 2007)." This resonated with me as I struggled on the brink of burn out. While one could argue I wasn't 'healing' my students (past, present, and future), I was offering much of my time, compassion, and empathy to them. Given my clinical responsibilities, I was also offering the same to my patients. The pandemic coinciding with my new role as chairperson required me to give more of myself to my colleagues in need of support as well. What was left for those outside of my work life? Didn't they deserve a piece of me? Didn't I deserve a piece of me? I needed to do something before there were no more pieces left. And so, I chose. Or rather, my overwhelmed nervous system chose for me. I froze and simply could not bring myself to reply to the alumni email mentioned in the introduction. This led to stepping back from some of the care work of academia. I no longer organized alumni events or attended as many student events as I had previously. And when I did, I brought my son along. The current cohort of students seems to love having him around. But, we shall see what the exit and course surveys bring.

As I begin to step back from some of my care work, I am unable to step back from the academic mom guilt. I find myself apologizing to former students when I do finally connect with them after too long a period of silence on my end of the email chain. "It's not you, it's me!" I keep saying to them. I apologize to my faculty when I don't know what every single alum is 'up to nowadays' because I quit social media the same time I stopped responding to alumni emails in a timely manner. I wonder if my current students would be more passionate about my discipline if I were able to invest more time in my academic mom role. It is difficult to accept this new version of my professional self, but I am working toward it as best I can.

The focus of this book is defining moments in women leaders in higher education. Many women before me (and likely after me) have stories of how sexism in the academy, motherhood, student perceptions and generational needs, and the pandemic have influenced their career paths as academics and leaders. However, there is a snapshot of time where a cohort of women experienced all of these at once. Much like my own experiences, Aldossari and Chaudhry (2021) identified disengagement, denial, and energy conservation as key coping mechanisms for academic women with children suffering from burn-out during the pandemic. As these are not ideal coping strategies for emotional well-being and professional success, questions remain on how this will bode for this cohort of women who experienced 'everything everywhere all at once' and are mothered out. Myself included.

REFERENCES

Acker, S., & Feuerverger, G. (1996). Doing Good and Feeling Bad: The work of women university teachers. *Cambridge Journal of Education*, 26(3), 401–422. DOI: 10.1080/0305764960260309

Aldossari, M., & Chaudhry, S. (2021). Women and burnout in the context of a pandemic. *Gender, Work and Organization*, 28(2), 826–834. DOI: 10.1111/gwao.12567

Bernard, J. (1964). *Academic women*. Pennsylvania State University Press.

Chinetti, S. (2023). The gender gap in academic productivity during the pandemic: Is childcare responsible? *IZA Journal of Labor Economics*, 12(1), 117–154. DOI: 10.2478/izajole-2023-0007

Clance, P. R., & Imes, S. A. (1978). The imposter phenomenon in high achieving women: Dynamics and therapeutic intervention. *Psychotherapy (Chicago, Ill.)*, 15(3), 241–247. DOI: 10.1037/h0086006

Docka-Filipek, D., Draper, C., Snow, J., & Stone, L. B. (2023). 'Professor moms' & 'hidden service' in pandemic times: Students report women faculty more supportive & accommodating amid US COVID crisis onset. *Innovative Higher Education*, 48(5), 787–811. DOI: 10.1007/s10755-023-09652-x PMID: 37361116

Docka-Filipek, D., & Stone, L. B. (2021). Twice a "housewife": On academic precarity, "hysterical" women, faculty mental health, and service as gendered care work for the "university family" in pandemic times. *Gender, Work and Organization*, 28(6), 2158–2179. DOI: 10.1111/gwao.12723

Dunn, T. R. (2020). When professor guilt and mom guilt collide: Pandemic pedagogy from a precarious place. *Communication Education*, 69(4), 491–501. DOI: 10.1080/03634523.2020.1803385

Fan, W., & Moen, P. (2024). The Shifting Stress of Working Parents: An Examination of Dual Pandemic Disruptions—Remote Work and Remote Schooling. *Social Sciences (Basel, Switzerland)*, 13(1), 36. DOI: 10.3390/socsci13010036

Gabrielova, K., & Buchko, A. A. (2021). Here comes Generation Z: Millennials as managers. *Business Horizons*, 64(4), 489–499. DOI: 10.1016/j.bushor.2021.02.013

Gilbert, J. (2008). Why I Feel Guilty All the Time: Performing Academic Motherhood. *Women's Studies in Communication*, 31(2), 203–208. DOI: 10.1080/07491409.2008.10162533

Grummell, B., Devine, D., & Lynch, K. (2009). The care-less manager: Gender, care and new managerialism in higher education. *Gender and Education*, 21(2), 191–208. DOI: 10.1080/09540250802392273

Heffernan, T. (2023). Abusive comments in student evaluations of courses and teaching: The attacks women and marginalised academics endure. *Higher Education*, 85(1), 225–239. DOI: 10.1007/s10734-022-00831-x

Heijstra, T. M., Steinthorsdóttir, F. S., & Einarsdóttir, T. (2017). Academic career making and the double-edged role of academic housework. *Gender and Education*, 29(6), 764–780. DOI: 10.1080/09540253.2016.1171825

Hwang, W. Y., Choi, S. Y., & An, H. J. (2022). Concept analysis of transition to motherhood: A methodological study. *Korean Journal of Women Health Nursing*, 28(1), 8–17. DOI: 10.4069/kjwhn.2022.01.04 PMID: 36312044

Lopes, M., & de Camargo Santos, C. (2023). Academic housework in pandemic times: COVID-19 effects on the gendered distribution of academic work in Portugal. *European Educational Research Journal*, •••, 14749041231191888. DOI: 10.1177/14749041231191888

Miller, A. C., & Mills, B. (2019). 'If They Don't Care, I Don't Care': Millennial and Generation Z Students and the Impact of Faculty Caring. *The Journal of Scholarship of Teaching and Learning*, 19(4), 78-. DOI: 10.14434/josotl.v19i4.24167

Modak, A., Ronghe, V., Gomase, K. P., Mahakalkar, M. G., & Taksande, V. (2023). A Comprehensive Review of Motherhood and Mental Health: Postpartum Mood Disorders in Focus. *Cureus*, 15(9), e46209. DOI: 10.7759/cureus.46209 PMID: 37905286

Philipsen, M., Case, S., Oetama-Paul, A., & Sugiyama, K. (2017). Academic womanhood across career stages: A work-in-life perspective on what was, is, and could be. *Community Work & Family*, 20(5), 623–644. DOI: 10.1080/13668803.2017.1378619

Romsa, K., Bremer, K. L., Lewis, J., & Romsa, B. (2017). The Evolution of Student-Faculty Interactions: What Matters to Millennial College Students? *The College Student Affairs Journal*, 35(2), 85–99. DOI: 10.1353/csj.2017.0015

Stebnicki, M. A. (2007). Empathy Fatigue: Healing the Mind, Body, and Spirit of Professional Counselors. *American Journal of Psychiatric Rehabilitation*, 10(4), 317–338. DOI: 10.1080/15487760701680570

Tulgan, B. (2016). *Not everyone gets a trophy: How to manage the millennials*. Wiley. DOI: 10.1002/9781119215073

Twenge, J. M. (2018). *IGen: Why today's super-connected kids are growing up less rebellious, more tolerant, less happy—and completely unprepared for adulthood : And what that means for the rest of us*. Atria Paperback.

Varallo, S. M. (2008). Motherwork in Academe: Intensive Caring for the Millenial Student. *Women's Studies in Communication*, 31(2), 151–157. DOI: 10.1080/07491409.2008.10162527

Wilkinson, C. (2020). Imposter syndrome and the accidental academic: An autoethnographic account. *The International Journal for Academic Development*, 25(4), 363–374. DOI: 10.1080/1360144X.2020.1762087

Zabak, S., Varma, A., Bansod, S., & Pohane, M. R. (2023). Exploring the Complex Landscape of Delayed Childbearing: Factors, History, and Long-Term Implications. *Cureus*, 15(9), e46291. DOI: 10.7759/cureus.46291 PMID: 37915872

Chapter 7
Narratives of Women Higher Education Teachers in Karnataka:
A Study on Self-Esteem, Small Group Socialization, and Workplace Communication Behaviour

Vishnu Achutha Menon
https://orcid.org/0000-0003-4028-3685
Institute for Educational and Developmental Studies, Noida, India

ABSTRACT

This chapter investigates the relationships between self-esteem, small group socialization, and workplace communication behaviour among women teachers in higher education institutions in Karnataka, India. Using standardized instruments, data was collected from 509 participants through offline and online surveys. Results reveal strong positive correlations between self-esteem and both small group socialization and workplace communication behaviour. Linear regression analyses confirm the predictive capabilities of self-esteem on these variables. The findings contribute to understanding professional dynamics among women educators and offer insights for supporting their career development.

DOI: 10.4018/979-8-3693-3144-6.ch007

INTRODUCTION

India is characterized by a complex and rich array of narratives that constitute the nation's diverse cultural, historical, and social fabric. The societal structure of India is marked by a multifaceted composition of traditions, customs, and social norms. The nation encompasses a plethora of religions, languages, and ethnic groups, each contributing to its vibrant diversity. Although the caste system has been legally abolished, its remnants continue to exert influence on social interactions and hierarchies. Urbanization and modernization are progressively altering traditional social frameworks, yet rural areas still uphold village communities as central to social governance and daily life. Urban centers, in contrast, reflect a confluence of traditional values and modern practices.

Within this intricate societal framework, women in India navigate their lives shaped by dominant historical and contemporary narratives. Historically, women's roles and statuses have varied widely across different regions and communities, often dictated by traditional narratives that emphasize domestic responsibilities and virtues such as modesty, obedience, and self-sacrifice. However, contemporary narratives are increasingly contesting these conventions, advocating for gender equality and the empowerment of women. In urban regions, women are progressively overcoming barriers, excelling in education, professional careers, and leadership roles. The rise of feminist movements and the implementation of legal reforms have significantly bolstered efforts to eradicate gender discrimination and combat violence against women. Despite these advancements, women in rural and conservative areas continue to confront substantial challenges, including restricted access to education and healthcare, early marriage, and limited economic opportunities.

Women in India are active agents in engaging with and reshaping societal narratives. Through their resilience and agency, they contribute to the ongoing transformation of India's societal structure, creating new paradigms and redefining their roles within both traditional and modern contexts. As India continues to evolve, the narratives surrounding women are anticipated to reflect broader societal shifts towards inclusivity, equality, and empowerment.

Women's experiences in higher education are deeply intertwined with self-esteem, small group socialization, and workplace communication behavior. Academic success significantly shapes self-worth for many women. Achieving high grades, receiving scholarships, and gaining recognition can boost self-confidence, while facing academic challenges or discrimination can negatively impact self-esteem. Mentorship is crucial, as female mentors and role models in higher education can enhance self-esteem by providing inspiration and a blueprint for personal and professional growth. However, many women experience imposter syndrome, particularly in male-dominated fields like STEM, which can cause them to doubt their abilities despite evident success. Support systems such as women's groups, academic clubs, and counseling services are essential in helping women build and maintain healthy self-esteem.

Socialization is another critical aspect of women's narratives in higher education. Peer networks offer emotional support, academic collaboration, and a sense of belonging, which are especially important in fields where women are underrepresented. However, gender dynamics within small groups can influence women's participation and leadership roles, as they may face challenges such as being talked over or not taken seriously. Women often excel in collaborative and cooperative learning environments, and participation in group projects and study groups can create a sense of community and shared purpose. Involvement in student organizations, clubs, and societies enhances socialization skills, leadership abilities, and creates lasting professional and personal relationships.

Women often develop communication styles that they carry into their professional lives, typically being more collaborative, empathetic, and inclusive. Nevertheless, they may face difficulties such as being interrupted, having their ideas overlooked, or being judged more harshly for assertive behavior. Training and awareness programs in universities can help prepare women for these challenges. Effective communication is key for women aspiring to leadership roles, and higher education provides platforms for developing these skills through presentations, group discussions, and leadership roles in student organizations. Workshops and courses on professional communication, negotiation, and public speaking are invaluable in equipping women with the skills needed to navigate workplace communication effectively.

The intersection of self-esteem, small group socialization, and workplace communication behavior highlights the complex and interconnected nature of women's experiences in higher education. A woman's self-esteem can influence her participation in group settings and her communication style in the workplace. Positive experiences in small group socialization can enhance self-esteem and lead to more effective workplace communication. Conversely, challenges in any of these areas can create a cycle of negative reinforcement, making it crucial for educational institutions to provide comprehensive support systems.

Self-esteem in India is profoundly influenced by cultural, familial, and societal expectations. Traditional Indian society places significant emphasis on collectivism, family honor, and societal norms, which can shape an individual's self-worth and self-perception. Self-esteem is often derived from fulfilling one's roles and responsibilities within the family and community. For instance, in many Indian families, academic achievement is highly valued and seen as a source of pride and self-esteem. Children are encouraged to excel in their studies, and success in this domain is often equated with personal worth. However, this emphasis can also lead to pressure and stress, impacting self-esteem negatively if expectations are not met.

Small group socialization typically emphasizes close-knit relationships, mutual support, and collective well-being. Groups such as extended families, peer circles, and local community groups play a crucial role in shaping social behavior and norms. For example, in rural areas, self-help groups (SHGs) are common, particularly among women. These groups provide a platform for social interaction, mutual support, and economic cooperation. Women in SHGs often engage in activities such as microfinancing, skill development, and community welfare projects, fostering a sense of solidarity and collective empowerment.

Workplace communication behavior in India is influenced by hierarchical structures, cultural norms, and the diversity of the workforce. Indian workplaces often reflect a blend of traditional hierarchical relationships and modern, collaborative approaches. Respect for authority and seniority is typically emphasized, while younger employees are encouraged to show deference to their superiors. For instance, in many Indian organizations, it is common for employees to address their superiors with titles such as "Sir" or "Madam," reflecting the cultural norm of respect for authority. However, multinational companies operating in India may adopt more egalitarian communication styles, encouraging open dialogue and feedback across all levels of the hierarchy. Another example is the use of English as the primary medium of communication in many Indian workplaces, especially in urban areas and multinational corporations. This practice accommodates the linguistic diversity of the Indian workforce and aligns with global business standards. However, regional languages may still be used in informal settings or among employees who share a common linguistic background, reflecting India's cultural diversity.

According to the All-India Survey on Higher Education (AISHE), India boasts 1,043 universities, 42,343 colleges, and 11,779 standalone institutions listed on the AISHE web portal. Out of these, 1,019 universities, 39,955 colleges, and 9,599 standalone institutions participated in the survey. Of the universities, 307 are affiliating, while 396 are privately managed, and 420 are situated in rural areas. Notably, 17 universities cater exclusively to women, distributed across various states. Additionally, there are 110 dual-mode universities offering distance education, with Tamil Nadu hosting the highest number. The universities span various categories, including general, technical, agriculture, medical, law, Sanskrit, and language universities. Uttar Pradesh, Maharashtra, Karnataka, Rajasthan, Andhra Pradesh, Tamil Nadu, Madhya Pradesh, and Gujarat lead in terms of college numbers, with Bangalore Urban district topping the list with 1,009 colleges, followed by Jaipur. However, despite these figures, the gender ratio among teachers remains imbalanced, with only 74 female teachers per 100 male teachers at the national level (AISHE, 2020). In school education 2019-20, the number of female school teachers in India surpassed that of males for the first time, as per the Unified District Information System for Education Plus (UDISE+) report. The report indicates a 2.72 percent increase in the total number of teachers compared to the previous year, totalling 96.87 lakh teachers. Of these, 49.15 lakh were female teachers, marking a notable rise from the previous year. Uttar Pradesh had the highest number of female teachers, with 6.42 lakh, followed by Tamil Nadu and Maharashtra with 4.22 lakh and 3.75 lakh respectively (Moneycontrol News, 2021).

In Karnataka's higher education sector, women hold various positions across different categories. As of the latest data available, 18.40 percent of women occupy roles in the Higher Category, which encompasses positions such as Vice-Chancellor, Director, Pro-Vice-Chancellor, Principal, Professor & Equivalent, and Associate Professor. In the Middle Category, consisting of roles like Reader, Lecturer (Selection Grade), Assistant Professor, Lecturer (Senior Scale), and Lecturer, women represent 56.86 percent. Meanwhile, in the Lower Category, which includes positions such as Tutor, Demonstrator, Part-Time Teacher, Ad hoc Teacher, Temporary Teacher, Contract Teacher, and Visiting Teacher, women account for 24.65 percent. Overall, women constitute 41.43 percent of the workforce in Karnataka's higher education sector (Ghara, 2016).

In the context of Karnataka, women hold various positions in higher education, with significant representation in middle-category roles. However, the gender ratio among teachers remains imbalanced, reflecting broader societal challenges. This research aims to investigate the relationship between self-esteem, small group socialization, and workplace communication behavior among women teachers in higher education in Karnataka. By examining these interconnected aspects, the study seeks to understand how women navigate and reshape societal narratives within both traditional and modern contexts, contributing to the ongoing transformation towards inclusivity, equality, and empowerment.

REVIEW OF LITERATURE

Research on the relationship between self-esteem and small group socialization and workplace communication behavior among women teachers in higher education in Karnataka is scarce. However, existing studies offer valuable insights into the potential influence of self-esteem on communication dynamics and professional interactions. Giri (2003) suggests that self-esteem can shape one's communication style, indicating that individuals with varying levels of self-esteem may exhibit distinct patterns of verbal and nonverbal communication. Mossholder (1982) posits that self-esteem may moderate the effects of peer group interaction on job performance and job strain, highlighting the interplay between individual self-perceptions and social dynamics in the workplace. Studies indicate that self-esteem plays a multi-faceted role in occupational choice and satisfaction. Greenhaus (1971) suggests that individuals with high self-esteem are more likely to pursue careers aligned with their interests and values, leading to greater job satisfaction. Guindon (1994) argues that high self-esteem buffers individuals from experiencing workplace demands as stressful, enabling them to effectively navigate challenging situations and maintain psychological well-being.

However, Schwalbe and Staples (1991) found no significant linear relationship between self-esteem and small group socialization in their study population, suggesting that contextual factors may moderate the association between these variables. Similarly, Duffy et al. (2000) observed that low self-esteem attenuated the negative relationship between relationship conflict and peer evaluations, highlighting the complex interplay between self-esteem, interpersonal dynamics, and performance evaluations in group settings. Burnett (1996) found that parental communication styles influence children's self-perceptions, underscoring the importance of early socialization experiences in shaping self-esteem. Callahan and Kidd (1986) found that job-satisfied women exhibit specific personality traits such as achievement orientation, cooperativeness, and self-confidence, suggesting that individual differences in self-esteem may contribute to job satisfaction and professional success. Hintsanen et al. (2010) found that social functioning and peer relations are associated with individual differences in self-concept and temperament dimensions, emphasizing the intricate relationship between self-esteem and social integration. Conversely, Myers et al. (2010) observed that students who perceived their group members as information peers reported higher levels of group animosity, indicating that perceptions of social hierarchy may influence group dynamics and intergroup relations.

Tafani et al. (2002) found that induction of low self-esteem diminishes the importance attributed to higher education, highlighting the role of self-esteem in educational aspirations and achievement motivation. Román et al. (2008) demonstrated that self-esteem and family support positively influence university students' learning and achievement, underscoring the importance of psychosocial factors in academic success. Similarly, Pasha and Munaf (2013) found that various aspects of self-esteem, including competence, lovability, personal power, moral self-approval, and body functioning, are significantly related to overall adjustment and well-being. Upshaw and Yates (1968) found that self-esteem influences success in creating a false impression in a "managed impression" situation, suggesting that self-esteem may impact impression management strategies and social interactions. Vishalakshi et al. (2011) observed a positive relationship between self-esteem and academic achievement among students from Mysore city, indicating that self-esteem may contribute to academic success and performance outcomes.

The influence of various psychosocial factors on self-esteem and its implications for interpersonal relationships and academic performance among individuals, particularly in educational and professional contexts, has been a subject of extensive research. Studies have revealed nuanced insights into the multifaceted nature of self-esteem and its associations with social dynamics, communication skills, academic achievement, and psychological well-being. Zuffianò et al. (2016) found that the quality of friendship serves as a mediating factor in the relationship between pro-social behavior and subsequent self-esteem development over time. Riggio et al. (1990) observed a positive correlation between social skills and self-esteem, highlighting the importance of effective interpersonal communication in shaping one's self-concept. Social anxiety and loneliness were negatively correlated with both social skills and self-esteem, underscoring the detrimental impact of social isolation on psychological well-being. However, Khan et al. (2019) found no significant positive correlation between academic achievement and self-esteem when considering male and female students collectively, suggesting that other factors may influence the relationship between academic performance and self-perception.

Nyadanu et al. (2014) noted that certain associations appeared to enhance students' self-esteem, indicating the potential role of environmental factors and interpersonal interactions in shaping self-esteem development. Supportive supervisory communication was found to enhance employees' self-esteem, reduce uncertainty, and foster a sense of meaning in the workplace (Rajesh & Suganthi, 2013), highlighting the importance of positive feedback and clear communication in promoting professional growth and job satisfaction. Tahir et al. (2015) observed a correlation between social support and self-esteem among adolescent girls, emphasizing the significance of social relationships in fostering positive self-regard during critical developmental stages. Knightley and Whitelock (2007) suggested that a mixed-method approach may be the most effective way to uncover and understand the mediators of self-esteem, highlighting the importance of integrating quantitative and qualitative research methods to gain a comprehensive understanding of self-esteem dynamics. The relationship between communication skills and self-esteem was found to predict clinical competency in nursing students (Park & Chung, 2015), underscoring the importance of interpersonal competence in professional practice.

Losa-Iglesias et al. (2017) identified a relationship between self-esteem and self-concept among nurses, suggesting that individuals' perceptions of themselves influence their overall psychological well-being. Meisenhelder (1986) found that perceived reflected appraisals from spouses strongly predicted self-esteem among women, indicating the significant influence of intimate relationships on self-perception. Troth et al. (2012) highlighted the mediating role of communication effectiveness in the relationship between the management of others' emotions and team cohesion, emphasizing the importance of effective communication in fostering positive team dynamics.

However, low self-esteem was associated with defensive behavior and poor communication among first-year nursing students (Sator, 2017), suggesting that addressing self-esteem issues is crucial for promoting effective interpersonal relationships and professional development. Moreover, cooperative learning environments were found to promote higher achievement and greater academic support from peers compared to individualistic learning approaches (Bertucci et al., 2010), highlighting the role of peer interactions in fostering academic success and self-esteem. Psychosocial variables predicting low self-esteem were found to be consistent across different demographic groups (Romans et al., 1996), indicating the universality of certain risk factors for self-esteem disturbances. Shackelford (2001) proposed that self-esteem evolved as an adaptive solution to tracking reproductively relevant costs inflicted by a spouse, suggesting an evolutionary basis for self-esteem dynamics in interpersonal relationships. Wagner et al. (2018) emphasized the importance of social inclusion as a fundamental human need, highlighting the role of social relationships in fostering positive self-esteem and psychological well-being.

Salavera et al. (2017) found that self-efficacy was positively correlated with social skills and emotional intelligence among secondary education students, highlighting the role of perceived competence in shaping interpersonal competencies. Bi et al. (2016) identified perceived stress as a mediator in the relationship between self-esteem and different types of interpersonal relationships, suggesting that stress perceptions may influence how individuals navigate social interactions. Khatib (2012) observed that lower levels of self-esteem and self-efficacy were associated with increased feelings of loneliness among college students, underscoring the importance of positive self-regard in fostering social connections. Son and Sung (2014) demonstrated that higher levels of teacher self-efficacy were linked to greater job satisfaction and higher-quality teacher-child interactions, highlighting the significance of educators' self-perceptions in shaping classroom dynamics. Vatankhah et al. (2013) implemented communication skills training sessions, indicating that targeted interventions can enhance individuals' communication competencies and potentially improve their interpersonal relationships. Cribb and Haase (2016) suggested that protective factors may mitigate the negative impact of socio-cultural attitudes towards appearance on self-esteem among adolescent girls, emphasizing the importance of creating supportive environments for positive self-development. Schwalbe et al. (1986) found that self-perceived competence was more salient to women than men, indicating gender differences in the importance attributed to self-concept. The statistical significance of self-esteem and workplace communication behavior affirms the reliability of these associations among media professionals in Karnataka (Kunnumpurath et al., 2024).

Lam et al. (2004) discovered that groups with higher levels of group self-esteem tended to attribute positive outcomes to internal factors, emphasizing the role of collective self-perception in shaping group dynamics. Schwartz et al. (1980) noted that moderate levels of self-concept were associated with greater success compared to both high and low levels of self-concept, suggesting that a balanced self-perception may be optimal for achieving goals. Liu et al. (2021) found that perceived social support was partially mediated by psychological suzhi, indicating the complex interplay between social relationships and individual psychological attributes in shaping self-esteem. Glotova and Wilhelm (2014) suggested that teachers with low self-esteem may benefit from psychological interventions aimed at enhancing their well-being and job satisfaction, highlighting the importance of addressing educators' mental health. Çiçek (2022) emphasized the role of self-esteem in promoting university students' psychological well-being, particularly in mitigating experiences of loneliness. Rusmana et al. (2020) demonstrated that assertive training techniques could empower individuals to assert their rights and enhance their sense of self-worth, contributing to greater life satisfaction. Hyun and Park (2008) found that interpersonal relationships and communication curricula had a positive impact on individuals' interpersonal skills and self-esteem, suggesting the potential benefits of targeted educational programs. Taghizadeh and Kalhori (2015) highlighted the association between low self-esteem and marital dissatisfaction, indicating the broader implications of self-esteem for intimate relationships. Kwal and Fleshler (1973) observed that groups with high self-esteem tended to share leadership functions more evenly, emphasizing the role of collective self-perception in group dynamics. Seshadri et al. (2019) suggested that the findings of such studies could be applied in various settings, including schools, colleges, and corporate offices, to promote positive self-esteem and interpersonal relationships. The cumulative findings underscore the multifaceted nature of self-esteem and its significant implications for individuals' social, emotional, and professional well-being. Understanding these dynamics can inform targeted interventions aimed at fostering positive self-perception and promoting healthy interpersonal relationships in diverse contexts.

Assertiveness training has been shown to be significantly effective in improving the rate of assertiveness and self-esteem among students. Self-esteem holds a pivotal position as an academic construct within the educational process. Notably, self-esteem demonstrates an increase in tandem with behavioral conformity to gender standards for personality, as evidenced by Witt and Wood (2010). Self-confidence and parental social support emerge as vital contributors to interpersonal communication, as highlighted by Oktary et al. (2019). Despite modest academic achievement, the domains of family, social, and overall self-esteem remain largely unaffected, as indicated by Akoul et al. (2021). Moreover, consistent engagement in regular sporting activities has been found to have a positive correlation with self-esteem, as demonstrated by

İbili et al. (2019). The readiness of teachers for change acts as a mediator in the relationship between self-esteem and technology readiness among South Korean teachers, according to the findings of Kim & Kim (2022). Social support plays a significant role in improving self-esteem and consequently affecting internalizing and externalizing problems during emerging adulthood, as observed by Szkody and McKinney (2019). Teaching styles appear to exert a stronger influence on fostering self-concept in female students compared to male students, as suggested by Alrajhi and Aldhafri (2015). Crane (1974) found consistent correlations between scales measuring attitudes and three different estimates of job satisfaction across various population samples. Schwager et al. (2020) noted that self-esteem mediated the effect of social integration on the mental and physical well-being of students. Interpersonal communication skills training has been shown to significantly enhance the social development of students in the experimental group during post-test and follow-up assessments. Jan and Ashraf (2008) highlighted the substantial influence of self-esteem on the mental health of women. Gorbett and Kruczek (2008) found that high levels of family cohesion and the number of siblings predicted strong social self-esteem among college-aged young adults. Self-esteem tends to be a more significant determinant of life satisfaction among females compared to males, as indicated by Huo and Kong (2014).

Classroom participation emerges as a crucial mediator between self-esteem and peer responses in classroom loneliness, as evidenced by a study involving 704 pre-adolescent boys and girls conducted by Stoeckli (2009). Salmela and Nurmi (1996) observed that socially uncertain women reported more negative interactions with their parents and partners compared to socially confident women. Addressing the needs of introverted students becomes imperative, particularly when they engage in group work within educational settings, as emphasized by Tuovinen et al. (2020). Interestingly, Ukeh et al. (2011) found that stress and gender did not significantly impact students' self-esteem levels. Yahne & Long (1988) highlighted that woman who participated in structured sessions experienced a significant increase in self-esteem compared to those in a control group. Han & Kim (2017) underscored the importance of communication competence in enhancing the self-esteem of nursing students. Bitonti (1992) observed that discrepancies between ideal self-concept and self-perceptions could lead to cognitive dissonance. Liang et al. (2016) discovered a positive association between growth-fostering mentoring relationships and the self-esteem of adolescent female students from affluent communities. Contrary to gender stereotypes, Tam et al. (2011) found no gender differences in perceived social support and self-esteem among adolescents. Akoul (2021) revealed a negative correlation between self-esteem and social anxiety among adolescent students, highlighting the stability of self-esteem within the family and social domains. Ayça (2022) noted that female students demonstrate a lower tolerance for inequality and are relatively more adept at dealing with uncertainty compared to their male counterparts. Additionally, Subon et al. (2020) highlighted the interconnectedness between self-esteem and academic achievement among undergraduates in Malaysia. Bukhari et al. (2023) found that teachers with higher self-esteem tend to exhibit greater assertiveness ratings compared to those with average or low self-esteem levels.

Communication plays a pivotal role in shaping the socialization of preservice teachers, as evidenced by discussions centered around self-reflection, task orientation, and the perceived impact of their teaching practices (Staton & Darling, 1986). Student behavior in small-group settings often mirrors the communication styles and expectations set by their instructors, influencing collaborative learning dynamics within the classroom (Webb et al., 2006). Examining the impact of mobile phone usage on social behavior and communication patterns among millennial future teachers, Roxå and Mårtensson (2009) highlighted how technology influences interpersonal interactions and professional relationships within educational contexts.

Further exploring workplace communication, Pluszczyk's study (2020) investigated the role of small talk in enhancing socialization and effective communication among Polish workers. This research underscores how informal conversations contribute to team cohesion and organizational culture in professional environments.In professional development, Trybulkevych (2020) demonstrated that peer feedback training among in-service teachers improves the efficiency and effectiveness of their communication practices. This training not only enhances collaboration but also cultivates a supportive environment for continuous professional growth and learning.

Teachers play a pivotal role in facilitating collaborative dialogue and learning within small student groups (Webb, 2009). This involves guiding interactions that promote cooperative learning among students, where teachers actively engage in facilitating roles that students then emulate within their groups (Gillies, 2006).Small stories and positioning analysis, as explored by Watson (2007), reveal how student teachers construct their professional identities through everyday interactions. These narratives not only help teachers manage dialectical tensions within evolving educational systems but also aid in understanding group identity through shared narratives (Gilmore & Kramer, 2019). Social identification among teachers, as studied by Van and Wagner (2002), correlates with improved work motivation, satisfaction, and adherence to in-group norms. Narrative group discussions, as highlighted by Uitto et al. (2015), assist beginning teachers in recognizing diverse dimensions of their professional identity within the micropolitical context of schools.

HYPOTHESIS

1) There is no significant linear relationship between self-esteem and small group socialization in the population.
2) There is no significant linear relationship between self-esteem and workplace communication behaviour in the population.

METHODOLOGY

The study utilized a set of standardized instruments to measure key variables. The Self-Esteem Scale gauges individuals' self-perceptions and confidence levels, and the Small Group Socialization Scale measures engagement and interactions in small group settings (Riddle et al., 2016). The Workplace Communication Behaviour Inventory Scale evaluates communication behaviors within a professional context (Walter, 2019). The participants in this study were women teachers affiliated with higher education institutions in Karnataka, totaling 509 individuals and recruited through stratified random sampling. The survey was conducted over a period spanning from March 2023 to November 2023. Both offline and online survey methods were employed to gather responses, providing flexibility to the participants. Prior to participation, informed consent was obtained from each respondent, ensuring ethical research practices and compliance with ethical guidelines. The data analysis techniques employed in the study encompassed both correlation analysis and linear regression analysis. Correlation analysis was utilized to investigate the relationships between self-esteem and both small group socialization and workplace communication behavior. The study observed strong positive correlations, indicating a substantial association between these variables. Linear regression analysis was then applied to delve deeper into the predictive relationships. The robustness of these relationships was emphasized by significant coefficients (β) and high t-values, confirming the statistical significance of the associations.

RESULTS

Table 1. Descriptive statistics and correlation matrix

Variable	Mean	SD	(1)	(2)	(3)
Self esteem	34.0138	5.66918	1	.951**	.500**
Small group socialization	47.6699	7.48181		1	.526**
Workplace communication behaviour	107.0079	20.06593			1

The descriptive statistics reveal key insights into the measured variables. The mean self-esteem score stands at approximately 34.01, demonstrating the central tendency of individuals' self-esteem in the given context, with a standard deviation of 5.67 indicating the degree of variability. Likewise, the mean small group socialization score is around 47.67, showcasing the average level of engagement in small group interactions, accompanied by a standard deviation of 7.48. Additionally, the mean workplace communication behaviours score registers at approximately 107.01, representing the central value of observed communication behaviours in the workplace, with a standard deviation of 20.07 reflecting the extent of dispersion in these behaviours. Moving on to the correlation coefficients, compelling relationships emerge. Between self-esteem and small group socialization, a robust positive correlation ($r = 0.951^{**}$) signifies that individuals with higher self-esteem are notably inclined to engage positively in small group socialization. This correlation is highly significant at the 0.01 level (2-tailed), reinforcing the strength and reliability of the association. Similarly, the moderately strong positive correlation ($r = 0.500^{**}$) between self-esteem and workplace communication behaviours indicates that individuals with elevated self-esteem tend to exhibit more positive workplace communication behaviours. Again, this correlation is highly significant at the 0.01 level (2-tailed), underscoring the robustness of the relationship. Lastly, the moderate positive correlation ($r = 0.526^{**}$) between small group socialization and workplace communication behaviours implies that positive small group socialization is connected with favourable workplace communication behaviours. This correlation is also highly significant at the 0.01 level (2-tailed), emphasizing the interrelated nature of these two variables.

Table 2. Linear regression predicting small group socialization from self-esteem

Predictor	β	t	R^2	Adj. R^2	F	Sig.
Self-esteem	.951	69.078	.904	.904	4771.770	<0.001

In the linear regression analysis, "Self-esteem" serves as the predictor variable, and its associated coefficient (β) is calculated to be 0.951. The statistical significance of this relationship is underscored by a substantial t-value of 69.078 and a significance level (Sig.) less than 0.001, denoted as <0.001. The remarkably low p-value (<0.001) further confirms the statistical significance, affirming that the connection between self-esteem and small group socialization is highly robust. Moving to the model fit and the extent of variance explained, the R-squared (R^2) value stands at 0.904, signifying that approximately 90.4% of the variability observed in small group socialization can be elucidated by the linear regression model employing self-esteem as the predictor. This high explanatory power is corroborated by an identical Adjusted R-squared (Adj. R^2) of 0.904, indicating that the model adeptly captures the variability in small group socialization while adjusting for the number of predictors involved. The model fit statistics further affirm the overall significance of the regression model, as reflected by the substantial F-statistic of 4771.770. This is coupled with a p-value of less than 0.001, emphasizing the model's statistical significance.

Table 3. Linear regression predicting workplace communication behaviour from self-esteem

Predictor	β	t	R^2	Adj. R^2	F	Sig.
Self-esteem	.500	12.983	.250	.248	168.557	<0.001

In the analysis of the linear regression model predicting workplace communication behaviours from self-esteem, self-esteem serves as the predictor variable, and its associated coefficient (β) is determined to be 0.500. The statistical significance of this relationship is robustly affirmed by a considerable t-value of 12.983 and a significance level (Sig.) less than 0.001 (indicated as <0.001). The remarkably low p-value (<0.001) further emphasizes the statistical significance, indicating that the observed relationship between self-esteem and workplace communication behaviour is highly unlikely to be due to chance. Moving on to the model fit and the extent of variance explained, the R-squared (R^2) value stands at 0.250, revealing that approximately 25% of the variability observed in workplace communication behaviour can be elucidated by the linear regression model employing self-esteem as the predictor. The Adjusted R-squared (Adj. R^2) corroborates this, registering at 0.248, suggesting that the model adeptly accounts for the variability in workplace communication behaviour while adjusting for the number of predictors involved. The model fit statistics further underscore the overall significance of the regression model. The F-statistic, reflecting the significance of the model, is substantial at 168.557. This is complemented by a p-value of less than 0.001, reinforcing the statistical significance of the model and affirming that the observed relationship between self-esteem and workplace communication behaviour is not merely a result of chance.

DISCUSSIONS

The narratives surrounding women teachers in Karnataka reflect a blend of respect for their contributions, challenges faced due to gender norms, and evolving dynamics in the educational sector. They are often respected for their dedication and commitment to educating the younger generation. Seen as nurturers and mentors, they play a crucial role in the holistic development of students. This respect extends beyond the classroom, where they are regarded as pillars of the community, contributing to social and moral values. Despite the respect, women teachers in Karnataka face several challenges stemming from traditional gender norms. Balancing professional responsibilities with familial duties remains a significant hurdle for many. Societal expectations often dictate that women manage household chores, childcare, and elder care, in addition to their teaching duties. This dual burden can lead to stress and burnout, impacting their overall well-being and professional growth. For example, a woman teacher in a rural school might have to manage long commutes, handle large class sizes with limited resources, and simultaneously fulfill domestic responsibilities. These challenges are further exacerbated by societal attitudes that sometimes undervalue women's professional contributions compared to their male counterparts.

The narrative is gradually shifting as more women take on leadership roles within the educational sector in Karnataka. Increased access to higher education, professional development opportunities, and supportive policies are empowering women teachers to advance in their careers. An example of this evolving dynamic can be seen in the increasing number of women occupying administrative positions in schools and colleges. Their leadership is not only enhancing the quality of education but also serving as an inspiration for the next generation of female educators and students. Women teachers in Karnataka also play a vital role in community development. Through initiatives like literacy programs, health awareness campaigns, and vocational training, they contribute significantly to the upliftment of their communities. Their involvement in such programs underscores the broader impact of women educators beyond the confines of the classroom. In rural areas, women teachers often spearhead community meetings and workshops, addressing issues like women's health, financial literacy, and child welfare.

The significance of the observed linear relationship between self-esteem and small group socialization among women higher education teachers in Karnataka can be critically analyzed from several perspectives. Firstly, the contextual specificity of the study, focusing exclusively on women educators in Karnataka, suggests that cultural, institutional, and socio-economic factors unique to this context may influence the findings. Understanding how these contextual factors shape the observed relationship is crucial for interpreting the results and considering their applicability to different populations or settings. Given the study's focus on women higher education teachers, it's important to consider the role of gender dynamics in shaping self-esteem and small group interactions. Women in academia may face distinct challenges and experiences that impact their self-esteem and interactions within small groups. Societal expectations, gender roles, and power dynamics within academic institutions can provide valuable insights into the observed relationship. The professional environment of higher education institutions in Karnataka is likely to influence the relationship between self-esteem and small group socialization among women teachers. Factors such as departmental culture, institutional support, leadership dynamics, and workload pressures may impact both self-esteem and opportunities for social interaction within small groups. These organizational factors intersect with individual characteristics can deepen our understanding of the observed relationship. The significance of the observed linear relationship between self-esteem and workplace communication behavior among women higher education teachers in Karnataka warrants a comprehensive exploration from various angles to fully understand its implications.

CONCLUSIONS

The narratives surrounding women teachers in Karnataka reveal a significant association between self-esteem and both small group socialization and workplace communication behavior. The study's findings illuminate that individuals with higher self-esteem tend to engage more positively in small group settings and exhibit enhanced communication skills in the workplace. This suggests that women teachers with robust self-esteem not only excel in creating supportive and effective educational environments but also demonstrate strong communication abilities in their professional interactions. The positive correlation observed between small group socialization and workplace communication behavior indicates a link between these two domains. Women teachers who excel in small group settings, such as collaborative teaching and community initiatives, are likely to demonstrate similar strengths in workplace communication. Linear regression analyses provide further depth to these relationships, revealing strong and statistically significant positive associations between self-esteem and both small group socialization and workplace communication behavior. The robustness of these relationships is underscored by high regression coefficients, significant t-values, and low p-values, indicating that the observed associations are not likely due to chance. Moreover, the high explanatory power of the regression models, as reflected in the substantial R-squared values, suggests that a considerable proportion of the variability in small group socialization and workplace communication behavior can be attributed to variations in self-esteem. The Adjusted R-squared values further validate the reliability of the models, accounting for the number of predictors included.

DATA AVAILABILITY

Data is available from the author.

REFERENCES

AISHE. (2020). *All India Survey on Higher Education 2019-20*.

Akoul, M. (2021). Correlations of self-esteem with academic competencies and gender variations. *Global Journal of Guidance and Counseling in Schools Current Perspectives*, 11(1), 15–26. DOI: 10.18844/gjgc.v11i1.5077

Akoul, M., Lotfi, S., & Radid, M. (2021). Correlations of self-esteem with academic competencies and gender variations. *International Journal of Learning & Teaching*, 13(1), 01–12. DOI: 10.18844/ijlt.v13i1.5204

Al Khatib, S. A. (2012). Exploring the relationship among loneliness, self-esteem, self-efficacy and gender in United Arab Emirates college students. *Europe's Journal of Psychology*, 8(1). Advance online publication. DOI: 10.5964/ejop.v8i1.301

Alrajhi, M., & Aldhafri, S. (2015). Academic and social self-concept: effects of teaching styles and gender in English as a foreign language setting. *Journal of Psychology in Africa (South of the Sahara, the Caribbean, and Afro-Latin America)*, 25(1), 44–49. DOI: 10.1080/14330237.2014.997009

Ayça, B. (2022). Sosyal Bilimler Öğrencilerinin Sosyo-Kültürel Boyutlar, Benlik Saygısı ve Akademik Öz Yeterlikleri Arasındaki İlişkinin İncelenmesi. *Ankara Hacı Bayram Veli Üniversitesi İktisadi ve İdari Bilimler Fakültesi Dergisi*, 24(2), 889–916. DOI: 10.26745/ahbvuibfd.1120436

Bertucci, A., Conte, S., Johnson, D. W., & Johnson, R. T. (2010). The impact of size of cooperative group on achievement, social support, and self-esteem. *The Journal of General Psychology*, 137(3), 256–272. DOI: 10.1080/00221309.2010.484448 PMID: 20718226

Bi, Y., Ma, L., Yuan, F., & Zhang, B. (2016). Self-esteem, perceived stress, and gender during adolescence: Interactive links to different types of interpersonal relationships. *The Journal of Psychology*, 150(1), 36–57. DOI: 10.1080/00223980.2014.996512 PMID: 25584816

Bitonti, C. (1992). The self-esteem of women: A cognitive-phenomenological study. *Smith College Studies in Social Work*, 63(1), 295–311. DOI: 10.1080/00377319209517375

Bukhari, M., Farooq, U., & Kouser, T. (2023). The relationship between public school teachers self esteem and their assertiveness. *Global Educational Studies Review*, VIII(I), 1–9. DOI: 10.31703/gesr.2023(VIII-I).01

Burnett, P. C. (1996). An investigation of the social learning and symbolic interaction models for the development of self-concepts and self-esteem. *Journal of Family Studies*, 2(1), 57–64. DOI: 10.5172/jfs.2.1.57

Callahan, S. D., & Kidd, A. H. (1986). Relationship between job satisfaction and self-esteem in women. *Psychological Reports*, 59(2), 663–668. DOI: 10.2466/pr0.1986.59.2.663

Çiçek, İ. (2022). Mediating role of self-esteem in the association between loneliness and psychological and subjective well-being in university students. *International Journal of Contemporary Educational Research*, 8(2), 83–97. DOI: 10.33200/ijcer.817660

Clark, J. V., & Arkowitz, H. (1975). Social anxiety and self-evaluation of interpersonal performance. *Psychological Reports*, 36(1), 211–221. DOI: 10.2466/pr0.1975.36.1.211 PMID: 1121542

Crane, C. (1974). Attitudes towards acceptance of self and others and adjustment to teaching. *The British Journal of Educational Psychology*, 44(1), 31–36. DOI: 10.1111/j.2044-8279.1974.tb00763.x PMID: 4817534

Cribb, V. L., & Haase, A. M. (2016). Girls feeling good at school: School gender environment, internalization and awareness of socio-cultural attitudes associations with self-esteem in adolescent girls. *Journal of Adolescence*, 46(1), 107–114. DOI: 10.1016/j.adolescence.2015.10.019 PMID: 26684660

de Jong, P. J. (2002). Implicit self-esteem and social anxiety: Differential self-favouring effects in high and low anxious individuals. *Behaviour Research and Therapy*, 40(5), 501–508. DOI: 10.1016/S0005-7967(01)00022-5 PMID: 12038643

Doherty, J., & Parker, K. (1977). An investigation into the effect of certain selected variables on the self-esteem of a group of student teachers. *Educational Review*, 29(4), 307–315. DOI: 10.1080/0013191770290408

Duffy, M. K., Shaw, J. D., & Stark, E. M. (2000). Performance and satisfaction in conflicted interdependent groups: When and how does self-esteem make a difference? *Academy of Management Journal*, 43(4), 772–782. DOI: 10.2307/1556367

Ghara, T. K. (2016). Status of Indian Women in Higher Education. *Journal of Education and Practice*, 7(34), 58–64.

Gillies, R. M. (2006). Teachers' and students' verbal behaviours during cooperative and small-group learning. *The British Journal of Educational Psychology*, 76(2), 271–287. DOI: 10.1348/000709905X52337 PMID: 16719964

Gilmore, B., & Kramer, M. W. (2019). We are who we say we are: Teachers' shared identity in the workplace. *Communication Education*, 68(1), 1–19. DOI: 10.1080/03634523.2018.1536271

Giri, V. N. (2003). Associations of self-esteem with communication style. *Psychological Reports*, 92(3, suppl), 1089–1090. DOI: 10.2466/PR0.92.3.1089-1090 PMID: 12931921

Glotova, G., & Wilhelm, A. (2014). Teacher's self-concept and self-esteem in pedagogical communication. *Procedia: Social and Behavioral Sciences*, 132, 509–514. DOI: 10.1016/j.sbspro.2014.04.345

Gorbett, K., & Kruczek, T. (2008). Family factors predicting social self-esteem in young adults. *The Family Journal (Alexandria, Va.)*, 16(1), 58–65. DOI: 10.1177/1066480707309603

Greenhaus, J. H. (1971). Self-esteem as an influence on occupational choice and occupational satisfaction. *Journal of Vocational Behavior*, 1(1), 75–83. DOI: 10.1016/0001-8791(71)90008-X

Guindon, M. H. (1994). Understanding the role of self-esteem in managing communication quality. *IEEE Transactions on Professional Communication*, 37(1), 21–27. DOI: 10.1109/47.272855

Han, M.-R., & Kim, H.-G. (2017). Mediating effect of communication competence on the relationship between emotional intelligence and self-esteem among nursing students. *Journal of Digital Convergence*, 15(2), 263–272. DOI: 10.14400/JDC.2017.15.2.263

Hintsanen, M., Alatupa, S., Pullmann, H., Hirstiö-Snellman, P., & Keltikangas-Järvinen, L. (2010). Associations of self-esteem and temperament traits to self- and teacher-reported social status among classmates: Self-esteem, temperament and social status. *Scandinavian Journal of Psychology*, 51(6), 488–494. DOI: 10.1111/j.1467-9450.2010.00820.x PMID: 20584152

Huo, Y., & Kong, F. (2014). Moderating effects of gender and loneliness on the relationship between self-esteem and life satisfaction in Chinese university students. *Social Indicators Research*, 118(1), 305–314. DOI: 10.1007/s11205-013-0404-x

Hyun, M.-Y., & Park, E.-O. (2008). The effect of interpersonal relationships and communication curriculum. *Journal of Korean Academic Society of Nursing Education*, 14(1), 5–11. DOI: 10.5977/JKASNE.2008.14.1.005

Ibili, E., & Billinghurst, M. (2019). The Relationship between Self-Esteem and Social Network Loneliness: A Study of Trainee School Counsellors. *Malaysian Online Journal of Educational Technology*, 7(3), 39–56.

Jan, M., & Ashraf, A. (2008). An assessment of self-esteem among women. *Studies on Home and Community Science*, 2(2), 133–139. DOI: 10.1080/09737189.2008.11885264

Khan, I., Mahmood, A., & Zaib, U. (2019). Interplay of self-esteem with the academic achievements between male and female secondary school students. *Journal of Human Behavior in the Social Environment*, 29(8), 971–978. DOI: 10.1080/10911359.2019.1611517

Kim, J., & Kim, E. (2022). Relationship between self-esteem and technological readiness: Mediation effect of readiness for change and moderated mediation effect of gender in South Korean teachers. *International Journal of Environmental Research and Public Health*, 19(14), 8463. DOI: 10.3390/ijerph19148463 PMID: 35886326

Knightley, W. M., & Whitelock, D. M. (2007). Assessing the self-esteem of female undergraduate students: An issue of methodology. *Educational Studies*, 33(2), 217–231. DOI: 10.1080/03055690601068485

Kunnumpurath, B., Prasad, A., Menon, V. A., & Thomas, J. (2024). Cultivating self-esteem: Exploring the intersection of culture, neurocognition, and behavior among female media professionals. In *Cognitive Behavioral Neuroscience in Organizational Settings* (pp. 65–82). IGI Global. DOI: 10.4018/979-8-3693-1858-4.ch004

Kwal, T., & Fleshler, H. (1973). The influence of self-esteem on emergent leadership patterns. *The Speech Teacher*, 22(2), 100–106. DOI: 10.1080/03634527309377997

Lam, S. S. K., Schaubroeck, J., & Brown, A. D. (2004). Esteem maintenance among groups: Laboratory and field studies of group performance cognitions. *Organizational Behavior and Human Decision Processes*, 94(2), 86–101. DOI: 10.1016/j.obhdp.2004.03.004

Liang, B., Lund, T. J., Mousseau, A. M. D., & Spencer, R. (2016). The mediating role of engagement in mentoring relationships and self-esteem among affluent adolescent girls: Mentoring relationships. *Psychology in the Schools*, 53(8), 848–860. DOI: 10.1002/pits.21949

Liu, G., Pan, Y., Ma, Y., & Zhang, D. (2021). Mediating effect of psychological *suzhi* on the relationship between perceived social support and self-esteem. *Journal of Health Psychology*, 26(3), 378–389. DOI: 10.1177/1359105318807962 PMID: 30557075

Losa-Iglesias, M. E., López López, D., Rodriguez Vazquez, R., & Becerro de Bengoa-Vallejo, R. (2017). Relationships between social skills and self-esteem in nurses: A questionnaire study. *Contemporary Nurse*, 53(6), 681–690. DOI: 10.1080/10376178.2018.1441729 PMID: 29451080

Meisenhelder, J. B. (1986). Self-esteem in women: The influence of employment and perception of husband's appraisals. *Image—the Journal of Nursing Scholarship*, 18(1), 8–14. DOI: 10.1111/j.1547-5069.1986.tb00532.x PMID: 3633863

Moneycontrol News. (2021). *Women teachers in Indian schools outnumber men in 2019-20, shows UDISE report*. Moneycontrol. https://www.moneycontrol.com/news/india/women-teachers-in-indian-schools-outnumber-men-in-2019-20-shows-udise-report-7124421.html

Morrison, T. L., & Duane Thomas, M. (1975). Self-esteem and classroom participation[1]. *The Journal of Educational Research*, 68(10), 374–377. DOI: 10.1080/00220671.1975.10884805

Mossholder, K. W., Bedeian, A. G., & Armenakis, A. A. (1982). Group process-work outcome relationships: A note on the moderating impact of self-esteem. *Academy of Management Journal*, 25(3), 575–585. DOI: 10.2307/256081 PMID: 10298752

Myers, S. A., Shimotsu, S., Byrnes, K., Frisby, B. N., Durbin, J., & Loy, B. N. (2010). Assessing the role of peer relationships in the small group communication course. *Communication Teacher*, 24(1), 43–57. DOI: 10.1080/17404620903468214

Nyadanu, S. D., Garglo, M. Y., Adampah, T., & Garglo, R. L. (2014). The impact of lecturer-student relationship on self-esteem and academic performance at higher education. *Journal of Social Science Studies*, 2(1), 264. DOI: 10.5296/jsss.v2i1.6772

Ogunsanmi, B. A. A. (2014). Influence of self-esteem on academic performance among secondary school students. [IOSRJRME]. *IOSR Journal of Research & Method in Education*, 4(5), 48–51. DOI: 10.9790/7388-04564851

Oktary, D., Marjohan, M., & Syahniar, S. (2019). The effects of self-confidence and social support of parents on interpersonal communication of students. *Journal of Educational and Learning Studies*, 2(1), 5. DOI: 10.32698/0352

Park, J. H., & Chung, S. K. (2015). The relationship among self-esteem, empathy, communication skill and clinical competency of nursing students. *Journal of the Korea Academia-Industrial Cooperation Society*, 16(11), 7698–7707. DOI: 10.5762/KAIS.2015.16.11.7698

Pasha, H. S., & Munaf, S. (2013). Relationship of self-esteem and adjustment in traditional university students. *Procedia: Social and Behavioral Sciences*, 84, 999–1004. DOI: 10.1016/j.sbspro.2013.06.688

Pluszczyk, A. (2020). Socializing at work—an investigation of small talk phenomenon in the workplace. In *Second Language Learning and Teaching* (pp. 201–217). Springer International Publishing.

Rajesh, J. I., & Suganthi, L. (2013). The satisfaction of teachers with their supervisors' interpersonal communication skills in relation to job burn-out and growth satisfaction in southern India. *Management in Education*, 27(4), 128–137. DOI: 10.1177/0892020613498521

Riddle, B. L., Anderson, C., & Martin, M. M. (2016). Small group socialization scale [Data set]. In *PsycTESTS Dataset*. American Psychological Association (APA).

Riggio, R. E., Throckmorton, B., & DePaola, S. (1990). Social skills and self-esteem. *Personality and Individual Differences*, 11(8), 799–804. DOI: 10.1016/0191-8869(90)90188-W

Román, S., Cuestas, P. J., & Fenollar, P. (2008). An examination of the interrelationships between self-esteem, others' expectations, family support, learning approaches and academic achievement. *Studies in Higher Education*, 33(2), 127–138. DOI: 10.1080/03075070801915882

Romans, S. E., Martin, J., & Mullen, P. (1996). Women's Self-Esteem: A Community Study of Women who Report and do not Report Childhood Sexual Abuse. *The British Journal of Psychiatry*, 169(6), 696–704. DOI: 10.1192/bjp.169.6.696 PMID: 8968626

Roxå, T., & Mårtensson, K. (2009). Significant conversations and significant networks – exploring the backstage of the teaching arena. *Studies in Higher Education*, 34(5), 547–559. DOI: 10.1080/03075070802597200

Rusmana, N., Hafina, A., Siddik, R. R., & Nur, L. (2020). Self-esteem development of vocational high school students in Indonesia: Does group counseling with assertive training technique help? *Jurnal Cakrawala Pendidikan*, 39(3), 573–582. DOI: 10.21831/cp.v39i3.31363

Salavera, C., Usán, P., & Jarie, L. (2017). Emotional intelligence and social skills on self-efficacy in Secondary Education students. Are there gender differences? *Journal of Adolescence*, 60(1), 39–46. DOI: 10.1016/j.adolescence.2017.07.009 PMID: 28750267

Salmela-Aro, K., & Nurmi, J.-E. (1996). Uncertainty and confidence in interpersonal projects: Consequences for social relationships and well-being. *Journal of Social and Personal Relationships*, 13(1), 109–122. DOI: 10.1177/0265407596131006

Sator, P. (2017). The effect of low self-esteem on clinical performance among first year nursing students in a private college at Kota Kinabalu, Sabah. [BJMS]. *Borneo Journal of Medical Sciences*, 11(1), 11–23. DOI: 10.51200/bjms.v11i1.634

Schwager, S., Wick, K., Glaeser, A., Schoenherr, D., Strauss, B., & Berger, U. (2020). Self-esteem as a potential mediator of the association between social integration, mental well-being, and physical well-being. *Psychological Reports*, 123(4), 1160–1175. DOI: 10.1177/0033294119849015 PMID: 31161961

Schwalbe, M. L., Gecas, V., & Baxter, R. (1986). The effects of occupational conditions and individual characteristics on the importance of self-esteem sources in the workplace. *Basic and Applied Social Psychology*, 7(1), 63–84. DOI: 10.1207/s15324834basp0701_5

Schwalbe, M. L., & Staples, C. L. (1991). Gender differences in sources of self-esteem. *Social Psychology Quarterly*, 54(2), 158. DOI: 10.2307/2786933

Schwartz, T. M., Wullwick, V. J., & Shapiro, H. J. (1980). Self-esteem and group decision making: An empirical study. *Psychological Reports*, 46(3), 951–956. DOI: 10.2466/pr0.1980.46.3.951

Seshadri, R., Srinivasan, R., & Kumar, V. (2019). Original Research Article: An exploratory study to understand and examine the nature and type of relationship between self-esteem, life satisfaction and adjustment among male and female migrant students. [IJMH]. *Indian Journal of Mental Health*, 7(2), 105. DOI: 10.30877/IJMH.7.2.2020.105-111

Shackelford, T. K. (2001). Self-esteem in marriage. *Personality and Individual Differences*, 30(3), 371–390. DOI: 10.1016/S0191-8869(00)00023-4

Son, H., & Sung, J. (2014). The effects of teacher's self-efficacy on children's sociality : The serial multiple mediating effects of job-satisfaction and the quality of teacher-child interaction. *Korean Journal of Child Studies*, 35(2), 191–209. DOI: 10.5723/KJCS.2014.35.2.191

Staton-Spicer, A. Q., & Darling, A. L. (1986). Communication in the socialization of preservice teachers. *Communication Education*, 35(3), 215–230. DOI: 10.1080/03634528609388345

Stoeckli, G. (2009). The role of individual and social factors in classroom loneliness. *The Journal of Educational Research*, 103(1), 28–39. DOI: 10.1080/00220670903231169

Subon, F., Unin, N., & Sulaiman, N. H. B. (2020). Self-esteem and academic achievement: The relationship and gender differences of Malaysian university undergraduates. *IAFOR Journal of Psychology & the Behavioral Sciences*, 6(1), 43–54. DOI: 10.22492/ijpbs.6.1.03

Szkody, E., & McKinney, C. (2019). Indirect effects of social support on psychological health through self-esteem in emerging adulthood. *Journal of Family Issues*, 40(17), 2439–2455. DOI: 10.1177/0192513X19859612

Tafani, E., Bellon, S., & Moliner, P. (2002). The role of self-esteem in the dynamics of social representations of higher education: An experimental approach. [Swiss Journal of Psychology]. *Swiss Journal of Psychology*, 61(3), 177–188. DOI: 10.1024//1421-0185.61.3.177

Taghizadeh, M. E., & Kalhori, E. (2015). Relation between self esteem with marital satisfaction of employed women in Payam-e-Noor university. *Mediterranean Journal of Social Sciences*. Advance online publication. DOI: 10.5901/mjss.2015.v6n6s6p41

Tahir, W. B.-E., Inam, A., & Raana, T. (2015). Relationship between social support and self-esteem of adolescent girls [Data set]. *Figshare*. DOI: 10.6084/M9.FIGSHARE.1353182

Tam, C.-L., Lee, T.-H., Har, W.-M., & Pook, W.-L. (2011). Perceived social support and self-esteem towards gender roles: Contributing factors in adolescents. *Asian Social Science*, 7(8). Advance online publication. DOI: 10.5539/ass.v7n8p49

Terra, F. de S., Marziale, M. H. P., & Robazzi, M. L. do C. C. (2013). Evaluation of self-esteem in Nursing teachers at public and private universities. *Revista Latino-Americana de Enfermagem, 21*(spe), 71–78. https://doi.org/DOI: 10.1590/s0104-11692013000700010

Troth, A. C., Jordan, P. J., & Lawrence, S. A. (2012). Emotional intelligence, communication competence, and student perceptions of team social cohesion. *Journal of Psychoeducational Assessment*, 30(4), 414–424. DOI: 10.1177/0734282912449447

Trybulkevych, K. H. (2020). *The influence of social reflection to enhance the efficiency of professional communication of the in-service teachers in the settings of methodical work*. Applied Linguistics Research Journal., DOI: 10.14744/alrj.2020.87894

Tuovinen, S., Tang, X., & Salmela-Aro, K. (2020). Introversion and social engagement: Scale validation, their interaction, and positive association with self-esteem. *Frontiers in Psychology*, 11, 590748. Advance online publication. DOI: 10.3389/fpsyg.2020.590748 PMID: 33329251

Uitto, M., Kaunisto, S.-L., Syrjälä, L., & Estola, E. (2015). Silenced truths: Relational and emotional dimensions of a beginning teacher's identity as part of the micropolitical context of school. *Scandinavian Journal of Educational Research*, 59(2), 162–176. DOI: 10.1080/00313831.2014.904414

Ukeh, M. I., Aloh, P. K., & Kwahar, N. (2011). Stress and gender in relation to self-esteem of university business students. *Gender & Behaviour*, 9(1). Advance online publication. DOI: 10.4314/gab.v9i1.67471

Upshaw, H. S., & Yates, L. A. (1968). Self-persuasion, social approval, and task success as determinants of self-esteem following impression management. *Journal of Experimental Social Psychology*, 4(2), 143–152. DOI: 10.1016/0022-1031(68)90038-3

van Dick, R., & Wagner, U. (2002). Social identification among school teachers: Dimensions, foci, and correlates. *European Journal of Work and Organizational Psychology*, 11(2), 129–149. DOI: 10.1080/13594320143000889

Vatankhah, H., Daryabari, D., Ghadami, V., & Naderifar, N. (2013). The effectiveness of communication skills training on self-concept, self-esteem and assertiveness of female students in guidance school in Rasht. *Procedia: Social and Behavioral Sciences*, 84, 885–889. DOI: 10.1016/j.sbspro.2013.06.667

Vishalakshi, K. K., & Yeshodhara, K. (2012). Relationship between self-esteem and academic achievement of secondary school students. *Education*, 1(12), 83–84.

Wagner, J., Lüdtke, O., Robitzsch, A., Göllner, R., & Trautwein, U. (2018). Self-esteem development in the school context: The roles of intrapersonal and interpersonal social predictors. *Journal of Personality*, 86(3), 481–497. DOI: 10.1111/jopy.12330 PMID: 28555752

Walter, H. L. (2019). Workplace communication behavior inventory. In *Communication Research Measures III* (pp. 515–520). Routledge. DOI: 10.4324/9780203730188-74

Watson, C. (2006). Narratives of practice and the construction of identity in teaching. *Teachers and Teaching*, 12(5), 509–526. DOI: 10.1080/13540600600832213

Watson, C. (2007). Small stories, positioning analysis, and the doing of professional identities in learning to teach. *Narrative Inquiry*, 17(2), 371–389. DOI: 10.1075/ni.17.2.11wat

Webb, N. M. (2009). The teacher's role in promoting collaborative dialogue in the classroom. *The British Journal of Educational Psychology*, 79(1), 1–28. DOI: 10.1348/000709908X380772 PMID: 19054431

Webb, N. M., Nemer, K. M., & Ing, M. (2006). Small-group reflections: Parallels between teacher discourse and student behavior in peer-directed groups. *Journal of the Learning Sciences*, 15(1), 63–119. DOI: 10.1207/s15327809jls1501_8

Witt, M. G., & Wood, W. (2010). Self-regulation of gendered behavior in everyday life. *Sex Roles*, 62(9–10), 635–646. DOI: 10.1007/s11199-010-9761-y

Yahne, C. E., & Long, V. O. (1988). The use of support groups to raise self-esteem for women clients. *Journal of American College Health*, 37(2), 79–84. DOI: 10.1080/07448481.1988.9939046 PMID: 3241029

Zuckerman, D. M. (1980). Self-esteem, personal traits, and college women's life goals. *Journal of Vocational Behavior*, 17(3), 310–319. DOI: 10.1016/0001-8791(80)90024-X

Zuffianò, A., Eisenberg, N., Alessandri, G., Luengo Kanacri, B. P., Pastorelli, C., Milioni, M., & Caprara, G. V. (2016). The relation of pro-sociality to self-esteem: The mediational role of quality of friendships. *Journal of Personality*, 84(1), 59–70. DOI: 10.1111/jopy.12137 PMID: 25234333

Chapter 8
Dichotomies, Power Structures, and Change-Focused Intentionality:
A Personal Narrative in Support of Ongoing Student Status and Reflection While Simultaneously Serving in Leadership Roles in Higher Education

Jennifer Schneider
Community College of Philadelphia, USA

ABSTRACT

This chapter shares a blend of evidence-based theory and reflexive, narrative first-person experiences in support of simultaneously adopting a formal position of student while serving as a leader and teacher in systems of higher education. The article does not argue for any one particular approach to intentionally adopting and maintaining an identity and status as student while also leading in teaching and administrative roles. Instead, the breadth of possible ways to simultaneously adopt a student identity while teaching and leading is highlighted and an ongoing state of reflexive and iterative student status is encouraged. The focus is on spaces in which the intersection of dual identities can further support and strengthen individual experiences as student, leader, and teacher within educational institutions.

DOI: 10.4018/979-8-3693-3144-6.ch008

Copyright © 2025, IGI Global. Copying or distributing in print or electronic forms without written permission of IGI Global is prohibited.

INTRODUCTION

Just because you have a choice, it doesn't mean that any of them has to be right.
— The Dodecahedron, *The Phantom Tollbooth*

In *Black Feminist Thought: Knowledge, Consciousness, and the Politics of Empowerment*, Patricia Hill Collins (1991) writes of either/or dichotomous thinking that effectively categorizes people, things, and ideas in terms of their difference(s) from one another. Category examples are broadly applied, from arguably objective characteristics to more nuanced, subjective concepts, and include, by way of example, race, gender, and mental states (1991). Whether either/or dichotomies are presented with reference to objective or subjective concepts, the outcome is the same: ideas, characteristics, and individuals conceptualized, analyzed, and/or contextualized as such gain meaning *only* in relation to their counterparts (1991). Collins shares a variety of illustrative examples, some of which align with characteristics that are somewhat and sometimes objective and/or visual (hair texture and/or color, skin tone, sex at birth) and others which are more subjective conceptual ("reason/emotion" and "culture/nature") (p. 68). The list of examples, not presented as comprehensive, is both suggestive and provocative – prompting thinking on a wide range of applications, including in educational contexts.

The teacher/student dichotomy as well as the educational leader (administrator)/faculty dichotomy is no exception to this binary, both as stated and in connection with its nuanced implications. Relatedly, in *Feminism and the False Dichotomy of Victimization and Agency*, Elizabeth Schneider (1993) argued in support of the need to "reject simple dichotomies, give up either/ors, learn to accept contradiction, ambiguity, and ambivalence in women's lives, and explore more 'grays' in our conceptions of women's experience" (p. 397). When working in contexts that define stakeholders for an educational institution of higher learning as part of specific categories, for example, student, faculty, *or* administrator, either/or dichotomies are inevitably both created and reinforced. In these situations, what could otherwise yield textured, nuanced, and richly detailed insights, learning, and analysis has the potential to not only result in conversations that are one-dimensional and potentially, even dangerously, narrow, reductionist, and confrontational, but also miss out on opportunities to do more for the benefit of students served in and by those same educational institutions.

In this chapter, I share a blend of evidence-based theory and reflexive, narrative first-person experiences in support of simultaneously adopting a formal position of student while serving as a leader and teacher in systems of higher education. The chapter does not propose an argument for any single approach to intentionally adopting and maintaining an identity and status as student while also leading in teaching and administrative roles. Instead, I share personal narratives, highlight a breadth of possible ways by which to simultaneously adopt a student identity while teaching and leading, and encourage an ongoing state of reflexive and iterative student status. The focus is on spaces in which the intersection of dual identities can further support and strengthen individual experiences as student, leader, administrator, *and* (as distinct from *or*) teacher within educational institutions. In addition to personal experiences, the chapter highlights examples of women leaders throughout history who, for a variety of personal and professional reasons, simultaneously pursued studies as a student within and alongside the structures and systems they led, thereby furthering their own narratives in this context. The chapter also highlights a variety of ways through which further formal education might be pursued while maintaining and continuing in a variety of educational leadership roles.

BACKGROUND

Seymour Papert's "learning manifesto", and constructivist theory more generally, suggests that learning is contextual and that, for one to truly learn something new, connections must be made to existing knowledge (Gollub, 2002; Picard et al., 2004). Specifically, "learners construct new knowledge most effectively when they are in the process of constructing something external which they can examine for themselves and discuss with others" (Picard et al., 2004, p. 262). As one who identifies strongly with this perspective on learning and who also spends most of her time working in spaces of higher education, perhaps I should not be surprised that another (possible) example, though not explicitly addressed in Collins's (1991) aforementioned examples of either/or dichotomies, finds itself at the forefront of my mind – student/teacher dichotomies. While it is no secret that "teacher-student relationships matter" (Will, 2021, p. 1), this acknowledgment, if taken at face value, begs and, perhaps, overlooks an equally important question of the role and impact of the teacher/student dichotomy in the first instance. Moreover, the acknowledgment also raises a related question of the many ways in which continued growth and learning might manifest, evolve, and "matter" not only for students but for teachers and leaders in educational spaces. Collins's work simultaneously prompts thinking about choice of language and words in any individual dichotomy (for example, why "reason/emotion" rather than "logic/feeling" and why "male/female" rather than "man/woman" similar to, as a further example, why "student/teacher" rather than "learner/instructor" or "teacher/educator", with many more variations possible). It strikes me that not only are the dichotomies potentially fundamentally oppositional in nature, and under-analyzed if not flawed as such, but the words chosen to describe those dichotomies (including identity as "either" an administrator, a faculty/teacher/instructor/educator, "or" a student/learner – rather than "and") potentially are, as well.

Relatedly, language used to describe roles and related dichotomies should also be analyzed, or, at a minimum, acknowledged, both iteratively and reflexively for potential ambiguity in intent and meaning, as well as for associated implications, especially those with outcomes discordant with intentions. For example, throughout education, educators hold a host of titles including teacher, instructor, lecturer, professor (adjunct, assistant, associate, full, visiting), among others, and each term simultaneously conveys unique and often deeply imbalanced and discordant power structures, meaning, and associated judgment. It is notable that the choice of address for an educator works, as well, to create and perhaps reinforce dichotomies and associated dynamics within the profession. Externally, the choice of phrasing sets up a variety of dichotomous relationships between students and instructors that are much more complex and nuanced than any one single dichotomy could accurately characterize – where the two are posed as oppositional with differences that are inherently opposed to one another. Whatever the subject, the language and naming rituals used to characterize a dichotomy are, often, just as powerful, and as power-centric, as the dichotomy itself.

Beyond further reflection and dialogue surrounding the language used to frame educations and roles in institutions of higher learning, it is my hope that this chapter and related personal reflections also serve to, potentially, inspire and encourage women leaders in higher education to consider more intentionally adopting, when personally and professionally feasible to do so, formal student-status and identity while serving, both as a part of nomenclature when describing their work and roles and as part of a sustained way of being and of crafting narratives in ways that will further enrich the learning experience for all stakeholders. In doing so, women leaders can simultaneously push back against either/or dichotomies, engage in overt opportunities to experience and enhance the student perspective, create and contribute to found community, and continue to embrace intersectional pluralities and identities both within and without their roles and titles as leaders in higher education. The chapter explores a range of potential reasons, ways, and opportunities to do so, including but not limited to issues of agency, efficacy, intersectionality, power dynamics, and equity in systems of higher education, and also shares narrative accounts unique to my own experiences while doing so.

REFLECTION: STUDENT/TEACHER/ADMINISTRATOR STATUS

Lorraine Hansberry, cited in Collins (1991), writes of the challenges, and the inherent impossibility, of knowing another's perspective, even more so if we do not ask. Beyond asking questions to learn, it is just as important to develop sufficient contextual experiences and understanding so as to know what is otherwise beyond the scope of understanding and/or awareness and, therefore, outside any realistic frame of query or inquiry. Hansberry (1969) writes that "[i]n order to create the universal, you must pay very great attention to the specific. Universality, I think, emerges from the truthful identity of what is" (p. 234).

As an extension of this inquiry, and as I share my experiences as simultaneous student, teacher, administrator, and leader in higher education, I wonder what is more specific, more truthful, and more personal than one's name and preferred manner of address, including as a part of leading, teaching, and learning in this context? If, in our classrooms, we hope to promote true learning, a somewhat logical initial first step seems, to me, to require that we begin by recognizing – and seeing (whether virtually or face to face) the individuals in front of us as well as the inherently complex and intersectional nature of their state of being, leading, and learning in educational spaces. The concept of "seeing", though, cannot be assumed nor taken for granted. Collins (1991) writes relatedly of this point when exploring matrices of domination:

The overarching matrix of domination houses multiple groups, each with varying experiences with penalty and privilege that produce corresponding partial perspectives, situated knowledges, and, for clearly identifiable subordinate groups, subjugated knowledges. No one group has a clear angle of vision. No one group possesses the theory or methodology that allows it to discover the absolute "truth" or, worse yet, proclaim its theories and methodologies as the universal norm evaluating other groups' experiences. (pp. 234-235)

It is both challenging for those seeking to be heard as well as for those seeking to hear. This fundamental challenge presents itself in all manners and forms of communication (and, with great significance in my own work, in online discussion board interactions with and among diverse student voices. As an example, Merryfield (2003) cautions against overlooked voices in online discussion forums and reminds educators to be watchful for "the lesson of isolates" in student responses. In a world where "dialogue is critical", online discussion boards, as one example, are open forums often with no guidelines as to whose ideas are explored (Collins, 1991, p. 236). Simultaneously identifying and experiencing systems as a student could, I suggest and encourage, promote an environment which, as Elsa Barkley Brown claims, "all people can learn to center in another experience, validate it, and judge it by its own standards without need of comparison or need to adopt that framework as their own" (as cited in Collins, 1991, p. 236). Regardless of the strategies that are ultimately chosen, educators and leaders in educational spaces, no matter the official title or role that defines the work of the individual's days, should be both aware of the possibility and watchful for silent corners in all classrooms (virtual and face to face). For silent corners to be offered voice, however, those corners must be identified and, arguably, experienced to be understood and then empowered in productive and safe ways. Collins (1991) writes relatedly on the challenges and importance of doing so:

Although most individuals have little difficulty identifying their own victimization within some major system of oppression – whether it be by race, social class, religion, physical ability, sexual orientation, ethnicity, age, or gender – they typically fail to see how their thoughts and actions uphold someone else's subordination. (p. 229)

It is increasingly clear that interactions in higher education must also be intentionally structured so that all voices are heard, all students are free to "produce specialized thought", and that each student's "thought is equally valid" and treated as such (Collins, 1991, p. 235). One way of doing so is working to covert "either-or" dichotomies to "and-but" perspectives on learning and learning community interactions. However, the structures and systems within which we teach, study, and learn, are set up in ways which make the dichotomies Collins describes hard to neutralize. On whom does the responsibility fall to ensure all students, learners, scholars, citizens have the vocabulary so necessary to discuss these complex and complicated issues with nuanced terms? Collins (1991) writes that

[s]chools, the media, corporations, and government agencies are essential sites for transmitting ideologies objectifying Black woman as the Other. These institutions are not controlled by African-Americans and are clearly the source of and ultimate beneficiaries of these externally defined controlling images. Confronting the controlling images forwarded by institutions external to African-American communities should continue as a fundamental concern of Black feminist thought. (p. 85)

The notion of creating alternative and empowering communities through daily action is powerful and broadly applied. In all learning environments (both formal and informal), community must be intentionally created. Similarly, nonbinary relationships and associated power structures must be both initiated, explored, and nurtured.

My practice to simultaneously take courses as I teach and lead in higher education has been iterative as well as transformative to my teaching practices and leadership style. Questions have led to answers which have led to new and personally transformative questions surrounding policy, pedagogy, and purpose. My simultaneous status as "student" in addition to "leader" in higher education has been a defining moment for me and the focus of this chapter.

The remaining sections in this chapter elaborate on simultaneously serving as student and leader for women in higher education as "creative acts of resistance" with associated positive intentionality and impact (p. 223). Personal experiences and narrative accounts are shared and opportunities for ongoing learning are also explored, as are examples of women leaders throughout history who simultaneously pursued studies as a student within the structures and systems they led, for the benefit of all. The chapter concludes with a series of experimental and interactive poems that further explore the issues raised herein. Sylvia Plath has said that "Poems are moments' monuments" (Inspirational Poetry Quotes, 2019) and the shared pieces are snapshots into how creative writing has further smoothed dichotomies previously constructed by either-or thinking and, instead, have helped shape alternative conceptualizations of moments and lived experiences in student, teacher, and leader spaces into monuments that guide my work and thinking.

CONSIDERATIONS

For readers interested in pursuing additional formal coursework and education while serving as educator, administrator, and other leadership roles, there is obviously no one single recommended approach or way to do so. For some considerations, it might be beneficial to consider issues of place, space, and content, all as tools to further inform teaching, pedagogy, and leadership styles as well as support unique personal and professional interests. For some, it might be worthwhile to consider taking a course in a new discipline as a reminder of the many complex feelings that accompany learning new materials as well as to gain new strategies on managing cognitive load in educational courses, programs, and support services. For others, convenience might be a primary factor. Irrespective of the decisions and decision-making process, much can be gained from a sustained approach to ongoing learning.

Quigley (2020) writes of the challenges associated with typical one-off professional development deliveries. While the referenced study focuses on challenging during COVID-quarantine, the takeaways and reminders of the importance of sustained relationships and ongoing learning are applicable far and well beyond any singular point in time. In a recent study exploring the value of mentorship as a part of professional development, for example, participants noted that concepts including peer personal growth and development along with recognition and acknowledgments that successful mentoring relationships, in its most ideal forms, lasts a lifetime (Mantzourani et. al, 2022). As another example, in a 10-month study that explored the ways in which participating in a yearlong leadership development program contributed to the leader identity development of individuals who had previously been identified as "emerging leaders of color" in Predominantly White Institutions, Longman et. al (2021) identified, in part, benefits associated with developmental relationships as well as an enhanced commitment of participants to strategic self-advocacy and risk taking. The sustained nature of a course and/or associated program, alongside associated relationship building that naturally presents when engaged in formal study as part of a group and community, is also valuable in and of itself as a learning tool, with the potential for similar benefits and sustained learning through the student lens. In the *Outliers*, Malcolm Gladwell writes that becoming an expert at a particular task takes at least 10,000 hours of practice. Similarly, in *The Personal MBA*, Josh Kaufman notes that at least 20 hours of sustained practice is necessary in order to move from zero knowledge on a topic to a state of proficiency. Relatedly, exercising personal choice in terms of how, when, and where to pursue further study even in formal contexts is also a powerful motivator and can return agency to educators in ways traditional professional development often fails to do (Martinelle & Stevens, 2024). Martinelle and Stevens make the case to transform professional development by focusing on principled resistance, where teachers assert agency and values when confronted with conflicting policies. In many ways, the act of undertaking sustained coursework on topics of personal interest by educators and leaders reflects similar strategies.

For example, completing coursework often served as a refresher course in instructional design as well as a reminder of power dynamics in classroom settings. Personal examples include confusing directions on assessments, hidden curriculum that manifested repeatedly across courses in a program, and unanswered emails at important points in time all served as moments that were more memorable than the underlying content. In massive open online education courses with, in some cases, hundreds of students, I was reminded of the power of individual connections and the potential to create them even in large settings. Similarly, in synchronous classes with no more than ten or fifteen students, I experienced moments of overwhelming feelings of isolation and solitariness. In each, the dynamics were set, sustained, and them crafted/molded by classroom leaders – of varying roles and titles, some named, most lacking any formal denomination.

To be big, or small, I was reminded, was entirely contextual and dependent upon the actions and inactions of every member of a classroom community. While stars produce light by creating their own energy, in classrooms energy is co-created. Just how big or how small each individual star in the universe of a classroom can shine depends upon the complex interaction of forces, both seen and unseen, at play. To be both student, teacher, and leader is to co-exist in a universe in which complexity can be more deeply appreciated and energy more productively expended and co-created.

the north star
both guide and guarded

the eclipse
Both shield and focal point

the smallest star
in the universe
both teacher and student

radio waves
as powerful in silence
as in sound

Energy, too, is co-produced and nurtured through processes. For a star in the night sky, energy is produced through nuclear fusion and a process dominated by a sequence of events that transforms atoms. When leading in educational spaces, energy can be produced, and, importantly, reproduced, through sustained engagement as student. I have found that the experiences of studying while teaching and leading also reinforces the collaborative, co-dependent nature of energy, potential for light to shine, and community vitality, both production and cessation.

For example, when an instructor responded to an email inquiry with a simple "NO", feelings of inadequacy and imposter identify almost immediately bubbled like bitter coffee. When a fellow student in a class with over 200 students responded to a discussion board post with encouragement, I reimagined my own potential to contribute, with my own energy highly interconnected with and dependent on the feedback loops generated in the classroom processes and dynamics. I have drawn energy from both positive and negative interactions in my learning journey. These interactions have also inspired confidence for intentional risk taking, creative empowerment, and bureaucratic resistance in the interests of students in my own responses to administrative proposals and policies.

energy –
the physics of performance
at play

The word "narrative" is derived from the Latin verb narrare, which means "to tell" as well as the adjective gnarus, which means "knowing or skilled" (Webster's Seventh New Collegiate Dictionary, 1969). When reflecting on the experience of enrolling, participating, and producing new work for classes in addition to maintaining my other commitments both "telling" and "knowing or skilled" are equally applicable phrases that resonate with all stages of the process. The experience of studying while teaching and leading also reiterates the incredibly complex dynamics of educational spaces. This reminder is one that continues to layer my day-to-day interactions, choices, and decisions in ways that are more purposeful, reflective, and nuanced. My recollections of times that I have fallen asleep in class, sent emails asking for extensions, and struggled to find copies of assigned materials have all profoundly impacted my current teaching and leading philosophies. Beyond pedagogy, I have relearned and reexperienced the challenges, including physical and emotional and mental tolls as well as time demands navigating incorrect billing amounts in account statements, petitioning for adjustment, and confirming schedules. I have been reintroduced to the cognitive dissonance inherent to the start of every new course and new teacher interaction. Titles have become both less important and more nuanced as identities, including and especially within my institution, have emerged as more contextual and complicated than ever before.

I have also been continuously reminded just how critical mentorship and support networks are, both for access to information and community, and that they need to be supported themselves. I have experienced the frustration of paying for required texts that turned out not to be needed as well as the frustration of being unable to access a copy of optional texts that turned out to be needed. I've also experienced the potential complexity of a system described in simple terms and the frustrations that emerge when a warm handoff turns complex and cold. The iterative and compounding impact of the first-person experience as student, teacher, and leader and all associated learning extend far beyond the semester and course content.

As evidenced by the repeated use of the first person throughout the shared recollections, my takeaways are deep and deeply personally. Most of all, I have learned that every Venn diagram has more than one point of intersection and interaction and that Crenshaw's intersectionality, "a lens through which you can see where power comes and collides, where it interlocks and intersects," (Columbia Law School, 2017, para. 3) is never bounded by, but only informed by context. We all exist in states of interlocking Venn diagrams. I have found that maintaining student status while teaching and leading in educational spaces helps keep the boundaries – both where they divide and collide in complex ways, more present in my daily decision-making.

While I share my experiences with the hope readers find them beneficial, I recognize and appreciate that nothing I share in novel or groundbreaking. For me though the experience of continuing as student in institutions where I teach and lead has served to keep all of these issues and concepts, including across content, discipline, pedagogy, curriculum, instruction and equity, at the forefront of my thinking.

Beyond topical and discipline-specific considerations, it might also be worthwhile to consider, as well, taking courses in a variety of modalities, including in-person, online synchronous, and online asynchronous, hybrid, and/or bichronous online learning. While naming conventions vary by and across institutions and accrediting bodies, there are three broad types of online learning, including synchronous, asynchronous, and bichronous online learning (Martin & Bolliger, 2023). Sometimes referred to as hybrid, bichronous online learning blends synchronous and asynchronous online learning by leveraging in a variety of ways the relative advantages of individual modalities and learning formats (Martin et al., 2020).

In my own experiences with distance, remote and online learning, for example, I found I learned just as much about ways to conduct remote asynchronous and synchronous online classes instructional strategies as I did about substantive course content. Doing so, for me, was not only an opportunity to continuously grow skills, but it also served a humbling reminder of just how challenging it can be to juggle multiple responsibilities, including work, school, family, and more, and also how difficult it can be to manage cognitive dissonance and to process new information (Treacy & Leavy, 2023). The experience served as an ongoing crash course in instructional design (both do's and don'ts) and fundamentally transformed my thinking on late penalties, grading, and curricular transparency.

Similar to Gutshall (2020) who highlights the positive impact on teachers' mindset, teaching efficacy, and teachers' approach to learning and grit, when teachers become students, I also benefited beyond lessons in pedagogy, new content areas, and teaching modalities. In many respects, simultaneously serving as faculty, administrator, and student has provided ongoing opportunities to refine, improve and strengthen my own pedagogy, curriculum, and instructional design. The best teachers have motivated me to want to be better, and those experiences that were lacking have helped me be more aware of avoiding similar situations in my own courses.

In *What Makes a Great Principal*, George Couros and Allyson Apsey (2024) write that "if you are in a role that make decisions for what the environment looks like in a classroom, you need to be present in those classrooms". This sentiment and advice are shared widely in primary and secondary educational spaces. For post-secondary applications the logistics might be more challenging, but there is a wonderful opportunity to not only be present but to be one (rather than either-or) as student. That is, presence can take the form of active engagement and involvement as a student, moving beyond that of a passive observer or ad hoc participant that sometimes manifests with in class observations of faculty and students rather than full adoption of student identities and roles.

REFLECTIONS

I believe that my lowest points and moments as a student are also the origins of my relative strengths as a teacher and leader. I also attribute characteristics and values such as empathy, flexibility, and authentic inclusive pedagogy to my own experiences as a student. My experience taking a series of classes ranging from one to two in a semester also highlighted just how challenging it can be when instructors have varying and potentially inconsistent expectations regarding, for example but by no means comprehensively, name expectations, late penalties, submission procedures, and required citation formats. I have revisited how I introduce material, how often I include reminders, and the pace at which I start new courses. I am also decidedly more empathetic and my thinking much more layered and nuanced when resolving disputes and working through practical challenges.

Participating as a student in formal education has also offered me an opportunity to experience higher education from the lens of a student, albeit with different positionality, while also serving as teacher and an administrator. My experiences fell across a wide spectrum of very positive to very negative. My takeaways continued to include much more than substantive content. My perspectives on teaching, learning, and leading for all students were impacted significantly as a result of my formal classroom experiences. Even the activity of completing individual course and teacher evaluation surveys, an area in which research has consistently shown than women experience persistent gender bias and are consistently evaluated more critically than male counterparts, influenced my thinking (Calling Attention to Gender Bias, 2019). Minorities and non-native English speakers, among other groups, experience similar bias (Course survey reforms, 2016).

As additional examples, the degree to which I reflect on tone in feedback, as well as other factors such as specificity, personalization, detail, and timeliness, all characteristics of strong feedback (Wiggins, 2012) is much more nuanced and complex, due largely to having experienced both "good" and "bad" feedback in my role as a student. My experience as a student and adult learner has also added deeper meaning, beyond what research can suggest, to many tasks including grading, feedback, and student (formerly called office) hours. Asking for feedback so that I could improve also felt, somehow, different when I added because as I student I also understand the importance of feedback on the learning process and I am also more present and, I think, more aware of the range of emotions and experiences that accompany student, educator, and administrator spaces and places. My student experiences have also helped crystallize and highlight topics such as cognitive overload, assignment transparency, and implicit bias in my own courses, as well. My course designs have benefited, as well. I am much more attuned to issues of clarity, scaffolding, and seamlessness in instructional design choices and decision making. I have learned to better differentiate, to be more empathetic as a teacher and a leader, and how to simultaneously slow down and to speed up, depending upon context. The lessons aren't necessarily new, but they feel more pressing. My choice of language has also become much more intentional and focused. It has become impossible for me to leave my student identity even while teaching and leading. I have also become more comfortable with vulnerability, my own, my students, and the faculty in my program.

As another example, introductions and naming conventions come to mind. From naming practices, to requests for pronunciation and student pronouns, to changing office hours to student hours, I became much more aware of the power and power dynamics inherent to the language used in the student, teacher, learner, relationship. Naming conventions is one of many examples that have yielded new ways of thinking as a result of my own student experiences.

Collins (1991) writes that "deference rituals such as calling Black domestic workers 'girls' and by their first names enable employers to treat their employees like children, as less capable human beings" (p. 69). In educational contexts, rituals such as calling instructors by more formal names arguably set up similar relationships where the educator is deemed more capable, too. While this might be true (at least in connection with subject matter expertise), extensive research on how students learn suggests that the best learning is co-created and not uni-directional (Picard et al., 2004). Educational research also suggests student agency, efficacy, and choice are important components of successful learning experiences (Bandura, 1989). When thinking about the importance of mutual decision making, agency, and choice for learning, I have also revisited manners of address as a possible way to neutralize domination, objectification, and an opportunity to "document ... everyday resistance to ... attempted objectification" (Collins, 1991, p. 70). Relatedly, adopting a broad perspective and "[v]iewing the world through a both/and conceptual lens of the simultaneity of race, class, and gender oppression and of the need for a humanist vision of community creates new possibilities", presents new questions, and offers new opportunities for growth in a wide realm of contexts, including education (Collins, 1991, p. 121). For example, might altered and reconceptualized language that expressly encourages students to consider themselves as partners in learning, co-creators of knowledge, and peer instructors in classroom settings (perhaps *learners and learning guides* or *students and lead students*) be both more valuable and empowering – for all stakeholders?

Collins further cites Dona Richards (1980) and "suggests that Western thought requires objectification, a process she describes as the 'separation of the knowing self' from the 'known object'" (p. 69). Western schooling and educational organizations appear to have adopted this train of thought. However, I wonder whether the often-dictated manners of address (whether in syllabi, school handbooks, or netiquette guidelines), identity as "either" student or teacher, and student responses, are adopted out a desire for respect or simply another way to perpetuate existing hierarchies, power structures, and control (Worthen, 2017).

For some time, I relied upon the use of my first name to, hopefully, remove barriers and further connections with students. While research suggests that practices differ by country, region, and even school, in many locales, students may adopt a first name basis with their teachers (Moore, 2019). However, and while I do not doubt the truth of these findings, this has not been my experience working with faculty as well as students in both U.S. and international higher education institutions. In my own teaching experiences, I had made it a practice to invite students to address me by my first name. I also recognize the important dynamics associated with names and naming conventions and I realize now that I may have inadvertently overlooked the power embedded within (and inherent to) naming conventions and their impact of ways of thinking (i.e., either/or versus and/but).

At the same time, I recognize perspectives on this topic vary widely and, in my own experiences as student, my own reactions to instructors that insisted on being addressed in certain ways further complicated my thinking in positive ways. Once I began taking classes, instead of looking to first names to further connect with students, I began to share my identity as both professor, department leader, and student. Through the relaying and retelling of shared experiences, I was able to bridge and build relationships in ways that felt more authentic.

Of course, taking courses while working is not, and has not been, without its challenges. I have questioned my own abilities and experienced, anew, feelings of imposter syndrome. Indeed, it is also a demonstrable privilege to include doing so as part of my own lived experiences and one I recognize. Despite the benefits, moreover, it is abundantly clear that these recommendations are, while I believe advantageous and beneficial, deeply challenging absent at-home support networks. I returned to the classroom as student at the age of 40 and was only able to do so when I had access to professional development funding opportunities and online learning options. As noted in Channing (2022), informal mentorship, support networks, and strategies to mitigate barriers all were, and remain, critical components of my experiences. I was only able to undertake additional courses once my own children were grown. For most of the time during which my children were at home, I taught and led a team of part-time instructors in an adjunct role, due, in part, to the challenges of work-life balance and related responsibilities. I am fortunate in that the opportunities for further formal coursework offered by my employer also opened opportunities for eventual full-time employment and leadership responsibilities in a system not traditionally designed to support women and career trajectories in this way.

Subsequent sections in this chapter highlight some free opportunities through which anyone interested can participate in formal, structured coursework. However, while there are wonderful free opportunities for continued learning and credentialing, this does not address the typically unpaid nature of the time and associated opportunity costs of further study. With women leaders already being paid less than men and also bearing a disproportionate degree of labor, service work, and challenges with work-life balance, the challenges of pursuing education of this nature, even while its potential benefits are acknowledged, must also be confronted and acknowledged (The Chronicle of Higher Education, 2022).

The simultaneous experience of student, teacher, and leader has also impacted my own expectations for students and the student experience in ways I could not have predicted. For example, I have modified assignment submission due dates, adjusted scaffolding, and revisited instruction transparency all as a direct consequence of experiences as a student. Additionally, by better understanding the student experience I also feel more empowered to argue for change for students. By utilizing student support services, I better understood the challenges. Instead of only warm handoffs, I knew that the writing center might not respond with enough time to process updates due to my own lived experiences. I understand what's it is like to see a grade with no explanation. And what it's like to craft an email advocating for oneself. Outside of my own classroom, I have become more adept at navigating the system and can now better steer my students through it, as well.

I have learned that all dots have pixels, and that transparency is not always what it seems. Forward movement on the part of a university is as much elastic as it is dependent upon every individual's energy. Trust is always fragile, and respect demands repetition. For a connected classroom to become a community of learners, strangers stitched of schedules thread opportunities that multiple identities, when embraced, can leverage. I've also been reenergized as a leader. Just as I draw energy from my peers as a student, my lived experience of continuing as student has made me more energized as a teacher, administrator, and associated leader. It has also complicated my roles and associated identity, while crystallizing the type of supportive teacher, leader, and educator I strive to be.

While my roles might have varied, they still held relative degrees of power inherent to titles. In every learning context, I have always disclosed my multiple roles whether through classroom introductions or by default due to university systems. My signature line has remained the same and shared in transparent ways. Beyond the transparency of formal roles and responsibilities and the intentions of formal university policies, though, it has been the choices made by individual stakeholders when provided an opportunity to impact in both positive and negative ways that have taught me the most. For example, I remember the professor that refused an extension when I asked for the first time after a rough time with a virus as well as the inflexibility and distance of the professor that had a no late work policy and the one that insisted on being addressed as "Doctor" while refusing to call anyone by anything other than their first name as reflected in the college's official system. I remember the formalized strength of my informal peer groups. My peer WhatsApp group chat, for example, has provided more real time support and answers than my instructors in many cases. My "Critique Group", a WhatsApp chat that originated with an initial purpose of providing feedback on written work to peers, transformed and expanded its purpose, both formal and informal, into equal parts craft and camaraderie. In a short period of time post-formation, the group's name ("Critique Group") no longer accurately reflected the adopted roles and purposes and benefits served.

Similar arguments, in my experience, can be made in connection with titles such as teacher, administrator, leader, and/or student and the associated either/or dichotomies that traditionally accompany these titles. My peer group was not solely a critique group, despite its given name. We were supporters, mentors, guides, sounding boards, and university navigators, among other roles. The university as a system is far too complex for any one role to be thought of as no more and no less than a title. To exist in a university system is to be A and B and __ (insert a leader, teacher, administrator, and student). In my experiences, taking formal classes and formally adopting the student role helped reinforce the importance of this perspective and the deeply interconnected and complex reality that is higher education.

Each interaction, however smooth or rocky, influences my own work as a leader and teacher. I've become more empathetic and more presently aware that the higher education experience is never either/or, but always and. Every student has the posed question, course, or assignment before them and more. Whenever a student emails, I know that email is always part of a more complex whole. I've always known this to be true, but maintaining an active student status strengthens my mindfulness in student-centric ways. Most of all, experiencing higher education as leader, teacher, administrator, and student has made me more whole -- both in ways I respond and react as well as how I plan and protect the spaces that we curate, with good intentions to do what I can to preserve them and improve upon them

The support networks previously discussed and formed through formal study have also served as a sounding board and a mechanism for strengthened resiliency as well as critical exposure to other narratives. In many ways, the classroom became a respite and a place of defined time for contemplation, meditative reflection, and storytelling with tremendous impact. Work done as part of my coursework emerged from time and space I would not otherwise have had for intentional reflection, growth, and deepening resiliency and confidence as well as the introduction to additional narratives on the part of female leaders in similar spaces. The next section introduces further narratives to explore and inspire in this context.

FEMALE LEADERS

Women leaders throughout history who simultaneously pursued studies as a student within the structures and systems they led. In this section, I highlight a few illustrative female leaders, some more well-known than others, who have simultaneously embraced lifelong learning as a part of their journey. This list is by no means comprehensive. Rather, it seeks to highlight a few of many worthy and notable examples and further narratives to explore in this context.

1. Eleanor Roosevelt. Roosevelt served as First Lady of the United States from 1933 through 1945. She also worked as a diplomat and activist, and she played a critical role in drafting the Universal Declaration of Human Rights (Luscombe, 2018). Although Roosevelt never attended college, she pursued learning throughout her entire life and took courses at the Todhunter School for Girls in New York City where she also taught history and literature (Wolfgarth, 2011)
2. Diana Natalicio. Natalicio served as President of the University of Texas at El Paso (UTEP) from 1988 to 2019. Before working at UTEP, Natalicio taught at University of Texas at Austin (UT). While she worked at UT, she also studied and earned a master's degree in Portuguese. After further study, she completed her doctorate degree in linguistics at UT (de la Teja, 2022). During her three-decade tenure as President at UTEP, Natalicio was deeply involved in all aspects of the university and often present and an actively participant adopting multiple roles, including leader, teacher, and student deeply engaged with courses, seminars, and similar learning experiences offered at UTEP (Pennamon, 2019; Smith, 2008). Natalicio attributed passion, tenacity, and perseverance to her leadership success, along with her commitment to education (Román, 2018). In a 2018 interview with Michaela Román, she said, "You have to have a passion of a certain kind for the work that you do," and continued to note

   > I have a real passion for education because I knew what it did for me. If I hadn't gotten that degree at St. Louis University, I wouldn't be sitting here right now and I wouldn't have had this wonderful life at UTEP. (para. 10)
3. Donna Shalala. Shalala served, in part, as chancellor of the University of Wisconsin-Madison (1988-1993) and President of the University of Miami (2001-2015). She also taught while serving as President. More recently, she has served as Interim President at The New School. She credits her non-traditional path to leadership, in part, to reframing the question of whether or not she was qualified to hold a particular position to "whether she was qualified to learn the job" (Radin, 2007, p. 504). Shalala's leadership trajectory and roles demonstrated an ability "to apply experiences and lessons from diverse settings to new positions" (Radin, 2007, p. 504) while continuing to learn in and from those around her.

While serving in educational leadership roles, Shalala reportedly maintained an active presence on campus and sometimes sat in on classes, examples including those on public health and policy (Radin, 2007). Serving as interim president at The New School, Shalala continues to blur lines between student, faculty, and leader spaces and associated dichotomies and either-or thinking. As Kini and Suvarna (2023) note, while the president's office is typically a lesser known and less accessible space to students, "Interim President Donna Shalala has opened the palace gates to students in efforts to change that" (para. 1).

4. Juliet García. Garcia was the first Mexican American woman to be president of a college or university in the United States. She was appointed president of Texas southmost College in 1986 (Carriuolo, 2022). She later served as President of the University of Texas at Brownsville (1992-2014) (Carriuolo, 2022). In a 2022 interview, Garcia states:

I am 52 and still learning. It is important for faculty and administrators to take classes. Some of our own faculty are taking Spanish and working toward becoming biliterate. Some who have never before taught in Spanish are beginning to do so. In addition to learning Spanish, it is good for faculty to spend time on the other side of the desk. Becoming a student again helps us as academics to experience the students' vulnerability in the classroom (para. 21).

Noting "the bigger the goal, the more help needed" (2022), García emphasizes the critical importance of questions, support networks, and continued learning in her leadership journey.

5. Nancy Zimpher. Zimpher was the first woman to serve as Chancellor of the State University of New York (SUNY) System (2009-2017). She was also the first woman to serve as chancellor at the University of Wisconsin in Milwaukee, as well as the first woman president at The University of Cincinnati (Kahn, 2009). Despite, or, perhaps, in spite of, her tremendous accomplishments, Zimpher has noted that her "accomplishments are nothing compared with what woman need to overcome to gain parity" (Kahn, 2009, para. 2).

While serving, Zimpher was deeply involved and engaged in all aspects of university life, described as "ubiquitous" and adopting a wide range of roles in "and" rather than "or" status, including "courtside basketball fan", "radio commentator" and "magazine cover girl" (Chandler, 2003, p. 69). She describes herself as "a nuisance" and a "pest" and as someone as a way to get things done (p. 71). She also adopted a persistent learner perspective and self-described as an avid reader of "make-me-better books on institutional change and leadership" (p. 71). Quoting Woody Allen, she noted that the key to success is "showing up" and "to keep showing up" (Chandler, 2003, p. 71), advice she adopted whole heartedly in roles that expanded understanding of the many ways in which a leader in higher education can embrace a role and serve as a leader, resisting narrow constructions of how to do so and, instead, adopting a much more expansive interpretation of a leader's day-to-day involvement in a university.

6. Dr. Ruth Simmons. Simmons served as President of Brown University from 2001 through 2012. She was the first African-American president of an Ivy League institution (Flakes, 2023). She also served as President of Smith College (1995-2001) and of Prairie View A&M University (2017-2023) (Finding Your Roots, n.d.). Simmons characterizes and describes leadership as grounded in learning. In a 2018 New York Times interview she notes that, for her, leadership is "more of a disposition — the ability to step into a situation to learn about the history of the enterprise, the opportunities that it faces, the culture that exists and the people who are served by it." (para. 14).

These examples and illustrative female leaders highlight the range of experiences and pathways through which an ongoing and formal status as student might be maintained and sustained while also holding educational leadership roles. Hopefully, they also illustrate the energy and motivation that ongoing learning and shared narratives can initiate. In the next section, I share some additional opportunities and pathways through which further study might be explored.

OPPORTUNITIES

Many institutions offer opportunities for free tuition and coursework within the institution. Beyond such opportunities, there are often "hidden" benefits in fine print (not unlike many services in systems of higher education, another lesson-learned from student status). Outside of formal roles, there are many opportunities for free courses online. Some sample sites follow.

1. EdX: https://www.edx.org
2. Coursera: https://www.coursera.org/
3. Harvard University Online, Free Courses: https://pll.harvard.edu/catalog/free
4. Stanford University Online, Free Courses: https://online.stanford.edu/free-courses
5. LinkedIn Learning: https://learning.linkedin.com/
6. Khan Academy: https://www.khanacademy.org/
7. OpenLearn, The Open University: https://www.open.edu/openlearn/free-courses/full-catalogue
8. FutureLearn: https://www.futurelearn.com/
9. Udacity: https://www.udacity.com/
10. Udemy: https://www.udemy.com/
11. Canvas: https://www.canvas.net/
12. Codecademy: https://www.codecademy.com/
13. YouTube: https://www.youtube.com/
14. Class Central: https://www.classcentral.com/collection/top-free-online-courses
15. Memrise: https://www.memrise.com/en-us/
16. 7000: https://www.7000.org/
17. Free Online Courses with Certificates: https://careerservices.upenn.edu/blog/2024/05/09/12-free-online-courses-with-certificates-to-boost-your-resume/
18. Writer's Workshops and Classes: for some free examples: https://www.theforeverworkshop.com/?utm_source=substack&utm_medium=email
19. Community colleges
20. Tuition reimbursement programs at home or partners institutions
21. Discipline specific training (many options)
22. New and/or revisited hobbies and related skills (many options)

This list is illustrative only. It is neither all inclusive nor comprehensive. There are many more options to explore, as well as many more narratives to share.

CREATIVE WRITING AS A TOOL FOR THINKING

In this section, I share a sampling of interactive, experimental, and prose poetry that provides accounts of both my personal responses and experiences in simultaneous student, faculty, administrator, and associated leadership roles and moments and that are shared with the hopes of prompting further inquiry regarding positionality, impact, and the intersectionality of simultaneous statuses in educational spaces.

The experimental and interactive poems are intended to further personalize the experiences shared in this chapter and, perhaps, encourage further exploration of creative writing as a tool to understand the interconnectedness of multiple identifies including student, teacher, and leader in higher education and to process thinking as it emerges in these interconnected spaces and places and across persistent and sometimes deeply entrenched dichotomies.

Shape of X

Robert Frost -- "The only way through is through."
As Written. Through. Ready. Set. Go.

```
Remember.                                        Weave.
    Understand.                              Wonder.
        Apply.                             Wander.
            Analyze.            Timelines.
                Evaluate. Learn. Lead.
                       Create.
                        Read.
                        Write.
                      Calculate.
               Assess. Grade. Explain.
                   Ready.       Score.
              Teach.                   Set.
         Gather.                          Go.
      Rigor.                                Reality.
Skills.                                          Mindsets.
Training.                                        Trauma.
```

Go. Set. Ready. Through. As Written.

How to Score a D

Study. Study more.
Sweat. Sweat more.
Master 60% of all material.
Add another percent.
Perhaps two. Maybe three.
Blend. Mix. Stir.

A Collection of Curiosities

1. Student scratches at paper, answering all asked questions. No questions asked until the paper, scored, is returned. I wrote and wrote and wrote, the student said. I wrote at least 1000 words. Why do I only get one, one letter in return?
2. Grading Scales

    teacher paces
    as she
    lectures writes
    and illustrates
    math equations
    teaches us
    to solve
    for X
    Y and
    Z using
    logic formulas
    and creativity
    I'm here
    to help
    she states
    ask questions
    says revisions
    are welcome
    to show
    our work
    is what
    matters but
    when she
    returns exams
    she stands
    at the
    front of
    the room
    as we
    listen carefully
    lead cautiously
    learn collectively
    I catch

her eye
times two
she blinks
a series
of *Why*s
my response
I tried
there's always
a single
number converted
to a
solitary letter
that incorporates
none of
the foregoing
no matter
what I
do or
what she
says we
remain on
parallel planes
with no
inter section

3. Students scratch, calculate,

   Circle, and rehash content
   Previously distributed
   They fill pages with
   Letters from A to Z and then,
   Anticipate their return
   The puzzle remains, with so
   Many letters written, how come
   the difference between an A
   B C and D will remain
   one letter only

4. Teacher says to read widely. Counselor says to expand my horizons.

Mother encourages far-flung aspirations. Father says to get a head-start, don't waste a minute. The recommendations share yet-to-be-explored latitude and longitude in common. Why then, do we sit in chairs in a room with no windows?

    5.

Revision opportunities are welcome,
but please don't revise me.
I'm content with my formative
years and this version of me.

    6.

(p)late
If I eat from an empty plate, all I know is late.

Bloom

I'm an expert skateboarder,
capable of competing all sorts
of tricks and routines. I bloom
in concrete quarters. Rocks
and rolls my preferred plot twist.
Bloom's taxonomy still,
surprisingly steep.

Ways to Grade a Paper

1. Apply red ink to vulnerable expressions of thought and think. Watch pupils sink.
2. Peer reviews. Provide open-ended opportunities for students to acknowledge others' work product.
3. On a bell curve. From behind a curtain.
4. Automatically. From a position of observation.
5. Subjectively score an objective exam.
6. Objectively score a subjective paper.
7. In accordance with unstated benchmarks and a hidden curriculum.
8. At irregular instances and decimals.
9. At regular insistences and intervals.

10. In response to administrative insistence.
11. Pursuant to iridescent standards.
12. In a non-defined doses of rigor and relevance.
13. In accordance with a twelve-point rubric.
14. With a Bic point pen.
15. With a freshly sharpened pencil, No. 3.
16. Only after a cup of coffee.
17. Only before a liter of levity.
18. Music on.
19. Muscle memory off.
20. While consistently asking yourself who am I am to score and why.
21. After three readings.
22. Anonymously.
23. Rigorously.
24. Tenderly.
25. Sorted by date of submission.
26. Returned by ease of delivery.
27. Minds closed.
28. Eyes open.
29. Roles on.
30. Titles tilted.
31. Seats reversed.
32. Names revealed.
33. One paper at a time.
34. One question at a time.
35. On a preset scale.
36. Weighted.
37. Only after waiting, hoping for more time.

ON LEARNING WHAT TEACHING CAN BE

When I was a girl, I thought that all instructors were teachers and that all teachers were instructors. And that learning was the main course – to quiet growling tummies and nourish hungry minds – with childhood favorites.

Spaghetti laces and bow tie noodles. Seasoned with *Salt. Butter*, too. *Mac n cheese* mountains and *marshmallow* bridges. *Squishy* to the touch. Circular soup bowls - stacked on waist high buffet shelves – hosted glass beads, Lego blocks, and wooden letters.

1, 2, 3. A, B, C. United we stand. Right hands on chests. All eyes on me. Listen. Closely.

When I was a girl, I'd repeat spoken words – as they floated in the air and settled in a puff – created by my own breath. The words educator, instructor, and teacher would roll off my rosy, red lips - our lips – eager to taste, to drink, to consume - the language teacher spoke - effortlessly and interchangeably.

'Venture to Room 12 to consume science, Social studies is served down the hall.'

'Out of graph paper in Room 10? Grab some construction sheets, please.'

Eat, children. Eat.

When I was a girl, I received instructions. *Perform* calculations. *Write* prose. *Repeat* experiments. I'd solve Algebraic equations. Compose five-paragraph essays. Simulate flight. Following carefully crafted *Recipes*, printed on laminated five by eight cards. Though I don't believe I was Taught. My recollection blurs, my mind wonders - when, where, and how - did I - do we - learn?

Terms such as Teacher, Instructor, and Educator are tossed together like spice blends. *Pepper, Oregano, and Cumin*, mixed with blends of *Behaviorism, Cognitivism, and Constructivism* - like a daily special, and delivered vending machine style to rows upon rows of ravenous children.

Why, then, did I always leave hungry?

ON LEARNING WHAT TEACHING MIGHT HAVE BEEN

No longer a girl, I now know that not all instructors are teachers and that not all teachers are instructors.

Like any good Venn diagram, though, some centers – like Tropical Fruit jellybeans and handfuls of Skittles - burst with potential and Teachers who not only instruct but inspire.

I was one of the more fortunate *Oats*. A fridge stocked with cold milk – *Whole* - and a pantry with stacked boxes of *Lucky Charms*. Seven days a week. A middle school probability textbook - Chapter One – elementary, of course - spoke of those. A rare occurrence. Often fleeting in nature. I feared my milk would sour and my pantry might run dry. An unwelcome move: cross-town, down two floors, up another four – a converted one bedroom, with room for three - yielded a welcome surprise.

A real-life Lesson, prepped and cooked unlike any before. Cooked to order. New words. Project-based lessons, Problem-based learning, Anchored Instruction. Spices began to blend in savory ways. My nose was drawn to the scent. My tongue craved a taste. Delicious.

All eyes on Me. Face front. Listen, not to me, but to your heart, your vision, closely.

Sensory overload, grilled to perfection. I liked what I saw, heard, smelled, touched, and tasted. A room of hungry learners, eyes wide before the open buffet.

Choose your own adventure. *Pen* your own story. *Construct* a building, not to scale. *Draft* your own plans. *Imagine* your own tower.

Follow your own recipe. A work in progress. Taste as you go. Caution, the mess-hall floor might get dirty. The walls, too. If you slip, we'll catch you. And help with clean-up.

Ready. Set. Go.

A recipe like no other. An original.

ON LEARNING WHAT TEACHING SHOULD BE

After a crosstown move and a palette craving tastes and comforts of home,
I discovered the joys of new cuisines.

Teacher stood at the front of the room and shared a story. One of his time as a boy, in a neighborhood not unlike our own. Densely packed apartment blocks, with units of one, two, and three beds and often many more bodies. Galley kitchens - blends of gray, beige, and mocha linoleum - with stovetops simmering savory soups - chicken noodle, vegetable, chowder - and complex stews - fresh vegetables - plum tomatoes, broccoli spears, green peppers, celery stalks - chopped, diced, and sliced. Left on the pot to simmer, like the ideas we share as we raise our hands during period two - English class, my favorite - a time to talk, share, and write - five days a week.

Teacher talked to us like no other teacher before. No lectures or directives full of canned goods. Real talk - homemade, for us - Joey, Jules, Bianca, Mannie, Me. Real words - life wasn't fair, but we could do something about it. Real worlds. Real stories. Real plans. We read books with characters that lived the lives we lived. What Mama always called *Real Talk, in the kitchen.*

Immersed in a crowded classroom of novel faces and new flavors, I consumed – greedily.

I was hungry. No more stale goods. Fresh offerings on a daily basis. I constantly sought more – we all did.

Authentic plots that lacked fairy tale endings. Fiery city settings. Dense concrete arcs. Novels of the night and the streets. Curfew, anyone? We cooked – and feasted - late into the night.

Most of all, we consumed words – *Alphabet Soup* – and numbers – recipes unique to our zip code – the one on the other side of the tracks - that blended together just right.

Dog-eared chapter books
form bridges to and from worlds

hidden around corners

WORLDS OF FOUR WALLS

In worlds of four walls and chairs in preset formation, formal letters linger. Theory turns to policy turns to practice. My vision blurs of dizzy letters. Gazes shift to the chained window. I struggle to catch my breath. Systems maintain balance as students stumble on untied laces.
tiny blue bird
pecks fingerprint smudged glass
chalk scratches blackboard

Rulers turn to rules and bells bely balance.
on the inside out
and the outside in
tiny souls cut fresh marks
as stray words crack hopes just so

Wrap fingers around nearby No. 2. Ready. Set. Go.
1. Favorite teacher 2. Grade school memory 3. Classroom supply 4. Another word for lesson 5. Writing instrument 6. Drawing instrument 7. Elementary subject 8. Non-elementary subject 9. Favorite author from childhood 10. Favorite author from young adulthood 11. Poet 12. Poetic device 13. Grammatical concept 14. Important public, historical event. One word 15. An important private past experience. One word 16. A level of Bloom's Hierarchy (bottom half) 17. A level of Bloom's Hierarchy (top half) 18. The color of recess 19. The flavor of a school lunch 20. The taste of learning 21. Favorite season 22. The smell of a new school year 23. Another word for vulnerability 24. The sound of writing 25. Another word for chalk 26. A low level on Maslow's Hierarchy 27. A high level on Maslow's Hierarchy 28. Song lyrics from a school teaching, leading, and/or learning experience

Days of _1_, _2_, and _3_ weave _4_ with_5__ and _6_. Mornings of _7_. Late nights of __8__. Bookcases lined of _9__ and _10__. _11__, too. Lessons on _12__ and _13__. Projects grounded in theory where _14_ meets _15_. Exercises designed to _16__ and _17__ prompt bells and play of _18__, _19__, and __20_. With new beginnings and seasons, _21__ most of all, that come and ago, we open mouths and minds wide and inhale _22__ in rooms full of _23__. Seeking both _24__ and __25__, we consume/name/memorize __26__, apply/demonstrate _27___, and justify/sing __28___.

A Series of Inquiries

1. Which of the following words is least like the others? Why?

    Muse / Maze / Misery / Mystery / Mercury

2. Which of the following words is least like the others? Why?

    Inspire / Infuse / Impart / Imperfect

3. Define inspiration. Define perspiration.

    How are the two terms similar? Different?

4. Define blank. Define page.

    How are the two terms similar? Different?

5. How does a pencil differ from a ballpoint pen?
6. How does a keyboard differ from a composition notebook?
7. Define composition (noun). Define composition (adjective).

    Does inspiration reside most often in nouns or adjectives?

8. Which of the following items is least like the others?

    Composition / Notebook / Keyboard / Desktop

9. Which of the following items is least like the others?

    Pencil, Pen, Finger, Tip

10. Define erasure. Define eraser. How are the two terms similar? Different?
11. Which of the following terms is least like the others?

    Pedagogy, Pedantic, Pedestrian, Pedestal

12. Which of the following terms is least like the others?

    Foundations / Findings / Flavors / Feelings

13. What term is missing from the following list of terms?

    Inspiration / Creativity / Deadlines / _____

14. Define education. Define inspiration. How do the terms differ? How are the terms similar?
15. How does an educator differ from an instigator?
16. In what ways is a leader a learner?
17. In what ways is a learner a leader?
18. How does the source of education differ from the source of inspiration?
19. Define inspire. Define educate. Identify a single word (noun) that unites the two terms.
20. What qualities (adjectives) are found at the intersection of education and inspiration?

HINDSIGHT IS INDEED 2020

On a cold December day, in a year with unrelenting ails and still vast unknowns, I was, again, reminded of the joy that there is no end to the affronts of which humankind, often those of the most unpromising titles, is capable. Blood boils despite the season. Biting winds and unpredictable storms move not only mountains but people. No end, too, to the possibility. Joy not in the act but in the public response and the potential for change.

From the lectern, the podium, the printing press – they write. Of wars both near and far. Turns out the home front has never been friendly and not all weapons make sounds. Though waves roar. The Internet was loud last night. The night before, too. And will be for nights to come. Rough seas shall persist for the fight continues. Often in the dark of the night. By those too cowardly to stand. And those who find strength through solidarity. Because there is no other way. Ink on the page, egos on display. Words simultaneously large and small, with power to move not only mountains but miles. Digital divides fuse if for but a moment. A moment both long overdue and whose time is now. His pen expands and fills berths long known.

Take notes and prepare. Organize both in private and in public. Our union awaits. First, we quiz ourselves. We reflect. We query. We ready ourselves for life's many tests. The winter/winner and the wait lie long ahead. We check. Glasses. Gazes. We play. 20 (plus) Questions. Ready. Set. Go.

Quizzes, Queries, and Questions

Question 1. What do the following words have in common?

Madame / First / Lady / Title

Question 2. Which of the following words is most like the other? Least?

Madame / Mrs. / Kiddo / Doctor

Question 3. Define Class.
Question 4. What do the following have in common?

Earned / Doctorate / Title / Promising

Question 5.

Define Promise.
Define Promising.
How are the two similar? How are the two different?

Question 6. Which word doesn't belong?

Position / Proposition / Premonition / Predisposition / Predilection

Question 7. Given a series of firsts, does order ever cease to matter? Explain.
Question 8. What do the following words have in common?

Journal / Journey / Street / Wall

Question 9. What word is missing from the following list?

Solicit / Sequester / Silence / Stun / Stand

Question 10. What one word describes the offering of unsolicited advice?
Question 11. Arrange the following words in order.

Organize / Public / Stigma / Response / Bargain

Question 12. What do the following words have in common?

Doctor / Degree / Dignitary / Dignified / Dynamite

Question 13. What do the following words have in common?

Solidarity / Support / Schema / Stand / Stance

Question 14. What word is missing from the following list?

Work / Women / Union / Seat

Question 15. Choose one of the following. Prepare a short answer response.

To what degree might one expect one with an honorary doctorate to question another?
To what degree is affront a symptom of affluence? Of arrogance?
For what is ignorance an excuse?
For what is ignorance a defense?
For what is ignorance if not a call to action?
What do ignorance and irony have in common?

Question 16. Define Opinion.
Question 17. What word would you add to the following list?

Opinion / Opine / Ode / Obnoxiate

Question 18. What do the following words have in common? Which word is least like the others?

Publish / Perish / Polish / Promise

Question 19. How much is an opinion worth?
Question 20. What is a synonym for Teacher? One word.
Question 21. Where does "defend an opinion" fall on Bloom's Hierarchy?
Question 22. Where does self-actualization fall on Maslow's Hierarchy?

Note: This letter and the associated quiz were both inspired by and an outcome of the following opinion piece: https://www.wsj.com/articles/is-there-a-doctor-in-the-white-house-not-if-you-need-an-m-d-11607727380

These pieces seek to convey insights, reflections, accounts, and recollections that emerged as part of the student-teacher-leader educational communities of which I have been a participant in varying roles and to varied degrees. The pieces are attempts to capture thoughts in progress and to process thinking as what I previously understood to be dichotomies began to blend from "either/or" identities into "and" identities. As defining moments and student/teacher/leader experiences unfolded in real time, I would often find it hard if not impossible to process my related thinking. Creative writing emerged as a tool to both remember and to better understand a range of high-impact moments that have helped shaped my thinking and experiences as a woman working, learning, teaching, and leading in higher education. The experimental nature of the writing has helped me reframe and reinvent my thinking and become more comfortable with a journey which is neither linear nor traditionally and which also does not necessarily fall within traditional or any one definition of how to teach, lead, and learn as a woman in higher education. As my own understanding of leadership and resilience in higher education continues to transform, I also continue to embrace the uncertainty and the challenges that are inherent in academia as I continue to learn from the successes as well as the struggles of those around me and those that have served before me.

In addition to the support networks formed through formal study, and as described earlier in this chapter, opportunities to engage in the practice of creative writing also led to new learning and insights that extended (and continue to extend) beyond the study of craft to include insights on the practices of teaching and leading in higher education. Given the openness and flexibility inherent to creative writing, assessments themselves became opportunities for ongoing growth as a teacher and leader. Not only did the support networks help build resiliency and provide much-needed energy, assigned writing exercises as well as associated peer workshop feedback helped refine and sharpen my thinking and understanding of how to lead and teach in higher education as well as how to balance competing responsibilities. It feels odd to frame the practice of formal study in creative writing as both therapeutic and targeted training for higher education leadership, but in my experiences, I believe both to be true. In terms of what one might draw from my own personal experiences, it is hard to say. What I feel more confident suggesting, though, is that formal study while leading has the potential to yield many benefits, including surprising positive bonuses outcomes above and beyond the acquisition of additional content-specific skills and knowledge.

While I have found the process of creative writing to be therapeutic, reflexive, and an especially helpful thinking tool while teaching, leading, and learning in higher education, publication, especially in spaces that are outside of the typical academic journal publication pathway, is also a way to build community and further conversations in this space.

There are many opportunities to publish and share creative reflections and written work to further build community and shared reflections regarding multiple identities and ways of leading in this context. Doing so is also an opportunity to explore alternative conceptions of what it means to engage in scholarly work in academic spaces. For example, there are numerous outlets, many of which adopt a feminist perspective, that welcome creative writing as a tool to explore issues of education and leadership in educational spaces. Sample journals include WSQ (themed) published by the Feminist Press (https://www.feministpress.org/), NCTE (https://ncte.org/resources/journals/english-journal/call-for-manuscripts/), and Practicing Anthropology, among others. Trish Hopkinson publishes a list of additional outlets and lit mags accepting feminist poetry. See: https://trishhopkinson.com/feminist-lit-mags-journals/.

CONCLUDING (FUTURE-FORWARD-FOCUSED) THOUGHTS

In conclusion, it is critical to note that the insights shared herein are by no means unique. While the experiences I have had as a student have transformed my work as an educator as well as a leader in higher education, nothing I suggest is novel. Similarly, arguments against binary thinking are strong and long-standing. While I hope that the shared experiences encourage further discourse surrounding both the benefits and challenges of pursuing further education while teaching and leading, I also hope the experiences prompts ongoing conversation, community, and collaboration as well as related research into the benefits, challenges, and lived experiences of a dual identity of higher education leader and student, beyond a focus on professional development sessions and conferences, like similar research done in the context of student athletes. Engelke and Frederickson (2022), for example, explore the lived experience of nursing student athletes. DeGrande and Painter (2023) undertake an evaluation of the experiences of working nurses attending graduate school during COVID-19. Quinaud et a. (2023) examine the influence of both individual and contextual characteristics on student-athlete identities during the undergraduate college years. Relatedly, Lee-Johnson (2022), conducts an analysis of the lived experiences of immigrant mothers of color who became certified English Language Learner teachers and argues in support of intersectionality, drawing upon Crenshaw (1989) as an avenue and opportunity to transform teaching and learning practices, drawing upon Mezirow's (1991) transformative learning, and ideologies in teacher preparation programs.

Moreover, much of my own reflection on the student, faculty, administrator, and leader experience has crystallized, at least initially, in the form of creative writing and poetry. Some argue that writing and the act of writing is a way to further crystallize thinking and to deepen active engagement, presence, and mindfulness. In my own experiences, this has proven true and, for anyone pursuing education alongside their roles as teaching faculty and/or administrator, I encourage writing to accompany the learning and reflection process. As an example, and also as a way to further encourage reflective thinking in connection with either/or dichotomies, binary thinking, and intersectionality in educational teaching, leading, and learning spaces, the illustrative series of interactive and experimental poetry reflects both my personal responses and experiences in simultaneous student, faculty, and administrator roles and moments and that are shared with the hopes of prompting further inquiry regarding positionality, impact, and the intersectionality of simultaneous statuses in educational spaces.

The same, I think, can be said for simultaneously experiencing education as a student while teaching and leading in similar spaces. Recognizing, acknowledging, and embracing the positive benefits associated with adopting multiple identities as student, teacher, and leader has transformed my own experiences as a woman in higher education. As discussed, I have grown into a space where part of my intentionality and reflexive practice as a teacher and leader means I also simultaneously adopt a student identity and take courses as I teach and lead in higher education. The intentional process of deliberately adopting and maintaining multiple identities and roles has offered additional opportunities to draw strength from reflexive analysis of similarities and shared experiences. My simultaneous status as "student" in addition to "leader" in higher education has been a defining moment for me and I hope the reflections and personal accounts shared throughout this chapter have prompted further reflection on the issue of shared identities as teacher, leader, and student in educational institutions of higher learning.

REFERENCES

Apsey, A., & Couros, G. (2024). *What Makes a Great Principal: The Five Pillars of Effective School Leadership*. Impress Press.

Bandura, A. (1989). Human agency in social cognitive theory. *The American Psychologist*, 44(9), 1175–1184. http://www.stiftelsen-hvasser.no/documents/Bandura_Human_Agency_in_social_Cognitiv_theory.pdf. DOI: 10.1037/0003-066X.44.9.1175 PMID: 2782727

Calling attention to gender bias dramatically changes course evaluations. (2019, May 30). *Politics & Government Business*.

Carriuolo, N. E., Rodgers, A., Stout, C. M., & Garcia, J. (2002). Valuing and Building from Strengths of Hispanic Students: An Interview with Juliet Garcia. *Journal of Developmental Education*, 25(3), 20–42.

Chandler, K. (2003). Spin Cycle. *Cincinnati Magazine*, 37(3), 66–71.

Channing, J. ""Oh, I'm a Damsel in Distress": Women Higher Education Leaders' Narratives" (2022). Journal of Women in Educational Leadership. 281. https://digitalcommons.unl.edu/jwel/281

Collins, P. H. (1991). *Black feminist thought: Knowledge, consciousness, and the politics of empowerment*. Routledge.

Columbia Law School. (2017). Kimberlé Crenshaw on Intersectionality, More than Two Decades Later. https://www.law.columbia.edu/news/archive/kimberle-crenshaw-intersectionality-more-two-decades-later

Course survey reforms aim to reduce gender, other bias in evaluation process. (2016, April 29). *UWIRE Text*, 1.

Crenshaw, K. (1989) "Demarginalizing the Intersection of Race and Sex: A Black Feminist Critique of Antidiscrimination Doctrine, Feminist Theory and Antiracist Politics," University of Chicago Legal Forum: Vol. 1989: Iss. 1, Article 8. Available at: https://chicagounbound.uchicago.edu/uclf/vol1989/iss1/8

de la Teja, M. H. (2022) "Natalicio, Eleanor Diana Siedhoff," *Handbook of Texas Online*. https://www.tshaonline.org/handbook/entries/natalicio-eleanor-diana-siedhoff

DeGrande, H., Seifert, M., & Painter, E. (2023). The Experience of Working Nurses Attending Graduate School During COVID-19: A Hermeneutic Phenomenology Study. *SAGE Open Nursing*, 9, 1–12. DOI: 10.1177/23779608231186676 PMID: 37435583

Engelke, E. C., & Frederickson, K. (2022). Dual Collegiate Roles? The Lived Experience of Nursing Student Athletes. *The Journal of Nursing Education*, 61(3), 117–122. https://doi-org.ezproxy.snhu.edu/10.3928/01484834-20220109-01. DOI: 10.3928/01484834-20220109-01 PMID: 35254153

Finding Your Roots with Henry Louis Gates. Jr. (n.d.). Season 1, Episode 7: "Samuel L. Jackson, Condoleezza Rice and Ruth Simmons". https://www.pbs.org/weta/finding-your-roots/about/meet-our-guests/ruth-simmons

Flakes, K. (2023). 11 Leadership Takeaways from Dr. Ruth Simmons, the First Black Woman to Lead an Ivy League College. https://www.kennethflakes.com/post/11-leadership-lessons-from-dr-ruth-simmons

Gladwell, M. (2011). *Outliers*. Back Bay Books.

Gollub, J. P. (2002). *Learning and understanding: Improving advanced study of mathematics and science in U.S. high schools*. National Academy Press.

Gutshall, C. A. (2020). When Teachers Become Students: Impacts of Neuroscience Learning on Elementary Teachers' Mindset Beliefs, Approach to Learning, Teaching Efficacy, and Grit. *European Journal of Psychology and Educational Research*, 3(1), 39–48. DOI: 10.12973/ejper.3.1.39

Hattie (2020). Visible learning. Retrieved from https://visible-learning.org/

Inspirational Poetry Quotes. (2019). https://paulathewriter.com/2019/04/17/inspirational-quotes-poetry/

Joutz, M. (2018). Ruth Simmons on Cultivating the Next Generation of College Students. *The New York Times*.https://www.nytimes.com/2018/02/28/opinion/hbcu-ruth-simmons-interview.html

Kahn, K. (2009). Shattering glass ceilings nothing new for SUNY chancellor. *Westchester County Business Journal*, 48(32), 31–34.

Kauffman, J. (2020). *The Personal MBA*. Portfolio.

Kini, A., & Suvarna, R. (2023). Interim President Donna Shalala wants to improve life at The New School by listening to what students want. New School Free Press. https://www.newschoolfreepress.com/2023/11/27/interim-president-donna-shalala-wants-to-improve-life-at-the-new-school-by-listening-to-what-students-want/

Lee-Johnson, Y. I. N. L. A. M. (2022). When Immigrant Mothers of Color Become Public School Teachers for English Language Learners: Intersectionality for Transformative Teacher Preparation. *TESOL Quarterly*.

Longman, K. A., Terrill, K., Mallet, G., Tchindebet, J., & Fernando, R. (2021). Developing a Leader Identity: The Lived Experiences of People of Color Identified as "Emerging Leaders.". *Journal of Ethnographic and Qualitative Research*, 15(4), 264–283.

Luscombe, A. (2018). Eleanor Roosevelt: A Crusading Spirit to Move Human Rights Forward. *Netherlands Quarterly of Human Rights*, 36(4), 241–246. DOI: 10.1177/0924051918801610

Mantzourani, E., Chang, H., Desselle, S., Canedo, J., & Fleming, G. (2022). Reflections of mentors and mentees on a national mentoring programme for pharmacists: An examination into relationships, personal and professional development. *Research in Social & Administrative Pharmacy*, 18(3), 2495–2504. DOI: 10.1016/j.sapharm.2021.04.019 PMID: 34120869

Martin, F., & Bolliger, D. U. (2023). Designing online learning in higher education. In Zawacki-Richter, O., & Jung, I. (Eds.), *Handbook of Open* (pp. 1217–1236). Distance and Digital Education., DOI: 10.1007/978-981-19-2080-6_72

Martin, F., Polly, D., & Ritzhaupt, A. (2020). Bichronous online learning: Blending asynchronous and synchronous online learning. Educause Review. https://er.educause.edu/articles/2020/9/bichronous-online-learning-blending asynchronous-and-synchronous-online-learning

Martinelle, R., & Stevens, K. (2024). Making Space for Principled Resistance: When leaders reimagine PD, they can help teachers become strategic activists for themselves and their students. *Educational Leadership*, 81(8), 16–21.

Merryfield, M. (2003). Like a veil: Cross-cultural experiential learning online. *Contemporary Issues in Technology & Teacher Education*, 3(2), 146–171.

Mezirow, J. (1991). *Transformative Dimensions of Adult Learning*. Jossey-Bass.

Moore, C. (2019). How to address a teacher around the world. Retrieved from https://www.expatica.com/education/children-education/how-do-children-address-their-teachers-across-the-globe-472217/

28% of Women in Higher Ed Fault Gender Bias. (2022, April 15). *The Chronicle of Higher Education*, 68(16), 14.

Pennamon, T. (2019). A Champion for Access and Excellence in Public Higher Education. *Diverse Issues in Higher Education*, 36(10), 14–15.

Picard, R. W., Papert, S., Bender, W., Blumberg, B., Breazeal, C., Cavallo, D., Machover, T., Resnick, M., Roy, D., & Strohecker, C. (2004). Affective Learning — A Manifesto. *BT Technology Journal*, 22(4), 253–269. DOI: 10.1023/B:BTTJ.0000047603.37042.33

Quigley, A. (2020). Is this a brave new world for teacher CPD? Schools have innovated amazingly well to allow staff development to continue over recent months - but studies show that effective CPD requires more than just one-off video sessions. *TES: Magazine*, 5411, 29.

Quinaud, R. T., Possamai, K., Gonçalves, C. E., & Carvalho, H. M. (2023). Student-Athlete Identity Variation Across the Undergraduate Period: A Mixed-Methods Study. *Perceptual & Motor Skills*, 130(2), 876–901. Radin, B. A. (2007). Qualified to Learn the Job: Donna Shalala. *Public Administration Review*, 67(3), 504–510.

Román, M. (2018). President Diana Natalicio reflects on the last 30 years leading UTEP. *The Prospector Daily*. https://www.theprospectordaily.com/2018/03/20/president-diana-natalicio-reflects-on-the-last-30-years-leading-utep/

Schneider, E. (1993). *Feminism and the False Dichotomy of Victimization and Agency*. 38 N.Y.L. Sch. L. Rev. 387.

Smith, E. (2008). Diana Natalicio. *Texas Monthly (Austin, Tex.)*, 36(2), 90–96.

Treacy, M., & Leavy, A. (2023). Student voice and its role in creating cognitive dissonance: The neglected narrative in teacher professional development. *Professional Development in Education*, 49(3), 458–477. DOI: 10.1080/19415257.2021.1876147

Webster's Seventh New Collegiate Dictionary. (1969). G. & C. Merriam Company.

Wiggins, G. (2012). Seven keys to effective feedback. Retrieved from http://www.ascd.org/publications/educational-leadership/sept12/vol70/num01/seven-keys-to-effective-feedback.aspx

Will, M. (2021, August 18). When Teachers and School Counselors Become Informal Mentors, Students Thrive. *Education Week*, 40(1), 16.

Wolfgarth, M. (2011). An Appealing Profession. *Cobblestone*, 32(3), 16–17.

Worthen, M. (2017). U can't talk to ur professor like this. Retrieved from https://www.nytimes.com/2017/05/13/opinion/sunday/u-cant-talk-to-ur-professor-like-this.html/

Chapter 9
Mentoring the Next Generation of Women Leaders
Investigating the Role of Women Leaders in Supporting the Development of Future Generations

Mohit Yadav
 https://orcid.org/0000-0002-9341-2527
O.P. Jindal Global University, India

Parth Sharma
 https://orcid.org/0000-0002-1955-9408
University of Petroleum and Energy Studies, India

Phuong Mai Nguyen
 https://orcid.org/0000-0002-2704-9707
International School, Vietnam National University, Hanoi, Vietnam

ABSTRACT

This chapter explores the pivotal role of mentorship in developing the next generation of women leaders. It examines how mentorship programs can empower women to overcome barriers, build confidence, and advance in their careers. Key themes include the integration of technological advancements, the emphasis on diversity and inclusivity, and the evolution of mentorship models. The chapter also addresses the future of mentorship, focusing on global networks, the impact of remote work,

DOI: 10.4018/979-8-3693-3144-6.ch009

and emerging challenges. By analyzing best practices and providing actionable insights, this chapter offers a roadmap for organizations to create effective mentorship programs that support women's leadership development. The ultimate goal is to foster a more equitable and innovative leadership landscape, where diverse voices and experiences contribute to organizational success and societal progress.

INTRODUCTION

Mentoring is identified as a great practice in leadership development in providing guidance, support, and knowledge transfer to burgeoning leaders (Pickett, 2022). Mentorship is even more critical for women who aim to reach leadership statuses since it offers them pathways to navigate the unique difficulties and system barriers they are always found to face in life. Although women have broken into leadership across diverse sectors, many still remain grossly underrepresented. This underrepresentation in such sectors recognizes a continuous require effective strategies that can promote gender variety and inclusiveness in leadership. Women leaders play a critical role in mentoring the next generation, not only through sharing their experiences and insights but also by challenging and reshaping the organizational cultures that have traditionally impeded women's advancement. The discussion in the next chapter further elaborates on the leadership role of women in terms of their mentoring, using both personal narrations and expert interviews to understand the kind of impact the mentoring relationships have on the mentor and the mentee. These stories illustrate the transformative power of mentorship and, it is hoped, will help to increase the continued participation of women leaders in this important work to support the next generation.

THE CURRENT STATE OF WOMEN IN LEADERSHIP

There have been great advances for women in leadership in the last few decades, but women stay far from parity in the world's top environments. Despite the huge efforts taken in promoting gender inclusiveness, underrepresentation of women at the executive and board levels compared to their male counterparts remains (Kakabadse, Figueira, Nicolopoulou, Hong Yang, Kakabadse & Özbilgin, 2015). In recent statistics, though women made almost half the global labor share, they held negligible proportions in the senior leadership. It is even more significant within male-dominated sectors such as technology, finance, and manufacturing, which are the so-called 'glass ceiling' causing the much sticky path on the forefront of the battle.

Numerous forces contribute to a woman's leadership profile these days. Cultural and social stereotypes determine the way in which Women's competencies to handle and occupy leading positions are projected within social perspectives; this ultimately impacts recruitment and promotion (Adom, & Anambane, 2020). Moreover, some other barriers that uniquely affect this part of the workforce are work–life imbalance, lack of focuses on building professional networks, and a dearth of role models supporting their advancement. Women of colour and other minorities, LGBTQ+ women, and women with disabilities face heightened discriminatory and bias practices that make levelling the playing field for them an even bigger challenge.

Despite those challenges, many women have carved their paths to leadership and have served as exemplars and change agents in their respective areas of interest. In addition to breaking down barriers, such women become strong role models for the next generation and serve as examples that with resilience, determination, and the aid of support, it can be done.

Interviews with experts for this chapter offer important insights concerning the current situation of women in leadership. Many of these leaders emphasized the importance of mentorship and sponsorship in their own career progression, saying that these relationships really gave them a lot of visibility, increased their own self-belief, and helped them navigate complex organizational dynamics. The interviews also provide, in women leaders, evidence of the growing realization of the need to create environments that can be supportive for other women, instilling a culture of inclusion and collaboration that may help in abolishing the barriers that are systemic.

Still another factor that can be attached is the fact that business cases for diversity are, in all increasing cases, gradually putting in place more inclusive leadership models that value different perspectives and experiences. Early indications are that companies with aggressive diversity and inclusion policies are already seeing concrete returns from increasingly gender-neutral leadership teams in terms of decision quality, innovation, and financial performance. These changes, although very incremental, stand in evidence of the hope of an improved future for women in leadership.

While the landscape of women in leadership is changing, it will really take some work to accomplish real gender parity. A lot can be done to develop the next generation of women leaders and to bring inclusivity and diversity into the leadership landscape by knowing where we are in the present and learning from those who have gone before.

THE ROLE OF MENTORSHIP IN DEVELOPING WOMEN LEADERS

Mentorship is the major building block for women leaders in developing available critical guidance, needed support, and inspiration throughout the professional journey they undertake (Brizuela, Chebet, & Thorson, 2023). In leadership development, mentorship goes beyond the simple transfer of knowledge and skills to the building of relationships that are empowering to the mentee to be able to confront, with success, special challenges and tasks in their careers at the critical points in their development. Mentorship, in its various forms, is considered a great opportunity for women to develop confidence, visibility, and access to opportunities which are usually beyond their reach (Bhatti, & Ali, 2021). For women, who often have to battle gender biases and restricted access to key informal networks for advancement, mentorship opens doors to developing confidence, visibility, and access to opportunities that, in other circumstances, would be beyond their reach. Mentorship for women leaders could mean formal and structured one-on-one pairings or informal and organically growing relationships. Each form has its benefits. Formal mentorship usually involves the pairing of experienced leaders with rising talents through clear boundaries and objectives with which to help guide the relationship (Zachary, & Fain, 2022). These are often wrapped in with regular check-ins, goals, and structured feedback—all toward the one-on-one mentee's professional growth. On the other hand, an informal mentorship relationship can be initiated from common interests or shared experiences, and thus it can take a very personal and flexible course, allowing for a deeper connection and more tailored guidance.

One of the important gains of mentorship in cases of women is the engagement of a mentee with someone who understands better about treading challenges. Women mentors, therefore, can give an account of their stories: how they overcame gender biases, balanced work and personal life, and broke through the glass ceiling with real-life advice and strategies for their mentees (Dashper, 2020). These shared experiences assure the mentees that they are understood and hence supported, drawing away from the feeling of isolation and self-doubt that is brought about by such environments. In addition, mentors can advocate or sponsor by opening doors for mentees, recommending projects, promotions, or leadership opportunities in some way that advance the progress of one's career. Mentorships provide a boost to confidence-building among aspiring women leaders. Positive reinforcement and constructive feedback from mentors help increase the self-efficacy and belief in one's potential. The confidence that ensues from the above is crucial because it will enable women to take up challenges, flow with the crowd, and be seen and felt in instances where they are probably the minority. The mentors come in to help the mentees in navigating organizational politics and culture, enabling them to have insights into unwritten rules and norms that usually determine up-or-out systems in careers.

Moreover, having a mentor in the organization very much helps by cultivating a culture of both learning and development for the mentor himself. If mentees get knowledge and acquire experience, mentors also gain the traits of leadership, the power of broader thinking, and derive a feeling of personal victory from the success of others. It places a mentor at the very center of learning and development and moves him or her to a new level of knowledge. This interactive nature of mentoring forms a positive feedback loop that contributes to the overall inclusiveness and support of the workplace environment.

Powerful interviews done in this chapter have emphasized the kind of transformational changes that have taken place because of mentorship for women leaders. This is supported by the fact that a majority of the women leaders have credited their success to mentorship early in their career. They say that having somebody to believe in them and guide them through was a critical factor that helped overcome barriers and capitalize on the opportunity. These stories underline the role of mentorship in creating not just technical and professional ability but also in developing a leadership identity with congruent purpose.

Mentorship is a key element of leadership development for women, which provides an opportunity, a guideline, and a way to get over the hurdles and emerge successful in careers. Organizations that can develop a strong partnership of mentorship will again have the ability to create a pipeline of talented women leaders in which the mantle is held high with confidence, creativity, and resilience. At the end of it all, this goes a mile to build a richer, more diverse, and inclusive leadership landscape, which is beneficial to all.

WOMEN LEADERS AS MENTORS: MOTIVATIONS AND APPROACHES

Indeed, activity within women leader mentoring is taken to be purposeful and committed to the future of the next generation of women. Their motivations for mentoring are wide and relate to life and world experiences, professional goals, and a desire to give back to the communities. In short, many women leaders view mentoring to be a means of bringing about change—one that corrects the inequalities based on gender—and one way that they can leave their mark, among what they have done through mentorship. Indeed, learning such motivations and the diverse strategies women employ can be highly instructive for understanding the effect of mentorship, and the most useful way of its practice.

A key motivation for many women leaders to become a mentor is a desire to pay this forward. Such leaders typically are well accustomed, due to gender bias, lack of representation, and unequal access to opportunities, to overcoming immense odds themselves and so have personal experiences that place a great deal of value on support and mentoring. They know from real-life experiences just how positively a mentor can affect a career for a woman, amounting to more than advice but also forthcoming with encouragement and advocacy. This might help them get the understanding that drives them to want to mentor others, be that support that at one time mentored them or that they in their minds felt could have made the difference. They hope that by advising another woman on how to handle similar situations, that may smoothen or bring more success to the journey for the person that comes later.

Further, women leaders are driven by the urge to eliminate gender imbalances in selling some leadership positions (Bodalina, & Mestry, 2022). Through mentoring of women, they will directly impact the creation of a leadership pipeline that is more diverse and inclusive. Most importantly, it is of great significance in places where the numbers of women are below par. Mentoring allows infrastructural leaders to fight quite actively against systemic barriers that have historically held women back, whether they are gender stereotypes or the lack of role models. In empowering other women to leadership, they are having a stake in individual careers, but by extension, they are motivating cultural and organizational change.

Another motivating factor for women in leadership positions to mentor others is the personal and professional development that can be achieved through the mentorship process (Read, Fisher & Juran, 2020). Mentoring encourages self-reflection and self-awareness, whereby mentor learns as much as the mentee does. This interchange allows mentors to gain new perspectives, keep in touch with emerging trends, and improve their own leadership and communication skills. Additionally, having the experience of mentoring can be personally gratifying because it brings a sense of fulfillment and satisfaction in that one knows he or she is making a difference tangibly in someone's life and career (Sarathi, 2023).

Women tend to mentor in ways that best suit their needs and the needs of their mentees, and the environments they find themselves in (Saffie-Robertson, 2020). Others gravitate more to the formal in terms of clearly setting expectations, defining certain goals and meeting on a regular basis to ensure the goals are being met. This approach works well in any form of corporate or organizational context where formalized mentorship has been established to facilitate the growth of emerging competent employees. In such scenarios, the protégés can focus on one or two critical competencies such as strategic thinking or leadership, where mentors provide a more specific direction on guidance and coaching towards achieving short-term and long-term professional goals for the mentee.

Some women take a more flexible, relationship-based approach to mentorship. These are symbolized by a vague, organic rhythm characterized by the development of trust and encouragement on the need basis. Informal mentoring usually develops with time, linking a mentor and mentee through a shared interest, experience, or professional affinity. In all other aspects, informal mentoring lets the mentor act as a confidante and sounding board in the needs or challenges the mentee has at the moment, without providing any kind of plotted-out agenda for what is to be done (Starr, 2021) This method can be especially effective when it comes to making mentees free to express any ideas and concerns open-hearted and without judgment.

Aside from these, a few women leaders had been using the model of mentorship, which is known as the sponsorship model (Singh & Vanka, 2020). Unlike the mentorship model, where mentors guide and advice mentees, this model goes a step further, whereby the mentor advocates for the mentees and ensures that some work areas are visible to the mentee and linking them to very powerful networks and opportunities. Sponsors use their power and authority to advance and advocate for their protégés' careers by putting them forward for promotions, high-profile projects, and other important assignments that further their overall learning. This kind of mentorship can be considered the keen help for women to break the glass ceiling, so they are prepared for leadership positions and even attain them.

Expert interviews highlight that the most effective mentors are adaptive in their approach to meet the needs of the person they are working with. They are good listeners, show empathy, and have a willingness to share their experience, if necessary, with successes and failures to build rapport and trust. They understand that mentoring is not something that you can cut to a template and that each mentoring case is uniquely different, requiring different strategies and levels of engagement.

To sum up, women leaders mentor for different reasons, ranging from giving back and the issue of gender inequities to personal growth and gaining satisfaction from the same (House, Dracup, Burkinshaw, Ward, & Bryant, 2021). Their practices of mentoring are as diverse as the use of formal, informal relationship-based interactions, and sponsorship programs. Understanding these reasons and strategies will enable organizations to guide these activities with more support and motivation, ultimately serving toward a more equal and inclusive leadership network.

CHALLENGES AND OPPORTUNITIES IN MENTORING WOMEN LEADERS

Mentoring women leaders is both a privilege and an effective channel for nurturing the next crop of women leaders. However, it is not free of challenges. For a mentor and mentee, one is exposed to different barriers that tend to have an effect, at times, on the effectiveness of the mentoring relationship. Nonetheless, for every challenge, such opportunities are viewed to make available numerous valuable lessons and thoughts that may be integrated into the reinforcement of a mentoring process. It is in knowing these challenges and opportunities that a perfect and empowered environment can be developed for these women leaders. Although times have significantly changed in terms of achieving gender equality, many preconceived ideas remain in place about a woman's ability and leadership style. These biases may drive not just colleagues' treatment and view of the mentee but also the treatment and view of many other mentees' superiors and mentors. The resultant effect is one where mentors have to help their mentees navigate through such professional biases, offering strategies to use perception management and self-advocacy in the workplace. Mentors also have to be watchful on unconscious bias in their interactions with people so that everyone, especially women receive equal measures of support and motivation.

Another very significant barrier is that in some industries, there are very few women leaders. If there are fewer women at the helm, then obviously the scope for aspiring women leaders to get a mentor who resonates with their concerns more and who has similar advice to give to them is low (Durbin, Lopes, & Warren, 2020). In this regard, as a consequence, women face an enormous problem in terms of their adequate imagination of leading roles and identification with a role model within the context of their career pathways. For this reason, organizations need to go out of their way to include women in leadership and provide formal mentorship programs that will link up potential women leaders with experienced mentors.

This might also hold true for work-life balance, which often, for both mentor and mentee, becomes challenging in the case of women's mentoring relationships. Almost all the women leaders have multiple roles in society, which comprises family obligations, professional ambitions, and personal development (Abalkhail, 2020). These roles might consume a lot of time and energies of the women, leaving limited opportunities for mentoring. In this context, a question arises as to how to keep in regular contact and meaningful interactions. Secondly, mentees may also be very busy balancing their career development and many other pursuits; this potentially hampers their active involvement in their mentoring process. To continue the mentoring process despite this phenomenon, the development of boundary distance between each other must be set by the mentors and mentees through open communication, open commitment, flexibility in scheduling to speak or communicate by mail, and to meet each other's need.

Challenges apart, mentoring women leaders is an opportunity carrying out enormous scope for growing and developing women to fulfill their potential. One fundamental value is being able to build strong, alternating networks beyond the immediate mentoring relationship. With a mentor, a woman can always reach out to somebody with a like mind, share resources, and work upon projects together to create a net of support that mutually makes one another succeed. Such networks can further offer the ability to reach other diverse opportunities like talking engagements, drive programs, and also provide people with a chance to flourish their careers that they never would.

Mentoring, in other aspects, allows one challenge or transform the already set norms and sometimes bad practices that might be in place and have been seen to disrupt the womens' prosperity in their place of work. In so doing, women leaders can role-model to others the way to lead inclusively and equitably, making the point that a range of leadership styles is effective and valuable. This encouragement would also offer an opportunity to mentor by demonstrating a stand in solidarity with organizational policies and practices supporting gender diversity—flexible working, clear promotion policies, and anti-bias review processes—to influence organizational culture. These efforts create a more inclusive environment not only beneficial to women but also to all employees.

On top of this, mentoring relationships are an amazing platform for personal and professional growth: mentees get invaluable insights into leadership and career management due to the examples and mistakes their mentors make and share (Soran & Kara, 2022). The course can help the mentees become more confident, develop basic skills, and develop career focus. On the other hand, mentors are also enriched by the young talent's new ideas on the ground, coupled with having their way of leadership enhanced and instilled in the innovation spirit. There is mutual gain here, which is an exchange of expertise and experience.

The other opportunity of mentoring the women in leadership is that it goes a long way in terms of impact and legacy. Women can also contribute to the long-term success and sustainability of their organizations and industries by building the next generation of female leaders (Pierli, Murmura & Palazzi, 2022). The success in the talent life cycle of women can also shape the future of leadership by building a talent pipeline filled with diversified and talented women. The goal is not only to advocate gender equity but also to make organizations benefit from a wider pool of perspectives and experiences that enhance quality in decision-making and bring about innovative solutions.

While mentoring women leaders comes with many challenges, it is in these very ones that opportunities for growth, learning, and positive change can be found. It is in understanding and addressing such challenges that mentors and mentees can create more effective and empowering relationships that support the development of women leaders. Embracing such opportunities arising out of challenges will have transformative outcomes on individuals, organizations, and society at large.

RESEARCH METHODOLOGY

This qualitative study deploys two methods: expert interviews and narrations, to identify the role of mentorship in developing women leaders. These methods bring out extensive information about the experiences, practices, and views of the people who participate in mentorship programs. The following sections describe the design of the research, data collection, and analysis procedures applied in this work.

1. Design of the Study

The research design taps into the intricacies of mentorship and its power in women leaders by drawing from experts and practitioners in the field. This paper, therefore, captures the depth stories and expertise that speak to complexities of mentorship in the varying organizational contexts by data collection for qualitative data.

2. Data Collection

Expert Interviews: Seven senior experts in leadership and mentorship were subjected to an in-depth, semiformal interview. The experts are senior leaders, program directors, and consultants who have accumulated considerable experience in the development and implementation of mentorship programs. The interview was designed to elicit detailed responses about the efficiency of mentorship practices, challenges faced, and future trends. The semi-structured format allows for flexibility—probing deeper into specific topics based on the expert's response.

Narrations: Interviews are complemented by personal narrations from mentors and mentees who have gone through mentorship programs. The narrations give a firsthand account of individual experiences, thus capturing both the emotional and practical aspects of the mentoring relationship. Individuals were encouraged to tell their stories of success, challenges, and how mentorship has impacted their personal and professional development. The narrations were captured in writing and audio recordings to fully capture their experiences.

3. Data Analysis

Thematic Analysis: The data from the expert interviews and narrations were analyzed using thematic analysis. It is a methodology wherein the researcher identifies, analyzes, and reports patterns or themes within the data. It consisted of the transcription of the interviews and narrations, followed by text coding to identify key themes and sub-themes related to mentorship practices, challenges, and future directions. Thematic analysis gave meaningful insights that could be elicited and developed in a coherent narrative about the role of mentorship in supporting women leaders.

Triangulation: This approach was used to increase the credibility and validity of the findings. The technique involved checking for consistency and reliability by comparing and contrasting data from the two different sources: expert interviews and personal narrations. Such a study could also have been undertaken to achieve a more firmly grounded insight into the mentorship landscape by cross-referencing insights from multiple perspectives.

4. Ethical Considerations

The investigation followed all ethical criteria for research on human participants. Written informed consent was sought from all interviewees and narrators about the purpose of the study and the rights of research subjects. All respondents' answers were kept confidential by anonymizing their responses and ensuring security measures for the storage of the data. In addition, respondents had a chance to go through and approve their contributions before publication.

Such methodology will allow the combination of expert interviews and personal narrations to be performed comprehensively in order to explore mentorship as a critical leadership development initiative for women. The above approach is likely to project nuanced insight into challenges, successes, and future directions of mentorship programs that add meaningfully to the greater discourse on leadership and gender equity.

DATA ANALYSIS

Table 1 showcases the Quotes from 7 experts with the names and designations. Also, based upon analysis themes were generated and later discussed in detail as well. The themes are also mentioned in the table 1.

Table 1. Expert Quotes

No.	Name	Designation	Quotes	Themes
1	Dr. Aisha Verma	CEO	"Mentoring is not just about providing guidance but about empowering women to realize their full potential and shatter glass ceilings."	Empowerment and Breaking Barriers
2	Priya Deshmukh	Director of Operation	"Creating a safe and supportive space for women leaders to grow is essential for nurturing talent and building a strong leadership pipeline."	Creating Supportive Environments
3	Radhika Iyer	Founder	"We need to actively seek out and support young women leaders, showing them that leadership is attainable and that their voices matter."	Advocacy and Inclusivity
4	Anjali Kapoor	CSO	"Mentorship should focus on skill-building and confidence enhancement, equipping women with tools to navigate complex professional landscapes."	Skill Development and Confidence Building
5	Meera Joshi	MD	"Diverse mentoring approaches, including sponsorship, are crucial in providing women with the opportunities they need to succeed."	Diversity in Mentorship Approaches
6	Sneha Rao	HR Head	"As mentors, we have a responsibility to challenge biases and advocate for policies that support gender equality in the workplace."	Challenging Biases and Policy Advocacy
7	Kavita Patel	Senior VP	"Mentoring is a two-way street; it's about learning and growing together, fostering mutual respect, and sharing knowledge across generations."	Mutual Growth and Knowledge Sharing

ANALYSIS AND ELABORATION OF THEMES FROM EXPERT INTERVIEWS

Analysis of the expert interviews regarding the chapter on "Mentoring the Next Generation of Women Leaders" identified a number of critical themes, which therefore bring out the complications, opportunities, and scope for mentoring women leaders. These themes give a broad outline of contemporary practices, challenges, and future directions in mentorship. The following is an expanded argument about the identified themes:

1. Empowerment and Breaking Barriers

Analysis from experts has it that mentorship should go beyond career advice to mentoring that empowers women to break systemic barriers for their full potential to be harnessed. It is essential for the mentors to help the mentees recognize the barriers along their way for them to grow, like gender biases and workplace inequalities.

Empowerment programs typically include components to increase self-esteem, hardiness, and assertiveness among women leaders. Mentoring helps in overcoming these primary constraints with interventions that encompass salary negotiation, handling workplace conflicts, and self-affirming one's leadership. Components of advocacy, involving mentors in a more structured way to back mentees' visibility and access to opportunities that might otherwise be out of reach for them to form part of such effective programs.

2. Creating Supportive Environments

Analysis: Experts say that the most important factor of a mentorship program is a supportive and enabling environment. An appropriate environment fosters a feeling of trust, openness, and respect between mentors and mentees.

Supportive environments are those that contain a good communication network, feedback, and a culture of inclusivity. The mentoring program, therefore, should ensure the availability of resources and support from mentor and mentee to engage fully in the mentoring relationship. This could be through access to networking, professional development workshops, and organizational support. Finally, this also helps mentees to address their concerns and challenges through the creation of safe spaces for candid discussions without being judged or penalized.

3. Advocacy and Inclusivity

This calls for the active promotion of inclusivity and advocacy of diverse talents by the mentorship program. Mentorship practices should be sensitive to the diverse cultural, social, and demographic advocates that impact the experiences of women.

Inclusion-oriented programs sensitize mentors to recognize and modulate any unconscious bias, thereby promoting a work culture where women from various backgrounds feel valued and are provided with support. It also refers to the recognition and accommodation of the difficulties faced by intersectional women from various cultural, financial, and physical abilities. Advocacy could also involve policy-level changes within the organizations. It could be seen in terms of collaboration with organizational leadership to bring about policies ensuring gender diversity with equal opportunity for both genders in climbing the corporate ladder.

4. Skill Development and Confidence Building

Analysis: Mentorship is noted to be associated with skill development and building confidence among women leaders. Literature available agrees that specific skill-building activities and confidence-enhancing strategies take center stage in mentorship.

A mentor program usually involves the development of soft and hard skills. Soft skills, such as those related to leadership, communication, and emotional intelligence, are instrumental in effective leadership. Hard skills include specific industry knowledge and technical-specific skills. Training sessions, workshops, or real-world projects would allow a mentee to build and finesse these skills. Elements of confidence building can include achieving incremental goals and receiving positive reinforcement, coupled with public speaking activities.

5. Diversity in Mentorship Approaches

Critique: It has been cited that today more recognition is being given for more diverse approaches to mentoring such as group mentoring, peer mentoring, and perhaps even reverse mentoring. These different models can provide different ways for supporting women leaders and diversifying needs.

Variants: group mentoring, which helps multiple mentees through the experience of a single mentor while facilitating peer learning and networking. Peer mentoring helps peers, i.e., colleagues at comparable career stages, to support each other by sharing their insights and opportunities that come across. Reverse mentoring enables junior staff to mentor senior leadership, opening up a channel for new perspectives while allowing mutual learning to take place. Each has underpinning distinct advantages, that may be flexibly applied within many differing organizational contexts and objectives.

6. Challenging Biases and Policy Advocacy

Discussion: Mentorship programs that have to work even on difficult organizational biases and help to enforce supportive policies are mentioned from time to time. Mentors are seen as a vital ingredient in the struggle for systemic changes.

Clarification: A good mentorship program will feature a way in which all of the biases in an organization are to be indentified and do something about those biases. Mentors can educate mentees on positive ways of going about these biases, which could be regarding performance appraisal, promotion, and daily interactions. Policy advocacy involves a mentor working with organizational leadership to develop and enact policies to assist in achieving gender equity in flexibility of work arrangements, transparent promotion criteria, and provision of anti-bias training. Mentors will set a highly responsive and supportive work environment conducive to the mentee through the aid of advocacy.

7. Mutual Growth and Knowledge Sharing

Interpretation: The authors argue that the mentor, as well as the mentee, both learned and grew in the process. Bidirectional learning sustains the mentoring effort and reaps the maximum benefits out of the program.

Expansion: Each party benefits from the dynamic interplay of ideas, experiences, and feedback. Though benefiting scientifically, the mentee receives wisdom and experience. The mentor benefits from gaining new perspectives, leading to growth in both personal and professional life. This bi-directional relationship fosters an environment of collaborative learning where both both parties can develop and thrive.

8. Measuring Impact and Continuous Improvement

Some experts have indicated the importance of always measuring the impact of the mentoring programs and iterating program design based on feedback and outcomes; in layman's terms, this is to ensure that the programs remain still effective and relevant.

Programs must have strong evaluation frameworks, whereby they are able to prove effectiveness or success in satisfying the needs of the mentor and protégé. Sources of evaluation metrics will include such things as career progression, increasing ability and skill, measurements of satisfaction, and reaching the set objectives. Regular reviews and feedback from participants are needed to point out the necessary improvements and modifications in programs. Continuous improvement includes the uptake of best practices, the filtering in of emerging challenges, and the ability to adapt according to the organizational environment and changing industrial trends.

These themes and expert interviews allude to a good foundation for sharing in-depth insights about mentorship programs for women leaders. Building on these themes, it is possible for organizations to develop more effective and inclusive strategies around mentorship to facilitate growth and progression for women leaders and hence create a more just and dynamic leadership landscape.

NARRATIONS

The private stories shared by women who benefited from the mentor are a testament to the changes the mentor brought in terms of career and leadership development by the relationship. Their stories provoke a way in which the mentorship has helped one to overcome the hurdles that exist in her career, build confidence, and shape up her path to leadership.

1. Transformative Career Trajectories

Many women recount how mentorship has been pivotal in shaping their career trajectories. In one instance, Ananya Sharma, senior project manager in a technology company, narrates how her mentor, one seasoned top executive, counselled and guided her at a very important point of her career: "When I was planning a move from technical jobs into a leadership role, my mentor explained the intricacies of handling teams and inculcating strategic thinking into my way of working". His mentor's guidance was very useful in securing her that role as a leader, and the skills and confidence with which to manage her new role. It facilitated Ananya to keep pace with immense career advancements, and recently, she has been promoted to the role of a director.

To that end, Meera Joshi explains how mentoring was central in the development of her own enterprise: "My mentor has great experience within this start-up ecosystem, and she gave key advice about business strategy to fundraising," Meera shared. "Otherwise, I would struggle to even make my way through the somewhat initial struggles of being an entrepreneur." The mentorship gave Meera domain insights and operational strategies that are important factors for the success and growth of an enterprise.

2. Direction and Assistance

Mentoring involves receiving concrete direction and assistance from mentors in the form of pragmatic counseling, emotional empathy, and strategical vision. For example, Priya Patel is a mid-level manager in an MNC, and she remembers the kind of support her mentor gave her on one really challenging project. To quote Priya: "My mentor was not only a sounding board for my ideas but also helped me refine my project management skills.". "She gave me good feedback, and she always challenged me to be able to own the project, which is key to getting it done." Such development provides a focused way in which Priya could work on being a good leader and becoming visible in her company.

In one other case, Ayesha Khan a young leader, who has emerged in the developmental sector, reflects on the emotional and strategic help she is getting. "My mentor helped me navigate organizational politics and provided a safe space to discuss my concerns," Ayesha said. "She inspired and advised me on how to build confidence and resilience." This support helped Ayesha surmount the challenges that lay in her workplace and grow her career.

3. Overcoming Obstacles and Building Confidence

In most cases, mentorship helps women believe more in themselves and helps build confidence that was lacking before. Nisha Reddy, an engineering lead, gives an example of how mentorship helped her address imposter syndrome and show up much more strongly in her leadership. "I struggled with self-doubt and felt like I didn't belong in my leadership role," Nisha admits. "My mentor made me aware of my accomplishments and worth; he gave me tools to learn how to handle things as they came." With her mentor standing by her, Nisha started feeling more empowered to lead better and to voice her ideas within the company.

For example, it is through mentorship that Rina Gupta, a health professional, found an answer to job-related gender challenges. "My mentor, who had faced similar challenges, offered practical advice and moral support," Rina says. "Her mentorship empowered me to speak up and take on leadership roles that I previously shied away from." This support was key to Rina's professional development and her raising a voice on women's issues concerning healthcare.

The personal stories demonstrate the significance of mentorship in women's career development and leadership. The mentors are a driving force in providing clear directions, emotional, and strategic support by way of guidance and role modeling, allowing women to break new ground, build confidence, and pursue rightful career goals. To share such experiences is to underline the reordering impact that mentorship has and the pivotal role of responsibility in the next generation of female leadership.

BUILDING EFFECTIVE MENTORSHIP PROGRAMS FOR WOMEN LEADERS

Powerful mentorship programs for women leaders are a major strategy in the development of female talent within an organizational framework (Ford, Dannels, Morahan, & Magrane, 2021). Initiating the development of such programs does not only enhance the scope of individual career development but also takes the organization toward a more inclusive, if not totally equal, work environment. A number of critical elements are to be added to constitute an organizational mentoring program, from the stage of its formulation and pilot implementation to the stage of its evaluation and improvement phase.

1. Program Design and Goals

A good mentorship program will highly depend on good design and clear objectives. The first step is to have an understanding of what it is the program is supposed to meet: improvement of one's leadership skills, improvement of the chances of career development and advancement, or the creation of a strong network of women leaders. Organizational objectives have to be in harmony with broader corporate objectives of diversity and inclusion.

A successful Mentorship program will generally have the following:

- Structure and Format: Decide on the structure of the program- the nature of its orientation –either formal or informal, one-on-one or group, and how often they should meet. The proposed program format should be formal or informal, and the one-to-one or group and the frequency. The former is typically established with the set timelines and the mandatory meetings normally have milestones whereas the latter may be loose and less structured. How many available resources for the programs will be the guide for the appropriate format.
- Matching Process: Effective matching of mentors and mentees is paramount. When matching mentors and mentees, a consideration of factors such as career goals, industry experience, and personal interests should come into play. Use surveys, assessments, or interviews to gather relevant information and ensure compatibility. Involving both in the matching process will also lead to a likely success rate of the relationship.
- Clear Expectations: Clear expectations from the beginning of the process should be set. The expectations for mentors and mentees should include defined roles, such as frequency of meetings, the format of meetings, confidentiality agreements, and goals expected from the mentorship relationship. Guiding or an agreement that is detailed would promote prevention measures against misunderstandings and ensure alignment on the part of both parties.

2. Training And Resources for Both Mentors And Mentees

Effective mentoring should be done by adequately training the mentor. This training may include training in any of the following parties:

- Mentoring skills: Training the mentor how to support the mentee effectively, like training how to listen actively, give good feedback, and setting goals. The training should also aim at supporting the mentee so that they can help the mentee navigate challenges in the organization and advance their career.
- Diversity and Inclusion: Explain to the Mentors, sensitize them on the issues of gender inclusion and diversity, and train them to institute strategies that will help them address "unconsciously" biased people, advocate and support an inclusive environment at the workplace, and uphold gender equity.
- Resources and Tools: Make resources available that include workshops, webinars, and networking events, which can be used to supplement the mentorship. There should be an ability to access tools and resources such as career development plans or industry research that would equally facilitate growth for the mentees.

3. Support and Involvement

Two aspects must stay alive in a mentorship program to be effective: continued support and involvement. The ways to continue involvement

- Continuous Monitoring and Support: There should be regular check-ins with both mentor and mentee to monitor the progress of the process, troubleshoot any problems, and ensure that added support can be accorded. One can have a survey on that, a feedback session, or an appointment set with a particular mentorship program coordinator.
- Information and Feedback Mechanisms: Establish mechanisms for information collection and obtaining feedback from the clients regarding their views and perceptions of the project and the effectiveness of the program. Use them to make the changes and improvements that may be deemed necessary. Frequent and periodic evaluations will help identify where the program performs well and areas of the program that require attention.
- Recognition and Incentives: Help in recognizing and rewarding the efforts put in by both mentors and mentees. Incentives like awards, certificates, or public acknowledgment of participants will let your audience remain motivated and attached to your program. Some accolades for their achievement or on completion of a particular milestone will also help raise your program to be much more visible and attractive.

4. Evaluation and Continuous Improvement

- Success Measurements: Design the measurements from the program and the benchmarks used for understanding the program's success. These metrics may encompass such phenomena as successful mentor relationships, career goal attainment for the aspiring mentees, and participant satisfaction among other considerations. This calls for regular reviews to measure the value of the program.
- Adaptation to feedback: The feedback from participants will be used to make any iterative improvisation in the program. Adaptive program: requirements change all the time due to either industry trends or best practices. Flexibility and responsiveness to the feedback would mean the program remains relevant and effective all along this period.
- Share Best Practices with Organizations or Within an Industry: Sharing best practices and lessons learned not only reinforces the need for sharing stories but can learn from the experience of other successful programs to bring out positive change in your own mentorship initiatives.

BUILDING A MENTORING CULTURE

Mentoring culture should be more than a formal program and must foster for an extended period within the company as part of its organizational fabric. Leaders must be motivated to mentor from top to bottom. The value of mentoring must be promoted, and the environment must therefore be created whereby it is cool to see mentoring as a development source. By facilitating an organizational culture where one can develop a network, a supportive ecosystem is created, which entirely benefits each employee (Pinna, Simone, Cicotto & Malik, 2020).

In conclusion, effective mentorship programs in building women leaders entail design, trained support for mentorship, and continuous improvement. Having such a focus will help organizations design mentorship programs that help foster and develop female leaders into an inclusive and just workplace environment. Investing in programs such as these cultivates a diverse pipeline of talent and helps to boost organizational success.

THE FUTURE OF WOMEN LEADERS AND MENTORSHIP

As the landscape of leadership continues to change, so does the future of women leaders and mentorship. With new trends emerging, organizational cultures changing, and technological amenities, new paradigms of how women are mentored and how they advance into positions of leadership are being formed. Getting the hang of these dynamics will be of essence in availing excellence in the next generation of leaders in ensuring that mentorship is upheld as a valuable prime mover towards empowerment and growth.

1. Technology Advancements

The inclusion of technology in mentorship is expected to change how women leaders connect, learn, and grow (Valerio, 2022). The development of digital platforms and tools, on the other hand, has helped to expand access to mentorship opportunities beyond geographical limitations and enabled virtual mentoring relationships bridging the gap between mentors and mentees across different regions and time zones. Generally, online mentorship platforms and apps make available both structured programs for goal setting as well as resources for both mentors and mentees, which make the whole process of mentoring accessible and efficient.

The most help in the betterment of mentorship programs is being contributed by artificial intelligence in combination with data analytics. AI-driven tools help in the matching process by analysing the vast data on career goals, experiences, and preferences more effectively, steering clear of matching mentors with mentees. Further, it calls for data analytics that can track progress, measure the impact of mentorship, and locate areas for further advantage, rendering more customized and targeted backup.

2. Fostering Inclusive and Diverse Mentoring

Increasingly, the future of mentoring lies in inclusivity and diversity. The field is beginning to appreciate the value of mentoring as a relationship indicative of a variety of experience, perspective, and background. Most likely, mentor programs will receive an intersectionality focus and address the issues that women of color, LGBTQ+ women, and women with disabilities face specifically. Inclusive mentoring environments better mentor all women leaders, making attainable, accessible, and equitable mentorship opportunities.

In addition to this, mentorship is expected to go beyond conventional career development to other core areas of importance such as personal development, wellness, and the integration of well-being with work–life balance. These programs would likely include holistic approaches to the broad scale of both challenges and opportunities for women leaders that provide for health and an overall ability to be resilient.

3. Expanding Mentorship Models

The future of mentorship will see the expansion and diversification of mentorship models. Traditional one-on-one mentoring relationships will be complemented by group mentoring, peer mentoring, and reverse mentoring. Group mentoring allows multiple mentees to benefit from the collective wisdom of a mentor and from interactions with other mentees, fostering collaborative learning and networking.

Peer mentoring among colleagues at the same levels is very effective since it offers support and insights while building strong professional networks. Reverse mentoring, where younger or less experienced employees mentor senior leaders, can offer fresh perspectives and foster mutual learning across generation areas.

4. Integrating Mentorship into Organizational Culture

It will ensure that mentorship increasingly becomes part of the organizational culture to be taken as an integral component of leadership development and talent management. The organizations will institute a culture in which mentoring is important and greatly encouraged at all levels. This will involve embedding mentorship into frameworks of performance management, succession planning, and career development.

Mentorship will be inculcated into leadership development programs across the spectrum, with senior leaders actively engaged in mentorship programs and themselves being mentored to reinforce a good example. This incorporation will help embed the importance of mentorship, support it naturally, and ensure that mentoring becomes a key element of career progression.

5. Measuring and Enhancing Impact

In this role, mentorship impact measurement is going to get more sophisticated and data-driven. The work concerning metrics development and an evaluation framework stands complete at ensuring the expected value from mentorship programs is realized. That entails tracing outcomes in career progression, skill development, and satisfaction levels for both mentors and mentees.

In strengthening the power of mentorship, refinement will be on an ongoing basis from feedback and data. Leveraging the learning from the evaluations, organizations will continuously refine programs, close gaps, and share best practices. It is through this commitment to measure and refine that mentorship initiatives will be responsive and impactful to support women leaders.

6. Building International Mentorship Networks

In future, there will be global large-scale mentorship networks that link women leaders across borders. It will become possible for mentors and mentees to both gain insights through diverse perspectives and experiences within and across such networks. Global mentoring programs will help women leaders navigate international opportunities, understand global industry trends, and create multi-country linkages.

These networks will also foster collaboration among organizations to share effort, resources, best practices, and stories of success. Global connections help to amplify the reach of these mentorship programs so that around the world, women leaders can find ways of support in managing increased complexity and to be active in an interconnected world.

7. Addressing Emerging Challenges

Mentor programs for an anticipated future must address emerging challenges such as remote work dynamics, changing career paths, economic fluctuations, etc. Mentorship will be pivotal in assisting women leaders to cope with a changed work environment, such as managing remote teams, skills required for the hybrid work model, and skills for new and evolving roles.

Also the programs will be made resilient to thrive in the face of economic uncertainties that may occur, and ensures that women leaders are supported to continue their lead in the wake of such changes. Mentors will also be on call to give advice on the transition of the career, managing stress and maintaining good work-life balance.

In conclusion, the future of women leaders and mentorship includes technological advancement, greater emphasis on inclusivity, diversifying of mentorship models, and integration with organizational culture. In adopting such trends and addressing emerging challenges, the organization will find the most effective means to build mentorship programs that support the increased growth and success of women leaders, thus ensuring better and dynamic leadership landscape overall.

CONCLUSION

The role mentorship can play in the development of women as leaders is deep and potentially transformative, shaping the future directions of leadership both within a given organization and in society more generally. Truly effective mentoring goes beyond guidance; it empowers women to overcome roadblocks in building self-confidence as they reach toward their most ideal career aspirations. Mentoring of the future will leverage technological advancements further, adopt different practices, be more inclusive, and respond to the changing workplace dynamics. Organizations need to make the development of a supportive environment an integral part of the culture at every level so that women leaders can avail themselves of the tools, opportunities, and networks of support they need to be successful. By constantly examining and refining such approaches, it is possible to level the leadership playing field so that the needs of the individual woman are appropriately met and organizational success, as well as societal advancement at large, is well served. Focusing especially on and nurturing young, talented females with mentorship will, in the final analysis, create a more inclusive and innovative future through the development of diverse leadership.

REFERENCES

Abalkhail, J. M. (2020). Women managing women: Hierarchical relationships and career impact. *Career Development International*, 25(4), 389–413. DOI: 10.1108/CDI-01-2019-0020

Bhatti, A., & Ali, R. (2021). Women's leadership pathways in higher education: Role of mentoring and networking. *Asian Women*, 37(3), 25–50. DOI: 10.14431/aw.2021.9.37.3.25

Bodalina, K. N., & Mestry, R. (2022). A case study of the experiences of women leaders in senior leadership positions in the education district offices. *Educational Management Administration & Leadership*, 50(3), 452–468. DOI: 10.1177/1741143220940320

Brizuela, V., Chebet, J. J., & Thorson, A. (2023). Supporting early-career women researchers: Lessons from a global mentorship programme. *Global Health Action*, 16(1), 2162228. DOI: 10.1080/16549716.2022.2162228 PMID: 36705071

Dashper, K. (2020). Mentoring for gender equality: Supporting female leaders in the hospitality industry. *International Journal of Hospitality Management*, 88, 102397. DOI: 10.1016/j.ijhm.2019.102397

Durbin, S., Lopes, A., & Warren, S. (2020). Challenging male dominance through the substantive representation of women: The case of an online women's mentoring platform. *New Technology, Work and Employment*, 35(2), 215–231. DOI: 10.1111/ntwe.12166

Ford, A. Y., Dannels, S., Morahan, P., & Magrane, D. (2021). Leadership programs for academic women: Building self-efficacy and organizational leadership capacity. *Journal of Women's Health*, 30(5), 672–680. DOI: 10.1089/jwh.2020.8758 PMID: 33064580

House, A., Dracup, N., Burkinshaw, P., Ward, V., & Bryant, L. D. (2021). Mentoring as an intervention to promote gender equality in academic medicine: A systematic review. *BMJ Open*, 11(1), e040355. DOI: 10.1136/bmjopen-2020-040355 PMID: 33500280

Kakabadse, N. K., Figueira, C., Nicolopoulou, K., Hong Yang, J., Kakabadse, A. P., & Özbilgin, M. F. (2015). Gender diversity and board performance: Women's experiences and perspectives. *Human Resource Management*, 54(2), 265–281. DOI: 10.1002/hrm.21694

Pickett, A. (2022). The Relationship between Mentoring and Leadership.

Pierli, G., Murmura, F., & Palazzi, F. (2022). Women and Leadership: How Do Women Leaders Contribute to Companies' Sustainable Choices? *Frontiers in Sustainability*, 3, 930116. DOI: 10.3389/frsus.2022.930116

Pinna, R., De Simone, S., Cicotto, G., & Malik, A. (2020). Beyond organisational support: Exploring the supportive role of co-workers and supervisors in a multi-actor service ecosystem. *Journal of Business Research*, 121, 524–534. DOI: 10.1016/j.jbusres.2020.02.022

Read, D. C., Fisher, P. J., & Juran, L. (2020). How do women maximize the value of mentorship? Insights from mentees, mentors, and industry professionals. *Leadership and Organization Development Journal*, 41(2), 165–175. DOI: 10.1108/LODJ-02-2019-0094

Saffie-Robertson, M. C. (2020). It's not you, it's me: An exploration of mentoring experiences for women in STEM. *Sex Roles*, 83(9), 566–579. DOI: 10.1007/s11199-020-01129-x

Sarathi, P. (2023). *Responsive Mentoring*. BFC Publications.

Singh, S., & Vanka, S. (2020). Mentoring is essential but not sufficient: Sponsor women for leadership roles. *Development and Learning in Organizations*, 34(6), 25–28. DOI: 10.1108/DLO-05-2019-0100

Soran, A. A., & Kara, S. (2022). Mentor-mentee relationship: Fifteen career saving suggestions. *International Journal of Social Sciences & Educational Studies*, 9(3), 138.

Starr, J. (2021). *The mentoring manual*.

Valerio, A. M. (2022). Supporting women leaders: Research-based directions for gender inclusion in organizations. *Consulting Psychology Journal*, 74(2), 178–193. DOI: 10.1037/cpb0000208

Zachary, L. J., & Fain, L. Z. (2022). *The mentor's guide: Facilitating effective learning relationships*. John Wiley & Sons.

Chapter 10
Empowered to Lead
Navigating Psychological Safety and Resilience as a Black Woman Leader

Kendra Lewis-Strickland
Independent Researcher, USA

ABSTRACT

This chapter, written by a Black woman mid-career leader with more than a decade of experience in higher education, explores the intersection of resilience, psychological safety, and the challenges faced by Black women professionals. Through two defining moments in her career, the author highlights the crucial role of psychological safety in shaping her personal and professional journey. This chapter positions psychological safety and resilience as vital for Black women in higher education. It combines personal narratives, research, and practical strategies, stressing the need for leaders to create empowering environments and for institutions to be intentionally designed with Black women in mind. The author's two pivotal experiences—early career challenges and navigating personal difficulties —illustrate the impact of psychological safety on her confidence and professional growth. These accounts provide insights into resilient coping mechanisms and institutional culture change.

INTRODUCTION

Promoting healthy and nurturing workplace environments in higher education necessitates an understanding of all individual's experiences to understand existing nuances and to ensure interventions are inclusive for all. Despite the increasing focus on diversity, equity, inclusion, and belonging (DEIB), Black women continue to face

DOI: 10.4018/979-8-3693-3144-6.ch010

unique challenges and systemic barriers as faculty and professional staff (Chance, 2022, Williams, 2023). To address these challenges and barriers, it is crucial to foster supportive environments that ensure psychological safety, defined as the belief that one can speak up without risk of punishment or humiliation. Psychological safety not only enhances organizational innovation and creativity (Liu & Keller, 2021; Hora, Lemoine, Xu & Shalley, 2021) but also impacts individual overall well-being (Hasan & Kashif, 2021). Exploring the vital role of psychological safety in workplace mental health and well-being was emphasized in the 2022 US Surgeon General's Framework for Workplace Mental Health and Well-Being report (United States). Centering these experiences, enhances the ability to recognize the workplace nuances derived from the intersectionality of race and gender and encourage intentional interventions that create opportunities to support Black women's abilities to thrive and contribute to organizational innovation and effectiveness.

In 2022, the US Surgeon General's Framework for Workplace Mental Health and Well-Being report (United States) underscored the critical importance of workplace mental health and well-being, placing emphasis on the foundational 'Essential for Protection from Harm', namely, psychological safety in the workplace. This national focus on workplace well-being has continued to spotlight opportunities to support and protect all workers from mental and physical harm. According to American Psychological Association, most workers feel generally satisfied with their jobs, performance and productivity, especially in environments that are 'psychologically safe'; yet workers who lack psychological safety tend to report feeling tense and stressed out (American Psychological Association, 2014). This creates a unique opportunity for leaders to encourage, facilitate, and reinforce environments that build psychological safety for all employees.

In the context of higher education, these concepts hold particular significance for Black women who continue to navigate individual and systemic barriers to not only survive but thrive. Despite the growing presence of women and people of color among higher education professionals in recent years (National Association of Higher Education Professionals, 2023), Black women continue to encounter various forms of adversity, including microaggressions, racial trauma, stereotypes, and discrimination, stemming from their intersectional gendered and racial identities (Chance, 2021; Townsend, 2021). Universities and colleges are also facing challenges such as financial constraints, talent crisis, disruptive innovation, including AI, and increasing concerns over the value of higher education (Deloitte, 2024). These challenges require university and college leaders to be innovative and harness the talents and capabilities of all employees, including Black women. Hence, there is a need for continued intentional discussions to promote pathways to healthy and nurturing environments for Black women to contribute.

To effectively foster a supportive and empowering environment for Black women, it is crucial to engage in ongoing, examination of experiences and to understand the role of psychological safety to create supportive interventions. Such discussions and interventions promote the resilience needed for the well-being of Black women and the broader professoriate. Psychological safety acts as a cornerstone of well-being, ensuring that resilience is both supported and celebrated within these environments (Edmondson, 2018). By centering these elements, there is an opportunity to showcase individual strength, but also contribute to the overall health of the higher education leadership community; illustrating the well-being of Black women as beneficial to institutional success.

In this chapter, the author will advocate for healthy pathways to leadership in higher education by sharing two personal reflective narratives that highlight the role of psychological safety in personal and professional development. It will feature two examples drawn from the personal journey of a black millennial woman navigating a career in higher education, highlighting the pivotal role of psychological safety and resilience, particularly, highlighting times when these components were lacking. By weaving together personal anecdotes with research insights and practical strategies, the aim is to offer a comprehensive perspective. Centering the experiences of a millennial Black woman, provides a unique opportunity to delve into firsthand accounts of the roles of psychological safety and resilience. Through reflective narratives, the author will provide insights into how she navigated these situations, identified resilient coping mechanisms, and strategically channeled her experiences that fostered a commitment to future continued institutional culture change.

SCHOLARLY BACKGROUND

In this chapter, we delve into the contemporary applications of psychological safety within organizational contexts, emphasizing its role in shaping team dynamics and fostering healthy, nurturing environments. The concept of psychological safety, introduced by Edgar Schein and Warren Bennis in their 1965 work on change management, has been a cornerstone of organizational culture. It revolves around an individual's confidence in managing change without fear of adverse consequences. Amy Edmondson further refined this concept, suggesting that psychological safety is best explored at the team level, where it is defined as a 'shared belief held by members of a team that they are safe for interpersonal risk-taking' (1999). This widely accepted definition underscores the importance of creating an environment where individuals can voice their concerns, disagreements, and ideas without fear of personal or reputational harm.

It's important to recognize that experiences that may seem insignificant or non-traumatic to some can profoundly impact others. Trauma is subjective, defined by an individual's perception and its disruption to their psychological well-being and worldview (McCann and Pearlman, 1992). These experiences highlight the pivotal role of psychological safety in fostering leadership resilience.

Understanding psychological safety in the workplace requires an examination at the individual level, highlighting the unique approaches needed to cultivate it effectively. This understanding is particularly crucial for black women who navigate complex workplace challenges in pursuit of success. Resilience, the capacity to confront, overcome, and thrive despite adversities and traumas, is deeply interconnected with psychological safety. Exploring these intertwined concepts provides valuable insights into fostering inclusive and supportive work environments conducive to the well-being and success of all employees, especially those from marginalized backgrounds.

Numerous studies highlight the compounded impact of racism and discrimination on black women's professional growth. Black women often face a 'double jeopardy' of oppression, experiencing racial and gender discrimination simultaneously (Davis and Maldonado, 2015). Stereotypes labeling black women as strong, tough, and aggressive, while praised in others, are weaponized against them, undermining their experiences and leaving them to navigate challenges alone.

Resilience is a vital component for fostering a culture where black women can effectively confront, overcome, and navigate workplace challenges. Masten (2014) defines resilience as the 'ability to adapt successfully to disturbances that threaten one's function, viability, or development.' This capacity to rebound when faced with threats is not just about maintaining resilience; it's about thriving. A study on black women in university dean positions found that participants expanded the notion of resilience to include centering oneself, having a short memory, regrouping, recovering quickly, and self-protection (Lewis-Strickland, 2020). This expanded notion of resilience sheds light on how black women have learned to positively respond to stressors, surmount challenges, and operate at a heightened level even in the face of adversity.

In conclusion, it is imperative to prioritize the well-being and empowerment of all employees, particularly black women, by creating workplaces rooted in psychological safety and resilience. This approach will ensure that all employees feel valued, supported, and able to succeed.

HARNESSING RESILIENCE AND PSYCHOLOGICAL SAFETY: AN EVOLUTION

Throughout my career, I've relied on core values - hard work, resilience, toughness, and collaboration - instilled in me by my family and refined through life experiences. These principles have guided me as I've navigated the complexities of the professional world, teaching me when and how to use my voice to advocate for my psychological safety and build resilience. This has been instrumental in my leadership journey. While I haven't always made the right decisions or had all the answers, I've come to understand the critical importance of advocating for psychological safety and fostering resilience at both individual and systemic levels. This commitment is deeply personal to me and has far-reaching implications for higher education, the broader workforce, and especially for black women in the profession.

Like many, I didn't grow up discussing psychological safety or advocacy in professional contexts. However, early in my career, I intuitively recognized their importance, even without the precise terminology. Reflecting on pivotal moments in my journey as an emerging leader and a woman, I've realized that psychological safety and resilience have always been present. However, I lacked the mindset, tools, and skills to fully leverage these elements for my benefit and that of others. The following two examples will highlight my professional interest in advocating for psychological safety and resilience for individuals and teams in higher education.

NAVIGATING PROFESSIONAL CHALLENGES: A JOURNEY OF RESILIENCE AND PSYCHOLOGICAL SAFETY

My first job in a university, was everything a first job should be: abundant learning opportunities, networking prospects, and meaningful work within a supportive environment. Despite the pay and long hours, I was happy in the role and embraced the chances to grow and develop. Here, supervisors fostered a culture of learning by providing guidance and redirection when needed, emphasizing the importance of accuracy and efficacy in our tasks, yet an acceptance and support for making mistakes. Mistakes were opportunities for learning not for embarrassment or belittling. Although I had not initially envisioned a career in higher education, this experience illuminated the potential for personal growth and societal contribution.

However, my next role presented a stark contrast. My initial excitement quickly diminished as I began to feel 'othered' by my colleagues. The social dynamics among the team members engendered feelings of exclusion. Given my life stage, relationship status, and lengthy commute, I refrained from participating in after-hours social events, which were deemed crucial for team bonding and camaraderie.

Consequently, my non-participation resulted in limited opportunities to connect with my colleagues, leading to increasing isolation. This isolation marked the beginning of a shift in how I was treated. Initially manifesting as subtle microaggressions, the situation soon escalated to jokes about my preferences and interests. Comments like "I didn't know black people listened to country music" or constant inquiries about 'black topics' where I was expected to be the expert. Despite my attempts to educate my colleagues on microaggressions and foster inclusivity, my efforts fell short.

Upon reflection, I recognize that many of these microaggressions were likely unintentional, perceived by my colleagues as attempts to include me in conversations. However, irrespective of intent, I felt marginalized and othered. This defensive posture permeated my environment, leaving me apprehensive about future interactions. In an effort to assimilate, I refrained from expressing my opinions or sharing ideas, fearing further microaggressions. This defensive stance and silence tapped into two aspects: my core values and the ongoing opportunities for isolation and disconnection. As Saakvitne & Pearlman (1996) suggest, values shape how individuals perceive experiences. The values of working hard, paying my dues, and 'letting the work speak for itself' were ingrained in me during my formative years, prompted me to immerse myself further in my work during these challenging times.

Moreover, an ill-advised attempt to seek mentorship and guidance from a senior colleague resulted in unforeseen repercussions. I reached out with the previous individual in the role who had a great report with the team and was not a partner/client for a large-scale event for advice and support. To build camaraderie, I shared with her my concerns and leaned into my vulnerability to ask for advice and support, which I thought she graciously provided. Despite receiving and following the advice and reassurance, I found myself blindsided by a formal reprimand from executive leadership, based on disparaging remarks made by the very colleague I had trusted. Not only was I provided with a formal reprimand, but I was also not provided an opportunity to voice my concerns, perspective, or address any of the identified issues in my defense. This betrayal left me feeling vulnerable, embarrassed, and disheartened, further lowering my psychological safety and performance.

Reflecting on my past, I now understand that my sense of psychological safety was significantly lower than that of my clients and colleagues. The concept of "psychological safety" was then an alien term to me, and its importance in the workplace was something I failed to comprehend. I felt a constant unease at work, which I mistakenly accepted as normality. Upon reflection, I realize that this discomfort was a byproduct of the selective promotion of psychological safety within our departmental culture.

Dr. Timothy Clark's framework underscores the necessity for employees to experience at least one form of safety - inclusive, self, learning, contributor, or challenger - to take interpersonal risks (The 4 Stages, 2020). I now recognize that I was devoid of feelings of inclusiveness and challenger safety. I felt alienated and unaccepted in my role. During a formal reprimand, I felt unsafe to stand up for myself and rectify the situation. The shock of the incident left me bewildered and unsure of how to react in that heightened emotional state.

In a subsequent meeting with a partner/client to address challenges and reset expectations, the atmosphere turned hostile. I vividly recall her eye-rolling, loud sighs, and dismissive body language, left me feeling rushed, anxious, and uneasy. As the conversation progressed, she began to interrupt me and exhibit aggressive gestures towards me. I attempted to ease the tension by seeking common ground. However, she blamed me for her hostility. In that moment, I felt defeated and marginalized, especially since my supervisor, also a black woman, did not intervene. especially as my supervisor, also a black woman, remained silent. I left the meeting feeling unprotected, isolated, embarrassed, and furious.

This experience had a profound impact on me, shifting me from a state of high stress and anxiety to a deep realization. It highlighted the critical importance of psychological safety and resilience, particularly for black women like myself, and fueled my passion for researching resilient behaviors and leadership development in the workplace.

This professional journey underscores the pivotal role of psychological safety in team performance, a concept eloquently explored by Amy Edmondson in "The Fearless Organization." Edmondson delineates various team dynamics, emphasizing the importance of psychological safety. She describes four zones: the comfort zone, where teams feel safe but lack motivation for change; the anxiety zone, characterized by low safety and high-performance pressure, leading to increased stress and turnover; the high-performance or learning zone, where teams feel safe and are motivated to innovate and succeed; and the apathy zone, where teams lack both safety and motivation (Fig 1.)

Comfort Zone		High Performance
Apathy		Anxiety

Y-axis: PSYCHOLOGICAL SAFETY; X-axis: DRIVE

Reflecting on my experience, I found myself predominantly in the anxiety zone, wrestling with stress and anxiety that stifled my creativity and innovation. Striving for perfection, I exacerbated my anxiety due to fear of exclusion or microaggressions. Post this experience, I transitioned into the apathy zone, feeling disengaged and disconnected, doing the bare minimum and actively seeking a new role. It's crucial to note that psychological safety is subjective, and not every team member may share the same feelings. This experience underscores the criticality of continuously measuring or exploring a team's psychological safety and addressing root causes.

Despite feeling disengaged and isolated post this experience, I received unexpected positive feedback from clients on my work quality, collaboration skills, and ability to multitask within a complex organizational structure. This feedback served as validation and recognition, reaffirming my value and contribution within the organization. This feedback served as validation and recognition, reaffirming my value within the organization. As Beyoncé wisely said, "always stay gracious, the best revenge is your paper," emphasizing the power of letting one's work speak for itself. Delivering quality work consistently became a testament to my capabilities and worth.

A JOURNEY THROUGH RECOGNITION, REFLECTION, AND INTROSPECTION

Recognition, reflection, and introspection are three key concepts in this context organizations can strive to strengthen. Recognition involves acknowledging an individual's contribution to the organization's mission or goals, while appreciation expresses gratitude for their work contributions (Kezar & Elrod, 2020). While I felt appreciated by my clients and recognized by my leaders, public recognition did not alleviate my feelings towards the team or the urgency to seek a new role. It's crucial for leaders to acknowledge and recognize contributions in a timely manner, demonstrating genuine interest and value for their team members' efforts, even if the employee doesn't initiate the recognition. Continued recognition reinforces team members' self-perceptions and sense of belonging, encouraging them to speak up and share their ideas confidently. This fosters an environment where individuals feel welcomed to contribute and innovate.

In the instance when this colleague may have intended to offer feedback or criticism, her behavior crossed into bullying territory. Bullying is regrettably prevalent in university settings, manifesting in various forms of incivility (Heffernan, & Bosetti, L., 2021). While these behaviors have been extensively studied among faculty members, research on bullying among non-academic and professional staff is comparatively limited. My narrative serves as just one example of the challenges and instances of bullying that professional staff may encounter in their workplace environments. The role of black women in professional staff positions is of importance as the majority of black women in university staff positions occupy these positions (National Center for Education Statistics, 2023).

This professional encounter significantly shaped my interest in leadership development, particularly in exploring the components of leadership resilience, including the practice of reflection. Following this experience, I recognized the need for reflection to address the harm inflicted on both professional and personal mindsets. However, in the immediate aftermath, shock and trauma hindered productive reflection, and I made decisions that were not in my best interest. Time is essential for self-reflection (Pang, 2020), but often there is not enough time in our days to engage in effective self-reflection, even if only for a few minutes (Klaphaak, 2021) to sit with the experiences of the event.

Initially, I struggled to engage in productive reflection due to the shock and trauma from the experience and the desire to quickly move on. Now, with hindsight, I recognize the need for in-action reflection that I should have undertaken earlier. At the time, I understood that while this experience may not have been typical for me, it wasn't abnormal for so many others either. It became clear that I needed to find a way to overcome the situation and return to a state of thriving; which is a critical aspect of resilience, deeply rooted in adaptability (Ledesma, 2014).

Adapting to a traumatic experience involves a complex interplay between personality, personal history, and contextual factors (Saakvitne et al., 1998). Throughout this prolonged ordeal, I oscillated between the anxiety and apathy zones, significantly impacting my well-being. Self-awareness emerges as crucial in fostering both psychological safety and resilience. While I struggled to engage in reflection, ongoing efforts to reconnect with myself and understand my role in the experience proved beneficial. Engaging in that self-reflection, would have provided opportunities to distinguish between stories and the facts and to acknowledge the immediate feelings. These two actions empower self-compassion through mindfulness and self-kindness (Neff, 2011) that black women do not often show inwardly in the quest for perfection.

Allocating time and space for introspection is imperative for cultivating self-awareness, accountability, and building resilience. As leaders, integrating reflection into practice is essential, as it fosters an openness to understanding both others and ourselves, enabling more effective leadership. However, engaging in reflection can be challenging because readiness to confront emerging truths is paramount and something we may not be entirely prepared to do. While examining thoughts and feelings may be easily identifiable, transitioning to considering lessons learned and personal growth opportunities may prove daunting. Importantly, introspection is just as relevant and necessary as retrospection.

Whether leading people or projects, managing a large team or oneself, undergoing the reflective process facilitates an understanding of how one's base values and experiences influence and contribute to situations, both positively and negatively. Acknowledging imperfection and embracing introspection enable candid conversations with oneself, fostering personal and professional growth. Undergoing introspective behaviors can help leaders model how to hold space for similar moments and how to integrate the learnings into practice.

Reflection is a great tool to explore the foundation of our programming and how these personal histories intertwine with our workplace. Reflecting on my past experiences, I observed black female leaders embody traits of strength, assertiveness, and an unwavering commitment to hard work. Vulnerability was often viewed as a liability, and prioritizing others' needs above one's own was the norm. As criticism and exclusion became prevalent themes in my professional life, I leaned increasingly on these values and principles. It was my programming to in those times of shock and stress to control what I could, my work.

However, this programming towards silent perseverance came at a cost. While I diligently strived for perfection and outcomes, I inadvertently neglected to assertively communicate my achievements. The absence of self-advocacy allowed misconceptions to flourish unchecked. Leaders, uninformed about the extent of my contributions, crafted narratives that obscured my true impact. Meanwhile, my counterparts shared seemingly trivial accomplishments, garnering recognition and visibility.

INDIVIDUAL AND ORGANIZATIONAL INTERVENTIONS

At the individual level, black women in professional staff positions are encouraged to explore their frame of references, refine their purpose, and actively strive for fulfillment rather than mere survival. Building upon Oikelome's seminal work (2017), I suggest strategies such as mentorship, seizing opportunities, leadership development, and understanding institutional fit. Rather than relying on silent perseverance, it is important to find individuals or programs that can provide you with personal or professional development, provide opportunities for introspection, and support. Not only is fit about finding individuals that align with your professional and personal values and development. Fit is also about organizational fit. It is important to truly explore the organization, look at what they market, and what they highlight in their front webpage news. It is even more important to thoroughly pay attention to the culture of the department or unit you're interviewing for. Rather than using the interview to highlight all of your skills to combat imposter syndrome and show your value and worth to the hiring team, use this time to watch how the team interacts with each other. They will put their best foot forward, but are they talking over eachother, are individuals looking each other in the eye, smiling at one another, etc. Also, ask questions about culture.

This narrative underscores a critical aspect of workplace dynamics: the correlation between psychological safety and self-expression. While advocating for oneself and celebrating accomplishments is essential, it's equally crucial to acknowledge the barriers that hinder such actions. In environments where individuals don't feel psychologically secure, speaking up can feel daunting, if not impossible. Understanding the interplay between individual programming and organizational culture is paramount for fostering inclusivity, amplifying diverse voices, and creating belonging. Creating environments where all team members feel empowered to share their experiences and achievements requires a concerted effort to cultivate psychological safety and challenge existing norms.

In essence, navigating workplace dynamics involves a delicate balance between honoring personal values and challenging systemic barriers. By fostering environments that encourage authenticity and mutual respect, organizations can harness the full spectrum of talent and foster a culture of belonging. When individuals feel a part of the organization, and empowered to share their experiences, challenges, and achievements, this can serve as a catalyst for organizational agility. These insights can help to address current challenges and explore potential innovative solutions and interventions.

Transitioning from an individual to an organizational perspective, this example offers practical strategies tailored to address the unique challenges encountered by black women in professional staff positions, particularly within environments characterized by low psychological safety. Acknowledging that many black women face similar experiences across various university settings, there arises a pressing need for leaders to take a proactive approach in assessing and enhancing the psychological safety climate within their teams. Utilizing tools such as short surveys and deliberate crucial conversations, leaders can gather valuable insights into the current climate and pinpoint areas in need of improvement. Furthermore, collaborative action planning with teams becomes essential, enabling the development, implementation, and continuous evaluation of interventions aimed at nurturing psychological safety.

Through collective action and a commitment to inclusivity, organizations can harness the full potential of their diverse talent pool, fostering environments where all individuals feel valued, respected, and empowered to contribute their unique perspectives and talents.

As we explore the multifaceted realm of psychological safety and resilience in the workplace, it is imperative to recognize the delicate interplay between personal experiences and organizational dynamics. This professional narrative illuminates the profound impact of psychological safety on individual well-being and engagement. This narrative shares an experience that delves into the fabric of workplace culture, from navigating the complexities of workplace dynamics to grappling with challenges of inclusion and recognition. However, the exploration extends beyond the organizational level into the deeply personal realms of introspection and growth. Transitioning from professional narratives to personal reflections allows for a continued discussion of the nuances of resilience and self-awareness.

MY PERSONAL EXPERIENCE

The intersection of motherhood and academia has increasingly become a focal point of scholarly inquiry, illuminating the unique challenges faced by mother-scholars navigating academic settings. Amidst the backdrop of the COVID-19 pandemic, I found myself confronted with unprecedented challenges that tested my resilience and shaped my professional trajectory. Reflecting on my personal journey, it becomes evident that the presence of psychological safety played a transformative role, significantly influencing my ability to thrive amidst uncertainties.

In 2020, as the pandemic unfolded, what was initially anticipated as a weeks-long pause turned into a years-long disruption that is still looming today. I, like many mother-scholars, found myself navigating the demands of pregnancy, childbirth, postpartum, and dissertation research amidst the chaos of a global crisis and isolation. The pressure to complete my dissertation before accruing additional student loans added a layer of personal urgency to an already challenging situation.

The early weeks of the pandemic marked a period of profound adjustment as I grappled with the demands of new motherhood while striving to meet the rigorous demands of academic research. The birth of my child amidst the chaos served as a catalyst for a transformative journey—one characterized by resilience and adaptation. I can remember a day when my newborn was sleeping on my chest while I conducted a 90-minute interview for my dissertation research, running on only a few hours of sleep. This would not be the last time that I would have a newborn or bottle in one arm and a keyboard at my fingertips. Balancing the demands of motherhood with the pursuit of academic excellence tested my resilience, often leaving me feeling overwhelmed, exhausted, and anxious.

MOTHER-SCHOLARS: NAVIGATING ACADEMIA AMIDST MOTHERHOOD AND A GLOBAL PANDEMIC

While navigating these complexities, the pivotal importance of psychological safety emerged as a guiding light. Amidst the challenges of managing a newborn alongside the demands of my dissertation process, I encountered further hurdles when a new committee member redirected my existing research path. Balancing the commitments of motherhood, the shifting committee priorities, and the fears related to black maternal health led to mounting burnout, as I struggled to maintain control while fearing the consequences of appearing inadequate. I realized that I was taking on too much. I spent hours crafting narratives and charts, attempting to project an image of unwavering competence in meetings. However, the truth of my emotional exhaustion could not be concealed. A pivotal conversation with my committee chair, who was also a mother-scholar, proved transformative. In this supportive environment characterized by open dialogue, trust, and collaborative problem-solving, I found solace. Her reassurance allowed me to embrace my overwhelmed state without fear of damaging my self-image. This experience underscored the vital role of psychological safety in academia, where leaders serve as catalysts for fostering collaborative problem-solving among colleagues.

Psychological safety is not merely established in moments of crisis when immediate action is required; but rather, it is during time when little risk exists. In this safe space, not only did I find the courage and language to voice my concerns, but my committee chair also fostered an atmosphere where I felt comfortable sharing my challenges and providing context. Through her mentorship, I learned to advocate for myself as a mother and scholar, set realistic boundaries, and prioritize self-care amidst competing academic demands. Trust, a foundational element of psychological safety, permeated our interactions, empowering me to navigate uncertainties with resilience, purpose, and growing confidence. Through collaborative effort, we devised a comprehensive plan that not only addressed the committee's requirements and institutional graduation criteria but also contributed to my main academic goal—the advancement of existing knowledge in the field.

Her support, perspective, and demonstration of resilience as a 'mother-scholar' not only boosted my confidence but also validated the difficulties I encountered. Embracing the interconnectedness of the roles of 'mother' and 'scholar', my committee chair shared her own challenges and triumphs in similar situations, creating a psychologically safe space for me to seek support and advocate for myself. Black women were central to my dissertation research, many who navigated the complexities of 'mother-scholarship' alongside the unique challenges of being Black women. With guidance from my committee chair, I refined my focus on exploring resilient leadership, aiming to amplify the experiences and valuable contributions of Black women. I was able to complete my dissertation, feel empowered to continue to explore my chosen topic area, and advocate for healthy boundaries as a mother.

This experience served as a reminder of the potent impact women can have when they advocate for each other and use their experiences to educate others. My professional goal was refined in these moments to extend opportunities for Black women, and other marginalized groups, to thrive in environments that are psychologically safe and empowering. These spaces should respect and nurture their multifaceted identities. Rather than just securing representation, I aim to support universities to foster an environment where Black women can voice their concerns, advocate for their needs, and contribute to the collective advancement of all marginalized identities. This narrative emphasizes the significant influence of psychological safety on mother-scholars who are navigating the intricacies of academia.

In conclusion, the journey of mother-scholars is a testament to resilience, adaptation, and the transformative power of psychological safety in academia. The challenges of navigating motherhood and academic pursuits, particularly amidst a global crisis, are immense. Yet, these challenges also provide opportunities for growth, self-advocacy, and the strengthening of resilience. The role of psychological safety, trust, and supportive mentorship cannot be overstated in this context. As mother-scholars, we not only contribute to the advancement of knowledge in our respective fields, but we also pave the way for future generations of women in academia. Our experiences underscore the importance of creating inclusive, supportive environments that recognize and validate the interconnected roles we play. Ultimately, our narrative is one of strength, perseverance, and the relentless pursuit of academic excellence amidst the complexities of motherhood. This journey, while challenging, is a powerful reminder of our capacity to thrive amidst uncertainties, contributing to a richer, more diverse academic landscape.

BALANCING PERSONAL AND PROFESSIONAL ROLES: A JOURNEY OF SELF-DISCOVERY AND GROWTH

Managing the complexities of my roles required a careful balance of time management, prioritization, and introspection to keep my sense of purpose and direction. I found myself switching between personal tasks like changing diapers and professional duties like data collection, blurring the lines between my personal and professional life within my home office.

While delving into my dissertation concepts, I was constantly reminded that our self-understanding forms the basis of our identities and how we perceive and relate to the world (Saakvitne et al., 1998). During my most overwhelming and vulnerable moments, I reflected on my needs as a mother and an emerging researcher. This led me to question my perceptions of these roles and my expectations of myself in each. By asking myself questions like 'How have you changed?' and 'What do you value about yourself now?', I was able to identify the values and needs of my current experience. This honesty facilitated self-discovery (Lewis-Strickland, 2021), enabling me to unlock inherent tools and gain new insights. Continuously revisiting these questions helped me to realize my strengths such as time management and task prioritization, but also helped me to identify areas where I could improve, such as asking for help and prioritizing self-care.

As I continue to ask myself these questions, I'm reminded of the mindset, skills, and tools that I developed during this period. I continually draw upon these resources to support myself, organizational leaders, and organizational cultures. As a leader, I continually engage in the often uncomfortable task of self-discovery to identify and reconnect with my strengths, opportunities, and boundaries. This mindset keeps continuous self-improvement at the forefront of my actions and conversations. I strive to prevent negative judgement from clouding my self-exploration to ensure I am being kind to myself and giving myself grace to be efficient, forming a basis for self-compassion. Professionally, this helps me to model self-discovery and reflection to clients and share relevant vulnerable moments, hoping that leaders can understand this value and try to implement and model it for their respective teams.

The skills of introspection and reflection, honed during this time, underscored the importance of self-knowledge as a way to understand and define my purpose. Often, in the workplace, we move from one deadline to another, making work seem very robotic and scripted. By intentionally engaging in introspection and reflection, we can stay connected with our purpose. For me, I realized that many scholars who are also mothers were facing similar challenges and constraints. When I explored my resilience, I reflected on my professional experiences and realized that my resilience had been tested in the past, and there were situations that I could have handled better.

Exploring my thoughts and feelings towards the scholarship and literature I was constantly engaged with, I began to articulate to others what my purpose and goals were in my professional life, something I had always struggled to articulate clearly. My goal was to help higher education leaders be better people leaders; to help these leaders create spaces where everyone could contribute and thrive, where everyone could bring their unique experiences and talents to the team and help to create innovative solutions for the purpose and goal of higher education. As a black woman, I realized I had a significant influence to bring my intersectional perspective to the conversation to influence authority to make choices that were inclusive of and benefited everyone. Black women are often stereotyped as having an attitude, being loud, confident, and assertive (Rosette, et al., 2016), which often leads to unwarranted negative associations and microaggressions. This leaves black women to control their own narrative.

In my professional experience, I realized that I had not advocated for myself, which left my narrative to be defined by others with a limited perspective. Hence, it is important for Black women to engage in the tiring but necessary act of asserting their psychological safety to manage the narrative others have of them in interpersonal situations (Saakvitne & Pearlman, 1996), in order to thrive. The skill of finding comfort in reflection resulted in my ability to express my thoughts and feelings towards the material, strengthening my confidence in my research and the ability to advocate for conceptual inclusions.

Creating a product that I am proud to share, discuss, and collaborate with others has transferred into my professional experiences, as I work with people leaders to share tactical strategies for individual and team development. As I reflect on my journey, it becomes evident that the intersection of psychological safety, resilience, and purpose-driven behavior profoundly influenced my personal and professional growth. By fostering an environment of trust and support, my committee chair enabled me to navigate challenges with confidence, ultimately shaping my trajectory in academia. This experience serves as a testament to the transformative power of psychological safety in fostering professional confidence, resilience, and well-being.

CONCLUSION

This chapter traces the author's growing comprehension of psychological safety and resilience in both personal and professional spheres. The chapter begins with brief relevant background explanation of key terms: psychological safety, black women's intersectionality, and resilience. The author shared two narratives that discussed psychological safety in organizational and personal settings. The author stresses the need for environments that empower individuals to share their experiences and achievements, acknowledging that obstacles to self-advocacy can impede both individual and organizational growth. The author advocates for inclusivity and the amplification of diverse voices to foster a sense of belonging.

The narrative then shifts from individual to organizational perspectives, offering practical strategies to address the unique challenges faced by Black women in professional staff positions within low psychological safety environments. The author urges leaders to proactively assess and enhance psychological safety climates within their teams, using tools such as surveys and crucial conversations to gather insights and collaborate on interventions that nurture psychological safety.

The chapter also candidly discusses the challenges of balancing motherhood with the demanding dissertation process. The author recognizes the crucial role of psychological safety in fostering collaborative problem-solving and resilience. By establishing a psychologically safe environment, the author was able to voice concerns, share challenges, and provide context. This underscores the transformative potential of psychological safety in nurturing professional confidence, resilience, and well-being.

In conclusion, this chapter serves as a powerful testament to the transformative power of psychological safety and resilience in both personal and professional contexts. It highlights the profound impact of introspection and development, and the pivotal role of psychological safety in shaping individual journeys and fostering environments of trust and encouragement. The author's journey exemplifies the transformative potential of psychological safety in tackling challenges with confidence and purpose. The chapter ends with a call to action for organizations to champion inclusivity and prioritize collective advancement, thereby unlocking the full potential of their diverse workforce and fostering cultures characterized by belongingness and innovation. This exploration of psychological safety and resilience serves as a poignant reminder of the significant role these concepts play in shaping individual paths and nurturing environments of trust and encouragement. Through introspection and professional evolution, the author's journey epitomizes the transformative potential of psychological safety in confronting challenges with assurance and purpose.

REFERENCES

American Psychological Association. (2024). *Work in America*. Retrieved from the American Psychological Association website: https://www.apa.org/pubs/reports/work-in-america/2024/2024-work-in-america-report.pdf

Chance, N. L. (2022). Resilient leadership: A phenomenological exploration into how black women in higher education leadership navigate cultural adversity. *Journal of Humanistic Psychology*, 62(1), 44–78. DOI: 10.1177/00221678211003000

Deloitte. (2024.). *Latest trends in higher education*. Deloitte Insights. Retrieved August 2, 2024, from https://www2.deloitte.com/us/en/insights/industry/public-sector/latest-trends-in-higher-education.html

Edmondson, A. (1999). Psychological safety and learning behavior in work teams. *Administrative Science Quarterly*, 44(2), 350–383. DOI: 10.2307/2666999

Edmondson, A. C. (2018). *The Fearless Organization: Creating Psychological Safety in the Workplace for Learning, Innovation, and Growth*. John Wiley & Sons.

Goodwin, E. V. (2016). The Effects of Male Leadership on Workplace Gender Identity, Self-Efficacy, and Career Aspirations of Women Working in College Athletics (Doctoral dissertation) Retrieved from Ohiolink.

Hasan, F., & Kashif, M. (2021). Psychological safety, meaningfulness and empowerment as predictors of employee well-being: A mediating role of promotive voice. *Asia-Pacific Journal of Business Administration*, 13(1), 40–59. DOI: 10.1108/APJBA-11-2019-0236

Heffernan, T., & Bosetti, L. (2021). Incivility: The new type of bullying in higher education. *Cambridge Journal of Education*, 51(5), 641–652. DOI: 10.1080/0305764X.2021.1897524

Hora, S., Lemoine, G. J., Xu, N., & Shalley, C. E. (2021). Unlocking and closing the gender gap in creative performance: A multilevel model. *Journal of Organizational Behavior*, 42(3), 297–312. DOI: 10.1002/job.2500

Kezar, A., & Elrod, S. (2020). Taken for Granted: Improving the Culture of Celebration, Appreciation, and Recognition in Higher Education. *Change*, 52(5), 29–36. DOI: 10.1080/00091383.2020.1807880

Klaphaak, A. (2021, August 25). How to self reflect. wikiHow. https://www.wikihow.com/Self-Reflect

Ledesma, J. (2014). Conceptual frameworks and research models on resilience in leadership. *SAGE Open*, 4(3), 1–8. DOI: 10.1177/2158244014545464

Liu, Y., & Keller, R. T. (2021). How psychological safety impacts R&D project teams' performance. *Research Technology Management*, 64(2), 39–45. DOI: 10.1080/08956308.2021.1863111

Masten, A. S. (2014). Global perspectives on resilience in children and youth. *Child Development*, 85(1), 6–20. DOI: 10.1111/cdev.12205 PMID: 24341286

National Center for Education Statistics. (2021.). Table 314.40. Percentage distribution of faculty, by race/ethnicity, sex, and faculty status in degree-granting postsecondary institutions, by control and level of institution: Fall 2019. Retrieved [June 8, 2024], from https://nces.ed.gov/programs/digest/d22/tables/dt22_314.40.asp

Neff, K. (2011). *Self-Compassion: The Proven Power of Being Kind to Yourself*. William Morrow.

Oikelome, G. (2017). Pathway to the President: The Perceived Impact of Identity Structures on the Journey Experiences of Women College Presidents. *International Journal of Multicultural Education*, 19(3), 23–40. DOI: 10.18251/ijme.v19i3.1377

Pang, N. S.-K. (2020). Teachers' reflective practices in implementing assessment for learning skills in classroom teaching. *ECNU Review of Education.*, (August), 1–21. DOI: 10.1177/2096531120936290

Saakvitne, K. W., & Pearlman, L. A. (1996). *Transforming the pain: A workbook on vicarious traumatization*. W. W. Norton & Co.

Schein, E., & Bennis, W. G. (1965). Personal and organizational change through group methods: The laboratory approach. New York: John Wiley and Sons. *Inc. Search in*.

Townsend, C. V. (2021). Identity politics: Why African American women are missing in administrative leadership in public higher education. *Educational Management Administration & Leadership*, 49(4), 584–600. DOI: 10.1177/1741143220935455

United States. Public Health Service. Office of the Surgeon General. (2022). The U.S. Surgeon General's Framework for Workplace Mental Health & Well-Being. Department of Health and Human Services.

Williams, B. M. (2023). "It's Just My Face:" Workplace Policing of Black Professional Women in Higher Education. *Journal of Women and Gender in Higher Education*, 16(2), 67–89. DOI: 10.1080/26379112.2023.2172730

Chapter 11
Where There's a Will, There's a Way

Julie Lynn Richards
SUNY Plattsburgh, USA

ABSTRACT

This chapter traces my transformative journey to a leadership position in higher education. Unlike a singular defining moment, my path unfolded through events and a significant leap of faith, guiding me back to academia and culminating in a leadership role. Embracing change and adventure laid the groundwork, while an unwavering commitment to continuous learning became foundational. "Where There's a Will, There's a Way" explores the instrumental role of networking and mentorship in shaping my leadership trajectory, highlighting flexibility and adaptability through overcoming struggles. Defying age stereotypes and persevering formed another crucial aspect. Emphasizing personal fulfillment alongside professional achievement became pivotal, underscoring the multifaceted nature of my worldview. The continuous pursuit of harmonizing personal passions acted as a driving force, propelling me into leadership in higher education. This narrative provides insights into the interconnected dynamics of personal growth, resilience, and passion pursuit in academic leadership development.

INTRODUCTION

Leadership can be approached and defined in many different ways (Benmira and Agboola, 2021). My journey to a leadership role in higher education wasn't marked by a single defining moment, but rather a series of experiences and a significant leap of faith that steered me back to academia, eventually leading to a leadership position. This crucial leap involved embracing change and new opportunities, setting

DOI: 10.4018/979-8-3693-3144-6.ch011

the stage for my transformative journey. A strong commitment to lifelong learning, a trait common among successful leaders (Amey, 2005; Frick, Polizzi, and Frick, 2009), was vital. Networking strengths and actively pursuing mentorship were key in shaping my leadership path, while adaptability and flexibility were developed through considerable challenges. Overcoming age-related stereotypes and discouragement through determination, persistence, and resilience was another important aspect of my journey. The constant drive to align and integrate my passions was the force that propelled me forward, solidifying the multifaceted perspective that ultimately led me to leadership in higher education.

THE EARLY YEARS

Embarking on risks and embracing novel opportunities has been a constant theme in my academic and career journey. During my undergraduate years, I had a strong desire to explore social work within a socialized healthcare system overseas. Determined to realize this vision, I persuaded the faculty and administration to support my endeavor in developing an internship focused on geriatric social work in England. I also proposed a research project comparing the role of the social worker in a national health service with that in the American healthcare system.

At that time, the notion of students studying abroad was far less common than it is today (Engle & Engle, 2003). Venturing into uncharted territory, I became a trailblazer by initiating an international internship and research project as a sophomore. There was no precedent. Yet for me, the act of forging opportunities to pursue my professional and intellectual interests felt ingrained in my very nature. The allure of living abroad and navigating the challenges independently, all while actively pursuing my career and intellectual aspirations, was an adventure I couldn't resist. Perhaps this experience was the first sign of things to come in my academic career?

Following the completion of my undergraduate degree, I delved into the field of social work, accumulating a diverse range of experiences from a brief stint in the Middle East to residential care in the rural US and urban child welfare. However, it took just three years for my path to lead me to graduate school for a master's degree in social work in Canada. Each of these experiences presented unique challenges, periods of solitude, opportunities to forge new connections, and a continual test of my resilience, adaptability, and capacity for personal and professional growth, characteristics that would later serve me well in my leadership roles (Deshwal & Ali, 2020). Through navigating these diverse roles and challenges, I emerged as a more versatile and empathetic professional, shaped by the richness of my journey and the array of individuals I encountered along the way.

As a newly minted MSW, I returned to the US and was hired as the first official school social worker in the state where I resided. And even though I held an MSW, recognized as the terminal degree in Social Work, I had always intended to pursue a doctoral degree. While working as a school social worker, I found myself immersed in a research study designed to evaluate an innovative treatment approach to address school failure, truancy, and other behavioral issues. Through my active involvement in this research project, I caught the attention of a doctoral program in social work.

I was recruited to join the doctoral program in social work, where I could extend my research efforts with the principal investigator and research team. This arrangement would not only have allowed me to continue to explore innovative treatment approaches but would have also provided the opportunity for the principal investigator to mentor and guide my development as a scholar (Zipp, Cahill & Clark, 2009; Ocobock et al., 2022). I believed that this sort of mentorship relationship for a doctoral program would be essential for my professional growth and career as I tend to thrive in these types of intellectual mentorship opportunities. The invitation to pursue the doctoral degree became a pivotal moment in my academic journey.

However, despite my initial aspirations for a doctoral degree, I made the conscious decision to put those plans on hold as I had recently married and desired to start a family. Unlike many mothers who grapple with trying to balance the complexity of the various competing priorities of higher education, study, work and family, which requires economic, social, emotional and cultural family capital to support a mother's academic success (Webber and Dismore, 2020), I felt conflicted and under-equipped with the full range of capital required for success and therefore opted to prioritize my family life. I focused on my social work practice and emerging academic career. Ultimately, it's a decision I have never regretted, as it aligns with my holistic approach to success, valuing personal fulfillment alongside professional achievements (Bocheliuk et al., 2022; Glavinska et al, 2020; Mikolajczyk, 2021).

While I cherished my work in school social work and found fulfillment in training upcoming social workers through supervising field internships for both undergraduate and graduate students, a familiar urge for a new professional challenge began to surface. My inclination towards adventure and change led me to recognize that when my professional responsibilities became too comfortable, it signaled a readiness for transformation. Eager for something new, I started exploring possibilities, and it was during this exploration that I first turned my gaze toward a career in higher education. Higher education offered more flexible work hours than my school social work schedule, which was particularly important to me with a growing family. It was also known for providing opportunities to be creative and innovative, and the chance to shape the next generation of social workers and interventions.

MOVING ON TO ACADEMIA

Embarking on a new chapter in my academic and professional journey, I assumed a full-time university administrative position to coordinate and co-lead a statewide effort to build public schools' capacity to include children with severe emotional and behavioral issues. Simultaneously, I accepted a position as an adjunct instructor of social work at the same university. As my involvement deepened, I transitioned to a full-time role as the director of the undergraduate social work program at that same university. This shift allowed me to further contribute to the development and growth of the social work program, solidifying my commitment to both education and the advancement of social work practices.

As my career progressed in academia, I encountered challenges in advancing without the PhD., despite holding the 'terminal degree' of an MSW. Without a PhD, I could not enter a tenure track faculty position. Rather, I was a lecturer. And as with most faculty positions around the time of the Great Recession, the increasing teaching load (Giroux, 2014) made it difficult to pursue additional academic projects. As a program director with a teaching load of two courses per year prior to the Great Recession, and the majority of my time dedicated to administration, recruitment, advisement, and committee work, I had time to also pursue research and other creative academic projects. I was promoted to Senior Lecturer and after the recession, my teaching load expanded to three courses per semester along with my administrative duties.

Meanwhile, as my family grew and I was navigating the academic landscape, I found that despite outward expressions of support for faculty with young families, there were subtle messages conveying a different reality (Ainslie, 2022; Cardel et al, 2020; Gallardo, 2021; Toepell, 2003). The scheduling of courses, for example, posed a challenge for those wanting to be present for their children's bedtime, making it difficult to teach specific classes. Informal departmental interactions essential for faculty bonding, networking, and exchanging ideas, often occurred outside regular business hours. Unfortunately, this created a dilemma for me as I couldn't stay late due to my children's schedules and family responsibilities.

Expressing my aspirations to connect with fellow faculty, teach certain courses, and engage in academic pursuits was, at times, met with skepticism. On one occasion, a comment implying that my priority as a mother would hinder being taken seriously in academia was disheartening and infuriating, although perhaps not uncommon in academia (Francis & Stulz, 2020; Keohane, 2020). What I found even more troublesome is that this comment came from an academic sister. I was surprised to find misogynic comments coming from female colleagues. I had thought my academic sisters would support my aspirations, but as some scholars note, female colleagues can sabotage a fellow sister's career (Allen and Flood, 2018; Brock, 2008), perhaps even more destructively than a misogynistic man. These experiences highlighted the need for a more inclusive and supportive academic environment that accommodates diverse responsibilities and aspirations of faculty members, particularly those with family commitments. I have made every effort to carry this important lesson forward throughout my career with my interactions with colleagues.

As my children continued to grow, the Department Chair at that time, a male, began encouraging me to rekindle my pursuit of a PhD. Adaptability, a recognized leadership quality (van Assen, 2020) emerged as a significant theme in my life, prompting me to navigate changing circumstances and remain open to growth in new directions. Recognizing the need for flexibility to succeed in my career, my husband and I had extensive conversations, and he ultimately supported the idea of managing the responsibilities of raising three children while I pursued a PhD.

PURSUING DOCTORAL STUDIES LATER IN LIFE

At the age of 46, I returned to school, marking another pivotal point in my journey. I decided to pursue an interdisciplinary doctoral degree in International Community and Family Studies. Balancing full-time work, raising a family, and staying happily married during this endeavor required meticulous juggling of priorities. I was keenly aware of the challenges, particularly the higher divorce rates among PhD students than their counterparts in the general public (Brannock, Litten & Smith, 2000). Nevertheless, I remained steadfast in my commitment not to compromise my family or marriage for career advancement.

In the middle of my academic pursuits, I developed an international service-learning program. This venture became the true highlight of my career thus far. Periodically bringing students to India, I collaborated with non-government organizations and schools, contributing to projects addressing human rights and advancing many of the Millennium Development Goals, and later the Sustainable Development Goals. This labor of love allowed me to advocate for global causes and build meaningful partnerships.

Simultaneously, I became involved in providing consultation and technical assistance to organizations in India, fostering collaboration and program development. This engagement evolved organically as I had the privilege of hosting some of my partners back in the US to help them further network and expand their repertoire of collaborating partners. During one such visit, I shared a paper that I had written for one of my doctoral community development courses. Sharing that paper led to an invitation from the executive director to provide consultation regarding program development. I began traveling to India, in between service-learning trips, to work with the executive director and staff on various consultation projects and provide technical assistance for several years. During some of these visits, my colleagues also facilitated additional consultation opportunities with other partner organizations.

As I concluded my doctoral studies, a defining moment began to crystalize. I envisioned integrating my passion for international practice and development with my calling to social work and educating the next generation of social workers. While I incorporated social work concepts and perspectives into my research and teaching, integrating them into the curriculum proved challenging. My colleagues did not fully embrace the interdisciplinary approach to international practice and development that I advocated during that time.

Further, while I remained at the rank of senior lecturer, I was explicitly informed that research could not be part of my workload, given my non-tenure track faculty status. What I found even more troublesome about this comment was that it came from a female administrator. It felt, in part, like the personification of the Queen Bee Syndrome, where female leaders avoid supporting their female subordinates to counteract the feelings of inadequacy and exclusion that male colleagues impose on them because of gender (Achhnani & Gupta, 2022; Baykal, Soyalp & Yeşil, 2020). I expected more from her; I expected that she would do everything possible to support my career advancement as I assumed she knew how difficult it was for a woman to thrive in higher education. The male administrators who came before her all supported my aspirations and me advancing my career through research and further education. However, this person refused to consider the human capital I offered, and, in fact, I felt quite sabotaged by her toward the end of my career at the university.

Recognizing that my academic career was at a stalemate at the university, I realized that it was time for a new adventure. The desire to align my professional calling and passion with a more supportive environment led me to seek fresh opportunities and avenues where I could truly integrate my expertise in social work, international practice, and development.

INTEGRATION OF PURPOSE

Embarking on a new chapter about a year after I completed my PhD, and with nearly 51 trips around the sun, I took a leap of faith and left academia to pursue a career in international development. What I hadn't anticipated was the formidable challenge of finding employment in this field, given my limited relevant experience and the fact that I had crossed the age threshold of 50 (McLaughlin & Neumark, 2022; Walker & Zelin, 2021). Ageism was real and I could find inspiration from, and relate to, much of Jane Pauley's Your Life Calling: Reimagining the Rest of Your Life (2014) in which she shares multiple anecdotes from interviews with people changing their careers after 50. I was fortunate enough to have the safety net of a supportive partner, and my entire family made financial sacrifices while we lived on just my husband's income for a while.

As many can attest, job hunting is a consuming endeavor. Engaging with networks and diligently exploring search engines catering to international humanitarian and relief communities became my daily routine. I meticulously expanded my digital network, reaching out to fellow members for insights, suggestions, and additional networking possibilities. The application process became a substantial part of my routine, with well over 200 applications submitted. Regrettably, my resume seldom advanced past the screening conducted by computer software.

During interviews, I encountered the paradox of being deemed overqualified for certain roles while simultaneously being informed that experience in Sub-Saharan Africa was a prerequisite for consideration in others. Undeterred, despite being perceived as potentially past mid-career, I remained open to entry level positions, driven by the desire to amass experience and contribute to my passion for fostering a just and equitable world. I acknowledged that international development embodies a reciprocal process, involving the exchange of ideas and adapting and sharing among many different innovations and locales that ultimately are mutually dependent, even if it isn't yet clear how and why.

Barriers persisted. My PhD and prior experience, which were predominantly in middle- and high-income countries, created perceptions of overqualification for the entry-level roles essential to my desired career shift. Moreover, the additional layer of being a woman over 50, though unspoken in professional settings, echoed in my interactions with practitioners and peers.

Undaunted, I refused to surrender. Seeking feedback from interviewers, I proactively inquired about potential organizations where they thought I might be a good fit or colleagues to connect with for network-building. Despite these efforts, the feeling of perpetually being a bridesmaid and never the bride lingered.

I found myself surrounded by friends who admired the courage of my leap of faith and by family members who praised my tenacity as I ventured into a career change at this stage of life. Oddly, I didn't perceive myself as particularly brave or tenacious; rather, I felt compelled to keep trying, as if there were no other viable option. Thankfully, my family served as a safety net, minimizing financial risks. My guiding mantra, "Where there's a will, there's a way," fueled my belief that the right opportunity was out there, and I just needed to cast a wide enough net.

Despite advice from career counselors and well-intentioned friends advocating for a more targeted approach, I found myself defaulting to the broader strategy. While diligently pursuing international development positions on a daily basis for two years, I also engaged in small consultation projects locally. It was during one of these projects, when I was in a coffee shop, that I overheard someone mentioning a local private, nonprofit organization that works internationally to eradicate unnecessary blindness. This snippet jogged my memory; I had read about the founder and the organization's mission several years earlier in a local paper, but it had slipped my mind until that moment.

Upon returning home, I wasted no time. I promptly emailed the organization expressing my interest, inquiring about potential consultation opportunities for program evaluation, and attached my resume. To my surprise, within a few days, I received a call from the Program Director inviting me for an interview. During our conversation, she shared the exciting news that the Board of Directors had just approved the creation of a new position. Instead of offering me a consultancy, they extended an offer for the position of Program Manager. My responsibilities would span across Ghana, Ethiopia and Bhutan. I would collaborate with country directors to plan, fund and facilitate cataract surgical events, capacity-building training, and ensure that each partner had the most effective and uptodate equipment available. I played a key role in crafting grant proposals and reports, monitoring outcomes, and developing standardized operating procedures.

This position provided an invaluable learning experience in international development and public health. I found myself traveling frequently to Sub-Saharan Africa and engaging in daily intercultural communication. However, a lingering sense of yearning for research persisted. Despite hopeful moments when it seemed my schedule might allow for research projects exploring the impact of our programs on workforce, poverty, and other critical issues, the pressing need to ensure continued access to surgeries for the most vulnerable community members took precedence. Understandably, the pursuit of research had to be shelved once again for the foreseeable future.

THE PRIME YEARS

Although I did not think that I would return to academia, one day I was casually browsing job postings (a habit formed over two years of job searching), when I stumbled upon an intriguing opportunity. A tenure track social work faculty position was available at a university just an hour and a half from my home. Aware of others who successfully navigated a similar commute without much complaint, I decided, on a whim, to submit an application and promptly forgot about it.

Fast forward to the spring of 2020, where I found myself teaching an international social work course as an adjunct professor at a local college. This experience, despite the unexpected pivot to an online video platform during the COVID lockdown, reminded me of how much I enjoyed teaching. This then became another pivotal and defining moment; not only did I crave research opportunities, but I had missed teaching.

Coincidentally, it was also during the onset of the COVID pandemic when the Faculty Search Committee Chairperson reached out to me about the tenure track faculty position. During the interview and hiring process, I discovered that the department and college truly valued international collaboration and development. I began to see a place for myself at this institution where I could thrive as a social worker working in international development. I accepted the position under the condition that I could apply for tenure within three years (I wasn't getting any younger!).

In some respects, it seemed like a return to academia, but in reality, it was a new beginning. I found myself in an institution that not only appreciated my unique perspective and experiences in social work but also provided an environment where I could truly thrive with them. This marked another defining moment in my journey. In the past, I had to choose between teaching social work or international development, but now in my new tenure track role, I discovered a space where I could seamlessly do both.

During my first semester in this role, I received an invitation from the vice president of one of the many non-profit organizations that I had applied to for an international development position. The offer was to undertake a six-month consultancy to support the Instructional Design Team. The task involved designing and testing teacher training and master trainer materials for evidence-based resilience training targeted at marginalized youth worldwide in preparation for program expansion. This experience reaffirmed my decision to embrace academia once again.

In a delightful twist, I not only continued to teach but also used my consultancy work as practical examples in the classroom. The non-profit organization expressed interest in hearing from my students about our international projects. This unique opportunity allowed me to integrate my two passions seamlessly, reinforcing the fulfillment of returning to academia.

The next pivotal moment in my journey came with the achievement of tenure. As previously mentioned, when I accepted the position, I negotiated a fast track to tenure; a decision driven by my willingness to take calculated risks and considering the successful outcome of my previous leap of faith when I left academia. Utilizing my scholarship in international development and international practice, I strategically advanced my career and successfully secured tenure. At the age of 56, I attained the rank of Associate Professor with the assurance and stability that tenure provides. This accomplishment not only validated my decision to return to academia but also showcased the positive outcomes of taking bold and calculated steps in one's professional journey. Further, I was able to integrate international development and practice with curriculum in such a way that I, along with twelve other colleagues from across the country, are promoting standards of excellence for international social work into curricula as we lead the infusion of global and intercultural content into existing social work courses.

The pace of my professional journey accelerated as swiftly as I secured tenure when my departmental colleagues approached me to assume the role of Chair, a position that had not been filled by a social worker for several years. This proposition posed an intriguing decision for me. My return to academia was driven by my desire to amalgamate my passion for international development with social work education. A significant portion of my teaching and research centered on equipping students with a global perspective and rights-based, sustainable approach to addressing, responding to, and ultimately preventing social problems. In fact, with support from my colleagues, I created a Global Social Action Certificate program. Additionally, my own teaching emphasized intercultural and interprofessional communication training and research to prepare students for careers in international practice, whether overseas or with local immigrant communities.

The question of whether to accept the Chair position arose, causing me to reflect on my original motivations for returning to academia. Was I prepared to momentarily set aside my focus on teaching and scholarship in order to delve into administration? Hadn't my return to academia been driven by the desire to engage in impactful teaching and dedicated scholarship?

While I was grappling with this decision, our department was experiencing an exhilarating period. We recently received approval for our Global Social Action Certificate Program from the state's Board of Education and had launched our online baccalaureate completion program. Additionally, there were discussions about the potential offering of an online MSW program. Taking on the role of department chair during this dynamic phase presented a leadership opportunity that hadn't crossed my mind before. Although I had engaged in program development throughout my practice career and had some experience as an undergraduate program director in my earlier academic role, envisioning myself in this leadership position at this particular level and stage in my career was a new consideration.

The prospect of guiding our department through these initiatives to expand our offerings and contribute to the growth of the social work workforce, all while supporting my colleagues in their professional development and scholarly pursuits, became compelling. Reflecting on the legacy I wished to leave as I approached the advanced stage of my career, I saw the opportunity to solidify the integration of social work with international development, build a robust workforce dedicated to supporting our most vulnerable community members, and address systemic issues perpetuating their challenges. Furthermore, the chance to support my colleagues as they worked towards their goals added to the appeal of this leadership position. I was interested in a feminine leadership style that emphasizes collaboration and faculty involvement, as opposed to a more traditional, authoritarian style associated with masculinity (Abdulraham & Amoush, 2020). Further, given my previous experience with Queen Bee leadership, the chance to encourage and foster my colleagues' continuous professional growth and the Department's internal human capital was incredibly appealing to me. After careful consideration, I made the decision to embrace the challenge, recognizing the privilege it offered to cap my career by enhancing our programs and fostering the growth of our faculty.

Through this journey, I have learned several things about myself. I do enjoy taking risks and embracing new opportunities. Taking a leap of faith not only challenged me but furthered my resolve in my personal motto of "Where there's a will, there's a way." Some of my strongest attributes, and the ones of which I am most proud, are my determination and persistence. My journey also taught me about balancing career and family. At certain points in my life, I made choices to prioritize my family that demonstrate a holistic approach to success. It was not easy to relinquish career timelines and postpone goals, but over the course of my journey, I was able to have it all through the path I chose. The ability to adapt and stay flexible, coupled with the establishment of new relationships, not only opened doors to emerging opportunities but also empowered me to pursue my goals, overcoming age-related stereotypes along the way.

In reflecting on my professional journey, there was not one, but several pivotal moments, each requiring resilience and flexibility, along with a steadfast commitment to my aspirational goals. From taking a profound leap of faith in pursuit of international development opportunities to negotiating an expedited track to tenure and eventually assuming the chairship of a department, my journey has been unconventional, yet tremendously rewarding.

The unconventional path I traveled in reaching a leadership position as a woman in higher education has underscored the importance of staying true to one's passions, taking calculated risks, and embracing opportunities that may not conform to traditional timelines. Balancing (or perhaps better phrased as juggling) career, family, and the pursuit of personal goals has been both challenging and gratifying, affirming that success can be achieved through a holistic approach. My circuitous journey through practice and academia never wavered from upholding the importance of personal fulfillment alongside professional achievement.

As I reflect on my experiences, I am reminded that there is no one-size-fits-all trajectory to leadership in academia. While the journey has not been a direct route, and in fact, quite circuitous and filled with unexpected turns, it is precisely this unpredictability that has fostered growth, resilience, and a unique set of skills and perspectives. In embracing the unexpected, not only have I overcome challenges, but I have also discovered opportunities that have enriched my career and hopefully contributed to the broader landscape of higher education leadership.

REFERENCES

Abdulrahman, M., & Amoush, A. H. (2020). Female characteristics and their new roles in leadership. *Journal of Business and Management Sciences*, 8(2), 38–47.

Achhnani, B., & Gupta, B. (2022). Queen bee: The culprit or the victim of sexism in the organisation. *British Journal of Administrative Management*.

Ainslie, K. M. (2022). 9 to 5 in Academia: Addressing barriers for women. *Molecular Pharmaceutics*, 20(1), 1–3. DOI: 10.1021/acs.molpharmaceut.2c00899 PMID: 36367381

Allen, T. G., & Flood, C. T. (2018). The Experiences of women in higher education: Who knew there wasn't a sisterhood? *Leadership and Research in Education*, 4, 10–27.

Amey, M. J. (2005). Leadership as learning: Conceptualizing the Process. *Community College Journal of Research and Practice*, 29(9-10), 689–704. DOI: 10.1080/10668920591006539

Baykal, E., Soyalp, E., & Yeşil, R. (2020). Queen Bee Syndrome: A Modern Dilemma of Working Women and Its Effects on Turnover Intentions. In Dincer, H., & Yüksel, S. (Eds.), *Strategic Outlook for Innovative Work Behaviours. Contributions to Management Science*. Springer., DOI: 10.1007/978-3-030-50131-0_9

Benmira, S., & Agboola, M. (2021). Evolution of leadership theory. *BMJ Leader*, •••, leader–2020.

Bocheliuk, V. Y., Spytska, L. V., Shaposhnykova, I. V., Turubarova, A. V., & Panov, M. S. (2022). Five stages of professional personality development: Comparative analysis. *Polish Psychological Bulletin*, 88–93.

Brannock, R. G., Litten, M. J., & Smith, J. (2000). The impact of doctoral study on marital satisfaction. *Journal of College Counseling*, 3(2), 123–130. DOI: 10.1002/j.2161-1882.2000.tb00172.x

Brock, B. L. (2008). When sisterly support changes to sabotage.

Cardel, M. I., Dhurandhar, E., Yarar-Fisher, C., Foster, M., Hidalgo, B., McClure, L. A., Pagoto, S., Brown, N., Pekmezi, D., Sharafeldin, N., Willig, A. L., & Angelini, C. (2020). Turning chutes into ladders for women faculty: A review and roadmap for equity in academia. *Journal of Women's Health*, 29(5), 721–733. DOI: 10.1089/jwh.2019.8027 PMID: 32043918

Deshwal, V., & Ali, M. A. (2020). A systematic review of various leadership theories. *Shanlax International Journal of Commerce*, 8(1), 38–43. DOI: 10.34293/commerce.v8i1.916

Engle, L., & Engle, J. (2003). Study abroad levels: Toward a classification of program types. *Frontiers: The Interdisciplinary Journal of Study Abroad*, 9(1), 1–20. DOI: 10.36366/frontiers.v9i1.113

Francis, L., & Stulz, V. (2020). Barriers and facilitators for women academics seeking promotion: Perspectives from the Inside. *Australian Universities Review*, 62(2), 47–60.

Frick, W. C., Polizzi, J. A., & Frick, J. E. (2009). Aspiring to a continuous learning ethic: Building authentic learning communities for faculty and administration. *Educational Leadership and Administration: Teaching and Program Development*, 21, 7–26.

Gallardo, M. (2021). Does maternity affect women's careers? Perceptions of working mothers in academia. *Educación XX1, 24*(1), 405-428.

Giroux, H. A. (2014). *Neoliberalism's war on higher education*. Haymarket Books.

Glavinska, O. D., Ovdiyenko, I. M., Brukhovetska, O. V., Chausova, T. V., & Didenko, M. S. V. (2020). Professional self-realization as a factor in the psychological well-being of specialists of caring professions. *Journal of Intellectual Disability - Diagnosis and Treatment, 8*(3), 548–559. https://doi.org/DOI: 10.6000/2292-2598.2020.08.03.32

Keohane, N. O. (2020). Women, power & leadership. *Daedalus*, 149(1), 236–250. DOI: 10.1162/daed_a_01785

McLaughlin, J. S., & Neumark, D. (2022). *Gendered Ageism and Disablism and Employment of Older Workers* (No. w30355). National Bureau of Economic Research.

Mikołajczyk, K. (2021). Sustainable development of an individual as a result of mutual enrichment of professional and personal life. *Sustainability (Basel)*, 13(2), 697. DOI: 10.3390/su13020697

Ocobock, C., Niclou, A., Loewen, T., Arslanian, K., Gibson, R., & Valeggia, C. (2022). Demystifying mentorship: Tips for successfully navigating the mentor–mentee journey. *American Journal of Human Biology*, 34(S1), e23690. DOI: 10.1002/ajhb.23690 PMID: 34664346

Pauley, J. (2014). *Your life calling: Reimagining the rest of your life*. Penguin Books.

Toepell, A. R. (2003). Academic mothers and their experiences navigating the academy. *Journal of the Motherhood Initiative for Research and Community Involvement*.

van Assen, M. F. (2020). Empowering leadership and contextual ambidexterity–The mediating role of committed leadership for continuous improvement. *European Management Journal*, 38(3), 435–449. DOI: 10.1016/j.emj.2019.12.002

Walker, R. V., & Zelin, A. I. (2021). "You're too young/old for this": The intersection of ageism and sexism in the workplace. In Cole, E., & Hollis-Sawyer, L. (Eds.), *Older women who work: Resilience, choice, and change* (pp. 161–187). American Psychological Association., DOI: 10.1037/0000212-010

Webber, L., & Dismore, H. (2020). Mothers and higher educations: Balancing time, study and space. *Journal of Further and Higher Education*, 45(6), 803–817. DOI: 10.1080/0309877X.2020.1820458

Zipp, G. P., Cahill, T., & Clark, M. (2009). The role of collaborative scholarship in the mentorship of doctoral students. [TLC]. *Journal of College Teaching and Learning*, 6(8). Advance online publication. DOI: 10.19030/tlc.v6i8.1111

Chapter 12
Balancing Lives:
A Thematic Analysis of Self-Care and Emotional Balance Among Female Professors

Shravani Minesh Kapse
https://orcid.org/0009-0006-4597-154X
Banasthali Vidyapith, India

Sandhya Gupta
Banasthali Vidyapith, India

Anu Raj Singh
Banasthali Vidyapith, India

Priyesh Kumar Singh
https://orcid.org/0000-0001-7552-5467
Banasthali Vidyapith, India

ABSTRACT

Female professors frequently experience extreme pressure and stressors when managing multiple duties, both personal and professional. They also think that they are more constrained because of their domestic duties. In fulfilling the demands of their personal and professional roles, female professors often struggle to maintain their self-care and emotional balance. This chapter has attempted to look into the self-care and emotional balance among female professors of two distinct groups, viz., 10 married female professors and 10 unmarried female professors, to explore whether there are any similarities and/or differences in their themes, and with the help of this thematic analysis, findings will be discussed.

DOI: 10.4018/979-8-3693-3144-6.ch012

1. INTRODUCTION

University faculty members are responsible for carrying out rigorous activities such as academic study, classroom instruction, and expert service. Significantly stressful situations pertaining to their workload as educators are typical scenarios for faculty members (Cladellas-Pros et al., 2018; Carrillo-Gonzalez et al., 2021). The well-being of university teachers may suffer from modifications to their working environment. Stress and job satisfaction seem to be correlated with aspects of the educational work environment, such as the inability to spend more time with students to solve their problems and the lack of effective task management (Sirajudeen et al., 2018). In addition, female professors think that they are more constrained because of their domestic duties. Moreover, there exists a belief that familial responsibilities obstruct professional progress and residual development. Monk-Turner and Fogerty (2010) stated in their study that it is difficult for women in academics to reconcile work and family responsibilities. Research has shown that female professors frequently experience extreme pressure and pressures when managing multiple duties, or both personal and professional (Beena and Poduval, 1992; Cushway and Tyler, 1994; Gadzella et al., 1990). As a result, individuals frequently find it difficult to make time for or engage in any self-care. It becomes difficult to keep emotional balance.

This chapter has attempted to look into the self care and emotional balance among female professors of two distinct groups viz. 10 married female professors and 10 unmarried female professors to explore whether there exist any kind of similarities and/or differences in their themes with the help of thematic analysis.

2. SELF-CARE

In this study, self-care is defined as actions done to lower stress levels brought on by daily life's pressures. Self-care, according to Orem (1995), is defined as acts people perform to maintain their safety and health on their own initiative or behalf. The act of practicing self-care involves adopting actions that uphold and maintain one's bodily and emotional well-being. These habits can be things like exercising, getting enough sleep, using social support, learning emotion-regulation skills, and engaging in mindfulness exercises. The Myers group (2012). This study has classified self-care into a number of categories, including academic, psychological, spiritual, emotional, interpersonal, cognitive, behavioural, and existential.

Self-care is acknowledged as a practical endeavour since it seeks to bring about specific controls of human functioning as well as growth through intentional activity seeking results under current or evolving environmental conditions. Orem,

Bekel, and Denyes (2001). Thus, it is clear that self-care has a variety of effects on a person's emotional equilibrium.

3. EMOTIONAL BALANCE

A person's ability to maintain emotional equilibrium is vital. Taking care of oneself naturally leads to emotional equilibrium. Two important psychological elements were included in the word "emotional balance": balance and emotions. The concept of balance sometimes referred to as stability, holds that a person has a suitable quantity of constant energy that tends to be dispersed equally throughout his body. When the person returns to this moderate condition, equilibrium is attained. This energy symbolizes the person's moderate level of stress. (1991) The Al-Obaidi, M. Retaining emotional equilibrium helps people deal with stress and demands, gives them constant resilience, and keeps emotions from being expressed excessively.

The capacity of the person to manage stress and demanding circumstances in life without endangering his mental health, disorder, self-control, or ability to cope with pleasant or unhappy circumstances (Mohammed, 2008).

4. METHODOLOGY

4.1. Sample Description

A sample of female university professors was incorporated in the study (10 married female professors and 10 unmarried female professors). 20 people were interviewed for this purpose. Purposive sampling technique was used to draw the sample. A varied sample with respect to race, ethnicity, and socioeconomic position was ensured through the selection of participants. Professors from different fields of study viz. law, management, finance, mathematics, social sciences were incorporated in the study to include different perspectives. Thematic analysis, or qualitative analysis, was carried out.

4.2. Procedure

This study used a qualitative research methodology to look into the self-care and emotional balance among female professors (10 married female professors and 10 unmarried female professors). Prior to the interview, the respondents were asked for their verbal consent and assured that the information they submitted would be kept private. The in-person interviews took place at the respective departments of the participants or at another appropriate location. The interviews were audio-recorded and analyzed. The data were examined using thematic analysis technique to identify recurrent themes and patterns in the responses provided by respondents.

5. RESULTS

The data was analysed using thematic analysis. From the audio recordings, themes and sub-themes were identified by in-depth examination and analysis.

Table 1. Themes and Sub-Themes for Behavioral Self Care among female professors (married)

Sr. No.	Themes	Sub-Themes	Findings
Behavioral Self Care among female professors			
1.	Engaging in activities other than work.	Outing, dancing, writing, eating out, watching OTT	Female professors do engage themselves in activities other than work
2.	Frequency of taking breaks	Long time gap, once a week, twice a month, very rarely	The frequency with which female professors take breaks is significantly lower

1.1. Engaging in Activities Other Than Work

Behavioural self-care for married female professors involves taking out time for their hobbies and other activities outside the realm of their work such as outings, dancing, and writing, dining out or watching OTT content in order to maintain their emotional and mental wellbeing.

Excerpt of participant 2 emphasizing on it; "I like to dance whenever I get time after coming back home from my lectures. It calms me."

Excerpt of participant 4 emphasizing on it; "I tend to watch Korean dramas, Thai dramas even while doing my work, I can multitask and it also trivializes the workload I have".

Excerpt of participant 10 emphasizing on it; "I am a foodie so whenever I feel stressed I go out to eat and I feel rejuvenated."

1.2. Frequency Of Taking Breaks

Behavioural self-care in married female professors involves intentionally taking out time for relaxation from daily workload, however the frequency varies from once/ twice or in a month to once in a week. This fluctuation depends upon the amount of work load and work pressure a female professor has to deal with on regular basis.

Excerpt of participant 14 emphasizing on it; "My tendency to take breaks varies to great extend, sometimes when there is too much work to do I hardly get time for myself. On most times it's once in 15-20 days.

Excerpt of participant 1 emphasizing on it; "I take breaks consciously whenever I feel the "work pressure" is getting to me I keep all of it aside and spend some time with my husband and children"

Excerpt of participant 20 emphasizing on it; "I take breaks twice a week sometimes the frequency may be less depending on my work demands, but yes once a week at any cost"

Table 2. Themes and Sub-Themes for Cognitive Self Care among female professors (married)

Sr. No.	Themes	Sub-Themes	Findings
Cognitive Self Care among female professors			
1.	Prioritization of internal aspects	Inner feeling, emotions, judgments, beliefs, thoughts, opinions	Female professors do prioritize their feelings, opinions, thoughts, believes judgments
2.	Self-Awareness/ Self-concept	Self-reflection, self-observation, self-scrutiny, introspection, thinking about life and goals	Female professors engage in self-reflection and introspection on nearly daily basis
3.	SWOT analysis	Strengths, weaknesses, positive traits, negative traits, weak points, pros and cons, deficiency,	Female professors are aware of their strengths and weaknesses and engage in its positive exploitation

2.1. Prioritization of Internal Aspects

Cognitive self-care in married female professors involves giving importance to and expressing their inner thoughts, emotions, beliefs, and judgments, understanding the significance of their overall being in both personal and professional lives.

Excerpt of participant 12 emphasizing on it; "yes, indeed my feelings, thoughts, beliefs, opinions are important to me and I don't hesitate to express them whenever I feel the need to do so"

Excerpt of participant 5 emphasizing on it; "being an independent woman, I feel prioritizing my beliefs and opinions comes very naturally to me… sometimes it just feels involuntary"

Excerpt of participant 3 emphasizing on it; "I express myself completely whenever I feel the person in front is going to understand what I tend to say otherwise I feel silence is bliss…"

2.2. Self-Awareness/Self-Concept

Cognitive self-care for married female professors involves self-reflection and introspection on daily basis, in order to understand their action, reactions, mistakes and upcoming goals. It helps them to preserve a sense of self awareness and positive self-concept and thus maintain healthy personal and professional lives.

Excerpt of participant 13 emphasizing on it; "every night before sleeping I have a habit to recap my whole day; what I did wrong and how I could have handled the situation differently; it makes me understand my action objectively…"

Excerpt of participant 3 emphasizing on it; "introspection is a part of my daily routine, at night I sit for 15 mins at least and put my mind into self reflection…."

Excerpt of participant 11 emphasizing on it; "yes self scrutiny is very important, I do it every day before sleeping and make my future goals and timetable sort of to achieve them..."

2.3. SWOT Analysis

Cognitive self-care in married female professors involves analyzing their strengthens, weaknesses, threats and opportunities through self-reflection in order to enhance their efficiency and effectiveness within both; personal and professional roles.

Excerpt of participant 8 emphasizing on it; "in these years of my career I have tried to understand my strengths and weaknesses and convert my weakness into something positive as well…"

Excerpt of participant 2 emphasizing on it; "by indulging in self reflection on daily basis I have come across my weaknesses and now I m trying to work on them.."

Excerpt of participant 9 emphasizing on it; "yes I know my strengths and weakness but I prefer to focus more on my strengths.."

Table 3. Themes and Sub-Themes for Psychological Self Care among female professors (married)

Sr. no.	Themes	Sub-Themes	Findings
Psychological Self Care among female professors			

1. Connection with self and others Sense of identity, feeling of detachment, trivializing emotions, emotional regulation, interpersonal relations Female professors feel connected to themselves. However, some Professors do detach themselves from other people who cause them inconvenience
2. Stress management Burnout, exhaustion, stress relieving activities, walking, music, nature Some female professors do face difficulty in putting efforts to reduce stress however, some tend to engage in leisure activities
3. Professional help Psychologist, Therapist, therapy, mental health and wellbeing, Advice, guidance, support Female professors have not felt the need to sort professional help. However, they seek support from friends and family

3.1. Connection With Self and Others

Psychological self-care in married female professors involves maintaining a strong sense of identity, emotional regulation and healthy interpersonal relations, it also involves enhancing connection with self and setting necessary boundaries with people who might undermine their emotional and mental wellbeing.

Excerpt of participant 19 emphasizing on it; "I definitely feel connected to myself mentally and emotionally and it enhances my self-concept.."

Excerpt of participant 14 emphasizing on it; "my mental health is very much important to me and my family, I make sure to keep sense of awareness about myself and exclude people to cause disharmony in my life.."

Excerpt of participant 13 emphasizing on it; "I believe in setting boundaries in order to maintain healthy interpersonal relations plus it also keeps my mental integrity safe.."

3.2. Stress Management

Psychological self-care for married female professors involves actively managing stress to prevent burnout and exhaustion by engaging in stress-relieving activities such as walking, listening to music, or spending time in nature, however some female professors struggle in prioritizing self-care due to overwhelmingly loaded professional roles.

Excerpt of participant 4 emphasizing on it; "for work related stress management, I engage myself in music, and taking a walk through nature…"

Excerpt of participant 19 emphasizing on it; "it gets difficult to put conscious efforts to reduce stress because there is lack of time for everything…"

Excerpt of participant 14 emphasizing on it; " yes its difficult most of the times but if I get time I relieve my stress through dancing…"

3.3. Professional Help

Psychological self-care in married female professors involves giving importance to mental health and emotional wellbeing by seeking support from mental health professionals like psychologists, therapists and counsellors whenever needed. Friends and family also come out to be a great support to maintain mental well being.

Excerpt of participant 10 emphasizing on it; "as of now I have never felt the need to visit a mental health professional, I talk to my parents and their suggestions help me the best.."

Excerpt of participant 7 emphasizing on it; " I have personally never been to a psychologists not that I am against it, I just never felt the need. Whenever I am in a dilemma simply talking my husband and parents calm me down…"

Excerpt of participant 1 emphasizing on it; " I have seek professional help till now I talk to my loved ones or write my feelings in my journal and I am good to go…"

Table 4. Themes and Sub-Themes for Emotional Self Care among female professors (married)

Sr. no.	Themes	Sub-Themes	Findings
Emotional Self Care among female professors			
1.	Professional expression	Work boundaries, limitations to personal emotional expression, professionalism, hierarchical restrictions	Female professors tend to limit their emotional expression in work environment and incline towards being more practical and professional
2.	Personal expression	Freedom to express, family decision making, opinions matter, no hierarchical restrictions	In personal environment female professors tend to express their emotions; positive and negative more freely without any restrictions

4.1. Professional Expression

Emotional self-care in married female professors involves understanding the distinction between personal and professional realms and thus limiting emotional expression that confines within the professional boundaries and thus maintaining professionalism within work environment

Excerpt of participant 8 emphasizing on it; "when I have to take any work related decisions I tend to be more practical and professional and I don't let my emotions come in between…"

Excerpt of participant 17 emphasizing on it; "I prefer to hide my emotions during my work hours because mixing emotions and work will not have perfect results as per my experience…"

Excerpt of participant 1 emphasizing on it; "in the department I prefer to be professional and not a emotional fool…."

4.2. Personal Expression

Emotional self-care for married female professors involves cultivating a supportive personal environment where they can freely express their feeling, emotions, and opinions without any professional or hierarchical restrictions. Ensuring that they are part of the decision-making process reflecting autonomy and freedom of personal expression.

Excerpt of participant 3 emphasizing on it; "any decisions to be taken in my family my husband and I decide it together.."

Excerpt of participant 18 emphasizing on it; "in personal environment I express my emotions, feelings and thoughts very openly without any restrictions…"

Excerpt of participant 10 emphasizing on it; "my feelings and emotions matter and I m heard in my family…."

Table 5. Themes and Sub-Themes for Spiritual Self Care among female professors (married)

Sr. no.	Themes	Sub-Themes	Findings
Spiritual Self Care among female professors			
1.	Worship	Daily idol worship, prayer, temple visit, aartis and mantra, chanting, regular hawans	Female professors do believe in God and daily idol worship, prayers, and other religious activities is mandate to them
2.	Life satisfaction	Able to find meaning to life, in difficult situation life seems meaningless	When in difficult situations some female professors are able to find meaning to their life but some find it difficult to do so

5.1. Worship

Spiritual self-care in married female professors involves engaging in practices such as daily idol worship, prayer, temple visits, aartis, mantra chanting, and regular hawans in order to keep enhancing the connection with god, the divine power and the universe and maintain a sense of inner balance and fulfilment

Excerpt of participant 12 emphasizing on it; "yes I do believe in god and my day does not start without lighting lamp and singing aarti in my temple…"

Excerpt of participant 14 emphasizing on it; "my whole family is religious and thus so is my daughter, we have regular poojas and hawans at our home…."

Excerpt of participant 1 emphasizing on it; "I won't come for lectures before I am done with my daily worship and rituals to god…"

5.2. Life Satisfaction

Spiritual self-care for married female professors involves practices that preserve their inner sense of meaning, help them find purpose and satisfaction in life even during difficult times, thus develop and maintain resilience and emotional well-being.

Excerpt of participant 17 emphasizing on it; "to be honest, it is difficult to not find life meaningless in difficult times everyone feels this way at some point in life…"

Excerpt of participant 11 emphasizing on it; "I know my life's worth so I have never felt that my life is meaningless whatever situation may come in life…."

Excerpt of participant 16 emphasizing on it; "I did feel my life was meaningless in one the toughest situations of my life but then I got through…"

Table 6. Themes and Sub-Themes for Social Self Care among female professors (married)

Sr. no	Themes	Sub-Themes	Findings
Social Self Care among female professors			
1.	Proximity	Distance, nearness, friends, colleagues, closeness, time	Female professors tend to make friends with colleagues and others who are in close proximity with them
2.	Telecommunications	Phone calls, video chat, texting	Female professors stay in contact with family members, parents, children and husband through telecommunication means
3.	Meeting frequency	Holidays, institutional offs, weekends, festivals	Female professors meet their family members, parents, children, husbands mostly on holidays and festivals

6.1. Proximity

Social self-care for married female professors involves fostering relationships with friends, colleagues and other people who are in close proximity. Making new connections through social interactions and maintain a safe and supportive environment for personal well being.

Excerpt of participant 1 emphasizing on it; "I have made new connections for myself through my seniors and colleagues, its goog to have some kind of support.."

Excerpt of participant 16 emphasizing on it; "having friends at work is beneficial in the sense that you have someone to understand your work related problems and also bring solutions to those problems…"

Excerpt of participant 15 emphasizing on it; "living away from home means you can't meet your family everyday so I have some friends in the department itself with whom I can spent some quality time…"

6.2. Telecommunications

Social self-care for married female professors involves maintaining contact with family members viz. parents, children, and partners through various telecommunication means such as phone calls, video chats, and texting to maintain and nurture existing relationships and overcome the geographical barriers arising due to career demands.

Excerpt of participant 5 emphasizing on it; "I make sure to take my family members on daily basis sometimes its more than twice daily…"

Excerpt of participant 17 emphasizing on it; "it's a compulsion for me and my parents and husband too that even for 10 mins at least we talk everyday…"

Excerpt of participant 4 emphasizing on it; "even if I am very tired one video call with family is enough to get me out of bed and do other things…"

6.3. Meeting Frequency

Social self-care for married female professors involves taking time out for family members and other significant people during weekends, vacation, institutional holidays and festivals to ensure a healthy work-life balance between interpersonal relationships and work.

Excerpt of participant 14 emphasizing on it; "on weekends I go to meet my family or they come to meet me and we spend nice quality time together.."

Excerpt of participant 20 emphasizing on it; "visiting family, parents, husband and children is limited to holidays, vacations and festivals due to busy schedule and living away from home…"

Excerpt of participant 9 emphasizing on it; "as I live in the campus I visit my children and husband every weekend…"

Table 7. Themes and Sub-Themes for Professional Self Care among female professors (married)

Sr. no	Themes	Sub-Themes	Findings
Professional Self Care among female professors			
1.	Intervals	Little relaxed work environment, in-between breaks, relaxing, coffee breaks, once in long time,	Female professors rarely take short breaks/ intervals while working; it may happen only once in a blue moon or when workload is relatively less.
2.	Boundaries	Seniority, institutional work, compulsion, authority-delegated	Female professors find it difficult to set boundaries in terms of work/tasks allotted to them

7.1. Intervals

Professional self-care for married female professors involves consciously taking regular short breaks between work throughout the day such as coffee breaks, moments of relaxation to relax one's mind and rejuvenate within the constraints of busy work schedule in order to work more efficiently for better outcomes.

Excerpt of participant 5 emphasizing on it; "no, while working in the department I rarely take breaks because then it just leads to more work…"

Excerpt of participant 2 emphasizing on it; "there I no time to take breaks while working as there are too many tasks to be completed except from taking lectures, like institutional responsibilities etc…"

Excerpt of participant 8 emphasizing on it; "I talk to my colleagues for some time or just drink tea while working that's the only break I take but even that's very rarely …"

7.2. Boundaries

Professional self-care for married female professors involves consciously establishing boundaries in terms of work and tasks allotted to them this encompasses factors such as seniority, institutional responsibilities and authority-delegated roles. This helps in controlling the amount of work load entrusted on oneself.

Excerpt of participant 18 emphasizing on it; "no I am unable to set boundaries because its not in my cup of tea to say no so easily…"

Excerpt of participant 3 emphasizing on it; setting boundaries gets a little tedious given the work environment we have here, its like family and so you can't say no to a "family member" then right…"

Excerpt of participant 11 emphasizing on it; "I try to set boundaries but it is not always possible, also if I can I help as much my potential allows me to…"

Table 8. Themes and Sub-Themes for Existential Self Care among female professors (married)

Sr. no.	Themes	Sub-Themes	Findings
Existential Self Care among female professors			
1.	Awareness	Meaning of life, sense, positive things, negative things,	Female professors have a sense of awareness of what is meaningful to them in life and what is not.

continued on following page

Table 8. Continued

Sr. no.	Themes	Sub-Themes	Findings
2.	Existential crisis	Initial career stage Career goals, professional identity, lagging behind, lack of experience, family, marriage, parenthood, competition	Female Professors did face existential crisis at some point of time in their career
3.	Balance	Personal wellbeing, career demands, self-care, work life balance	Female professors sometimes are able to balance their career demands and personal wellbeing, but sometimes they find it difficult to do so
4.	Extra burdens	Extra delegated work, seniors, institutional work, authority delegated work	Female professors sometimes set boundaries in terms of extra work delegated to them which is not originally theirs, sometimes they find it difficult to do so

8.1. Awareness

Existential self-care in married female professors encompasses of the sense of awareness about the meaning of life; both positive and negative aspects, and to gain an understanding of what contributes to the sense of fulfilment in personal and professional lives.

Excerpt of participant 8 emphasizing on it; "yes, I do know what is meaningful to me and what is not and I try to focus on the positive things in my life rather than to waste my time on the negativity…"

Excerpt of participant 14 emphasizing on it; "being married, having children I feel I have seen enough life and it is safe to say that I am aware about what is important to me…"

Excerpt of participant 12 emphasizing on it; "yes I am aware of what is meaningful to me in my life and what s not. My family, children, husband and my parents are important to me everything else is secondary…"

8.2. Existential Crisis

Existential self-care in married female professors involves facing existential crisis in their career especially in the initial stages of the career. This may be due intense competition, lack of experiences and lagging behind due to various reasons including family, marriage and parenthood which impacts their professional identity.

Excerpt of participant 4 emphasizing on it; "yes, I did face some existential crisis in the initial stages of my career because I was still try to get a grip on how things work, all the research, lectures etc…."

Excerpt of participant 16 emphasizing on it; "After my pregnancy, I felt I was really lagging behind with my papers and publication and stuff but then eventually I got on track…"

Excerpt of participant 15 emphasizing on it; "I got married during my PhD so that's when my career took a halt for a year and half, adjusting with new life and career demands was tough then…"

8.3. Balance

Existential self-care for married female professors involves preserving their personal wellbeing, taking care of self and maintaining emotional balance while sailing through the demands of career and professional role. While sometimes, they are able to mend the bridge between the two, other times female professors find it difficult to do so.

Excerpt of participant 5 emphasizing on it; "sometimes its manageable; my self-care and career but not always…"

Excerpt of participant 10 emphasizing on it; "there is never a balance, one has to be compromised for the other, sometimes it's the career and sometimes it's the self care.."

Excerpt of participant 17 emphasizing on it; "to be honest taking out time for self care is a bit tough, and career is more like a responsibility…"

8.4. Extra Burdens

Existential self-care for married female professors involves prioritizing personal wellbeing by establishing boundaries in professional realm in terms of accepting tasks which are not originally theirs and other extra institutional work in order to protect themselves from the extra burdens of delegated work and navigate through the complexities of authority dynamics and institutional responsibilities.

Excerpt of participant 1 emphasizing on it; "I don't say no to any tasks delegated to me by my seniors because I don't want to complicate things for myself…"

Excerpt of participant 19 emphasizing on it; "it's not really in our hands to say no to institutional work it's like a compulsory thing we need to do…"

Excerpt of participant 20 emphasizing on it; "I try to establish boundaries but it's not always possible to say no to your seniors and other authorities.."

Table 9. Themes and Sub-Themes for Physical Self Care among female professors (Unmarried)

Sr. no.	Themes	Sub-Themes	Findings
\multicolumn{4}{|l|}{Physical Self Care among female professors}			
1.	Physical Activity	Exercise, yoga, meditation, walking, dancing	Female professors engage themselves in some physical activity everyday
2.	Healthcare	Regular checkups, tests, Mediclaim, medical history, diagnosis	Female professors undergo medical checkups only related to their pre-existing conditions
3.	Sleep cycle	Everyday sleep, rem sleep, sound sleep, sleep hours, rest, 7-8 hours	Female professors tend to get minimum 7-8 hours sound sleep on daily basis

9.1. Physical Activity

Physical self-care for married female professors entails regular exercise, yoga, meditation, and walking in order to maintain their physical health and wellbeing.

Excerpt of participant 16 emphasizing on it; "I practice yoga and meditation everyday for an hour after coming back from lectures to relax..."

Excerpt of participant 11 emphasizing on it; "every night my husband and I go for a walk after dinner and we walk all around the campus...."

Excerpt of participant 2 emphasizing on it; "I ensure to have some physical activity everyday be it exercise, yoga or meditation..."

9.2. Healthcare

Physical self-care for married female professors involves regular checkups and tests, maintaining medical records, and ensuring appropriate medical coverage such as medical insurances, however, their healthcare is often limited to pre-existing health conditions due to time constraints and other responsibilities.

Excerpt of participant 6 emphasizing on it; "I don't really go for medical check-ups unless it needed...."

Excerpt of participant 7 emphasizing on it; "I was diagnosed with diabetes last year so for me it's kind of a compulsion to get myself tested every now and then..."

Excerpt of participant 19 emphasizing on it; "besides the checkups related to my medical history I don't prefer going to the doctor..."

9.3. Sleep Cycle

Physical self-care for married female professors involves ensuring proper rest, maintaining healthy sleep cycle and having sound sleep, Female professors consistently get 7-8 hours of sound sleep each night to support overall well-being and cognitive function.

Excerpt of participant 10 emphasizing on it; "I ensure to have 7 hrs sleep daily or I feel tired a grumpy the whole day…"

Excerpt of participant 7 emphasizing on it; "after being diagnosed with diabetes I have been prescribed by the doctor to have at least 7hrs sleep daily…"

Excerpt of participant 3 emphasizing on it; "earlier it was difficult because of research and other things but now being understood the importance of sleep I make sure to sleep at least 8hrs…"

Table 10. Themes and Sub-Themes for Emotional Balance among female professors (Married)

Emotional Balance among female professors			
1.	Emotional regulation	Work experience, Emotional stability, age factor	Female professors have emotional balance due to work experience and maturity with progressing age.
2.	Balance in work and personal wellbeing	Time management, occasional self-care boundaries, nonchalance, experience	Female professors maintain their emotional balance through time management, occasional self-care
3.	Work-load consequences directed to self	Transient and manageable frustration, anger, irritation, sudden outburst	Female professors do face self-directed negative emotions like anger, frustration, irritation but these are transient and manageable

10.1. Emotional Regulation

Emotional balance in married female professors refers to their capacity to meet the demands of their professional and personal lives with stability, regulating their emotional and mental wellbeing with resilience through years of accumulated work experience often enhanced by maturity and age.

Excerpt of participant 13 emphasizing on it; "with different experiences and ongoing learning I have understood myself better which has made it easy to have my emotions under control and be stable.."

Excerpt of participant 5 emphasizing on it; "with age, you tend to mature and your mental stability becomes utmost important to you, and thus the balance is maintained…"

Excerpt of participant 1 emphasizing on it; "emotional balance means to regulate your mental wellbeing and also not get affected by petty things, I got a grip of my emotions through my journey of teaching which was full of experiences.."

10.2. Balance In Work and Personal Wellbeing

Emotional balance in married female professors involves mastering the skill of time management to effectively maintain equilibrium between self care, emotional balance, personal wellbeing and dealing with the complexities of work, demands, dynamics and responsibilities associated with professional role.

Excerpt of participant 20 emphasizing on it; "maintaining the balance between self care and work is possible only with proper time management…"

Excerpt of participant 15 emphasizing on it; "I believe in respecting my time, which involves doing everything on time be it eating, sleeping, studying or any other task…."

Excerpt of participant 11 emphasizing on it; "I sleep on time and wake up early it makes me feel that I have extra time to do my chores and this way everything gets balanced.."

10.3. Work-Load Consequences Directed to Self

Emotional balance in married female professors involves effectively managing frustrations, anger, and irritations arising from work-related challenges such work pressure and work load; while maintaining stability and resilience in their personal and professional lives.

Excerpt of participant 8 emphasizing on it; "yes, sometimes it happens that I tend to get very angry and irritated when I am stuck at some point in my research or other work but eventually it's not that severe I can manage by giving myself some space.."

Excerpt of participant 4 emphasizing on it; "no I don't think I have ever faced a situation where my work had caused severe negative consequences directed to myself, a little bit of frustration and impatience is ought to occur but its transient…"

Excerpt of participant 3 emphasizing on it; " I feel it's natural to feel certain negative emotions when you are very stressed due to work, what I do is I talk to my loved ones, take a break calm myself down and everything becomes fine…"

5.1. Mental Worship

Spiritual self-care for unmarried female professors involve practices such as mental worship, where they engage in internal reflections, gratitude, and reverence without the requirement of compulsory prayers or traditional rituals like aartis or idol worship.

Excerpt of participant 12 emphasizing on it;"I do believe in god but I do not engage myself in everyday rituals and idol worship…"

Excerpt of participant 14 emphasizing on it;" I believe in god and pay my respects to god in my heart, as it gets difficult perform everyday pooja and aarti consistently…"

Excerpt of participant 18 emphasizing on it;"I don't perform aarti and pooja everyday but pray to god internally thanking him for everything…"

4. DISCUSSION

The present study looks into the differences and similarities in the themes of married and unmarried female university professors. On the basis of thematic analysis conducted it is seen that there no major differences in themes of married and unmarried female professors i.e. most of their themes are similar except for the theme Worship in married female professors and Mental Worship in unmarried female professors illustrating that married female professors tend to engage more in idol worship, performing rituals, aartis, poojas and hawans whereas unmarried female professors though believe in god, their tendency to engage in such religious activities is relatively low. This may be due to their single life; they are shouldered with many responsibilities which gives them very less time to engage in such religious rituals among other things. Secondly, increasing professional responsibilities of the present times leaves very little room for sufficient time management for these female professors to engage in religious activities. Thus, a part of their spiritual self-care takes a setback.

Moreover, apart from the marital status taken as a determinant in the study it was found that seniority, age factor and individual's temperament also plays an important role in determining the tendency of self-care and emotional balance in female university professors.

Reflecting on the factor of seniority, it was found that senior female professors were more proficient in managing their self care and emotional balance. Reasons for this can be their work experience; senior female professors have an experience of multiple work environments. They have devoted many years of their lives to the field. They are familiar with various novel situations and have faced numerous challenges in their professional life which has made them resilient and adaptive to everyday work load and stressors. Thus, they are able to preserve their self care and emotional wellbeing.

Similarly, discussing the age-related factor has same implications. Female professors who are in their late middle ages also display excellent self care and emotional balance. Reasoning for this is evident from the fact that with increasing age an individual is more prone to diseases and illnesses which automatically leads them to take proper care of themselves which includes healthy diet, harmonious sleep cycle, daily exercise, taking breaks between works, taking sufficient rest as per the body needs and lastly regular health checkups. All these activities encompass various dimensions of self care. Additionally drawing on the accumulated work experience of all the previous years of professional life female professors who are in their late middle ages have a stabilized emotional balance which helps them in dealing with severe emotional turmoil with calmness and composure.

Lastly, exploring the tendency of self care and emotional balance based on the temperament of female professors it was found that, Even if they are married, female professors with an inherently introspective and contemplative temperament could be more drawn to internal spiritual self-care practices like for instance, mental worship. This is consistent with the results of the thematic analysis, which show that unmarried female professors are more likely to practice internal worship than external religious activities. On the other hand, extroverted people may find greater comfort and rejuvenation in social interactions or outdoor pursuits than in conventional religious activities. Moreover, temperament might affect how female professors handle stress and take care of their emotional well-being. For instance, regardless of seniority or marital status, those with resilient temperaments may exhibit higher emotional stability and adaptability in the face of adversity. On the contrary, female professors with more sensitive or anxious temperaments can need more help and coping mechanisms to regulate their emotions, particularly in stressful work settings.

REFERENCES

Al-Masri, A. R. I. (2020). Impulsive Buying Behavior and Its Relation to the Emotional Balance. *Int. J. Psychol. Brain Sci*, 5(1), 5–20. DOI: 10.11648/j.ijpbs.20200501.12

Al-Obaidi, M. (1991). Measuring Emotional Balance among Martyrs' sons and relatives living with their parents, unpublished Master's Thesis, IbnRushd Faculty of Pedagogy, University of Baghdad.

Beena, C., & Poduval, P. R. (1992). Gender differences in work stress of executives. *Psychological Studies*, 37(2-3), 109–113.

Cushway, D., & Tyler, P. A. (1994). Stress and coping in clinical psychologists. *Stress Medicine*, 10(1), 35–42. DOI: 10.1002/smi.2460100107

Denyes, M. J., Orem, D. E., & Bekel, G. (2001). Self-care: A foundational science. *Nursing Science Quarterly*, 14(1), 48–54. DOI: 10.1177/089431840101400113 PMID: 11873354

Gadzella, B. M., Ginther, D. W., Tomcala, M., & Bryant, G. W. (1990). Stress as perceived by professionals. *Psychological Reports*, 67(3), 979–983. DOI: 10.2466/PR0.67.7.979-983 PMID: 2287691

Lease, S. H. (1999). Occupational role stressors, coping, support, and hardiness as predictors of strain in academic faculty: An emphasis on new and female faculty. *Research in Higher Education*, 40(3), 285–307. DOI: 10.1023/A:1018747000082

Mohammed, A. (2019). Emotional Balance and Its Relation with Self–Confidence for Special Education Students Department. Opción. *Revista de Ciencias Humanas y Sociales*, (21), 630–657.

Myers, S. B., Sweeney, A. C., Popick, V., Wesley, K., Bordfeld, A., & Fingerhut, R. (2012). Self-care practices and perceived stress levels among psychology graduate students. *Training and Education in Professional Psychology*, 6(1), 55–66. DOI: 10.1037/a0026534

Orem, D. (1995). *Nursing: Concepts of Practice* (5th ed.). Mosby Year Book.

Phd, F., & Ncama, B. (2011). Self, self-care and self-management concepts: Implications for self-management education. *Educational Researcher*, 2, 1733–1737.

Chapter 13
Becoming
How Leadership and Mentoring Influence the Perception of Self

Clair A. Stocks
https://orcid.org/0009-0006-8655-7791
Chapman University, USA

ABSTRACT

This chapter will use a single personal narrative and case study approach to analyze the challenges often faced by women in higher education and the impact of leadership in influencing the perception of self. A pivotal experience with a transformational leader and engaged mentor was the impetus for deep reflection that shepherded an evolution of individuals, teams, and an entire institution. This defining experience in the author's career will serve as a guide through literature that emphasizes the influence of leadership on individual perceptions and performance, cohesive team formation, and institutional success. The far-reaching effect of transformational leadership will be considered, as those who experience it adopt the practices of effective leadership and bring them to new teams and institutions. This chapter will include a specific focus on the lasting impact positive experiences with leadership and mentoring can have on confidence, achievement, and new leader development among women in higher education.

BECOMING: HOW LEADERSHIP AND MENTORING INFLUENCE THE PERCEPTION OF SELF

The percentage of women participating in the workforce, especially those with formal education, has been climbing for decades and is approaching parity with men's participation (U.S. Bureau of Labor Statistics, 2023). While women are well

DOI: 10.4018/979-8-3693-3144-6.ch013

Copyright © 2025, IGI Global. Copying or distributing in print or electronic forms without written permission of IGI Global is prohibited.

represented in academia, they are cloistered in entry and mid-level positions, lagging behind men who hold the majority of full-time and tenure-track faculty positions and senior administrative roles (American Association of University Women, n.d.). The dearth of women in higher education leadership contributes to an environment where the accomplishments of women are overlooked or misappropriated by men, leaving women to question their value and capabilities.

Longstanding gender biases have a significant impact on women in academia. The gender gap has practical consequences for career advancement and prestige and often leaves women feeling increasingly disillusioned until they abandon their careers in academia entirely (Llorens et al., 2021). After nearly 15 years in higher education, this is the position in which I found myself. In my years in academia, I had experienced a litany of micro and macro aggressions, bounced from one toxic environment to another, and grown weary in my stalled career. Even in the male-normed meritocracy where my performance was routinely lauded as exceptional, I found it difficult to advance. Men frequently spoke to me with condescension despite my expertise. The few women leaders I encountered often fell prey to queen bee syndrome to protect their limited influence and opportunity (Gomes Neto et al., 2022; Staines et al., 1974). I found myself languishing mid-career with many other women who were smart and capable but were faced with a labyrinth of obstacles that prevented them from advancement (Carli & Eagly, 2016).

THE TERMINUS

I had been working at the same institution for some time, a victim of the sticky floor phenomenon (Subbaye & Vithal, 2017) in which women find themselves languishing in entry and mid-level roles. While I had fallen victim to career stagnation due to a myriad of reasons from an organizational structure that was not suited to career advancement to becoming indispensable at my very particular job, I continued to stay at the institution.

I reported to a senior male leader who I respected, and I had developed a very strong informal mentoring network of women who provided critical social support that I had come to rely on personally and professionally (Madsen & Longman, 2020; Statti & Torres, 2019). I had accepted the status quo as inevitable and, as is the case with many women in academia, I lacked the confidence to advocate for my own advancement (Herbst, 2020).

However, as the institution experienced significant organizational challenges and changes, the environment became more toxic. Leadership became autocratic (Luqman et al., 2019) with a focus on self-promotion and deflecting blame to subordinates (Wolor et al., 2022). The interpersonal fulfillment of my job began to wane, and I found myself demoralized. During a meeting with the senior male leader who I had previously respected, I found myself gaslit and publicly chastised as he reversed course on a decision he had privately communicated to me (Hussain, 2024). This became the catalyst for my decision to finally seek employment elsewhere.

In what appeared to be a moment of fortuity, I very quickly found and accepted a position at an institution whose values and mission perfectly aligned with my own. Though the position was technically a step back in my career, there was ample opportunity for professional development and advancement at the institution, so I made the leap.

While my initial experience at this new institution was positive and I found myself surrounded by colleagues with a similar passion for the work we were doing, it became evident that the executive team was rife with toxic leadership. The dimensions of toxic leadership including deception, blame and scapegoating, suppression of dissent, dishonesty, and character assassination were overwhelming (Fahie, 2020). Within a year of my arrival, nearly the entire small staff had turned over through targeted dismissals and resignations. The institution I had positioned as a dream school with its inspirational mission had turned out to be another nightmare. Exhausted and demoralized (Koc et al., 2022), I found myself reconsidering my career in higher education and planning a pivot to a new industry. I joined institution after institution full of hope and enthusiasm. And time and again I found myself stifled by toxic leaders who lacked integrity or impeded my growth. Higher education, I had decided, was awash with malignant leaders and there was simply no way forward for me. I mourned the sector I had previously celebrated, but I could not see any alternative that would allow me to preserve my wellbeing.

THE CATALYST

As I planned my exit from higher education, the toxic environment of my institution bubbled over, and the board of directors brought in a consultant to assess the situation. On the consultant's recommendation, a new senior leader was brought in to help the institution grow and address turnover and the toxic culture perpetuated by the executive team. I was dubious about the new leader's intentions and his ability to affect any significant change at the institution. Initially, in my state of burnout and disillusionment, I barely registered his presence expecting the status quo to reign.

Six weeks after he began his tenure, the new leader eliminated several senior positions, including my director supervisor, a woman who I deeply respected but who also found herself with limited influence or power. My opinion about this leader shifted from indifference to incredulity. Immediately following these dismissals, the leader scheduled a meeting with me. Stone-faced and suspicious, I listened as he told me that he was going to turn the institution around and he wanted me to be a central part of that transformation. He wanted to build a team of highly capable and collaborative individuals who were unafraid of change, including a new dean he had hired to oversee multiple functional areas, including my own. He told me that if I placed my trust in him and his vision, he would teach me everything he knew about running a university and give me the tools to drive my career forward in any way I might imagine for myself. I was cautious and untrusting but intrigued. I would, I decided, continue to explore a transition to a new industry while tentatively considering the opportunity with which I was being presented.

Shortly thereafter the new dean arrived. I reacted to her presence with mistrust and uncertainty. But I also made note of the interactions I began to have with the new leader. He regularly sought me out to better understand the culture of the institution and to strategize about not only the future goals and success of our school, but the motivations and frustrations of the staff that we might address. Very slowly, I found myself letting my guard down. My suspicion about the new dean also began to ebb as I watched her assess and address issues and concerns with integrity and courage.

A couple months after my conversation with the new leader, I was in my office working, my flow interrupted by the occasional conversation with various colleagues as we all focused on an impending deadline. The leader stopped in my doorway smiled and observed, "You seem happy." As he walked away, I was stunned to find that I was, if not happy, then at least content. I was working hard, focused on new initiatives that my colleagues and I had been diligently crafting. I realized this new leader had been acting as a shield between his team and the toxic executives. The protective space he provided gave me the opportunity to redirect my attention from preserving my well-being in an unhealthy environment to tackling my work with renewed interest and motivation (Milosevic et al., 2019). That small observation, that I seemed happy, was the first inkling I had that I was on the precipice of a career-defining experience.

THE FAR-REACHING IMPACT OF POSITIVE LEADERSHIP

Toxic leadership is responsible for significant rates of employee dissatisfaction and attrition. In fact, toxic workplaces are ten times more likely to negatively impact employee retention than compensation (Sull et al., 2022). Toxic leaders damage employee morale, impede motivation, create career stagnation for employees, and damage the reputation and success of the organizations they manage (Erdal & Budak, 2021). The impact of toxic leaders is even more detrimental to women who already wield less power and face significant professional obstacles related to their gender (Herbst & Roux, 2023).

By contrast, effective leadership can have a dramatic impact on employee morale and performance, contributing not only to a culture of cooperation harmony but to increased productivity and organizational goal attainment (Sonmez Cakir et al., 2020). When employees have a strong leader, they are more likely to feel job satisfaction, form strong teams, and meet and exceed performance expectations (Ali et al., 2020; Rehman et al., 2020). The following narrative analysis highlights how one such leader served as the catalyst for not only my personal transformation during a critical period of professional disillusionment, but for setting into motion a highly collaborative and symbiotic team that propelled a previously stagnant institution forward.

Individual Impact

After 15 years, I had reached a critical period of wariness and cynicism about my career in higher education. Like many high performing women in academia, I experienced career stagnation marked by a cycle of praise and gaslighting (Docka-Filipek & Stone, 2021; Van Veelen & Derks, 2021). Having taken a role with an institution whose mission aligned closely with my personal values only to find myself in a profoundly toxic environment, I was drowning in imposter syndrome and disenchantment. With a mix of bitterness and sadness, I began to quietly plan my pivot out of higher education. My feelings about the importance of higher education had not changed, but I had reached the limit of my ability to endure an environment I consistently found to be plagued by egotistic and incompetent leaders at best, and narcissistic and abusive leaders at worst (Burns, 2017).

The arrival of a new leader who used an approach that was rooted in developing relationships and trust with followers was entirely new to me. While I was initially suspicious of the leader's honesty and motivations, as I assessed his words and actions over time, I found myself recognizing he was earnest in his enthusiasm and dedication to the well-being of not only the institution, but the individuals working for him.

At the time of the leader's arrival, our institution was languishing, and it was clear transformative change was necessary for its success. In a culture marred by toxicity with a demoralized team, creating motivation for change was a daunting task. Relational leadership, which focuses on mutually beneficial cooperative relationship building (Hollander, 1992; Uhl-Bien, 2006; Webb, 2021), provided a foundation for understanding the different strengths, needs, and aspirations of individuals. The evolution from relationship-building to authentic and purposeful action facilitated trust and served as the impetus for my transformation from apathy to empowerment (Jiang et al., 2020).

Despite my professional languor and discontent upon his arrival, the leader quickly noted that I was quite capable and ambitious. After so many years of relative stagnation, my drive to propel my career forward had stalled. Recognizing this, the leader actively removed constraints that had prevented me from exercising autonomy in my role and imbued me with decision-making authority in areas where I had demonstrated expertise. Through his empowerment, I began to develop a sense of purpose and commitment, viewing myself as an integral component in our success (Kim & Beehr, 2021). The more he provided a space for me to contribute and achieve, the more engaged and invested I became.

In addition to empowering me to perform and stretch my capabilities, the new leader also understood the importance of recognition on my development. Like many women, I had not only been denied recognition for work I had done, but I had also experienced men receiving credit for my ideas and work (Sarsons et al., 2021; University of Delaware, 2017). The new leader was vocal in recognizing my contributions in public settings and meetings which helped build my sense of self-efficacy while also positioning me as an authority in the organization (Abun et al., 2021). The recognition of my work included not only verbal affirmation, but promotion and financial rewards. Blending transformational leadership with transactional leadership created an intersection of social, professional, and practical benefits that had eluded me and showed a willingness to move beyond conversation to action (Nguyen et al., 2022).

The positive impact of the leader was magnified by his decision to bring in a dean to manage operational activities who was particularly skilled at interpersonal relationship building and mentoring. Though mentoring is a critical component in the success and leadership development of women (Statti & Torres, 2019), I had moved through my career without experiencing mentorship. While the leader had created the conditions for a career revitalization, it was the mentoring provided by the dean that allowed me to flourish.

My mentor's intercession in my career transformed my professional identity. She provided a model of a women pursuing her aspirations with ambition, determination, and integrity that created a guide for my own professional progression (O'Connor, 2018). Her openness and candor accelerated trust and communication between us. She showed an interest in who I was, what I was capable of, and what I wanted for myself personally and professionally. And I admired and respected her. Thus, when she advised me, I believed in and internalized her assessments. I was receptive even to her constructive criticism as it was clearly intended to challenge me to grow and enhance my leadership competency (Eiland et al., 2021). Under her tutelage, I found myself transforming into a confident, authentic, and self-assured leader.

While I had experienced supportive relationships with colleagues, often they did not result in any discernable change in our professional circumstances. Without power, we could only recognize the inherent value we saw in one another but had no ability to affect the changes necessary for broader recognition or growth. The positional authority the new leader brought allowed him to use his influence to advocate for me and disrupt the dysfunctional cycle in which I had found myself stuck (Early, 2020; Harris & Lee, 2019). I eagerly embraced the opportunity to transform and transcend and began to see a clear trajectory toward the aspirations I had nearly abandoned.

Team Impact

I was not alone in experiencing the transformational impact of the new leader and dean on my career. The existing and new members of the team received similar care and attention allowing each individual to thrive. The collective group of invigorated and confident individuals quickly assembled into a high performing team. Tasked with overcoming tremendous hurdles to meet institutional objectives, it was essential the team be willing to innovate and enthusiastically participate in radical change.

In the best of circumstances, building dynamic, synergistic teams who collaborate and manage conflict well can be a challenge. At our institution, employees were tense and stressed by a corrupt culture. Overcoming the tense atmosphere and creating an environment where current employees were both willing to embrace change, but also open to new individuals joining the team took finesse, commitment, and consistent communication and transparency. Resistance to change and conflict were successfully managed through adaptive leadership that recognized the needs of individuals and the team and the empowerment of individuals on the team to manage challenges together (Jung et al., 2020). There was no need for competition among the team as each member understood everyone was integral to its success. Fostering a cohesive vision and respect created a shared identity and promoted accountability among all members.

The leader approached the team with respect for their ideas and expertise, soliciting advice, promoting shared decision-making, and often deferring to the collective wisdom of the team. Though the positional leader and dean carried the most institutional authority, they willingly disbursed their power to members of the team to allow for the co-creation of a shared vision and strategy (Ali et al., 2020). In this environment, everyone was a leader. Where influence and opportunity were once scarce, this approach created a feeling of abundance that facilitated greater cooperation, sharing, and trust.

The empowered team the leader had assembled formed deep and lasting relationships with one another. They recognized the importance of the individual while remaining committed to the goals of the collective. Members collaborated, found innovative solutions to problems, enthusiastically championed members' ideas, and embraced leaders vision for the future (Mascareño et al., 2019). The team approached their work with creativity and vigor, which ultimately resulted in a transformation of the institution.

Institutional Impact

Toxic leadership depresses employee morale which has significant implications that go beyond individuals. Employees trapped in a negative work culture experience stress, exhaustion, and a lack of motivation that inhibits productivity and creativity, leading to unsatisfactory institutional performance (Koc et al., 2022). Rather than collaborating to generate new ideas to help our institution succeed, employees felt discouraged and feared retaliation if they made suggestions that did not align with the self-promoting agenda of senior leadership. Problems were ignored as addressing them would be to acknowledge a fundamental strategic failure. As a result, the institution was languishing, failing to grow its student population or meet regulatory standards and best practices.

During the first two years I spent at the institution, our student population and academic offerings remained stagnant. When the new leader arrived, we were in a dire situation with dwindling resources and no feasible plan for sustainability. It was clear a profound change was necessary, but employees were apprehensive, fearing reprisal. Loosely following Kotter's (1996) eight step method for change management, the new leader began to assemble his team, build trust, create a shared vision, and empower the team to reimagine how things could be done to help propel the institution forward.

While the fledgling team showed enthusiasm for implementing change, there was a persistent wariness that the initiative might rouse the ire of the toxic senior leaders who remained. However, as a member of the executive team, the new leader positioned himself between the existing toxic leaders and his employees. This allowed his team the necessary space to collaborate, strategize, and share ideas. The result was the vigorous undertaking of multiple projects to reposition the institution and drive enrollment, efficiencies, and to implement a framework to support best practices in compliance and standardization.

As the team experienced initial success with their change strategies, they became more cohesive and empowered. Their enthusiasm for innovation broadened and the individuals and collective experienced deepening confidence and energy (Errida & Lotfi, 2021). The fear that had permeated the toxic culture before the new leader's arrival dissipated and was replaced with courage and zeal as they tackled the institution's problems and impediments.

The result of the vitality and motivation of the team to the institution was profound. Over two years, the school's population grew seven-fold. Multiple new programs were successfully proposed and launched. The institution went from systems of regulatory inadequacy to developing sound processes and procedures that drove accreditation, state, and federal compliance. Key performance indicators were initiated and closely monitored to allow for swift intervention and action. Engagement in the community deepened and the institution's reputation flourished.

Transforming a culture mired by toxicity was a formidable undertaking. However, the new leader employed tactics of effective leadership to great success. As individuals transformed from alienated and disengaged employees to empowered and motivated, a cohesive coalition emerged to pursue a shared vision for success (Ambad et al., 2021). The impact of this experience transcended the moment of time during which it occurred and had long-lasting and far-reaching effects.

PAYING IT FORWARD

Over time, members of the team the leader had eloquently brought together began to pursue new opportunities, many in senior leadership positions. While most of the original team eventually branched out to new institutions and organizations, their experience remained transformational. The team's bonds persisted as they developed friendships independent of the institution. And their desire to collaborate carried forth with many of them working together at new institutions.

My career trajectory was profoundly altered by my experience with the leader and my mentor. The trust and empowerment I experienced allowed me to be open to coaching and reflection that enhanced my leadership capacity. With strong advocates bolstering me, I pursued and earned a doctoral degree, sought and accepted new and increasingly challenging roles with confidence, and found a renewed excitement for my future in higher education leadership. The way I saw myself as a professional was irrevocably altered and I developed a courageousness that allowed me to pursue my goals with tenacity.

The lessons I learned from this transformational time in my career continue to affect how I approach challenges and leadership. After years of seeing leaders model toxic behaviors driven by ego, scarcity, and competition, the notion that this simply was what leadership looked like was dispelled. I developed and found my voice as a leader who was interested in navigating professional challenges with integrity and innovation. I learned how to communicate and stand firm in my convictions while also empowering others to do the same. I approach small and big challenges with a mindset of opportunity and encourage others to do the same which has helped me drive my teams and organizations forward.

Perhaps the most significant realization I had was how powerful mentorship was, especially among women who often struggle to create harmony between the social expectations they face and their desire to lead (Eagly & Karau, 2002). Navigating the leadership terrain of the male-normed environment of the academy can be a tricky proposition for women (White & Burkinshaw, 2019). While the empowerment of the senior male leader I received was crucial, so too was the understanding and advice of my female mentor who understood the particular barriers and complexities I faced as a woman pursuing career advancement (Brue & Brue, 2018).

My experience being mentored created a commitment in me to provide other women with the same support and counsel I received. While these mentoring relationships are sometimes formalized in my work with junior colleagues, the informal mentoring relationships I participate in with colleagues are just as powerful and profound (Early 2020; Madsen & Longman, 2020). The result has been the formation of a vast network of engaged and deeply caring women who act as champions, advisors, and advocates for each other. We have eschewed the notion of the queen bee (Gomes Neto, 2022) and embraced a vision of abundance and resilience.

CONCLUSION

Toxic leadership is a blight upon academic institutions, extinguishing innovation, creativity, and motivation (Fahie, 2020). Women are especially burdened by toxic leadership as they already face gender bias and complex barriers that impede their progress and success (Herbst & Roux, 2023). Effective leadership strategies that recognize and embrace individual, team, and institutional needs can have a profound influence on performance and aspirations. Experiencing the transformational impact of authentic leadership built on trust and empowerment was a defining moment in my personal and professional life. It was through this experience that I was able to craft a new narrative about my professional identity and become the leader I had envisioned. The significance of this experience created a lasting ripple effect that reignited my passion for my career and inspired me to become a leader committed to supporting, encouraging, and developing others.

REFERENCES

Abun, D., Nicholas, T., Apollo, E. P., Magallanes, T., & Encarnacion, M. J. (2021). Employees' self-efficacy and work performance of employees as mediated by work environment. *International Journal of Research in Business & Social Science*, 10(7), 1–15. DOI: 10.20525/ijrbs.v10i7.1470

Ali, A., Wang, H., & Johnson, R. E. (2020). Empirical analysis of shared leadership promotion and team creativity: An adaptive leadership perspective. *Journal of Organizational Behavior*, 41(5), 405–423. DOI: 10.1002/job.2437

Ambad, S. N. A., Kalimin, K. M., Ag Damit, D. H. D., & Andrew, J. V. (2021). The mediating effect of psychological empowerment on leadership styles and task performance of academic staff. *Leadership and Organization Development Journal*, 42(5), 763–782. DOI: 10.1108/LODJ-05-2020-0197

American Association of University Women. (n.d.). *Fast facts: Women working in academia*.https://www.aauw.org/resources/article/fast-facts-academia/

Brue, K. L., & Brue, S. A. (2018). Leadership role identity construction in women's leadership development programs. *Journal of Leadership Education*, 17(1), 7–27. DOI: 10.12806/V17/I1/C2

Burns, W. A.Jr. (2017). A descriptive literature review of harmful leadership styles: Definitions, commonalities, measurements, negative impacts, and ways to improve these harmful leadership styles. *Creighton Journal of Interdisciplinary Leadership*, 3(1), 33–52. DOI: 10.17062/cjil.v3i1.53

Carli, L. L., & Eagly, A. H. (2016). Women face a labyrinth: An examination of metaphors for women leaders. *Gender in Management*, 31(8), 514–527. DOI: 10.1108/GM-02-2015-0007

Docka-Filipek, D., & Stone, L. B. (2021). Twice a "housewife": On academic precarity, "hysterical" women, faculty mental health, and service as gendered care work for the "university family" in pandemic times. *Gender, Work and Organization*, 28(6), 2158–2179. DOI: 10.1111/gwao.12723

Eagly, A. H., & Karau, S. J. (2002). Role congruity theory of prejudice toward female leaders. *Psychological Review*, 109(3), 573–598. DOI: 10.1037/0033-295X.109.3.573 PMID: 12088246

Early, S. L. (2020). Relational leadership reconsidered: The mentor-protégé connection. *Journal of Leadership Studies*, 13(4), 57–61. DOI: 10.1002/jls.21671

Eiland, L. S., Shields, K. M., Smith, S. E., Covington, E. W., Edwards, A., Kinney, S. R. M., & Haines, S. L. (2021). Development and assessment of a nationwide, cross-discipline women faculty mentoring program. *Currents in Pharmacy Teaching & Learning*, 13(12), 1555–1563. DOI: 10.1016/j.cptl.2021.09.031 PMID: 34895663

Erdal, N., & Budak, O. (2021). The mediating role of organizational trust in the effect of toxic leadership on job satisfaction. *Research in Business & Social Science*, 10(3), 139–155. DOI: 10.20525/ijrbs.v10i3.1144

Errida, A., & Lofti, B. (2021). The determinants of organizational change management success: Literature review and case study. *International Journal of Engineering and Business Management, 2021*(13). https://doi.org/DOI: 10.1177/18479790211016273

Fahie, D. (2020). The lived experience of toxic leadership in Irish higher education. *International Journal of Workplace Health Management*, 13(3), 341–355. DOI: 10.1108/IJWHM-07-2019-0096

Gomes Neto, M. B., Grangeiro, R. R., & Esnard, C. (2022). Academic women: A study on the queen bee phenomenon. *Human and Social Management, 23*(2), 1-30. https://doi.org/DOI: 10.1590/1678-6971/eramg220211.en

Harris, T. M., & Lee, C. N. (2019). Advocate-mentoring: A communicative response to diversity in higher education. *Communication Education*, 68(1), 103–113. DOI: 10.1080/03634523.2018.1536272

Herbst, T. H. H. (2020). Gender differences in self-perception accuracy: The confidence gap and women leaders' underrepresentation in academic. *SA Journal of Industrial Psychology*, 46(1), A1704. Advance online publication. DOI: 10.4102/sajip.v46i0.1704

Herbst, T. H. H., & Roux, T. (2023). Toxic leadership: A slow poison killing women leaders in higher education in South Africa? *Higher Education Policy*, 36(1), 164–189. DOI: 10.1057/s41307-021-00250-0

Hollander, E. P. (1992). The essential interdependence of leadership and followership. *Current Directions in Psychological Science*, 1(2), 71–75. DOI: 10.1111/1467-8721.ep11509752

Hussain, S. T. (2024). Challenging gaslighting of women in academia: A call for gender equality and inclusive environment. *International Journal of Innovation in Teaching and Learning*, 10(1), 40–63. DOI: 10.35993/ijitl.v10i1.3146

Jiang, H., & Shen, H. (2020). Toward a relational theory of employee engagement: Understanding authenticity, transparency, and employee behaviors. *International Journal of Business Communication*, 60(3), 948–975. DOI: 10.1177/2329488420954236

Jung, K. B., Kang, S., & Choi, S. B. (2020). Empowering leadership, risk-taking behavior, and employees' commitment to organizational change. The mediated moderating role of task complexity. *Sustainability (Basel)*, 12(6), 2340. Advance online publication. DOI: 10.3390/su12062340

Kim, M., & Beehr, T. A. (2021). The power of empowering leadership: Allowing and encouraging followers to take charge of their own jobs. *International Journal of Human Resource Management*, 32(9), 1865–1898. DOI: 10.1080/09585192.2019.1657166

Koc, O., Bozkurt, S., Tasdemir, D. D., & Günsel, A. (2022). The moderating role of intrinsic motivation on the relationship between toxic leadership and emotional exhaustion. *Frontiers in Psychology*, 13, 1047834. Advance online publication. DOI: 10.3389/fpsyg.2022.1047834 PMID: 36591061

Kotter, J. P. (1996). *Leading change*. Harvard University Press.

Llorens, A., Tzovara, A., Bellier, L., Bhaya-Grossman, I., Bidet-Caulet, A., Chang, W. K., Cross, Z. R., Dominguez-Faus, R., Flinker, A., Fonken, Y., Gorenstein, M. A., Holdgraf, C., Hoy, C. W., Ivanova, M. V., Jimenez, R. T., Jun, S., Kam, J. W. Y., Kidd, C., Marcelle, E., & Dronkers, N. F. (2021). Gender bias in academia: A lifetime problem that needs a solution. *Neuron*, 109(13), 2047–2074. DOI: 10.1016/j.neuron.2021.06.002 PMID: 34237278

Luqman, R., Fatima, S., Ahmed, S., Khalid, I., & Bhatti, A. (2019). The impact of autocratic leadership style on counterproductive work behavior: The mediating role of employee commitment and moderating role of emotional exhaustion. *Pollster Journal of Academic Research*, 6(1), 22–47.

Madsen, S., & Longman, K. (2020). Women's leadership in higher education: Status, barriers, and motivators. *Journal of Higher Education Management*, 35(1), 13–24.

Mascareño, J., Rietzschel, E., & Wisse, B. (2019). Envisioning innovation: Does visionary leadership engender team innovative performance through goal alignment? *Creativity and Innovation Management*, 29(1), 33–48. DOI: 10.1111/caim.12341

Milosevic, I., Maric, S., & Lončar, D. (2019). Defeating the toxic boss: The nature of toxic leadership and the role of followers. *Journal of Leadership & Organizational Studies*, 27(2), 117–137. DOI: 10.1177/1548051819833374

Nguyen, T. T., Berman, E. M., Plimmer, G., Samartini, A., Sabharwal, M., & Taylor, J. (2021). Enriching transactional leadership with public values. *Public Administration Review*, 82(6), 1058–1076. DOI: 10.1111/puar.13495

O'Connor, P. (2018). Gender imbalance in senior positions in higher education: What is the problem? What can be done? *Policy Reviews in Higher Education*, 3(1), 28–50. DOI: 10.1080/23322969.2018.1552084

Rehman, S. U. R., Shahzad, M., Farooq, M. S., & Javaid, M. E. (2020). Impact of leadership behavior of a project manager on his/her subordinate's job-attitudes and job-outcomes. *Asia Pacific Management Review*, 25(1), 38–47. DOI: 10.1016/j.apmrv.2019.06.004

Sarsons, H., Gërxhani, K., Reuben, E., & Schram, A. (2021). Gender differences in recognition for group work. *Journal of Political Economy*, 129(1), 101–147. DOI: 10.1086/711401

Sonmez Cakir, F., & Adiguzel, Z. (2020). Analysis of leader effectiveness in organization and knowledge sharing behavior on employees and organization. *SAGE Open*, 10(1). Advance online publication. DOI: 10.1177/2158244020914634

Staines, G., Tavris, C., & Jayaratne, T. E. (1974). The queen bee syndrome. *Psychology Today*, 7(8), 55–60. DOI: 10.1037/e400562009-003

Statti, A. L. C., & Torres, K. (2019). Innovative approaches to traditional mentoring practices of women in higher education. In Schnackenberg, H., & Simard, D. (Eds.), *Challenges and opportunities for women in higher education leadership* (pp. 1–19). IGI Global., DOI: 10.4018/978-1-5225-7056-1.ch001

Subbaye, R., & Vithal, R. (2017). Gender, teaching, and academic promotions in higher education. *Gender and Education*, 29(7), 926–951. DOI: 10.1080/09540253.2016.1184237

Sull, D., Sull, C., & Zweig, B. (2022, January 11). *Toxic culture is driving the great resignation.* MIT Sloan Management Review. https://sloanreview.mit.edu/article/toxic-culture-is-driving-the-great-resignation/

Uhl-Bien, M. (2006). Relational leadership theory: Exploring the social processes of leadership and organizing. *The Leadership Quarterly*, 17(6), 654–676. DOI: 10.1016/j.leaqua.2006.10.007

University of Delaware. (2017, December 13). Women get less credit than men in the workplace. *ScienceDaily.*https://www.sciencedaily.com/releases/2017/12/171213130252.htm

U.S. Bureau of Labor Statistics. (2023, March 24). Employment differences of men and women narrow with educational attainment. *TED: The Economics Daily.*https://www.bls.gov/opub/ted/2023/employment-differences-of-men-and-women-narrow-with-educational-attainment.htm

Van Veelen, R., & Derks, B. (2021). Academics as agentic superheroes: Female academics' lack of fit with the agentic stereotype of success limits their career advancement. *British Journal of Social Psychology*, 61(3), 748–767. DOI: 10.1111/bjso.12515 PMID: 34935167

Webb, O. (2021). Enacting relational leadership through restorative practices. *The Alberta Journal of Educational Research*, 67(2), 159–177. DOI: 10.55016/ojs/ajer.v67i2.68603

White, K., & Burkinshaw, P. (2019). Women and leadership in higher education: Special issue editorial. *Social Sciences (Basel, Switzerland)*, 8(204), 1–7. DOI: 10.3390/socsci8070204

Woller, C. W., Ardiansyah, A., Rofaida, R., Nurkhin, A., & Rababah, M. A. (2022). Impact of toxic leadership on employee performance. *Health Psychology Research*, 10(4), 57551. Advance online publication. DOI: 10.52965/001c.57551 PMID: 36540087

Compilation of References

28% of Women in Higher Ed Fault Gender Bias. (2022, April 15). *The Chronicle of Higher Education*, 68(16), 14.

Abalkhail, J. M. (2020). Women managing women: Hierarchical relationships and career impact. *Career Development International*, 25(4), 389–413. DOI: 10.1108/CDI-01-2019-0020

Abdulrahman, M., & Amoush, A. H. (2020). Female characteristics and their new roles in leadership. *Journal of Business and Management Sciences*, 8(2), 38–47.

Abun, D., Nicholas, T., Apollo, E. P., Magallanes, T., & Encarnacion, M. J. (2021). Employees' self-efficacy and work performance of employees as mediated by work environment. *International Journal of Research in Business & Social Science*, 10(7), 1–15. DOI: 10.20525/ijrbs.v10i7.1470

Achhnani, B., & Gupta, B. (2022). Queen bee: The culprit or the victim of sexism in the organisation. *British Journal of Administrative Management*.

Acker, S., & Feuerverger, G. (1996). Doing Good and Feeling Bad: The work of women university teachers. *Cambridge Journal of Education*, 26(3), 401–422. DOI: 10.1080/0305764960260309

Adekunle, J. O., Campbell, K., Chapman, S. J., Chávez, M., Dooley, K. L., Liu, P., & Williams, H. V. (2023). *Inequality and Governance in an Uncertain World: Perspectives on Democratic and Autocratic Governments*. Rowman & Littlefield.

Ainslie, K. M. (2022). 9 to 5 in Academia: Addressing barriers for women. *Molecular Pharmaceutics*, 20(1), 1–3. DOI: 10.1021/acs.molpharmaceut.2c00899 PMID: 36367381

AISHE. (2020). *All India Survey on Higher Education 2019-20*.

Akoul, M., Lotfi, S., & Radid, M. (2021). Correlations of self-esteem with academic competencies and gender variations. *International Journal of Learning & Teaching, 13*(1), 01–12. DOI: 10.18844/ijlt.v13i1.5204

Akoul, M. (2021). Correlations of self-esteem with academic competencies and gender variations. *Global Journal of Guidance and Counseling in Schools Current Perspectives*, 11(1), 15–26. DOI: 10.18844/gjgc.v11i1.5077

Al Khatib, S. A. (2012). Exploring the relationship among loneliness, self-esteem, self-efficacy and gender in United Arab Emirates college students. *Europe's Journal of Psychology*, 8(1). Advance online publication. DOI: 10.5964/ejop.v8i1.301

Aldossari, M., & Chaudhry, S. (2021). Women and burnout in the context of a pandemic. *Gender, Work and Organization*, 28(2), 826–834. DOI: 10.1111/gwao.12567

Ali, A., Wang, H., & Johnson, R. E. (2020). Empirical analysis of shared leadership promotion and team creativity: An adaptive leadership perspective. *Journal of Organizational Behavior*, 41(5), 405–423. DOI: 10.1002/job.2437

Allen, M., Smith, A., & Dika, S. (2023). Black Feminism and Black Women's Interactions With Faculty in Higher Education. In *Oxford Research Encyclopedia of Education*. DOI: 10.1093/acrefore/9780190264093.013.1723

Allen, T. G., & Flood, C. T. (2018). The Experiences of women in higher education: Who knew there wasn't a sisterhood? *Leadership and Research in Education*, 4, 10–27.

Al-Masri, A. R. I. (2020). Impulsive Buying Behavior and Its Relation to the Emotional Balance. *Int. J. Psychol. Brain Sci*, 5(1), 5–20. DOI: 10.11648/j.ijpbs.20200501.12

Al-Obaidi, M. (1991). Measuring Emotional Balance among Martyrs' sons and relatives living with their parents, unpublished Master's Thesis, IbnRushd Faculty of Pedagogy, University of Baghdad.

Alrajhi, M., & Aldhafri, S. (2015). Academic and social self-concept: effects of teaching styles and gender in English as a foreign language setting. *Journal of Psychology in Africa (South of the Sahara, the Caribbean, and Afro-Latin America), 25*(1), 44–49. DOI: 10.1080/14330237.2014.997009

Ambad, S. N. A., Kalimin, K. M., Ag Damit, D. H. D., & Andrew, J. V. (2021). The mediating effect of psychological empowerment on leadership styles and task performance of academic staff. *Leadership and Organization Development Journal*, 42(5), 763–782. DOI: 10.1108/LODJ-05-2020-0197

American Association of University Women. (n.d.). *Fast facts: Women working in academia.* https://www.aauw.org/resources/article/fast-facts-academia/

American Psychological Association. (2018). Stress affects on the body. Retrieved from: https://www.apa.org/topics/stress/body

American Psychological Association. (2024). *Work in America*. Retrieved from the American Psychological Association website: https://www.apa.org/pubs/reports/work-in-america/2024/2024-work-in-america-report.pdf

Amey, M. J. (2005). Leadership as learning: Conceptualizing the Process. *Community College Journal of Research and Practice*, 29(9-10), 689–704. DOI: 10.1080/10668920591006539

Anderson, E. (2022). *Black in white space: The enduring impact of color in everyday life*. University of Chicago Press.

Antecol, H., Bedard, K., & Stearns, J. (2018). Equal but inequitable: Who benefits from gender-neutral tenure clock stopping policies? *The American Economic Review*, 108(9), 2420–2441. DOI: 10.1257/aer.20160613

Apsey, A., & Couros, G. (2024). *What Makes a Great Principal: The Five Pillars of Effective School Leadership*. Impress Press.

Arnold, N. W., Crawford, E. R., & Khalifa, M. (2016). Psychological heuristics and Faculty of Color: Racial battle fatigue and tenure/promotion. *The Journal of Higher Education*, 87(6), 890–919. DOI: 10.1080/00221546.2016.11780891

Ayça, B. (2022). Sosyal Bilimler Öğrencilerinin Sosyo-Kültürel Boyutlar, Benlik Saygısı ve Akademik Öz Yeterlikleri Arasındaki İlişkinin İncelenmesi. *Ankara Hacı Bayram Veli Üniversitesi İktisadi ve İdari Bilimler Fakültesi Dergisi*, 24(2), 889–916. DOI: 10.26745/ahbvuibfd.1120436

Bandura, A. (1989). Human agency in social cognitive theory. *The American Psychologist*, 44(9), 1175–1184. http://www.stiftelsen-hvasser.no/documents/Bandura_Human_Agency_in_social_Cognitiv_theory.pdf. DOI: 10.1037/0003-066X.44.9.1175 PMID: 2782727

Barak, M. (2005). *Managing Diversity: Toward a globally inclusive workplace*. SAGE.

Baumann, N., Faulk, C., Vanderlan, J., & Bhayani, R. (2020). Small-group discussion sessions on imposter syndrome. *MedEdPORTAL: the Journal of Teaching and Learning Resources*, 11004. Advance online publication. DOI: 10.15766/mep_2374-8265.11004 PMID: 33204832

Baumgartner, K. (2022). In pursuit of knowledge: Black women and educational activism in antebellum []. NYU Press.]. *America*, 5, •••.

Baykal, E., Soyalp, E., & Yeşil, R. (2020). Queen Bee Syndrome: A Modern Dilemma of Working Women and Its Effects on Turnover Intentions. In Dincer, H., & Yüksel, S. (Eds.), *Strategic Outlook for Innovative Work Behaviours. Contributions to Management Science*. Springer., DOI: 10.1007/978-3-030-50131-0_9

Beena, C., & Poduval, P. R. (1992). Gender differences in work stress of executives. *Psychological Studies*, 37(2-3), 109–113.

Bender, S., Brown, K. S., Hensley Kasitz, D. L., & Vega, O. (2022). Academic women and their children: Parenting during COVID-19 and the impact on scholarly productivity. *Family Relations*, 71(1), 46–67. DOI: 10.1111/fare.12632

Benmira, S., & Agboola, M. (2021). Evolution of leadership theory. *BMJ Leader*, •••, leader–2020.

Bennis, W. G., & Thomas, R. J. (2002). *Geeks and Geezers: How Era, Values, and Defining Moments Shape Leaders*. Harvard Business School Publishing.

Bernard, J. (1964). *Academic women*. Pennsylvania State University Press.

Bertucci, A., Conte, S., Johnson, D. W., & Johnson, R. T. (2010). The impact of size of cooperative group on achievement, social support, and self-esteem. *The Journal of General Psychology*, 137(3), 256–272. DOI: 10.1080/00221309.2010.484448 PMID: 20718226

Bhatti, A., & Ali, R. (2021). Women's leadership pathways in higher education: Role of mentoring and networking. *Asian Women*, 37(3), 25–50. DOI: 10.14431/aw.2021.9.37.3.25

Bitonti, C. (1992). The self-esteem of women: A cognitive-phenomenological study. *Smith College Studies in Social Work*, 63(1), 295–311. DOI: 10.1080/00377319209517375

Bi, Y., Ma, L., Yuan, F., & Zhang, B. (2016). Self-esteem, perceived stress, and gender during adolescence: Interactive links to different types of interpersonal relationships. *The Journal of Psychology*, 150(1), 36–57. DOI: 10.1080/00223980.2014.996512 PMID: 25584816

Black, W. T. R. (2022). Retrieved from https://everylevelleads.com/wp-content/uploads/2022/06/Black-Women-Thriving-Report_2022.pdf

Bocheliuk, V. Y., Spytska, L. V., Shaposhnykova, I. V., Turubarova, A. V., & Panov, M. S. (2022). Five stages of professional personality development: Comparative analysis. *Polish Psychological Bulletin*, 88–93.

Bodalina, K. N., & Mestry, R. (2022). A case study of the experiences of women leaders in senior leadership positions in the education district offices. *Educational Management Administration & Leadership*, 50(3), 452–468. DOI: 10.1177/1741143220940320

Bookchin, M. (1980). *Toward an ecological society*. Black Rose.

Borelli, J. L., Nelson, S. K., River, L. M., Birken, S. A., & Moss-Racusin, C. (2017). Gender differences in work-family guilt in parents of young children. *Sex Roles*, 76(5-6), 356–368. DOI: 10.1007/s11199-016-0579-0

Brannock, R. G., Litten, M. J., & Smith, J. (2000). The impact of doctoral study on marital satisfaction. *Journal of College Counseling*, 3(2), 123–130. DOI: 10.1002/j.2161-1882.2000.tb00172.x

Bravata, D., Watts, S., Keefer, A., Madhusudhan, D., Taylor, K., Clark, D., Nelson, R. S., Cokley, K. O., & Hagg, H. (2019). Prevalence, predictors, and treatment of impostor syndrome: A systematic review. *Journal of General Internal Medicine*, 35(4), 1252–1275. DOI: 10.1007/s11606-019-05364-1 PMID: 31848865

Breeze, M., Taylor, Y., & Addison, M. (2022). Imposter agony aunts: ambivalent feminist advice., 611-630. DOI: 10.1007/978-3-030-86570-2_37

Bresman, H., & Edmondson, A. C. (2022). Research: To excel, diverse teams need psychological safety. *Harvard Business Review*. https://hbr.org/2022/03/research-to-excel-diverse-teams-need-psychological-safety

Brizuela, V., Chebet, J. J., & Thorson, A. (2023). Supporting early-career women researchers: Lessons from a global mentorship programme. *Global Health Action*, 16(1), 2162228. DOI: 10.1080/16549716.2022.2162228 PMID: 36705071

Brock, B. L. (2008). When sisterly support changes to sabotage.

Brock, R., Pratt-Clarke, M., & Maes, J. B. (Eds.). (2019). *Journeys of social justice: Women of color presidents in the academy*. Peter Lang Incorporated, International Academic Publishers.

Bronfenbrenner, U. (1977). Toward an experimental ecology of human development. *The American Psychologist*, 32(7), 513–531. DOI: 10.1037/0003-066X.32.7.513

Bronfenbrenner, U. (2001). The bioecological theory of human development. In Smelser, N. J., & Baltes, P. B. (Eds.), *International encyclopedia of the social and behavioral sciences* (Vol. 10, pp. 6963–6970). Elsevier. DOI: 10.1016/B0-08-043076-7/00359-4

Brooks, R. (2014). Social and spatial disparities in emotional responses to education: Feelings of guilt among student parents. *British Educational Research Journal*, 41(3), 505–519. DOI: 10.1002/berj.3154

Brown, N. (2006). *Private politics and public voices: Black women's activism from World War I to the New Deal*. Indiana University Press.

Brubacher, J. (2017). *Higher education in transition: History of American colleges and universities*. Routledge. DOI: 10.4324/9780203790076

Brue, K. L., & Brue, S. A. (2018). Leadership role identity construction in women's leadership development programs. *Journal of Leadership Education*, 17(1), 7–27. DOI: 10.12806/V17/I1/C2

Buchanan, N. T., & Settles, I. H. (2019). Managing (in) visibility and hypervisibility in the workplace. *Journal of Vocational Behavior*, 113, 1–5. DOI: 10.1016/j.jvb.2018.11.001

Budig, M. (2014). *The fatherhood bonus and the motherhood penalty: Parenthood and the gender gap in pay*. The Way. https://www.thirdway.org/report/the-fatherhood-bonus-and-the-motherhood-penalty-parenthood-and-the-gender-gap-in-pay?tpcc=nlbroadsheet

Bukhari, M., Farooq, U., & Kouser, T. (2023). The relationship between public school teachers self esteem and their assertiveness. *Global Educational Studies Review*, VIII(I), 1–9. DOI: 10.31703/gesr.2023(VIII-I).01

Burnett, P. C. (1996). An investigation of the social learning and symbolic interaction models for the development of self-concepts and self-esteem. *Journal of Family Studies*, 2(1), 57–64. DOI: 10.5172/jfs.2.1.57

Burns, W. A. Jr. (2017). A descriptive literature review of harmful leadership styles: Definitions, commonalities, measurements, negative impacts, and ways to improve these harmful leadership styles. *Creighton Journal of Interdisciplinary Leadership*, 3(1), 33–52. DOI: 10.17062/cjil.v3i1.53

Butcher, J. T. (Ed.). (2022). *Black Female Leaders in Academia: Eliminating the Glass Ceiling With Efficacy, Exuberance, and Excellence*. IGI Global., DOI: 10.4018/978-1-7998-9774-3

Callahan, S. D., & Kidd, A. H. (1986). Relationship between job satisfaction and self-esteem in women. *Psychological Reports*, 59(2), 663–668. DOI: 10.2466/pr0.1986.59.2.663

Calling attention to gender bias dramatically changes course evaluations. (2019, May 30). *Politics & Government Business*.

Canli, U., & Aquino, E. (2023). Barriers and challenges experienced by latina nurse leaders. *Hispanic Health Care International; the Official Journal of the National Association of Hispanic Nurses*, 22(2), 92–98. DOI: 10.1177/15404153231199175 PMID: 37728110

Carby, H. V. (1987). *Reconstructing womanhood: The emergence of the Afro-American woman novelist*. Oxford University Press.

Cardel, M. I., Dhurandhar, E., Yarar-Fisher, C., Foster, M., Hidalgo, B., McClure, L. A., Pagoto, S., Brown, N., Pekmezi, D., Sharafeldin, N., Willig, A. L., & Angelini, C. (2020). Turning chutes into ladders for women faculty: A review and roadmap for equity in academia. *Journal of Women's Health*, 29(5), 721–733. DOI: 10.1089/jwh.2019.8027 PMID: 32043918

Cardinal, B. J., & Thomas, J. D. (2016). Self-care strategies for maximizing human potential. *Journal of Physical Education, Recreation & Dance*, 87(9), 5–7. DOI: 10.1080/07303084.2016.1227198

Carducci, R., Harper, J., & Kezar, A. (2024). *Higher Education Leadership: Challenging Tradition and Forging Possibilities*. JHU Press. DOI: 10.56021/9781421448787

Carli, L. L., & Eagly, A. H. (2016). Women face a labyrinth: An examination of metaphors for women leaders. *Gender in Management*, 31(8), 514–527. DOI: 10.1108/GM-02-2015-0007

Carriuolo, N. E., Rodgers, A., Stout, C. M., & Garcia, J. (2002). Valuing and Building from Strengths of Hispanic Students: An Interview with Juliet Garcia. *Journal of Developmental Education*, 25(3), 20–42.

Chance, N. L. (2021). A phenomenological inquiry into the influence of crucible experiences on the leadership development of Black women in higher education senior leadership. *Educational Management Administration & Leadership*, 49(4), 601–623. DOI: 10.1177/17411432211019417

Chance, N. L. (2022). Resilient leadership: A phenomenological exploration into how black women in higher education leadership navigate cultural adversity. *Journal of Humanistic Psychology*, 62(1), 44–78. DOI: 10.1177/00221678211003000

Chandler, K. (2003). Spin Cycle. *Cincinnati Magazine*, 37(3), 66–71.

Channing, J. ""Oh, I'm a Damsel in Distress": Women Higher Education Leaders' Narratives" (2022). *Journal of Women in Educational Leadership*. 281. https://digitalcommons.unl.edu/jwel/281

Chapman, A. (2015). Using the assessment process to overcome imposter syndrome in mature students. *Journal of Further and Higher Education*, 41(2), 112–119. DOI: 10.1080/0309877X.2015.1062851

Chinetti, S. (2023). The gender gap in academic productivity during the pandemic: Is childcare responsible? *IZA Journal of Labor Economics*, 12(1), 117–154. DOI: 10.2478/izajole-2023-0007

Chinn, J. J., Martin, I. K., & Redmond, N. (2021). Health equity among Black women in the United States. *Journal of Women's Health*, 30(2), 212–219. DOI: 10.1089/jwh.2020.8868 PMID: 33237831

Çiçek, İ. (2022). Mediating role of self-esteem in the association between loneliness and psychological and subjective well-being in university students. *International Journal of Contemporary Educational Research*, 8(2), 83–97. DOI: 10.33200/ijcer.817660

Clance, P. R., & Imes, S. A. (1978). The imposter phenomenon in high achieving women: Dynamics and therapeutic intervention. *Psychotherapy (Chicago, Ill.)*, 15(3), 241–247. DOI: 10.1037/h0086006

Clanton, T. L., Shelton, R. N., & Franz, N. E. (2023). Thriving Despite the Odds: A Review of Literature on the Experiences of Black Women at Predominately White Institutions. *Handbook of Research on Exploring Gender Equity, Diversity, and Inclusion Through an Intersectional Lens*, 423–437.

Clark, J. V., & Arkowitz, H. (1975). Social anxiety and self-evaluation of interpersonal performance. *Psychological Reports*, 36(1), 211–221. DOI: 10.2466/pr0.1975.36.1.211 PMID: 1121542

CohenMiller. A.S. (October 25, 2019). *Gender equality & social justice: Raising awareness & empowering community*. Nazarbayev University Media and Information Literacy Forum 2019, Astana, Kazakhstan. DOI:DOI: 10.13140/RG.2.2.15965.15842

CohenMiller, A. S., Demers, D., Schnackenberg, H., & Izekenova, Z.CohenMiller. (2022). "You are seen; you matter": Applying the theory of gendered organizations to equity and inclusion for motherscholars in higher education. *Journal of Women and Gender in Higher Education*, 15(1), 87–109. DOI: 10.1080/26379112.2022.2025816

Collier, Z. (2021). "Don't Touch My Hair": An Examination of the Exercise of Privilege and Power Through Interracial Hair-Centered Communication Interactions. *Proceedings of the New York State Communication Association*, 2017(1), 11.

Collins, P. H. (1990). Black feminist thought in the matrix of domination. *Black feminist thought: Knowledge, consciousness, and the politics of empowerment, 138*(1990), 221-238.

Collins, C. (2021). Is maternal guilt a cross-national experience? *Qualitative Sociology*, 44(1), 1–29. DOI: 10.1007/s11133-020-09451-2

Collins, P. H. (1991). *Black feminist thought: Knowledge, consciousness, and the politics of empowerment*. Routledge.

Collins, P. H. (2020). Defining black feminist thought. In *Feminist Theory Reader* (pp. 278–290). Routledge.

Collins, P. H., & Bilge, S. (2020). *Intersectionality*. John Wiley & Sons.

Columbia Law School. (2017). Kimberlé Crenshaw on Intersectionality, More than Two Decades Later. https://www.law.columbia.edu/news/archive/kimberle-crenshaw-intersectionality-more-two-decades-later

Cooper, B. C. (2017). *Beyond respectability: The intellectual thought of race women*. University of Illinois Press. DOI: 10.5406/illinois/9780252040993.001.0001

Costa, K. (2024). Study protocol of "exploring the interplay between family responsibilities, personal vulnerabilities, and motivational theories in the publishing endeavours of women scholars: a qualitative evidence synthesis". DOI: 10.20944/preprints202402.0680.v1

Cottrill, K., Denise Lopez, P., & Hoffman, C., C. (. (2014). How authentic leadership and inclusion benefit organizations. *Equality, Diversity and Inclusion*, 33(3), 275–292. DOI: 10.1108/EDI-05-2012-0041

Course survey reforms aim to reduce gender, other bias in evaluation process. (2016, April 29). *UWIRE Text*, 1.

Crane, C. (1974). Attitudes towards acceptance of self and others and adjustment to teaching. *The British Journal of Educational Psychology*, 44(1), 31–36. DOI: 10.1111/j.2044-8279.1974.tb00763.x PMID: 4817534

Crenshaw, K. (1989) "Demarginalizing the Intersection of Race and Sex: A Black Feminist Critique of Antidiscrimination Doctrine, Feminist Theory and Antiracist Politics," University of Chicago Legal Forum: Vol. 1989: Iss. 1, Article 8. Available at: https://chicagounbound.uchicago.edu/uclf/vol1989/iss1/8

Cribb, V. L., & Haase, A. M. (2016). Girls feeling good at school: School gender environment, internalization and awareness of socio-cultural attitudes associations with self-esteem in adolescent girls. *Journal of Adolescence*, 46(1), 107–114. DOI: 10.1016/j.adolescence.2015.10.019 PMID: 26684660

Cui, R., Ding, H., & Zhu, F. (2022). Gender inequality in research productivity during the COVID-19 pandemic. *Manufacturing & Service Operations Management*, 24(2), 707–726. DOI: 10.1287/msom.2021.0991

Cushway, D., & Tyler, P. A. (1994). Stress and coping in clinical psychologists. *Stress Medicine*, 10(1), 35–42. DOI: 10.1002/smi.2460100107

Dagbovie, P. G. (2003). Black women, Carter G. Woodson, and the association for the study of Negro life and history, 1915-1950. *Journal of African American History*, 88(1), 21–41. DOI: 10.2307/3559046

Daniel, G. R., & Williams, H. V. (Eds.). (2014). *Race and the Obama phenomenon: The vision of a more perfect multiracial union*. Univ. Press of Mississippi. DOI: 10.14325/mississippi/9781628460216.001.0001

Dashper, K. (2020). Mentoring for gender equality: Supporting female leaders in the hospitality industry. *International Journal of Hospitality Management*, 88, 102397. DOI: 10.1016/j.ijhm.2019.102397

de Jong, P. J. (2002). Implicit self-esteem and social anxiety: Differential self-favouring effects in high and low anxious individuals. *Behaviour Research and Therapy*, 40(5), 501–508. DOI: 10.1016/S0005-7967(01)00022-5 PMID: 12038643

de la Teja, M. H. (2022) "Natalicio, Eleanor Diana Siedhoff," *Handbook of Texas Online*. https://www.tshaonline.org/handbook/entries/natalicio-eleanor-diana-siedhoff

DeGrande, H., Seifert, M., & Painter, E. (2023). The Experience of Working Nurses Attending Graduate School During COVID-19: A Hermeneutic Phenomenology Study. *SAGE Open Nursing*, 9, 1–12. DOI: 10.1177/23779608231186676 PMID: 37435583

Deloitte. (2024.). *Latest trends in higher education*. Deloitte Insights. Retrieved August 2, 2024, from https://www2.deloitte.com/us/en/insights/industry/public-sector/latest-trends-in-higher-education.html

Denyes, M. J., Orem, D. E., & Bekel, G. (2001). Self-care: A foundational science. *Nursing Science Quarterly*, 14(1), 48–54. DOI: 10.1177/089431840101400113 PMID: 11873354

Derrick, G.E., Chen, P., Leeuwen, T.N., Larivière, V., & Sugimoto, C.R. (2018). The academic motherload: Models of parenting engagement and the effect on academic productivity and performance. *ArXiv, abs/2108.05376*.

Deshwal, V., & Ali, M. A. (2020). A systematic review of various leadership theories. *Shanlax International Journal of Commerce*, 8(1), 38–43. DOI: 10.34293/commerce.v8i1.916

DeWitt, P. M. (2016). *Collaborative leadership: Six influences that matter most*. Corwin Press.

DiAngelo, R. (2015). White fragility: Why it's so hard to talk to White people about racism. *The Good Men Project,* 9.

Docka-Filipek, D., Draper, C., Snow, J., & Stone, L. B. (2023). 'Professor moms' & 'hidden service' in pandemic times: Students report women faculty more supportive & accommodating amid US COVID crisis onset. *Innovative Higher Education*, 48(5), 787–811. DOI: 10.1007/s10755-023-09652-x PMID: 37361116

Docka-Filipek, D., & Stone, L. B. (2021). Twice a "housewife": On academic precarity, "hysterical" women, faculty mental health, and service as gendered care work for the "university family" in pandemic times. *Gender, Work and Organization*, 28(6), 2158–2179. DOI: 10.1111/gwao.12723

Doherty, J., & Parker, K. (1977). An investigation into the effect of certain selected variables on the self-esteem of a group of student teachers. *Educational Review*, 29(4), 307–315. DOI: 10.1080/0013191770290408

Duffy, M. K., Shaw, J. D., & Stark, E. M. (2000). Performance and satisfaction in conflicted interdependent groups: When and how does self-esteem make a difference? *Academy of Management Journal*, 43(4), 772–782. DOI: 10.2307/1556367

Dunn, A. H. (2023). Teacher Self-Care Mandates as Institutional Gaslighting in a Neoliberal System. *Educational Researcher*, 52(8), 491–499. DOI: 10.3102/0013189X231174804

Dunn, T. R. (2020). When professor guilt and mom guilt collide: Pandemic pedagogy from a precarious place. *Communication Education*, 69(4), 491–501. DOI: 10.1080/03634523.2020.1803385

Durbin, S., Lopes, A., & Warren, S. (2020). Challenging male dominance through the substantive representation of women: The case of an online women's mentoring platform. *New Technology, Work and Employment*, 35(2), 215–231. DOI: 10.1111/ntwe.12166

Eagly, A. H., & Karau, S. J. (2002). Role congruity theory of prejudice toward female leaders. *Psychological Review*, 109(3), 573–598. DOI: 10.1037/0033-295X.109.3.573 PMID: 12088246

Early, S. L. (2020). Relational leadership reconsidered: The mentor-protégé connection. *Journal of Leadership Studies*, 13(4), 57–61. DOI: 10.1002/jls.21671

Edmondson, A. (1999). Psychological safety and learning behavior in work teams. *Administrative Science Quarterly*, 44(2), 350–383. DOI: 10.2307/2666999

Edmondson, A. C. (2018). *The Fearless Organization: Creating Psychological Safety in the Workplace for Learning, Innovation, and Growth*. John Wiley & Sons.

Eiland, L. S., Shields, K. M., Smith, S. E., Covington, E. W., Edwards, A., Kinney, S. R. M., & Haines, S. L. (2021). Development and assessment of a nationwide, cross-discipline women faculty mentoring program. *Currents in Pharmacy Teaching & Learning*, 13(12), 1555–1563. DOI: 10.1016/j.cptl.2021.09.031 PMID: 34895663

Eisenmann, L. (2023). Historical Considerations of Women and Gender in Higher Education. In Perna, L. W. (Ed.), *Higher Education: Handbook of Theory and Research. Higher Education: Handbook of Theory and Research* (Vol. 38). Springer., DOI: 10.1007/978-3-031-06696-2_6

Eltayeb, S. (2022). Recognizing the University's Role in Mental Health Promotion. 132, *(57)*6, , 143.

Engelke, E. C., & Frederickson, K. (2022). Dual Collegiate Roles? The Lived Experience of Nursing Student Athletes. *The Journal of Nursing Education*, 61(3), 117–122. https://doi-org.ezproxy.snhu.edu/10.3928/01484834-20220109-01. DOI: 10.3928/01484834-20220109-01 PMID: 35254153

England, P., Bearak, J., Budig, M. J., & Hodges, M. J. (2016). Do highly paid, highly skilled women experience the largest motherhood penalty? *American Sociological Review*, 81(6), 146–167. DOI: 10.1177/0003122416673598

Engle, L., & Engle, J. (2003). Study abroad levels: Toward a classification of program types. *Frontiers: The Interdisciplinary Journal of Study Abroad*, 9(1), 1–20. DOI: 10.36366/frontiers.v9i1.113

Erdal, N., & Budak, O. (2021). The mediating role of organizational trust in the effect of toxic leadership on job satisfaction. *Research in Business & Social Science*, 10(3), 139–155. DOI: 10.20525/ijrbs.v10i3.1144

Errida, A., & Lofti, B. (2021). The determinants of organizational change management success: Literature review and case study. *International Journal of Engineering and Business Management, 2021*(13). https://doi.org/DOI: 10.1177/18479790211016273

Essed, P., & Carberry, K. (2020). In the name of our humanity: Challenging academic racism and its effects on the emotional wellbeing of women of colour professors. In *The international handbook of black community mental health* (pp. 61–81). Emerald Publishing Limited. DOI: 10.1108/978-1-83909-964-920201005

Evans, S. Y. (2016). *Black women in the ivory tower, 1850–1954: An intellectual history*. University Press of Florida.

Fahie, D. (2020). The lived experience of toxic leadership in Irish higher education. *International Journal of Workplace Health Management*, 13(3), 341–355. DOI: 10.1108/IJWHM-07-2019-0096

Fan, W., & Moen, P. (2024). The Shifting Stress of Working Parents: An Examination of Dual Pandemic Disruptions—Remote Work and Remote Schooling. *Social Sciences (Basel, Switzerland)*, 13(1), 36. DOI: 10.3390/socsci13010036

Feldkamp, K., & Neusteter, S. B. (2021). *The little-known, racist history of the 911 emergency call system* (Doctoral dissertation, These Times).

Finding Your Roots with Henry Louis Gates. Jr. (n.d.). Season 1, Episode 7: "Samuel L. Jackson, Condoleezza Rice and Ruth Simmons". https://www.pbs.org/weta/finding-your-roots/about/meet-our-guests/ruth-simmons

Flaherty, C. (April 9, 2014). So much to do so little time. *Inside Higher Ed*. https://www.insidehighered.com/news/2014/04/09/research-shows-professors-work-long-hours-and-spend-much-day-meetings

Flakes, K. (2023). 11 Leadership Takeaways from Dr. Ruth Simmons, the First Black Woman to Lead an Ivy League College. https://www.kennethflakes.com/post/11-leadership-lessons-from-dr-ruth-simmons

Ford, A. Y., Dannels, S., Morahan, P., & Magrane, D. (2021). Leadership programs for academic women: Building self-efficacy and organizational leadership capacity. *Journal of Women's Health*, 30(5), 672–680. DOI: 10.1089/jwh.2020.8758 PMID: 33064580

Fox, M. (2022). 7 A community of practice-educators as self-care. *Reflections on Valuing Wellbeing in Higher Education: Reforming our Acts of Self-care*.

Francis, L., & Stulz, V. (2020). Barriers and facilitators for women academics seeking promotion: Perspectives from the Inside. *Australian Universities Review*, 62(2), 47–60.

Frick, W. C., Polizzi, J. A., & Frick, J. E. (2009). Aspiring to a continuous learning ethic: Building authentic learning communities for faculty and administration. *Educational Leadership and Administration: Teaching and Program Development*, 21, 7–26.

Friedman, S., O'Brien, D., & McDonald, I. (2021). Deflecting privilege: Class identity and the intergenerational self. *Sociology*, 55(4), 716–733. DOI: 10.1177/0038038520982225

Gabrielova, K., & Buchko, A. A. (2021). Here comes Generation Z: Millennials as managers. *Business Horizons*, 64(4), 489–499. DOI: 10.1016/j.bushor.2021.02.013

Gadzella, B. M., Ginther, D. W., Tomcala, M., & Bryant, G. W. (1990). Stress as perceived by professionals. *Psychological Reports*, 67(3), 979–983. DOI: 10.2466/PR0.67.7.979-983 PMID: 2287691

Gallardo, M. (2021). Does maternity affect women's careers? Perceptions of working mothers in academia. *Educación XX1*, 24(1), 405-428.

Gamble, E. D., & Turner, N. J. (2015). Career ascension of African American women in executive positions in postsecondary institutions. *Journal of Organizational Culture. Communications and Conflict*, 19(1), 82.

Ghara, T. K. (2016). Status of Indian Women in Higher Education. *Journal of Education and Practice*, 7(34), 58–64.

Giddings, P. (1988). In search of sisterhood: Delta Sigma Theta and the challenge of the Black sorority movement.

Gilbert, J. (2008). Why I Feel Guilty All the Time: Performing Academic Motherhood. *Women's Studies in Communication*, 31(2), 203–208. DOI: 10.1080/07491409.2008.10162533

Gillies, R. M. (2006). Teachers' and students' verbal behaviours during cooperative and small-group learning. *The British Journal of Educational Psychology*, 76(2), 271–287. DOI: 10.1348/000709905X52337 PMID: 16719964

Gilmore, B., & Kramer, M. W. (2019). We are who we say we are: Teachers' shared identity in the workplace. *Communication Education*, 68(1), 1–19. DOI: 10.1080/03634523.2018.1536271

Giri, V. N. (2003). Associations of self-esteem with communication style. *Psychological Reports*, 92(3, suppl), 1089–1090. DOI: 10.2466/PR0.92.3.1089-1090 PMID: 12931921

Giroux, H. A. (2014). *Neoliberalism's war on higher education*. Haymarket Books.

Gladwell, M. (2011). *Outliers*. Back Bay Books.

Glavinska, O. D., Ovdiyenko, I. M., Brukhovetska, O. V., Chausova, T. V., & Didenko, M. S. V. (2020). Professional self-realization as a factor in the psychological well-being of specialists of caring professions. *Journal of Intellectual Disability - Diagnosis and Treatment, 8*(3), 548–559. https://doi.org/DOI: 10.6000/2292-2598.2020.08.03.32

Glotova, G., & Wilhelm, A. (2014). Teacher's self-concept and self-esteem in pedagogical communication. *Procedia: Social and Behavioral Sciences*, 132, 509–514. DOI: 10.1016/j.sbspro.2014.04.345

Gollub, J. P. (2002). *Learning and understanding: Improving advanced study of mathematics and science in U.S. high schools*. National Academy Press.

Gomes Neto, M. B., Grangeiro, R. R., & Esnard, C. (2022). Academic women: A study on the queen bee phenomenon. *Human and Social Management, 23*(2), 1-30. https://doi.org/DOI: 10.1590/1678-6971/eramg220211.en

Goodreads. (2024). Popular quotes. Retrieved from https://www.goodreads.com/quotes

Goodwin, E. V. (2016). The Effects of Male Leadership on Workplace Gender Identity, Self-Efficacy, and Career Aspirations of Women Working in College Athletics (Doctoral dissertation) Retrieved from Ohiolink.

Gorbett, K., & Kruczek, T. (2008). Family factors predicting social self-esteem in young adults. *The Family Journal (Alexandria, Va.)*, 16(1), 58–65. DOI: 10.1177/1066480707309603

Gorsi, H., Ali, S. A., & Tariq, S. (2023). A conceptual model of impostor phenomenon and job performance: Role of vicarious learning, impression management, and self-reflection. *Journal of Professional & Applied Psychology*, 4(3), 460–477. DOI: 10.52053/jpap.v4i3.183

Grant, C. M. (2015). Smashing the glass ceiling: Accountability of institutional policies and practices to leadership diversity in higher education. In *Culturally Responsive Leadership in Higher Education* (pp. 167–179). Routledge. DOI: 10.4324/9781315720777-12

Gray-Nicolas, N. M., Modeste, M. E., Miles Nash, A., & Tabron, L. A. (2022). (Other) sistering: Black Women Education Leadership Faculty Aligning Identity, Scholarship, and Practice Through Peer Support and Accountability. *Journal of Education Human Resources*, 40(1), 90–113. DOI: 10.3138/jehr-2021-0017

Greenhaus, J. H. (1971). Self-esteem as an influence on occupational choice and occupational satisfaction. *Journal of Vocational Behavior*, 1(1), 75–83. DOI: 10.1016/0001-8791(71)90008-X

Greer, T. M. (2011). Coping strategies as moderators of the relationship between race-and gender-based discrimination and psychological symptoms for African American women. *The Journal of Black Psychology*, 37(1), 42–54. DOI: 10.1177/0095798410380202

Grottis, L. R. (2022). Black Women in Higher Education Leadership: A Critical Review of the Achievements and Barriers to Career Advancement. *Black Female Leaders in Academia: Eliminating the Glass Ceiling With Efficacy, Exuberance, and Excellence*, 58–72.

Grummell, B., Devine, D., & Lynch, K. (2009). The care-less manager: Gender, care and new managerialism in higher education. *Gender and Education*, 21(2), 191–208. DOI: 10.1080/09540250802392273

Guarino, C. M., & Borden, V. M. H. (2017). Faculty service loads and gender: Are women taking care of the academic family? *Research in Higher Education*, 58(6), 672–694. DOI: 10.1007/s11162-017-9454-2

Guindon, M. H. (1994). Understanding the role of self-esteem in managing communication quality. *IEEE Transactions on Professional Communication*, 37(1), 21–27. DOI: 10.1109/47.272855

Gutshall, C. A. (2020). When Teachers Become Students: Impacts of Neuroscience Learning on Elementary Teachers' Mindset Beliefs, Approach to Learning, Teaching Efficacy, and Grit. *European Journal of Psychology and Educational Research*, 3(1), 39–48. DOI: 10.12973/ejper.3.1.39

Hailu, M. F., & Cox, M. F. (2022). Black women in academic leadership: reflections of one department chair's journey in engineering. In *Black Feminist Epistemology, Research, and Praxis* (pp. 177–188). Routledge.

Han, M.-R., & Kim, H.-G. (2017). Mediating effect of communication competence on the relationship between emotional intelligence and self-esteem among nursing students. *Journal of Digital Convergence*, 15(2), 263–272. DOI: 10.14400/JDC.2017.15.2.263

Harris, T. M., & Lee, C. N. (2019). Advocate-mentoring: A communicative response to diversity in higher education. *Communication Education*, 68(1), 103–113. DOI: 10.1080/03634523.2018.1536272

Harvard Public Health. (2023). For Black Americans, homeownership can mean better health. Retrieved from: https://harvardpublichealth.org/equity/fighting-for-more-black-homeownership-and-less-systemic-racism/

Hasan, F., & Kashif, M. (2021). Psychological safety, meaningfulness and empowerment as predictors of employee well-being: A mediating role of promotive voice. *Asia-Pacific Journal of Business Administration*, 13(1), 40–59. DOI: 10.1108/APJBA-11-2019-0236

Hattie (2020). Visible learning. Retrieved from https://visible-learning.org/

Heffernan, T. (2023). Abusive comments in student evaluations of courses and teaching: The attacks women and marginalised academics endure. *Higher Education*, 85(1), 225–239. DOI: 10.1007/s10734-022-00831-x

Heffernan, T., & Bosetti, L. (2021). Incivility: The new type of bullying in higher education. *Cambridge Journal of Education*, 51(5), 641–652. DOI: 10.1080/0305764X.2021.1897524

Heijstra, T. M., Steinthorsdóttir, F. S., & Einarsdóttir, T. (2017). Academic career making and the double-edged role of academic housework. *Gender and Education*, 29(6), 764–780. DOI: 10.1080/09540253.2016.1171825

Herbst, T. H. H. (2020). Gender differences in self-perception accuracy: The confidence gap and women leaders' underrepresentation in academic. *SA Journal of Industrial Psychology*, 46(1), A1704. Advance online publication. DOI: 10.4102/sajip.v46i0.1704

Herbst, T. H. H., & Roux, T. (2023). Toxic leadership: A slow poison killing women leaders in higher education in South Africa? *Higher Education Policy*, 36(1), 164–189. DOI: 10.1057/s41307-021-00250-0

Hideg, I., & Shen, W. (2019). Why still so few? a theoretical model of the role of benevolent sexism and career support in the continued underrepresentation of women in leadership positions. *Journal of Leadership & Organizational Studies*, 26(3), 287–303. DOI: 10.1177/1548051819849006

Hill, C., Miller, K., Benson, K., & Handley, G. (2016). *Barriers and bias: The status of women in leadership*. American Association of University Women. https://www.aauw.org/resources/research/barrier-bias/

Hill, R. F. (2019). The danger of an untold story: Excerpts from my life as a Black academic. *Journal of Education for Library and Information Science*, 60(3), 208–214. DOI: 10.3138/jelis.2019-0008

Hintsanen, M., Alatupa, S., Pullmann, H., Hirstiö-Snellman, P., & Keltikangas-Järvinen, L. (2010). Associations of self-esteem and temperament traits to self- and teacher-reported social status among classmates: Self-esteem, temperament and social status. *Scandinavian Journal of Psychology*, 51(6), 488–494. DOI: 10.1111/j.1467-9450.2010.00820.x PMID: 20584152

Hochschild, A. (2012). The second shift: Working families and the revolution at home. Penguin Group., 978-0-14-312033-9.

Hollander, E. P. (1992). The essential interdependence of leadership and followership. *Current Directions in Psychological Science*, 1(2), 71–75. DOI: 10.1111/1467-8721.ep11509752

Holm, J. M., Prosek, E. A., & Godwin Weisberger, A. C. (2015). A phenomenological investigation of counseling doctoral students becoming mothers. *Counselor Education and Supervision*, 54(1), 2–16. DOI: 10.1002/j.1556-6978.2015.00066.x

Hora, S., Lemoine, G. J., Xu, N., & Shalley, C. E. (2021). Unlocking and closing the gender gap in creative performance: A multilevel model. *Journal of Organizational Behavior*, 42(3), 297–312. DOI: 10.1002/job.2500

Horhn, E. B., & Lassiter, S. (2022). A Tale of Two Black Women Seeking Solidarity within Academia. *The Ivory Tower: Perspectives of Women of Color in Higher Education*, 81.

House, A., Dracup, N., Burkinshaw, P., Ward, V., & Bryant, L. D. (2021). Mentoring as an intervention to promote gender equality in academic medicine: A systematic review. *BMJ Open*, 11(1), e040355. DOI: 10.1136/bmjopen-2020-040355 PMID: 33500280

Howard-Baptiste, S. D. (2014). Arctic space, lonely place: "Mammy moments" in higher education. *The Urban Review*, 46(4), 764–782. DOI: 10.1007/s11256-014-0298-1

Howard-Baptiste, S., & Harris, J. C. (2014). Teaching then and now: Black female scholars and the mission to move beyond borders. *Negro Educational Review*, 65(1–4), 5–22.

Howard-Hamilton, M. F. (2023). Black Women in higher education reclaiming our time. *New Directions for Student Services*, 2023(182), 5–8. DOI: 10.1002/ss.20462

Hunt, A. N. (2015). The role of theory in understanding the lived experiences of mothering in the academy. In Young, A. M. (Ed.), *Teacher, scholar, mother: Re-envisioning motherhood in the academy* (pp. 3–12). Lexington Books.

Huo, Y., & Kong, F. (2014). Moderating effects of gender and loneliness on the relationship between self-esteem and life satisfaction in Chinese university students. *Social Indicators Research*, 118(1), 305–314. DOI: 10.1007/s11205-013-0404-x

Hussain, S. T. (2024). Challenging gaslighting of women in academia: A call for gender equality and inclusive environment. *International Journal of Innovation in Teaching and Learning*, 10(1), 40–63. DOI: 10.35993/ijitl.v10i1.3146

Hutchins, H. (2015). Outing the imposter: A study exploring imposter phenomenon among higher education faculty. *New Horizons in Adult Education and Human Resource Development*, 27(2), 3–12. DOI: 10.1002/nha3.20098

Hwang, W. Y., Choi, S. Y., & An, H. J. (2022). Concept analysis of transition to motherhood: A methodological study. *Korean Journal of Women Health Nursing*, 28(1), 8–17. DOI: 10.4069/kjwhn.2022.01.04 PMID: 36312044

Hyun, M.-Y., & Park, E.-O. (2008). The effect of interpersonal relationships and communication curriculum. *Journal of Korean Academic Society of Nursing Education*, 14(1), 5–11. DOI: 10.5977/JKASNE.2008.14.1.005

Ibili, E., & Billinghurst, M. (2019). The Relationship between Self-Esteem and Social Network Loneliness: A Study of Trainee School Counsellors. *Malaysian Online Journal of Educational Technology*, 7(3), 39–56.

Idowu, B. D. (2023). A personal reflection upon navigating into a senior academic role. *Frontiers in Sociology*, 8, 979691. DOI: 10.3389/fsoc.2023.979691 PMID: 37415874

Inspirational Poetry Quotes. (2019). https://paulathewriter.com/2019/04/17/inspirational-quotes-poetry/

Isgro, K., & Casteñeda, M. (2015). Mothers in U.S. academia: Insights from lived experiences. *Women's Studies International Forum*, 53, 174–181. DOI: 10.1016/j.wsif.2014.12.002

Jan, M., & Ashraf, A. (2008). An assessment of self-esteem among women. *Studies on Home and Community Science*, 2(2), 133–139. DOI: 10.1080/09737189.2008.11885264

Jerald, M. C., Cole, E. R., Ward, L. M., & Avery, L. R. (2017). Controlling images: How awareness of group stereotypes affects Black women's well-being. *Journal of Counseling Psychology*, 64(5), 487–499. DOI: 10.1037/cou0000233 PMID: 29048195

Jiang, H., & Shen, H. (2020). Toward a relational theory of employee engagement: Understanding authenticity, transparency, and employee behaviors. *International Journal of Business Communication*, 60(3), 948–975. DOI: 10.1177/2329488420954236

Johnson, J. B., Castillo, N., Nagthall, N., & Negussie, H. (2024). Safeguarding black women educators' mental health. Retrieved from https://www.insidehighered.com/opinion/career-advice/conditionally-accepted/2024/03/01/how-and-why-advocate-and-support-black

Johnson, N. N. (2023). Intersectionality in Leadership: Spotlighting the Experiences of Black Women DEI Leaders in Historically White Academic Institutions. In *The Experiences of Black Women Diversity Practitioners in Historically White Institutions* (pp. 213–238). IGI Global.

Johnson, A., & Joseph-Salisbury, R. (2018). 'Are You Supposed to Be in Here?' Racial microaggressions and knowledge production in higher education. In *Dismantling race in higher education* (pp. 143–160). Palgrave Macmillan. DOI: 10.1007/978-3-319-60261-5_8

Johnson, L. (2023). Black Women and Theoretical Frameworks. *The Scholarship Without Borders Journal*, 1(2), 1. DOI: 10.57229/2834-2267.1018

Johnson, N. N. (2021). Balancing race, gender, and responsibility: Conversations with four Black women in educational leadership in the United States of America. *Educational Management Administration & Leadership*, 49(4), 624–643. DOI: 10.1177/1741143221991839

Johnson, N. N. (2024). Rooted in justice: One Black woman's unique, intersectional educational leadership journey. *School Leadership & Management*, 44(2), 140–158. DOI: 10.1080/13632434.2023.2290512

Johnson, N. N. (2025). Two Centuries of Defining Moments for Black Women Higher Education Leaders in the United States. In Schnackenberg, H. L. (Ed.), *Narratives on Defining Moments for Women Leaders in Higher Education*. IGI Global.

Johnson, N. N., & Fournillier, J. B. (2022). Increasing diversity in leadership: Perspectives of four Black women educational leaders in the context of the United States. *Journal of Educational Administration and History*, 54(2), 174–192. DOI: 10.1080/00220620.2021.1985976

Johnson, N. N., & Fournillier, J. B. (2023). Intersectionality and leadership in context: Examining the intricate paths of four Black women in educational leadership in the United States. *International Journal of Leadership in Education*, 26(2), 296–317. DOI: 10.1080/13603124.2020.1818132

Johnson, N. N., & Johnson, T. L. (2024). The Race-Gender-Equity-Leadership Matrix: Intersectionality and Its Application in Higher Education Literature. *Journal of Black Studies*. Advance online publication. DOI: 10.1177/00219347241259454

Joutz, M. (2018). Ruth Simmons on Cultivating the Next Generation of College Students. *The New York Times.* https://www.nytimes.com/2018/02/28/opinion/hbcu-ruth-simmons-interview.html

Jung, K. B., Kang, S., & Choi, S. B. (2020). Empowering leadership, risk-taking behavior, and employees' commitment to organizational change. The mediated moderating role of task complexity. *Sustainability (Basel)*, 12(6), 2340. Advance online publication. DOI: 10.3390/su12062340

Kahn, K. (2009). Shattering glass ceilings nothing new for SUNY chancellor. *Westchester County Business Journal*, 48(32), 31–34.

Kakabadse, N. K., Figueira, C., Nicolopoulou, K., Hong Yang, J., Kakabadse, A. P., & Özbilgin, M. F. (2015). Gender diversity and board performance: Women's experiences and perspectives. *Human Resource Management*, 54(2), 265–281. DOI: 10.1002/hrm.21694

Kapasi, I., Sang, K. J., & Sitko, R. (2016). Gender, authentic leadership and identity: Analysis of women leaders' autobiographies. *Gender in Management*, 31(5/6), 339–358. DOI: 10.1108/GM-06-2015-0058

Kauffman, J. (2020). *The Personal MBA*. Portfolio.

Keohane, N. O. (2020). Women, power & leadership. *Daedalus*, 149(1), 236–250. DOI: 10.1162/daed_a_01785

Kezar, A., & Elrod, S. (2020). Taken for Granted: Improving the Culture of Celebration, Appreciation, and Recognition in Higher Education. *Change*, 52(5), 29–36. DOI: 10.1080/00091383.2020.1807880

Khan, I., Mahmood, A., & Zaib, U. (2019). Interplay of self-esteem with the academic achievements between male and female secondary school students. *Journal of Human Behavior in the Social Environment*, 29(8), 971–978. DOI: 10.1080/10911359.2019.1611517

Kim, J., & Kim, E. (2022). Relationship between self-esteem and technological readiness: Mediation effect of readiness for change and moderated mediation effect of gender in South Korean teachers. *International Journal of Environmental Research and Public Health*, 19(14), 8463. DOI: 10.3390/ijerph19148463 PMID: 35886326

Kim, M., & Beehr, T. A. (2021). The power of empowering leadership: Allowing and encouraging followers to take charge of their own jobs. *International Journal of Human Resource Management*, 32(9), 1865–1898. DOI: 10.1080/09585192.2019.1657166

Kincade, L. L. (2023). At the Crossroads: A Social-Ecological Model of Support for Women of Color in Higher Education Leadership. In *Stabilizing and Empowering Women in Higher Education: Realigning, Recentering, and Rebuilding* (pp. 87-105). IGI Global. DOI:DOI: 10.4018/978-1-6684-8597-2.ch006

Kini, A., & Suvarna, R. (2023). Interim President Donna Shalala wants to improve life at The New School by listening to what students want. New School Free Press. https://www.newschoolfreepress.com/2023/11/27/interim-president-donna-shalala-wants-to-improve-life-at-the-new-school-by-listening-to-what-students-want/

Klaphaak, A. (2021, August 25). How to self reflect. wikiHow. https://www.wikihow.com/Self-Reflect

Knightley, W. M., & Whitelock, D. M. (2007). Assessing the self-esteem of female undergraduate students: An issue of methodology. *Educational Studies*, 33(2), 217–231. DOI: 10.1080/03055690601068485

Koc, O., Bozkurt, S., Tasdemir, D. D., & Günsel, A. (2022). The moderating role of intrinsic motivation on the relationship between toxic leadership and emotional exhaustion. *Frontiers in Psychology*, 13, 1047834. Advance online publication. DOI: 10.3389/fpsyg.2022.1047834 PMID: 36591061

Kolontari, F., Lawton, M., & Rhodes, S. (2023). Using developmental mentoring and coaching approaches in academic and professional development to address feelings of 'imposter syndrome'. *Journal of Perspectives in Applied Academic Practice*, 11(1), 34–41. DOI: 10.56433/jpaap.v11i1.537

Korabik, K. (2015). The intersection of gender and work–family guilt. In Mills, M. (Ed.), *Gender and the work-family experience.* Springer., DOI: 10.1007/978-3-319-08891-4_8

Kotter, J. P. (1996). *Leading change.* Harvard University Press.

Kramer, J., Yinusa-Nyahkoon, L., Olafsson, S., Penti, B., Woodhams, E., Bickmore, T., & Jack, B. W. (2021). Black men's experiences with health care: Individuals' accounts of challenges, suggestions for change, and the potential utility of virtual agent technology to assist black men with health management. *Qualitative Health Research*, 31(10), 1772–1785. DOI: 10.1177/10497323211013323 PMID: 34092141

Krukowski, R. A., Jagsi, R., & Cardel, M. I. (2021). Academic productivity differences by gender and child age in science, technology, engineering, mathematics, and medicine faculty during the COVID-19 pandemic. *Journal of Women's Health*, 30(3), 341–347. DOI: 10.1089/jwh.2020.8710 PMID: 33216682

Kunnumpurath, B., Prasad, A., Menon, V. A., & Thomas, J. (2024). Cultivating self-esteem: Exploring the intersection of culture, neurocognition, and behavior among female media professionals. In *Cognitive Behavioral Neuroscience in Organizational Settings* (pp. 65–82). IGI Global. DOI: 10.4018/979-8-3693-1858-4.ch004

Kvale, S. (1996). *Interviews: An Introduction to Qualitative Research Interviewing*. Sage.

Kwal, T., & Fleshler, H. (1973). The influence of self-esteem on emergent leadership patterns. *The Speech Teacher*, 22(2), 100–106. DOI: 10.1080/03634527309377997

La Freada, F. R. (2021). *Equipping African American Christian Women to Succeed in Predominantly White Institutions of Higher Education Within the United States of America* (Doctoral dissertation, Regent University).

Lam, S. S. K., Schaubroeck, J., & Brown, A. D. (2004). Esteem maintenance among groups: Laboratory and field studies of group performance cognitions. *Organizational Behavior and Human Decision Processes*, 94(2), 86–101. DOI: 10.1016/j.obhdp.2004.03.004

Lapayese, Y. (2017). Mother-scholars: Thinking and being in higher education. Cole, K. & Hassel, H. (Eds.) *Surviving sexism in academia: Strategies for feminist leadership*. Routledge.

Lawson, E. N. (1984). *The three Sarahs: Documents of antebellum black college women*. Mellen-Press.

Lease, S. H. (1999). Occupational role stressors, coping, support, and hardiness as predictors of strain in academic faculty: An emphasis on new and female faculty. *Research in Higher Education*, 40(3), 285–307. DOI: 10.1023/A:1018747000082

Ledesma, J. (2014). Conceptual frameworks and research models on resilience in leadership. *SAGE Open*, 4(3), 1–8. DOI: 10.1177/2158244014545464

Lee-Johnson, Y. I. N. L. A. M. (2022). When Immigrant Mothers of Color Become Public School Teachers for English Language Learners: Intersectionality for Transformative Teacher Preparation. *TESOL Quarterly*.

Leong, T., & Smallwood, N. (2021). Leading by example: The women of respiratory health in australia. *Respirology (Carlton, Vic.)*, 26(10), 997–998. DOI: 10.1111/resp.14135 PMID: 34459516

Lewis, J. A., Mendenhall, R., Harwood, S. A., & Browne Huntt, M. (2016). "Ain't I a woman?" Perceived gendered racial microaggressions experienced by Black women. *The Counseling Psychologist*, 44(5), 758–780. DOI: 10.1177/0011000016641193

Liang, B., Lund, T. J., Mousseau, A. M. D., & Spencer, R. (2016). The mediating role of engagement in mentoring relationships and self-esteem among affluent adolescent girls: Mentoring relationships. *Psychology in the Schools*, 53(8), 848–860. DOI: 10.1002/pits.21949

Liao, K. Y. H., Wei, M., & Yin, M. (2020). The misunderstood schema of the strong Black woman: Exploring its mental health consequences and coping responses among African American women. *Psychology of Women Quarterly*, 44(1), 84–104. DOI: 10.1177/0361684319883198

Liepina, E., & Martinsone, K. (2022, May). Teachers' self-Care Strategies And Supervision As A Self-Care Activity For Teachers. In *Society. Integration. Education.Proceedings of the International Scientific Conference* (Vol. 1, pp. 426-441).

Liu, G., Pan, Y., Ma, Y., & Zhang, D. (2021). Mediating effect of psychological *suzhi* on the relationship between perceived social support and self-esteem. *Journal of Health Psychology*, 26(3), 378–389. DOI: 10.1177/1359105318807962 PMID: 30557075

Liu, Y., & Keller, R. T. (2021). How psychological safety impacts R&D project teams' performance. *Research Technology Management*, 64(2), 39–45. DOI: 10.1080/08956308.2021.1863111

Llorens, A., Tzovara, A., Bellier, L., Bhaya-Grossman, I., Bidet-Caulet, A., Chang, W. K., Cross, Z. R., Dominguez-Faus, R., Flinker, A., Fonken, Y., Gorenstein, M. A., Holdgraf, C., Hoy, C. W., Ivanova, M. V., Jimenez, R. T., Jun, S., Kam, J. W. Y., Kidd, C., Marcelle, E., & Dronkers, N. F. (2021). Gender bias in academia: A lifetime problem that needs a solution. *Neuron*, 109(13), 2047–2074. DOI: 10.1016/j.neuron.2021.06.002 PMID: 34237278

Logan, S. W. (1999). *We are coming: The persuasive discourse of nineteenth-century Black women*. SIU Press.

Longman, K. A., Terrill, K., Mallet, G., Tchindebet, J., & Fernando, R. (2021). Developing a Leader Identity: The Lived Experiences of People of Color Identified as "Emerging Leaders.". *Journal of Ethnographic and Qualitative Research*, 15(4), 264–283.

Lopes, M., & de Camargo Santos, C. (2023). Academic housework in pandemic times: COVID-19 effects on the gendered distribution of academic work in Portugal. *European Educational Research Journal*, •••, 14749041231191888. DOI: 10.1177/14749041231191888

Losa-Iglesias, M. E., López López, D., Rodriguez Vazquez, R., & Becerro de Bengoa-Vallejo, R. (2017). Relationships between social skills and self-esteem in nurses: A questionnaire study. *Contemporary Nurse*, 53(6), 681–690. DOI: 10.1080/10376178.2018.1441729 PMID: 29451080

Love, B. H., Templeton, E., Ault, S., & Johnson, O. (2021). Bruised, not broken: Scholarly personal narratives of Black women in the academy. *International Journal of Qualitative Studies in Education : QSE*, •••, 1–23.

Luqman, R., Fatima, S., Ahmed, S., Khalid, I., & Bhatti, A. (2019). The impact of autocratic leadership style on counterproductive work behavior: The mediating role of employee commitment and moderating role of emotional exhaustion. *Pollster Journal of Academic Research*, 6(1), 22–47.

Luscombe, A. (2018). Eleanor Roosevelt: A Crusading Spirit to Move Human Rights Forward. *Netherlands Quarterly of Human Rights*, 36(4), 241–246. DOI: 10.1177/0924051918801610

Madsen, S., & Longman, K. (2020). Women's leadership in higher education: Status, barriers, and motivators. *Journal of Higher Education Management*, 35(1), 13–24.

Mantzourani, E., Chang, H., Desselle, S., Canedo, J., & Fleming, G. (2022). Reflections of mentors and mentees on a national mentoring programme for pharmacists: An examination into relationships, personal and professional development. *Research in Social & Administrative Pharmacy*, 18(3), 2495–2504. DOI: 10.1016/j.sapharm.2021.04.019 PMID: 34120869

Mapping Police Violence. (2024). Retrieved from https://mappingpoliceviolence.org

Maqsood, H., Shakeel, H., Hussain, H., Khan, A., Ali, B., Ishaq, A., & Shah, S. (2018). The descriptive study of imposter syndrome in medical students. *International Journal of Research in Medical Sciences*, 6(10), 3431. DOI: 10.18203/2320-6012.ijrms20184031

Martin, F., Polly, D., & Ritzhaupt, A. (2020). Bichronous online learning: Blending asynchronous and synchronous online learning. Educause Review. https://er.educause.edu/articles/2020/9/bichronous-online-learning-blending asynchronous-and-synchronous-online-learning

Martinelle, R., & Stevens, K. (2024). Making Space for Principled Resistance: When leaders reimagine PD, they can help teachers become strategic activists for themselves and their students. *Educational Leadership*, 81(8), 16–21.

Martin, F., & Bolliger, D. U. (2023). Designing online learning in higher education. In Zawacki-Richter, O., & Jung, I. (Eds.), *Handbook of Open* (pp. 1217–1236). Distance and Digital Education., DOI: 10.1007/978-981-19-2080-6_72

Mascareño, J., Rietzschel, E., & Wisse, B. (2019). Envisioning innovation: Does visionary leadership engender team innovative performance through goal alignment? *Creativity and Innovation Management*, 29(1), 33–48. DOI: 10.1111/caim.12341

Mason, M. A., & Goulden, M. (2002). Do babies matter? The effect of family formation on the lifelong careers of academic men and women. *Academe*, 88(6), 21–27. DOI: 10.2307/40252436

Mason, M. A., & Goulden, M. (2004). Do babies matter (Part 2)? Closing the baby gap. *Academe*, 90(6), 1–10. DOI: 10.2307/40252699

Mason, M. A., Wolfinger, N. H., & Goulden, M. (2013). *Do babies matter? Gender and family in the ivory tower*. Rutgers University Press.

Masten, A. S. (2014). Global perspectives on resilience in children and youth. *Child Development*, 85(1), 6–20. DOI: 10.1111/cdev.12205 PMID: 24341286

Matias, C. E. (2011, April 7 - April 11). *Paying it forward: Motherscholars navigating the academic terrain*. AERA Division G Highlighted Panel. American Educational Research Association 2011, Annual Meeting, New Orleans, LA, United States.

Matias, C. E. (2022). Birthing the motherscholar and motherscholarship. *Peabody Journal of Education*, 97(2), 246–250. DOI: 10.1080/0161956X.2022.2055897

Matias, C. E., & Nishi, N. W. (2018). ParentCrit epilog. *International Journal of Qualitative Studies in Education : QSE*, 31(1), 82–85. DOI: 10.1080/09518398.2017.1379625

McCluney, C. L., & Rabelo, V. C. (2019). Conditions of visibility: An intersectional examination of Black women's belongingness and distinctiveness at work. *Journal of Vocational Behavior*, 113, 143–152. DOI: 10.1016/j.jvb.2018.09.008

McCluskey, A. T. (2014). *A forgotten sisterhood: Pioneering Black women educators and activists in the Jim Crow South.* Rowman & Littlefield. DOI: 10.5771/9781442211407

McCullough, L. (2020). Barriers and assistance for female leaders in academic stem in the us. *Education Sciences*, 10(10), 264. DOI: 10.3390/educsci10100264

McLaughlin, J. S., & Neumark, D. (2022). *Gendered Ageism and Disablism and Employment of Older Workers* (No. w30355). National Bureau of Economic Research.

Mebane, B. (2019). *The Sisterhood Is Alive and Well at Spelman College: A Feminist Standpoint Case Study.* Ball State University.

Meisenhelder, J. B. (1986). Self-esteem in women: The influence of employment and perception of husband's appraisals. *Image—the Journal of Nursing Scholarship*, 18(1), 8–14. DOI: 10.1111/j.1547-5069.1986.tb00532.x PMID: 3633863

Merryfield, M. (2003). Like a veil: Cross-cultural experiential learning online. *Contemporary Issues in Technology & Teacher Education*, 3(2), 146–171.

Metz, C. L., & Jarvie, S. H. (2022). Ecological Approach to Higher Educator Wellness and Self-Care. In *Self-Care and Stress Management for Academic Well-Being* (pp. 214–229). IGI Global. DOI: 10.4018/978-1-6684-2334-9.ch013

Mezirow, J. (1991). *Transformative Dimensions of Adult Learning.* Jossey-Bass.

Mikołajczyk, K. (2021). Sustainable development of an individual as a result of mutual enrichment of professional and personal life. *Sustainability (Basel)*, 13(2), 697. DOI: 10.3390/su13020697

Miller, A. C., & Mills, B. (2019). 'If They Don't Care, I Don't Care': Millennial and Generation Z Students and the Impact of Faculty Caring. *The Journal of Scholarship of Teaching and Learning,* 19(4), 78-. DOI: 10.14434/josotl.v19i4.24167

Miller, R. A., Jones, V. A., Reddick, R. J., Lowe, T., Franks Flunder, B., Hogan, K., & Rosal, A. I. (2018). Educating through microaggressions: Self-care for diversity educators. *Journal of Student Affairs Research and Practice*, 55(1), 14–26. DOI: 10.1080/19496591.2017.1358634

Milosevic, I., Maric, S., & Lončar, D. (2019). Defeating the toxic boss: The nature of toxic leadership and the role of followers. *Journal of Leadership & Organizational Studies*, 27(2), 117–137. DOI: 10.1177/1548051819833374

Mitchell, J. A., & Perry, R. (2020). Disparities in patient-centered communication for Black and Latino men in the US: Cross-sectional results from the 2010 health and retirement study. *PLoS One*, 15(9), e0238356. DOI: 10.1371/journal.pone.0238356 PMID: 32991624

Modak, A., Ronghe, V., Gomase, K. P., Mahakalkar, M. G., & Taksande, V. (2023). A Comprehensive Review of Motherhood and Mental Health: Postpartum Mood Disorders in Focus. *Cureus*, 15(9), e46209. DOI: 10.7759/cureus.46209 PMID: 37905286

Mohammed, A. (2019). Emotional Balance and Its Relation with Self–Confidence for Special Education Students Department. Opción. *Revista de Ciencias Humanas y Sociales*, (21), 630–657.

Moneycontrol News. (2021). *Women teachers in Indian schools outnumber men in 2019-20, shows UDISE report*. Moneycontrol. https://www.moneycontrol.com/news/india/women-teachers-in-indian-schools-outnumber-men-in-2019-20-shows-udise-report-7124421.html

Moody, A. T., & Lewis, J. A. (2019). Gendered racial microaggressions and traumatic stress symptoms among Black women. *Psychology of Women Quarterly*, 43(2), 201–214. DOI: 10.1177/0361684319828288

Moore, C. (2019). How to address a teacher around the world. Retrieved from https://www.expatica.com/education/children-education/how-do-children-address-their-teachers-across-the-globe-472217/

Morrison, T. L., & Duane Thomas, M. (1975). Self-esteem and classroom participation[1]. *The Journal of Educational Research*, 68(10), 374–377. DOI: 10.1080/00220671.1975.10884805

Mossholder, K. W., Bedeian, A. G., & Armenakis, A. A. (1982). Group process-work outcome relationships: A note on the moderating impact of self-esteem. *Academy of Management Journal*, 25(3), 575–585. DOI: 10.2307/256081 PMID: 10298752

Motro, D., Evans, J. B., Ellis, A. P., & Benson, L.III. (2022). Race and reactions to women's expressions of anger at work: Examining the effects of the "angry Black woman" stereotype. *The Journal of Applied Psychology*, 107(1), 142–152. DOI: 10.1037/apl0000884 PMID: 33793257

Murray, Ó., Chiu, Y., Wong, B., & Horsburgh, J. (2022). Deindividualising imposter syndrome: Imposter work among marginalised stemm undergraduates in the uk. *Sociology*, 57(4), 749–766. DOI: 10.1177/00380385221117380

Myers, L. (2002). *A broken silence: Voices of African American women in the academy*. Bloomsbury Publishing USA. DOI: 10.5040/9798400621802

Myers, S. A., Shimotsu, S., Byrnes, K., Frisby, B. N., Durbin, J., & Loy, B. N. (2010). Assessing the role of peer relationships in the small group communication course. *Communication Teacher*, 24(1), 43–57. DOI: 10.1080/17404620903468214

Myers, S. B., Sweeney, A. C., Popick, V., Wesley, K., Bordfeld, A., & Fingerhut, R. (2012). Self-care practices and perceived stress levels among psychology graduate students. *Training and Education in Professional Psychology*, 6(1), 55–66. DOI: 10.1037/a0026534

Nataraj, B. M., & Reddy, K. J. (2022). Psychological Well-Being of School Teachers: Predictive Role of Mindfulness and Emotional Intelligence. *MIER Journal of Educational Studies Trends and Practices*, 242-262.

National Association of Real Estate Brokers. (2023). 2023 state of housing in black America. Retrieved from https://www.nareb.com/site-files/uploads/2023/11/SHIBA-Report-2023.pdf

National Center for Education Statistics. (2021.). Table 314.40. Percentage distribution of faculty, by race/ethnicity, sex, and faculty status in degree-granting postsecondary institutions, by control and level of institution: Fall 2019. Retrieved [June 8, 2024], from https://nces.ed.gov/programs/digest/d22/tables/dt22_314.40.asp

Neff, K. (2011). *Self-Compassion: The Proven Power of Being Kind to Yourself*. William Morrow.

Nguyen, M. (2023). Managing Our Mental Health Needs in Turbulent Times Through Self-Care: Importance of Practicing Self-Care in Education. In *Cases on Current Issues, Challenges, and Opportunities in School Counseling* (pp. 250-262). IGI Global.

Nguyen, T. T., Berman, E. M., Plimmer, G., Samartini, A., Sabharwal, M., & Taylor, J. (2021). Enriching transactional leadership with public values. *Public Administration Review*, 82(6), 1058–1076. DOI: 10.1111/puar.13495

Nickerson, J. C. (2020). Black women in higher education leadership: examining their lived experiences utilizing cross-race and cross-gender mentorship.

Noble, J. (1993). The higher education of African American women in the twentieth century. *Women in higher education: a feminist perspective*, 329-336.

Nuelle, J., Agnew, S., & Fishman, F. (2023). Challenges for women in hand surgery: Our perspective. *Journal of Hand and Microsurgery*, 15(4), 258–260. DOI: 10.1055/s-0042-1744209 PMID: 37701318

Nyadanu, S. D., Garglo, M. Y., Adampah, T., & Garglo, R. L. (2014). The impact of lecturer-student relationship on self-esteem and academic performance at higher education. *Journal of Social Science Studies*, 2(1), 264. DOI: 10.5296/jsss.v2i1.6772

O'Connor, P. (2018). Gender imbalance in senior positions in higher education: What is the problem? What can be done? *Policy Reviews in Higher Education*, 3(1), 28–50. DOI: 10.1080/23322969.2018.1552084

Obama, M. (2018). *Becoming*. Crown.

Ocobock, C., Niclou, A., Loewen, T., Arslanian, K., Gibson, R., & Valeggia, C. (2022). Demystifying mentorship: Tips for successfully navigating the mentor–mentee journey. *American Journal of Human Biology*, 34(S1), e23690. DOI: 10.1002/ajhb.23690 PMID: 34664346

Ogunsanmi, B. A. A. (2014). Influence of self-esteem on academic performance among secondary school students. [IOSRJRME]. *IOSR Journal of Research & Method in Education*, 4(5), 48–51. DOI: 10.9790/7388-04564851

Oikelome, G. (2017). Pathway to the President: The Perceived Impact of Identity Structures on the Journey Experiences of Women College Presidents. *International Journal of Multicultural Education*, 19(3), 23–40. DOI: 10.18251/ijme.v19i3.1377

Oktary, D., Marjohan, M., & Syahniar, S. (2019). The effects of self-confidence and social support of parents on interpersonal communication of students. *Journal of Educational and Learning Studies*, 2(1), 5. DOI: 10.32698/0352

Orem, D. (1995). *Nursing: Concepts of Practice* (5th ed.). Mosby Year Book.

Pang, N. S.-K. (2020). Teachers' reflective practices in implementing assessment for learning skills in classroom teaching. *ECNU Review of Education.*, (August), 1–21. DOI: 10.1177/2096531120936290

Parfait-Davis, M. (2022). A Framework for Contextualizing Black Women's Negative Experiences in the Academy. *The Ivory Tower: Perspectives of Women of Color in Higher Education*, 55.

Park, J. H., & Chung, S. K. (2015). The relationship among self-esteem, empathy, communication skill and clinical competency of nursing students. *Journal of the Korea Academia-Industrial Cooperation Society*, 16(11), 7698–7707. DOI: 10.5762/KAIS.2015.16.11.7698

Pasha, H. S., & Munaf, S. (2013). Relationship of self-esteem and adjustment in traditional university students. *Procedia: Social and Behavioral Sciences*, 84, 999–1004. DOI: 10.1016/j.sbspro.2013.06.688

Patton, L. D., Davison, C. H., Mackie, T., McCollum, S., & Nelson, B. (2024). *Black Women in Academia*. Oxford Bibliographies., DOI: 10.1093/obo/9780199756810-0320

Pauley, J. (2014). *Your life calling: Reimagining the rest of your life*. Penguin Books.

Pennamon, T. (2019). A Champion for Access and Excellence in Public Higher Education. *Diverse Issues in Higher Education*, 36(10), 14–15.

Perkins, L. M. (2015). "Bound to them by a common sorrow": African American women, higher education, and collective advancement. *Journal of African American History*, 100(4), 721–747. DOI: 10.5323/jafriamerhist.100.4.0721

Phd, F., & Ncama, B. (2011). Self, self-care and self-management concepts: Implications for self-management education. *Educational Researcher*, 2, 1733–1737.

Philipsen, M., Case, S., Oetama-Paul, A., & Sugiyama, K. (2017). Academic womanhood across career stages: A work-in-life perspective on what was, is, and could be. *Community Work & Family*, 20(5), 623–644. DOI: 10.1080/13668803.2017.1378619

Picard, R. W., Papert, S., Bender, W., Blumberg, B., Breazeal, C., Cavallo, D., Machover, T., Resnick, M., Roy, D., & Strohecker, C. (2004). Affective Learning — A Manifesto. *BT Technology Journal*, 22(4), 253–269. DOI: 10.1023/B:BTTJ.0000047603.37042.33

Pickett, A. (2022). The Relationship between Mentoring and Leadership.

Pierli, G., Murmura, F., & Palazzi, F. (2022). Women and Leadership: How Do Women Leaders Contribute to Companies' Sustainable Choices? *Frontiers in Sustainability*, 3, 930116. DOI: 10.3389/frsus.2022.930116

Pillay, D., & Vermeulen, C. (2023). Seeking support through solidarity: Female leader's experiences of workplace solidarity in male-dominated professions. *Frontiers in Psychology*, 14, 1119911. Advance online publication. DOI: 10.3389/fpsyg.2023.1119911 PMID: 37457071

Pinna, R., De Simone, S., Cicotto, G., & Malik, A. (2020). Beyond organisational support: Exploring the supportive role of co-workers and supervisors in a multi-actor service ecosystem. *Journal of Business Research*, 121, 524–534. DOI: 10.1016/j.jbusres.2020.02.022

Pinto, R., Douglas, T. R. M., Lane-Bonds, D., & McMillian, R. (2024). Yes She Can: Examining the Career Pathways of Black Women in Higher Education Senior Leadership Position. *Advances in Developing Human Resources*, 26(2-3), 15234223241254574. DOI: 10.1177/15234223241254574

Pluszczyk, A. (2020). Socializing at work—an investigation of small talk phenomenon in the workplace. In *Second Language Learning and Teaching* (pp. 201–217). Springer International Publishing.

Porter, C. J., Sulé, V. T., & Croom, N. N. (Eds.). (2022). *Black Feminist Epistemology, Research, and Praxis: Narratives in and Through the Academy*. Taylor & Francis. DOI: 10.4324/9781003184867

Puliatte, A. (2021). Women Academic Leaders and Self-Care During a Crisis. In *Women and Leadership in Higher Education During Global Crises* (pp. 175–189). IGI Global. DOI: 10.4018/978-1-7998-6491-2.ch011

Quaye, S. J., Karikari, S. N., Carter, K. D., Okello, W. K., & Allen, C. (2020). Why can't I just chill?": The visceral nature of racial battle fatigue. *Journal of College Student Development*, 61(5), 609–623. DOI: 10.1353/csd.2020.0058

Quigley, A. (2020). Is this a brave new world for teacher CPD? Schools have innovated amazingly well to allow staff development to continue over recent months - but studies show that effective CPD requires more than just one-off video sessions. *TES: Magazine*, 5411, 29.

Quinaud, R. T., Possamai, K., Gonçalves, C. E., & Carvalho, H. M. (2023). Student-Athlete Identity Variation Across the Undergraduate Period: A Mixed-Methods Study. *Perceptual & Motor Skills*, 130(2), 876–901. Radin, B. A. (2007). Qualified to Learn the Job: Donna Shalala. *Public Administration Review*, 67(3), 504–510.

Rajesh, J. I., & Suganthi, L. (2013). The satisfaction of teachers with their supervisors' interpersonal communication skills in relation to job burn-out and growth satisfaction in southern India. *Management in Education*, 27(4), 128–137. DOI: 10.1177/0892020613498521

Rasheed-Karim, W. (2023). Further Education Teachers' Wellbeing: A Discussion of Equal Opportunities and Career Progression. *Brock Journal of Education*, 11(8), 22–48. DOI: 10.37745/bje.2013/vol11n82248

Read, D. C., Fisher, P. J., & Juran, L. (2020). How do women maximize the value of mentorship? Insights from mentees, mentors, and industry professionals. *Leadership and Organization Development Journal*, 41(2), 165–175. DOI: 10.1108/LODJ-02-2019-0094

Rehman, S. U. R., Shahzad, M., Farooq, M. S., & Javaid, M. E. (2020). Impact of leadership behavior of a project manager on his/her subordinate's job-attitudes and job-outcomes. *Asia Pacific Management Review*, 25(1), 38–47. DOI: 10.1016/j.apmrv.2019.06.004

Richardson, S. D. (2023). Higher Education Leaders as Entre-Employees: A Narrative Study. *American Journal of Qualitative Research*, 7(3), 1–18. DOI: 10.29333/ajqr/13222

Riddle, B. L., Anderson, C., & Martin, M. M. (2016). Small group socialization scale [Data set]. In *PsycTESTS Dataset*. American Psychological Association (APA).

Riggio, R. E., Throckmorton, B., & DePaola, S. (1990). Social skills and self-esteem. *Personality and Individual Differences*, 11(8), 799–804. DOI: 10.1016/0191-8869(90)90188-W

Román, M. (2018). President Diana Natalicio reflects on the last 30 years leading UTEP. *The Prospector Daily*. https://www.theprospectordaily.com/2018/03/20/president-diana-natalicio-reflects-on-the-last-30-years-leading-utep/

Román, S., Cuestas, P. J., & Fenollar, P. (2008). An examination of the interrelationships between self-esteem, others' expectations, family support, learning approaches and academic achievement. *Studies in Higher Education*, 33(2), 127–138. DOI: 10.1080/03075070801915882

Romans, S. E., Martin, J., & Mullen, P. (1996). Women's Self-Esteem: A Community Study of Women who Report and do not Report Childhood Sexual Abuse. *The British Journal of Psychiatry*, 169(6), 696–704. DOI: 10.1192/bjp.169.6.696 PMID: 8968626

Romsa, K., Bremer, K. L., Lewis, J., & Romsa, B. (2017). The Evolution of Student-Faculty Interactions: What Matters to Millennial College Students? *The College Student Affairs Journal*, 35(2), 85–99. DOI: 10.1353/csj.2017.0015

Ronnie, L., Bam, A., & Walters, C. (2022, May). Emotional wellbeing: The impact of the COVID-19 pandemic on women academics in South Africa. [). Frontiers.]. *Frontiers in Education*, 7, 770447. DOI: 10.3389/feduc.2022.770447

Roxå, T., & Mårtensson, K. (2009). Significant conversations and significant networks – exploring the backstage of the teaching arena. *Studies in Higher Education*, 34(5), 547–559. DOI: 10.1080/03075070802597200

Ruffin, K. N. (2010). *Black on earth: African American ecoliterary traditions*. University of Georgia Press. DOI: 10.1353/book11452

Ruple, A. (2020). Overcoming imposter syndrome., 2020 Recent Graduate Proceeding. https://doi.org/DOI: 10.21423/aabppro20207954

Rusmana, N., Hafina, A., Siddik, R. R., & Nur, L. (2020). Self-esteem development of vocational high school students in Indonesia: Does group counseling with assertive training technique help? *Jurnal Cakrawala Pendidikan*, 39(3), 573–582. DOI: 10.21831/cp.v39i3.31363

Ryan, M., & Ryan, M. (2015). A model for reflection in the pedagogic field of higher education. In Ryan, M. E. (Ed.), *Teaching reflective learning in higher education* (pp. 15–27). Springer., DOI: 10.1007/978-3-319-09271-3_2

Saakvitne, K. W., & Pearlman, L. A. (1996). *Transforming the pain: A workbook on vicarious traumatization*. W. W. Norton & Co.

Saffie-Robertson, M. C. (2020). It's not you, it's me: An exploration of mentoring experiences for women in STEM. *Sex Roles*, 83(9), 566–579. DOI: 10.1007/s11199-020-01129-x

Salavera, C., Usán, P., & Jarie, L. (2017). Emotional intelligence and social skills on self-efficacy in Secondary Education students. Are there gender differences? *Journal of Adolescence*, 60(1), 39–46. DOI: 10.1016/j.adolescence.2017.07.009 PMID: 28750267

Sallee, M., Ward, K., & Wolf-Wendel, L. (2016). Can anyone have it all? Gendered views on parenting and academic careers. *Innovative Higher Education*, 41(3), 187–202. DOI: 10.1007/s10755-015-9345-4

Salmela-Aro, K., & Nurmi, J.-E. (1996). Uncertainty and confidence in interpersonal projects: Consequences for social relationships and well-being. *Journal of Social and Personal Relationships*, 13(1), 109–122. DOI: 10.1177/0265407596131006

Sanchez-Hucles, J. V., & Davis, D. D. (2010). Women and women of color in leadership: Complexity, identity, and intersectionality. *The American Psychologist*, 65(3), 171–181. DOI: 10.1037/a0017459 PMID: 20350016

Santos, G. G. (2015). Narratives about work and family life among Portuguese academics. *Gender, Work and Organization*, 22(1), 1–15. DOI: 10.1111/gwao.12061

Sarathi, P. (2023). *Responsive Mentoring*. BFC Publications.

Sarsons, H., Gërxhani, K., Reuben, E., & Schram, A. (2021). Gender differences in recognition for group work. *Journal of Political Economy*, 129(1), 101–147. DOI: 10.1086/711401

Sator, P. (2017). The effect of low self-esteem on clinical performance among first year nursing students in a private college at Kota Kinabalu, Sabah. [BJMS]. *Borneo Journal of Medical Sciences*, 11(1), 11–23. DOI: 10.51200/bjms.v11i1.634

Schein, E., & Bennis, W. G. (1965). Personal and organizational change through group methods: The laboratory approach. New York: JohnWiley and Sons. *Inc. Search in.*

Schnackenberg, H. L. (2018) motherscholar:MotherLeader. In Schnackenberg, H.L. & Simard, D.A. (Eds.), *Challenges and Opportunities for Women in Higher Education Leadership,* Hershey, PA: IGI Global.

Schnackenberg, H. L. (2020). motherscholar: MotherLeader and the Ethical Double-Bind. In Squires, M.E. & Yu, Y., & Schnackenberg, H.L. (Eds), *Ethics in Higher Education*, New York, NY: Nova Science Publishers.

Schnackenberg, H. L. (2021). motherscholar: MotherLeader and the Pandemic. In Schnackenberg, H.L. & Simard, D.A. (Eds), *Women and Leadership in Higher Education During Global Crises.* Hershey, PA: IGI Global.

Schnackenberg, H. L. (2022). motherscholar: MotherLeader Reflections from a Little Past the Middle. In Schnackenberg, H.L. (Ed.) *Women in Higher Education and the Journey to Mid-Career.* Hershey, PA: IGI Global.

Schnackenberg, H. L. (2023). motherscholar and MotherLeader: The more things change, the more they stay the same. In H.L. Schnackenberg & D.A. Simard (Eds), *Stabilizing and empowering women in higher education: Realigning, recentering, and rebuilding* (pp. 284-295). IGI Global. DOI: DOI: 10.4018/978-1-6684-8597-2

Schneider, E. (1993). *Feminism and the False Dichotomy of Victimization and Agency.* 38 N.Y.L. Sch. L. Rev. 387.

Schwager, S., Wick, K., Glaeser, A., Schoenherr, D., Strauss, B., & Berger, U. (2020). Self-esteem as a potential mediator of the association between social integration, mental well-being, and physical well-being. *Psychological Reports*, 123(4), 1160–1175. DOI: 10.1177/0033294119849015 PMID: 31161961

Schwalbe, M. L., Gecas, V., & Baxter, R. (1986). The effects of occupational conditions and individual characteristics on the importance of self-esteem sources in the workplace. *Basic and Applied Social Psychology*, 7(1), 63–84. DOI: 10.1207/s15324834basp0701_5

Schwalbe, M. L., & Staples, C. L. (1991). Gender differences in sources of self-esteem. *Social Psychology Quarterly*, 54(2), 158. DOI: 10.2307/2786933

Schwartz, T. M., Wullwick, V. J., & Shapiro, H. J. (1980). Self-esteem and group decision making: An empirical study. *Psychological Reports*, 46(3), 951–956. DOI: 10.2466/pr0.1980.46.3.951

Scott-Jones, G., & Kamara, M. R. (2020). The traumatic impact of structural racism on African Americans. *Delaware Journal of Public Health*, 6(5), 80–82. DOI: 10.32481/djph.2020.11.019 PMID: 34467171

Seshadri, R., Srinivasan, R., & Kumar, V. (2019). Original Research Article: An exploratory study to understand and examine the nature and type of relationship between self-esteem, life satisfaction and adjustment among male and female migrant students. [IJMH]. *Indian Journal of Mental Health*, 7(2), 105. DOI: 10.30877/IJMH.7.2.2020.105-111

Shackelford, T. K. (2001). Self-esteem in marriage. *Personality and Individual Differences*, 30(3), 371–390. DOI: 10.1016/S0191-8869(00)00023-4

Shahid, K. T. (2014). *Finding Eden: How Black women use spirituality to navigate academia* (Doctoral dissertation, Miami University).

Showunmi, V. (2023). Visible, invisible: Black women in higher education. *Frontiers in Sociology*, 8, 974617. DOI: 10.3389/fsoc.2023.974617 PMID: 37152206

Singh, S., & Vanka, S. (2020). Mentoring is essential but not sufficient: Sponsor women for leadership roles. *Development and Learning in Organizations*, 34(6), 25–28. DOI: 10.1108/DLO-05-2019-0100

Smith, E. (2008). Diana Natalicio. *Texas Monthly (Austin, Tex.)*, 36(2), 90–96.

Smith, J. C., & Phelps, S. (Eds.). (1992). *Notable Black American women* (Vol. 2). VNR AG.

Smith-Tran, A. (2023). "There's the Black Woman Thing, and There's the Age Thing": Professional Black Women on the Downsides of "Black Don't Crack" and Strategies for Confronting Ageism at Work. *Sociological Perspectives*, 66(3), 419–433. DOI: 10.1177/07311214221139441

Soares, L. (2023). "Tuskegee Is Her Monument": Gender and Leadership in Early Public Black Colleges. *History of Education Quarterly*, 63(3), 1–21. DOI: 10.1017/heq.2023.3

Solomon, B. M. (1985). *In the company of educated women: A history of women and higher education in America*. Yale University Press.

Son, H., & Sung, J. (2014). The effects of teacher's self-efficacy on children's sociality : The serial multiple mediating effects of job-satisfaction and the quality of teacher-child interaction. *Korean Journal of Child Studies*, 35(2), 191–209. DOI: 10.5723/KJCS.2014.35.2.191

Sonmez Cakir, F., & Adiguzel, Z. (2020). Analysis of leader effectiveness in organization and knowledge sharing behavior on employees and organization. *SAGE Open*, 10(1). Advance online publication. DOI: 10.1177/2158244020914634

Soran, A. A., & Kara, S. (2022). Mentor-mentee relationship: Fifteen career saving suggestions. *International Journal of Social Sciences & Educational Studies*, 9(3), 138.

Spates, K., Evans, N. T., James, T. A., & Martinez, K. (2020). Gendered racism in the lives of Black women: A qualitative exploration. *The Journal of Black Psychology*, 46(8), 583–606. DOI: 10.1177/0095798420962257

Staines, G., Tavris, C., & Jayaratne, T. E. (1974). The queen bee syndrome. *Psychology Today*, 7(8), 55–60. DOI: 10.1037/e400562009-003

Stark, K., Daulat, N., & King, S. (2022). A vision for teachers' emotional well-being. *Phi Delta Kappan*, 103(5), 24–30. DOI: 10.1177/00317217221079975

Starr, J. (2021). *The mentoring manual.*

Staton-Spicer, A. Q., & Darling, A. L. (1986). Communication in the socialization of preservice teachers. *Communication Education*, 35(3), 215–230. DOI: 10.1080/03634528609388345

Statti, A. L. C., & Torres, K. (2019). Innovative approaches to traditional mentoring practices of women in higher education. In Schnackenberg, H., & Simard, D. (Eds.), *Challenges and opportunities for women in higher education leadership* (pp. 1–19). IGI Global., DOI: 10.4018/978-1-5225-7056-1.ch001

Stebnicki, M. A. (2007). Empathy Fatigue: Healing the Mind, Body, and Spirit of Professional Counselors. *American Journal of Psychiatric Rehabilitation*, 10(4), 317–338. DOI: 10.1080/15487760701680570

Stoeckli, G. (2009). The role of individual and social factors in classroom loneliness. *The Journal of Educational Research*, 103(1), 28–39. DOI: 10.1080/00220670903231169

Subbaye, R., & Vithal, R. (2017). Gender, teaching, and academic promotions in higher education. *Gender and Education*, 29(7), 926–951. DOI: 10.1080/09540253.2016.1184237

Subon, F., Unin, N., & Sulaiman, N. H. B. (2020). Self-esteem and academic achievement: The relationship and gender differences of Malaysian university undergraduates. *IAFOR Journal of Psychology & the Behavioral Sciences*, 6(1), 43–54. DOI: 10.22492/ijpbs.6.1.03

Sull, D., Sull, C., & Zweig, B. (2022, January 11). *Toxic culture is driving the great resignation*. MIT Sloan Management Review. https://sloanreview.mit.edu/article/toxic-culture-is-driving-the-great-resignation/

Szkody, E., & McKinney, C. (2019). Indirect effects of social support on psychological health through self-esteem in emerging adulthood. *Journal of Family Issues*, 40(17), 2439–2455. DOI: 10.1177/0192513X19859612

Tafani, E., Bellon, S., & Moliner, P. (2002). The role of self-esteem in the dynamics of social representations of higher education: An experimental approach. [Swiss Journal of Psychology]. *Swiss Journal of Psychology*, 61(3), 177–188. DOI: 10.1024//1421-0185.61.3.177

Taghizadeh, M. E., & Kalhori, E. (2015). Relation between self esteem with marital satisfaction of employed women in Payam-e-Noor university. *Mediterranean Journal of Social Sciences*. Advance online publication. DOI: 10.5901/mjss.2015.v6n6s6p41

Tahir, W. B.-E., Inam, A., & Raana, T. (2015). Relationship between social support and self-esteem of adolescent girls [Data set]. *Figshare*. DOI: 10.6084/M9.FIGSHARE.1353182

Tam, C.-L., Lee, T.-H., Har, W.-M., & Pook, W.-L. (2011). Perceived social support and self-esteem towards gender roles: Contributing factors in adolescents. *Asian Social Science*, 7(8). Advance online publication. DOI: 10.5539/ass.v7n8p49

Tao, K., & Gloria, A. (2018). Should i stay or should i go? the role of impostorism in stem persistence. *Psychology of Women Quarterly*, 43(2), 151–164. DOI: 10.1177/0361684318802333

Taylor, Y., & Breeze, M. (2020). All imposters in the university? striking (out) claims on academic twitter. *Women's Studies International Forum*, 81, 102367. DOI: 10.1016/j.wsif.2020.102367

Terra, F. de S., Marziale, M. H. P., & Robazzi, M. L. do C. C. (2013). Evaluation of self-esteem in Nursing teachers at public and private universities. *Revista Latino-Americana de Enfermagem, 21*(spe), 71–78. https://doi.org/DOI: 10.1590/s0104-11692013000700010

Terry, D. (2023). On the Threshold of Education: Race and Antebellum Schooling in the Text and Context of the Colored American. *CEA Critic*, 85(1), 58–83. DOI: 10.1353/cea.2023.0004

Tevis, T., Hernandez, M., & Bryant, R. (2020). Reclaiming our time: An autoethnographic exploration of Black women higher education administrators. *The Journal of Negro Education*, 89(3), 282–297.

Thelin, J. R., & Gasman, M. (2003). Historical overview of American higher education. *Student services: A handbook for the profession, 4*, 3-22.

Toepell, A. R. (2003). Academic mothers and their experiences navigating the academy. *Journal of the Motherhood Initiative for Research and Community Involvement*.

Townsend, C. V. (2021). Identity politics: Why African American women are missing in administrative leadership in public higher education. *Educational Management Administration & Leadership*, 49(4), 584–600. DOI: 10.1177/1741143220935455

Treacy, M., & Leavy, A. (2023). Student voice and its role in creating cognitive dissonance: The neglected narrative in teacher professional development. *Professional Development in Education*, 49(3), 458–477. DOI: 10.1080/19415257.2021.1876147

Troth, A. C., Jordan, P. J., & Lawrence, S. A. (2012). Emotional intelligence, communication competence, and student perceptions of team social cohesion. *Journal of Psychoeducational Assessment*, 30(4), 414–424. DOI: 10.1177/0734282912449447

Trybulkevych, K. H. (2020). *The influence of social reflection to enhance the efficiency of professional communication of the in-service teachers in the settings of methodical work*. Applied Linguistics Research Journal., DOI: 10.14744/alrj.2020.87894

Tulgan, B. (2016). *Not everyone gets a trophy: How to manage the millennials*. Wiley. DOI: 10.1002/9781119215073

Tuovinen, S., Tang, X., & Salmela-Aro, K. (2020). Introversion and social engagement: Scale validation, their interaction, and positive association with self-esteem. *Frontiers in Psychology*, 11, 590748. Advance online publication. DOI: 10.3389/fpsyg.2020.590748 PMID: 33329251

Turner, C. S. V. (2002). Women of color in academe: Living with multiple marginality. *The Journal of Higher Education*, 73(1), 74–93. DOI: 10.1080/00221546.2002.11777131

Twenge, J. M. (2018). *IGen: Why today's super-connected kids are growing up less rebellious, more tolerant, less happy—and completely unprepared for adulthood : And what that means for the rest of us*. Atria Paperback.

U. S. Office of the Surgeon General. (2022). *The US Surgeon General's framework for workplace mental health & well-being*. Department of Health and Human Services.

U.S. Bureau of Labor Statistics. (2023, March 24). Employment differences of men and women narrow with educational attainment. *TED: The Economics Daily*. https://www.bls.gov/opub/ted/2023/employment-differences-of-men-and-women-narrow-with-educational-attainment.htm

Uhl-Bien, M. (2006). Relational leadership theory: Exploring the social processes of leadership and organizing. *The Leadership Quarterly*, 17(6), 654–676. DOI: 10.1016/j.leaqua.2006.10.007

Uitto, M., Kaunisto, S.-L., Syrjälä, L., & Estola, E. (2015). Silenced truths: Relational and emotional dimensions of a beginning teacher's identity as part of the micropolitical context of school. *Scandinavian Journal of Educational Research*, 59(2), 162–176. DOI: 10.1080/00313831.2014.904414

Ukeh, M. I., Aloh, P. K., & Kwahar, N. (2011). Stress and gender in relation to self-esteem of university business students. *Gender & Behaviour*, 9(1). Advance online publication. DOI: 10.4314/gab.v9i1.67471

United States. Public Health Service. Office of the Surgeon General. (2022). The U.S. Surgeon General's Framework for Workplace Mental Health & Well-Being. Department of Health and Human Services.

University of Delaware. (2017, December 13). Women get less credit than men in the workplace. *ScienceDaily*. https://www.sciencedaily.com/releases/2017/12/171213130252.htm

Upshaw, H. S., & Yates, L. A. (1968). Self-persuasion, social approval, and task success as determinants of self-esteem following impression management. *Journal of Experimental Social Psychology*, 4(2), 143–152. DOI: 10.1016/0022-1031(68)90038-3

Valerio, A. M. (2022). Supporting women leaders: Research-based directions for gender inclusion in organizations. *Consulting Psychology Journal*, 74(2), 178–193. DOI: 10.1037/cpb0000208

van Assen, M. F. (2020). Empowering leadership and contextual ambidexterity–The mediating role of committed leadership for continuous improvement. *European Management Journal*, 38(3), 435–449. DOI: 10.1016/j.emj.2019.12.002

van Dick, R., & Wagner, U. (2002). Social identification among school teachers: Dimensions, foci, and correlates. *European Journal of Work and Organizational Psychology*, 11(2), 129–149. DOI: 10.1080/13594320143000889

Van Veelen, R., & Derks, B. (2021). Academics as agentic superheroes: Female academics' lack of fit with the agentic stereotype of success limits their career advancement. *British Journal of Social Psychology*, 61(3), 748–767. DOI: 10.1111/bjso.12515 PMID: 34935167

Varallo, S. M. (2008). Motherwork in Academe: Intensive Caring for the Millenial Student. *Women's Studies in Communication*, 31(2), 151–157. DOI: 10.1080/07491409.2008.10162527

Vatankhah, H., Daryabari, D., Ghadami, V., & Naderifar, N. (2013). The effectiveness of communication skills training on self-concept, self-esteem and assertiveness of female students in guidance school in Rasht. *Procedia: Social and Behavioral Sciences*, 84, 885–889. DOI: 10.1016/j.sbspro.2013.06.667

Vishalakshi, K. K., & Yeshodhara, K. (2012). Relationship between self-esteem and academic achievement of secondary school students. *Education*, 1(12), 83–84.

Wagner, J., Lüdtke, O., Robitzsch, A., Göllner, R., & Trautwein, U. (2018). Self-esteem development in the school context: The roles of intrapersonal and interpersonal social predictors. *Journal of Personality*, 86(3), 481–497. DOI: 10.1111/jopy.12330 PMID: 28555752

Walker, R. V., & Zelin, A. I. (2021). "You're too young/old for this": The intersection of ageism and sexism in the workplace. In Cole, E., & Hollis-Sawyer, L. (Eds.), *Older women who work: Resilience, choice, and change* (pp. 161–187). American Psychological Association., DOI: 10.1037/0000212-010

Walkington, L. (2017). How far have we really come? Black women faculty and graduate students' experiences in higher education. *Humboldt Journal of Social Relations*, 39(39), 51–65. DOI: 10.55671/0160-4341.1022

Walser-Smith, J. (2019). *Transforming the Academy: Black Women Leaders at Predominantly White Institutions in the South* (Doctoral dissertation, Appalachian State University).

Walter, H. L. (2019). Workplace communication behavior inventory. In *Communication Research Measures III* (pp. 515–520). Routledge. DOI: 10.4324/9780203730188-74

Ward, K., & Wolf-Wendel, L. (2012). *Academic motherhood: How faculty manage work and family*. Rutgers University Press.

Watson, C. (2006). Narratives of practice and the construction of identity in teaching. *Teachers and Teaching*, 12(5), 509–526. DOI: 10.1080/13540600600832213

Watson, C. (2007). Small stories, positioning analysis, and the doing of professional identities in learning to teach. *Narrative Inquiry*, 17(2), 371–389. DOI: 10.1075/ni.17.2.11wat

Webber, L., & Dismore, H. (2020). Mothers and higher educations: Balancing time, study and space. *Journal of Further and Higher Education*, 45(6), 803–817. DOI: 10.1080/0309877X.2020.1820458

Webb, N. M. (2009). The teacher's role in promoting collaborative dialogue in the classroom. *The British Journal of Educational Psychology*, 79(1), 1–28. DOI: 10.1348/000709908X380772 PMID: 19054431

Webb, N. M., Nemer, K. M., & Ing, M. (2006). Small-group reflections: Parallels between teacher discourse and student behavior in peer-directed groups. *Journal of the Learning Sciences*, 15(1), 63–119. DOI: 10.1207/s15327809jls1501_8

Webb, O. (2021). Enacting relational leadership through restorative practices. *The Alberta Journal of Educational Research*, 67(2), 159–177. DOI: 10.55016/ojs/ajer.v67i2.68603

Webster's Seventh New Collegiate Dictionary. (1969). G. & C. Merriam Company.

West, N. M. (2020). A contemporary portrait of Black women student affairs administrators in the United States. *Journal of Women and Gender in Higher Education*, 13(1), 72–92. DOI: 10.1080/26379112.2020.1728699

West, N. M., & Porter, C. J. (2023). The state of Black women in higher education: A critical perspective 20 years later. *New Directions for Student Services*, 2023(182), 9–13. DOI: 10.1002/ss.20463

White, D. G. (1999). *Too heavy a load: Black women in defense of themselves 1894-1994*. WW Norton & Company.

White, K., & Burkinshaw, P. (2019). Women and leadership in higher education: Special issue editorial. *Social Sciences (Basel, Switzerland)*, 8(204), 1–7. DOI: 10.3390/socsci8070204

Wiggins, G. (2012). Seven keys to effective feedback. Retrieved from http://www.ascd.org/publications/educational-leadership/sept12/vol70/num01/seven-keys-to-effective-feedback.aspx

Wilder, J., Jones, T. B., & Osborne-Lampkin, L. T. (2013). A profile of Black women in the 21st-century academy: Still learning from the "Outsider-Within.". *Journal of Research Initiatives*, 1(1), 5.

Wilkinson, C. (2020). Imposter syndrome and the accidental academic: An autoethnographic account. *The International Journal for Academic Development*, 25(4), 363–374. DOI: 10.1080/1360144X.2020.1762087

Williams, J. C., & Jessica, L. (September 28, 2015). It's illegal, Yet it happens all the time: How Pregnant women and mothers get hounded out of higher education. *Chronicle of Higher Education*. https://www.chronicle.com/article/Its-Illegal-Yet-It-Happens/233445

Williams, B. M. (2023). "It's Just My Face:" Workplace Policing of Black Professional Women in Higher Education. *Journal of Women and Gender in Higher Education*, 16(2), 67–89. DOI: 10.1080/26379112.2023.2172730

Williams, H. V. (2023). *Black Women in Higher Education*. Oxford Bibliographies., DOI: 10.1093/obo/9780190280024-0115

Williams, H. V., & Ziobro, M. (Eds.). (2023). *A Seat at the Table: Black Women Public Intellectuals in US History and Culture*. Univ. Press of Mississippi. DOI: 10.14325/mississippi/9781496847515.001.0001

Will, M. (2021, August 18). When Teachers and School Counselors Become Informal Mentors, Students Thrive. *Education Week*, 40(1), 16.

Winkle-Wagner, R. (2015). Having their lives narrowed down? The state of Black women's college success. *Review of Educational Research*, 85(2), 171–204. DOI: 10.3102/0034654314551065

Winslow, S., & Davis, S. N. (2016). Gender inequality across the academic life course. *Sociology Compass*, 10(5), 404–416. DOI: 10.1111/soc4.12372

Witt, M. G., & Wood, W. (2010). Self-regulation of gendered behavior in everyday life. *Sex Roles*, 62(9–10), 635–646. DOI: 10.1007/s11199-010-9761-y

Wolfgarth, M. (2011). An Appealing Profession. *Cobblestone*, 32(3), 16–17.

Woller, C. W., Ardiansyah, A., Rofaida, R., Nurkhin, A., & Rababah, M. A. (2022). Impact of toxic leadership on employee performance. *Health Psychology Research*, 10(4), 57551. Advance online publication. DOI: 10.52965/001c.57551 PMID: 36540087

Worthen, M. (2017). U can't talk to ur professor like this. Retrieved from https://www.nytimes.com/2017/05/13/opinion/sunday/u-cant-talk-to-ur-professor-like-this.html/

Wright, D. A., & Salinas, C. (2016). African American women leaders in higher education. In *Racially and ethnically diverse women leading education* [). Emerald Group Publishing Limited.]. *Worldview*, 25, 91–105.

Wyatt, J. P., & Ampadu, G. G. (2022). Reclaiming self-care: Self-care as a social justice tool for Black wellness. *Community Mental Health Journal*, 58(2), 213–221. DOI: 10.1007/s10597-021-00884-9 PMID: 34478022

Yahne, C. E., & Long, V. O. (1988). The use of support groups to raise self-esteem for women clients. *Journal of American College Health*, 37(2), 79–84. DOI: 10.1080/07448481.1988.9939046 PMID: 3241029

Zabak, S., Varma, A., Bansod, S., & Pohane, M. R. (2023). Exploring the Complex Landscape of Delayed Childbearing: Factors, History, and Long-Term Implications. *Cureus*, 15(9), e46291. DOI: 10.7759/cureus.46291 PMID: 37915872

Zachary, L. J., & Fain, L. Z. (2022). *The mentor's guide: Facilitating effective learning relationships*. John Wiley & Sons.

Zipp, G. P., Cahill, T., & Clark, M. (2009). The role of collaborative scholarship in the mentorship of doctoral students. [TLC]. *Journal of College Teaching and Learning*, 6(8). Advance online publication. DOI: 10.19030/tlc.v6i8.1111

Zuckerman, D. M. (1980). Self-esteem, personal traits, and college women's life goals. *Journal of Vocational Behavior*, 17(3), 310–319. DOI: 10.1016/0001-8791(80)90024-X

Zuffianò, A., Eisenberg, N., Alessandri, G., Luengo Kanacri, B. P., Pastorelli, C., Milioni, M., & Caprara, G. V. (2016). The relation of pro-sociality to self-esteem: The mediational role of quality of friendships. *Journal of Personality*, 84(1), 59–70. DOI: 10.1111/jopy.12137 PMID: 25234333

About the Contributors

Heidi L. Schnackenberg, Ph.D., is a Professor and Department Chair in Education at SUNY Plattsburgh in Plattsburgh, NY. Specializing in educational technology, she currently teaches graduate courses on the use of technology to enhance teaching and learning in the P-12 classroom. Her various research interests include the integration of technology into pedagogical practices, the complexities of women in leadership in higher education, and the challenges faced by motherscholars and MotherLeaders in academia. She has published numerous articles on educational technology, co-authored Challenges Facing Female Department Chairs in Contemporary Higher Education: Emerging Research and Opportunities, and co-edited Best Practices for Education Professionals, Best Practices for Education Professionals Volume 2, The Ethics of Cultural Competence in Higher Education, Preparing the Education Space for Gen Z, Ethics in Higher Education, Challenges and Opportunities for Women in Higher Education Leadership, Women and Leadership in Higher Education During Global Crises, Women in Higher Education and the Journey to Mid-Career, and Challenges and Opportunities, and Stabilizing and Empowering Women in Higher Education: Realigning, Recentering, and Rebuilding. Dr. Schnackenberg began her education career as an elementary music teacher.

***

Vishnu Achutha Menon is an independent journalist, writer, researcher, and an Indian percussionist. He is a recipient of the Junior Scholarship the Ministry of Culture awarded. His research interests are film studies, verbal & nonverbal communication, south Asian performances, Natyasastra, media studies, media analysis techniques, Laban Movement Analysis, and Ethnomusicology.

Natasha N. Johnson is a Clinical Instructor of Criminal Justice and Criminology in the Andrew Young School of Policy Studies at Georgia State University. A career educator since 2001, her research focuses on critical theory, equity, and social justice leadership, particularly within the K-20 sector. Her other research areas include intersectionality, educational law, policy, and governance, and curriculum development. Dr. Johnson holds multi-state reciprocity and has previously worked as a teacher, guidance counselor, assistant dean, instructional leader, and curriculum developer domestically and abroad. She is a David L. Clark scholar, a CETLOE Faculty Teaching Fellow, and her work is published in JSTOR, SAGE, the Oxford Research Encyclopedia of Criminology and Criminal Justice, Taylor & Francis, the Routledge Focus series, Psychology of Violence, the popular press, and several highly acclaimed educational leadership journals.

Preet Kanwal completed her Post-Doctoral Fellowship at the ESG, University of Quebec in Montreal, Canada, furthering research expertise in her field. During her Post Doctoral Fellowship, she worked on exploring demographic sensitivity and its impact on discrimination in HEIs while considering insights from Canada and India. Dr. Kanwal is an academician and researcher with over 20 years of experience in Human Resource Management. She holds a PhD in Human Resource Management from I.K. Gujral Punjab Technical University, Punjab, India, where she conducted an empirical study on the quality of work life in the textile industry of Punjab, India. She also has international experience teaching MBA students from Victoria University (Online), Australia, and Sunway University (Online), Malaysia. Dr. Kanwal's research interests revolve around the quality of work-life, work-life balance, industrial relations, labour laws, social security and labour welfare, organizational stress, and behaviour, particularly in the context of the textile industry. She has presented her research at numerous national and international conferences and published her work in Scopus-indexed and UGC-listed Journals. Additionally, she has authored several book chapters on related topics, underscoring her commitment to advancing knowledge in her field. Her contributions extend beyond teaching and research; she has been actively involved in organizing and leading training sessions, workshops, and conferences, both as a participant and as a session chair.

Lolita L. Kincade, Ph.D., CFLE, PPS, NCC, LPC, is an Associate Professor and Chair of the Human Development and Family Relations Department at the State University of New York Plattsburgh in Plattsburgh, New York. She earned a Ph.D in Family Studies from Loma Linda University in Loma Linda, California. Dr. Kincade is certified as a Family Life Educator through the National Council on Family Relations (NCFR), and is also a Licensed Professional Counselor. Her professional interests include improving quality and standards of individual and family life. She has published research on diverse topics, including the intersection of race and gender, and social justice education and advocacy. She has worked with diverse populations in academic, hospital, and community settings, and is experienced in research consultation, program development and planning, non-profit administration, and policy advocacy. Dr. Kincade is motivated to impact and transform institutions of higher education in the interest of students, faculty, and leaders of color.

Kendra Lewis-Strickland is a dedicated practitioner and scholar with over a decade of experience in transforming organizational cultures to achieve strategic goals. She has successfully developed and executed programs that enhance stakeholder engagement, cultural development, and capabilities. Her work focuses on improving leadership and professional skills for a diverse audience, including staff and faculty. Dr. Lewis-Strickland holds a Doctorate of Education in Organizational Leadership, specializing in Higher Education. Her research emphasizes building resilience in leaders and institutions, particularly focusing on the experiences of black women. She is passionate about addressing the unique challenges in higher education and fostering agile, adaptable leaders. She has published in scholarly journals and presented at numerous conferences, sharing her insights with industry leaders.

Thi Minh Ngoc Luu is currently the Head of the Faculty of Economics and Management at the International School, Vietnam National University, Hanoi. She has 17 years of teaching and research experience in human resource management, corporate governance, business management, leadership, entrepreneurship, individual and organizational behavior, sustainable development, and e-commerce.

Elsy N.J. is an Assistant Professor at Jyoti Nivas Autonomous College, Bangalore. She is passionate for psychology and well-being. Currently, she is a Research Scholar at Christ University, Bangalore. She also leverages her expertise as a counseling psychologist and life skills trainer and extends her support to families and couples through her work as a therapist.

Julie Richards is an Associate Professor and Chair of the Department of Social Work, bringing over three decades of experience in educational, health, and behavioral health contexts. With an MSW and a PhD in International Family and Community Studies, Dr. Richards' leadership is characterized by a deep commitment to international development, intercultural and interprofessional growth, and applied learning. Her career includes diverse roles from urban child welfare in New York City to global community development and human rights advocacy. Dr. Richards is a recognized leader in higher education, guiding academic and programmatic initiatives that advance humanitarian practice, foster social inclusion, and strengthen organizational impact through strategic planning, curriculum design, and robust monitoring and evaluation frameworks.

Jennifer Schneider is an Assistant Professor at the Community College of Philadelphia where she teaches in the Social Science Department. She serves as Program and Legal Internship Coordinator for the Paralegal Studies Program. She earned her Doctorate in Education at the University of South Carolina and her Juris Doctorate at the New York University School of Law.

Parth Sharma is Associate Professor in School of Law at University of Petroleum and Energy Studies. He holds a doctorate degree in India-China relations from Aligarh Muslim University. He had published research papers in international and national journals of high repute. He is a gold medallist and has qualified UGC (JRF-NET) in Political Science. He also had participated in various workshops and conferences organized by U.G.C, British high commission, and premier think tanks like Centre for Policy Research New Delhi. His area of interest includes International Politics, Strategic Affairs, Political Theory, Media Studies, Politics of Development, Issues concerning Higher Education. etc.

Anu raj Singh is an Assistant professor of psychology at Banasthali University, where she has been teaching and conducting research for over 10 years. She earned her Ph.D. in Psychology from Banasthali University and done MPhil in Jawaharlal Nehru University,New Delhi. She has published numerous articles in prestigious academic journals on topics ranging from educational psychology to gender psychology.Dr. A.R. Singh is particularly known for her work in the area of Educational & gender psychology, with a focus on understanding the social and emotional development of children and adolescents. In addition to her research, Dr.Anu raj Singh is a dedicated teacher who is passionate about inspiring the next generation of psychologists. She has taught courses on Personality development, Indian psychology, and Human Values, among others.

Priyesh Kumar Singh (Ph.D; PGDGC; PGDVGCC; M.A.) is an assistant professor at Department of Psychology, Banasthali Vidyapith University, Rajasthan. He certified counseling psychologist as well as behavior therapist. He has published several research papers/articles/book chapters in various journals of repute and is associated with PubMed; Medknow and Elsevier. His areas of interest include Health psychology, Cognitive psychology, Neuroscience, Indian psychology and Psychotherapy. He is also certified NLP; Graphologist and Hypnotherapist.

Mohit Yadav is an Associate Professor in the area of Human Resource Management at Jindal Global Business School (JGBS). He has a rich blend of work experience from both Academics as well as Industry. Prof. Mohit holds a Ph.D. from Department of Management Studies, Indian Institute of Technology Roorkee (IIT Roorkee) and has completed Master of Human Resource and Organizational Development (MHROD) from prestigious Delhi School of Economics, University of Delhi. He also holds a B.Com (Hons.) degree from University of Delhi and UGC-JRF scholarship. He has published various research papers and book chapters with reputed publishers like Springer, Sage, Emerald, Elsevier, Inderscience etc. and presented research papers in national and International conferences both in India and abroad. He has many best paper awards on his credit too. He is reviewer of various international journals like Computers in Human Behavior, Policing etc. His areas of interest are Organizational Behavior, HRM, Recruitment and Selection, Organizational Citizenship Behavior, Quality of work life and role.

Index

A

academic mom 117, 119, 120, 121, 122, 123
academic mother 25
authenticity 54, 69, 71, 231, 286

B

Black Women 1, 2, 5, 6, 7, 8, 9, 11, 12, 13, 14, 15, 16, 17, 18, 19, 20, 21, 22, 91, 92, 93, 94, 95, 96, 97, 98, 99, 100, 101, 102, 103, 104, 105, 106, 107, 108, 109, 110, 111, 221, 222, 223, 224, 225, 227, 229, 230, 231, 232, 234, 236, 237, 238
Black Women Higher Education 91, 93, 108, 110
Black Women Higher Education Leaders 91, 93, 108

C

Career Advancement 84, 100, 102, 107, 122, 245, 246, 276, 284, 289
Case Study 59, 62, 85, 108, 219, 275, 286
Change 1, 2, 8, 10, 13, 16, 21, 32, 33, 38, 40, 43, 44, 61, 62, 67, 68, 83, 92, 103, 117, 136, 147, 155, 169, 172, 173, 184, 197, 199, 200, 204, 214, 215, 221, 223, 227, 238, 239, 241, 243, 247, 254, 277, 278, 279, 281, 282, 286, 287
cognitive restructuring 65, 80, 85
cognitive self care 259
collaboration 62, 129, 137, 188, 197, 207, 217, 225, 228, 245, 249, 250
college 14, 22, 27, 28, 31, 39, 40, 50, 93, 94, 95, 108, 111, 114, 118, 119, 125, 130, 134, 136, 144, 150, 153, 155, 170, 171, 172, 173, 188, 191, 222, 238, 239, 248, 249, 252, 254

D

Defying Age Stereotypes 241
Diversity 4, 11, 14, 17, 63, 69, 78, 81, 84, 92, 93, 102, 105, 106, 108, 128, 130, 195, 197, 203, 206, 207, 208, 212, 213, 215, 219, 221, 286
Dual Identities 155, 157

E

effective leadership 208, 230, 275, 279, 283, 284
emotional balance 255, 256, 257, 268, 270, 271, 272, 273, 274
Emotional Wellbeing 47, 51, 57, 61, 63, 64, 262, 273
Empowerment 20, 24, 57, 58, 99, 128, 130, 131, 156, 163, 190, 206, 207, 215, 224, 238, 280, 281, 283, 284, 285
existential self care 266

F

females 30, 94, 136, 218
Future Trends 204

H

higher education 1, 2, 3, 5, 6, 8, 9, 11, 12, 13, 14, 15, 16, 17, 19, 20, 21, 22, 24, 29, 30, 31, 32, 33, 34, 36, 37, 38, 39, 40, 41, 42, 43, 44, 45, 63, 64, 87, 88, 91, 92, 93, 94, 95, 96, 97, 98, 99, 100, 101, 102, 103, 104, 105, 106, 107, 108, 109, 110, 111, 118, 119, 123, 124, 125, 127, 128, 129, 130, 131, 132, 138, 141, 142, 144, 145, 148, 149, 151, 155, 156, 157, 158, 159, 160, 161, 166, 168, 169, 170, 173, 175, 187, 188, 189, 190, 192, 219, 221, 222, 223, 225, 236, 238, 239, 241, 242, 243, 246, 251, 252, 253, 254, 274, 275, 276, 277, 279, 283, 286, 287, 288, 289
Higher Education Leadership 1, 2, 3, 9, 16, 17, 21, 24, 38, 91, 92, 93, 97, 99,

100, 101, 102, 105, 107, 109, 187, 223, 238, 251, 276, 283, 288
Holistic Approach 243, 251

I

Identity 5, 7, 8, 14, 15, 22, 42, 45, 53, 54, 55, 60, 67, 68, 87, 100, 107, 108, 119, 120, 121, 137, 146, 152, 155, 156, 157, 158, 159, 162, 167, 168, 169, 188, 189, 192, 193, 199, 238, 239, 261, 267, 280, 281, 284, 285

Imposter Syndrome 65, 66, 67, 68, 69, 70, 71, 72, 74, 75, 76, 77, 79, 80, 81, 82, 83, 84, 85, 86, 87, 88, 115, 116, 126, 128, 168, 211, 231, 279

Inclusivity 128, 131, 195, 197, 206, 207, 215, 217, 226, 231, 232, 237

International Development 246, 247, 248, 249, 250, 251

intersectionality 14, 22, 65, 68, 72, 76, 79, 83, 86, 92, 93, 106, 108, 158, 164, 174, 188, 189, 190, 191, 215, 222, 237

K

Karnataka 127, 130, 131, 134, 138, 141, 142

L

Leader 2, 5, 31, 67, 74, 76, 88, 118, 155, 156, 157, 159, 161, 162, 163, 164, 166, 167, 168, 169, 170, 171, 172, 173, 175, 184, 187, 188, 189, 192, 199, 210, 211, 221, 225, 235, 252, 275, 276, 277, 278, 279, 280, 281, 282, 283, 284, 288

Leadership 1, 2, 3, 5, 6, 7, 9, 11, 15, 16, 17, 19, 20, 21, 22, 24, 31, 32, 33, 37, 38, 40, 41, 42, 43, 44, 45, 47, 62, 64, 65, 66, 67, 68, 71, 72, 74, 75, 76, 77, 78, 79, 84, 85, 86, 88, 91, 92, 93, 94, 96, 97, 98, 99, 100, 101, 102, 103, 104, 105, 106, 107, 108, 109, 113, 116, 117, 122, 128, 129, 135, 141, 142, 147, 155, 157, 161, 162, 168, 171, 172, 173, 174, 187, 188, 190, 191, 192, 193, 196, 197, 198, 199, 200, 201, 202, 203, 204, 205, 206, 207, 208, 209, 210, 211, 212, 215, 216, 217, 218, 219, 220, 223, 224, 225, 226, 227, 229, 230, 231, 234, 238, 239, 241, 242, 245, 250, 251, 252, 253, 254, 275, 276, 277, 278, 279, 280, 281, 282, 283, 284, 285, 286, 287, 288, 289

Leadership Roles 31, 65, 66, 91, 92, 96, 100, 101, 122, 128, 129, 141, 155, 157, 161, 172, 173, 174, 211, 220, 242

M

Mental Health 1, 2, 8, 9, 10, 11, 12, 13, 14, 15, 16, 17, 20, 21, 23, 24, 34, 47, 48, 50, 55, 56, 57, 60, 61, 62, 63, 64, 86, 114, 119, 120, 124, 125, 135, 136, 150, 222, 239, 257, 261, 262, 285

mentoring 24, 81, 84, 88, 100, 114, 115, 136, 147, 162, 192, 195, 196, 199, 200, 201, 202, 203, 204, 206, 207, 208, 209, 210, 212, 213, 214, 215, 216, 217, 218, 219, 220, 275, 276, 280, 284, 286, 288

mentorship 16, 17, 65, 71, 75, 77, 78, 79, 80, 81, 84, 85, 86, 109, 128, 161, 164, 168, 195, 196, 197, 198, 199, 200, 201, 202, 204, 205, 206, 207, 208, 209, 210, 211, 212, 213, 214, 215, 216, 217, 218, 219, 220, 226, 231, 234, 235, 241, 242, 243, 253, 254, 280, 284

mom guilt 122, 123, 124
MotherLeader 25, 31, 38
motherscholar 25, 29, 31, 38
mothers in academia 40, 253

O

organizational culture 68, 74, 75, 76, 78, 84, 106, 137, 203, 214, 216, 217, 223, 231

P

Phenomenological Analysis 47, 51
professor guilt 122, 124

Psychological Safety 1, 9, 10, 11, 16, 19, 221, 222, 223, 224, 225, 226, 227, 228, 230, 231, 232, 233, 234, 236, 237, 238, 239

R

relational leadership 279, 285, 288, 289
Resilience 13, 49, 56, 57, 61, 75, 79, 92, 99, 101, 128, 187, 197, 199, 211, 221, 223, 224, 225, 227, 229, 230, 232, 233, 234, 236, 237, 239, 241, 242, 249, 251, 254, 257, 264, 270, 271, 284

S

scarcity 283
self care 256, 258, 259, 260, 262, 263, 264, 265, 266, 268, 269, 271, 272, 273
Self-care 2, 12, 13, 14, 17, 23, 24, 47, 48, 49, 50, 51, 52, 53, 54, 55, 56, 57, 59, 60, 61, 62, 63, 64, 234, 235, 255, 256, 257, 258, 259, 260, 261, 262, 263, 264, 265, 266, 267, 268, 269, 270, 272, 273, 274
self-compassion 55, 58, 61, 62, 65, 72, 75, 79, 80, 85, 86, 230, 235, 239
self-doubt 65, 66, 67, 69, 71, 72, 73, 74, 75, 76, 77, 78, 79, 80, 83, 84, 85, 86, 198, 211
Self-esteem 13, 73, 77, 120, 127, 128, 129, 131, 132, 133, 134, 135, 136, 137, 138, 139, 140, 141, 142, 143, 144, 145, 146, 147, 148, 149, 150, 151, 152, 153, 207
Small group socialization 127, 128, 129, 130, 131, 132, 138, 139, 140, 141, 142, 143, 149
Social-Ecological Model 1, 2, 11, 12, 21
Social Work 46, 98, 144, 242, 243, 244, 246, 248, 249, 250

T

teams 19, 197, 210, 217, 225, 227, 232, 236, 237, 238, 239, 275, 279, 281, 284
Technology 13, 21, 37, 40, 84, 136, 137, 147, 192, 193, 197, 210, 215, 219, 239
toxic leadership 277, 278, 282, 284, 286, 287, 289
transformational leadership 275, 280
trust 169, 201, 207, 233, 234, 235, 236, 237, 278, 279, 280, 281, 282, 283, 284, 286

U

university 9, 11, 13, 14, 15, 17, 19, 20, 21, 22, 24, 36, 38, 39, 40, 41, 42, 44, 45, 46, 47, 48, 49, 50, 51, 54, 62, 63, 65, 73, 89, 91, 94, 95, 96, 105, 106, 108, 110, 114, 124, 132, 135, 145, 146, 149, 151, 152, 169, 170, 171, 172, 173, 174, 190, 195, 222, 224, 225, 229, 232, 244, 246, 248, 256, 257, 272, 274, 275, 276, 278, 280, 285, 287, 288
university professors 40, 42, 51, 257, 272

W

Women 1, 2, 5, 6, 7, 8, 9, 10, 11, 12, 13, 14, 15, 16, 17, 18, 19, 20, 21, 22, 24, 28, 29, 30, 31, 33, 34, 36, 37, 38, 39, 40, 41, 42, 43, 44, 45, 47, 48, 49, 50, 53, 59, 62, 63, 64, 65, 66, 67, 68, 69, 70, 71, 72, 73, 74, 75, 76, 77, 78, 79, 80, 81, 82, 83, 84, 85, 86, 87, 88, 89, 91, 92, 93, 94, 95, 96, 97, 98, 99, 100, 101, 102, 103, 104, 105, 106, 107, 108, 109, 110, 111, 113, 115, 116, 117, 118, 119, 120, 121, 122, 123, 124, 125, 126, 127, 128, 129, 130, 131, 132, 133, 134, 136, 138, 141, 142, 144, 145, 147, 148, 149, 151, 153, 156, 157, 158, 161, 166, 168, 169, 171, 186, 190, 192, 195, 196, 197, 198, 199, 200, 201, 202, 203, 204, 205, 206, 207, 208, 209, 210, 211, 212, 214, 215, 216, 217, 218, 219, 220, 221, 222, 223, 224, 225, 227, 229, 230, 231, 232, 234, 235, 236, 237, 238, 239, 252, 253, 254, 256, 275, 276, 278, 279, 280, 284, 285, 286, 287, 288, 289
Women Education Leadership 107

Women Higher Education Leaders 9, 91, 93, 108, 190
Women in Academia 5, 9, 47, 62, 96, 101, 103, 109, 122, 142, 235, 276, 279, 286
women in academic leadership 93, 107
women leaders 40, 41, 65, 66, 67, 68, 69, 70, 71, 74, 75, 76, 77, 78, 79, 80, 81, 82, 83, 84, 85, 86, 91, 92, 93, 94, 96, 100, 101, 102, 104, 108, 109, 110, 111, 123, 157, 158, 161, 169, 171, 195, 196, 197, 198, 199, 200, 201, 202, 203, 204, 205, 206, 207, 208, 209, 211, 212, 214, 215, 216, 217, 218, 219, 220, 276, 285, 286
Women of Color 1, 2, 5, 6, 9, 12, 15, 17, 21, 22, 24, 105, 107, 109, 215
Women teachers 127, 131, 138, 141, 142, 148
Workplace communication behaviour 127, 138, 139, 140, 141

Milton Keynes UK
Ingram Content Group UK Ltd.
UKHW051834211024
450061UK00009B/122

9 798369 331446